To John Edwards,

A good friend and a ~~very good~~ lawyer.

Wishing you and Chris all the best, both personally and professionally.

Brian Brincy
October 3, 2011

FINANCE & ACCOUNTING FOR LAWYERS

BRIAN P. BRINIG, J.D., C.P.A.

Business Valuation Resources, LLC
1000 SW Broadway, Suite 1200
Portland, OR 97205
(503) 291-7963 • Fax (503) 291-7955 • www.BVResources.com

What It's Worth

Managing Editor: Colin Murcray
Chair and CEO: David Foster
President: Lucretia Lyons
Sales: Linda Mendenhall
Customer Service Manager: Stephanie Crader
ISBN: 978-1-935081-71-5

Table of Contents

Chapter 9: General Principles of Appraisal and Valuation of Businesses

Chapter 10: Damages

Chapter 11: Personal Economic Losses

Chapter 1

Accounting, Finance and the Law

Introduction

Accounting is the system of recording and reporting the financial transactions of an entity. Accounting accumulates all of the financial transactions of the entity and summarizes them into financial statements, the primary mechanism for disclosing the entity's performance to management, investors and the public. Accounting is often referred to as the "language of business" because the vast majority of business activity can be summarized through the money measurement concept, one of the underlying principles of accounting. Because accounting only deals with money measurement, there are frequently important aspects of business that are not summarized through the accounting process, and a reader of financial statements must beware of these shortcomings. But as Tom Cruise said in the award winning movie, *Jerry McGuire*: "Show me the money!" It is through accounting documents and financial summaries that we see the "money," the financial status of the business and the financial results of its operations.

Accounting is sometimes thought to be rote or mechanistic, but in fact, the system relies heavily on the reasoned judgments, estimates and approximations of the accountant preparing the financial statements. The application of broad accounting principles to countless business transactions requires an understanding of the objectives of financial reporting and the needs of the users of financial information. Contrary to popular belief, accounting is not a mathematical formula or calculation, but rather an organized system that logically summarizes business transactions into useable information that is meaningful to management, creditors, business investors and other stakeholders.

This text will take the reader through the system of accounting and the development of financial statements. In Chapters 2 through 7, we will proceed through the accounting process to the preparation of financial statements. Some of the complexities and limitations of accounting information will also be explored, culminating in a study of ratio analysis of financial statements to glean relevant insights from them. We will briefly cover the complexities of accounting for fixed assets and inventories with the goal of introducing the concepts. The objective of this introductory study of accounting is to provide a broad, workable knowledge base that will facilitate the use of accounting information as it relates to the practice of law.

Finance is the science of funds management, and it involves the interrelationships of money, interest, time and risk. Corporate finance deals with the task of providing the funds for a company's activities, called capitalization. Corporate finance also involves the competing policies of risk management and profitability maximization. Monetary finance addresses the time value of money, a concept that underlies all economic transactions.

In this text, our discussion of finance will involve both corporate and monetary finance. In the area of monetary finance, our emphasis will relate to the time value of money because of its importance to all financial activities and the practice of law. Chapter 8 deals with time value concepts, but it also provides the reader with "hands on" application of the concepts with problems that require calculator and/or computer solutions. These concepts are most easily learned by applying them, and the problems enable the student to understand the concepts better.

Many students approach the practice of law with a foundation in the liberal arts, only to learn that much of the American legal system involves financial issues. Money is frequently the substance of the dispute; however, even when monetary issues are not at the forefront of the issues in the case, they are almost always part of the solution to the problem. The chapter on business valuation, Chapter 9, deals directly with determining the value of an entity through the process of income capitalization, a concept that is poorly understood by many law practitioners.

The principles of accounting and finance directly extend to contract issues, torts, business and securities matters, taxation issues, partnership disputes, gift and estate matters, to name only a partial list. These areas of jurisprudence are often based significantly on substantive financial questions, and their measurement can be the heart of the entire matter. Additionally, the calculation of commercial damages and personal economic losses is fundamentally a financial matter, involving the finance concepts of present and future value. Damages analysis is a critical aspect of litigation, both business and personal, and the lawyer's understanding of damage theories and calculations is vital to the success of these matters.

Finally, the intersection of finance, accounting and the law is very broad, involving opinion testimony of expert witnesses and cross-examination of experts at trial. The use of financial experts has exploded in recent decades, and practicing lawyers must be skilled in their interaction with these related professionals. Not only must lawyers be mindful of substantive financial issues, but they must be knowledgeable about procedural issues relating to the development of expert opinions, privileges relating to expert communications and techniques of examining and cross-examining opposing experts.

For all these reasons and more, it behooves the lawyer to have, at a minimum, a rudimentary understanding of finance and accounting concepts and knowledge of their far-reaching effects in the American legal system.

A Quick History of Accounting

The History of Accounting.[1] Modern accountancy has its roots in the 15th Century when an Italian monk named Luca Pacioli codified a system of double entry bookkeeping in his book, *Summa de Arithmetica*, one of the first books printed by the Gutenberg movable-type printing method. Pacioli was the first person to describe the double entry system, although it had evolved over two hundred years in Venetian commerce. Pacioli's method became known as the "Italian method" or the "Method of Venice" and it spread across Europe in the 15th and 16th centuries through Venetian trade. In fact, Venice and its importance as a financial epicenter was so world-renowned that it inspired one of Shakespeare's most famous works, *The Merchant of Venice*, whose quibble over a contract provision granting a party damages of a pound of flesh but nothing more, is a classic depiction of legal accounting.[2]

Over time, settlers to the New World imported the double entry system to colonial America. The importance of accounting grew as businesses increasingly used capital provided by others, such as lenders and investors, and the capital providers needed to know the financial results of their investments. Financial transactions were (and are) summarized and accumulated in a double entry bookkeeping system, and the results of the financial activity are presented in various financial statements. These different financial statements are the bedrock of financial accounting, and they will be discussed in detail in subsequent chapters of this text.

During the 19th Century, investors began to regard accounting data (primarily composed of balance sheets[3]) as providing important information and analytical content for assessing alternatives. Business leaders began to advocate expert accounting analysis and certification of financial information as a means to publicize and legitimize financial results. An industry of independent "public" accountants grew up around this need to audit the books and provide accounts of businesses. England had "chartered accountants," forerunners of the American Certified Public Accountant, by the mid-1800s. By the late 1800s, accountancy was an established profession in the United States.

The Institute of Accountants of New York was formed in 1882 and is the first known professional accounting organization in the U.S. In 1896, New York State became the first state to legislatively recognize a class of professionals, the "certified public accountants," and mandate that only accountants with this certificate be employed to examine accounts, or serve as expert accountants or auditors. By the mid-1920s, comparable legislation was in place in all 48 (existing) states.

---

1. This history of accounting adapts material presented in Mundstock, George, *A Finance Approach to Accounting for Lawyers*, Foundation Press, 1999, and Cunningham, Lawrence A., *Introductory Accounting, Finance and Auditing for Lawyers*, Fourth Ed., Thomson West, 2002.
2. Shakespeare, William, *The Merchant of Venice*.
3. A balance sheet is so named because it is usually presented with assets in one column and liabilities and equity in the other column, the two columns balancing each other out.

The turn of the 20th Century also saw the beginnings of the modern public capital markets in the U.S. Stocks and securities were being bought and sold by investors who had little knowledge of, or contact with, the issuing business. Financial statements were being used, not only by capital providers to supervise management, but also by investors determining whether to buy or sell securities. In 1913, The New York Stock Exchange imposed reporting obligations as a condition of listing on the exchange. Thus, accounting became even more important. As a consequence, states began to license the practice of accountancy, and accountancy began to regulate itself.

In 1916, in response to increasing public criticism of the accounting profession as exclusive and ineffective, arising out of substantial infighting between various state accounting organizations, the American Association of Public Accountants was reorganized and became the *American Institute of Accountants* ("AIA"). In 1917, the Federal Reserve Board published a document called *Uniform Accounting,* proposing to establish uniform standards for the profession. The document promulgated rules for measuring assets and liabilities and limited verification to be rendered by accountants registered with a federal agency, such as the Federal Reserve Board. In response to the threat of meddling government regulation, the accounting profession, through the AIA, published its own *Uniform Accounting.* This self-regulating standard managed to circumvent the federal registration of accountants at that time. However, the victory was short-lived.

In response to the stock market crash of 1929 and the ensuing Great Depression, a more elaborate financial reporting system emerged. Between 1932 and 1934, the AIA and the New York Stock Exchange ("NYSE") engaged in wide-ranging discussion concerning the accounting profession's responsibilities. In 1932, the AIA crafted five broad accounting principles, which were endorsed by the NYSE and became the first "accepted principles of accounting." This was the first formal attempt at articulating *"generally accepted accounting principles."*[4] In 1933 and 1934, Congress enacted the basic federal securities laws,[5] The Securities Act of 1933 and The Securities Exchange Act of 1934, which also created the Securities and Exchange Commission ("SEC") to administer the newly enacted legal restrictions on corporations. These legislative reforms, often referred to as the "truth in securities" laws,[6] sought to give public investors access to all information relevant to evaluating their investments and to add transparency to perceived insider abuse. Because of the central importance of accounting information to the stock market and the stock market to the economy, the SEC became the final arbiter of financial accounting rules for businesses subject to its jurisdiction (basically businesses that sell securities to the public or have publicly traded securities). Financial statements of these businesses are filed with the SEC and are available to the public.

In 1938, the SEC formally (but not irrevocably) delegated its authority to determine financial reporting standards to the AIA. The SEC concluded that where substantial authoritative support existed for a company's accounting practices and the SEC had not taken a position on a matter,

---

4. These principles have become known as GAAP, and they have evolved to be the foundation of modern accounting. The broad concepts of GAAP are discussed in Chapter 2.

5. www.sec.gov/about/laws.shtml

6. www.sec.gov/about/laws.shtml

the SEC would not dispute the practices. In 1939, the AIA began to issue Accounting Research Bulletins (ARBs) and emerged as the first official rule-making body for accounting pronouncements in the United States.

Over the decades of the 1930s, 1940s and 1950s, accountants insisted that management was responsible for determining the prudence of accounting principles selected by a company and that the accountant's role was limited to determining whether a particular approach was an accepted practice and had been properly applied. Regarding the accountant's role in the external audit of financial statements, the accountant's view was that the auditor was responsible for the expression of an informed and independent judgment on the question of whether the accounts which he approves are a full and fair presentation. In 1936, in response to Congressional threats of a federal licensing regime for auditors, the AIA issued a bulletin entitled "Examination of Financial Statements," which tended to state the role of auditors negatively (i.e., it limited the responsibility of auditors). The general perception was that auditing was not operating effectively. The AIA tried to respond and foreclose federal intervention through promulgation of generally accepted auditing standards (GAAS).

In 1957, the AIA was renamed the *American Institute of Certified Public Accountants* ("AICPA"). The next year it created the *Accounting Principles Board* ("APB") to adopt rules for financial reporting. This body adopted industry authoritative pronouncements that addressed both accounting (GAAP[7]) and auditing (GAAS[8]). In 1973, the AICPA established a separate, permanent, independent entity to regulate accounting principles: the *Financial Accounting Standards Board* ("FASB"). In 1973, the AICPA adopted Rule 203 of its Code of Professional Conduct, requiring AICPA members to follow FASB pronouncements (unless doing so would result in material misstatement of financial statements).

Throughout the 1980s and 1990s, the frequency of corporate accounting scandals, such as the savings and loan crisis, multiplied. The scandals featured such accounting tricks as recognizing revenue prematurely, creating fictitious revenue through phony invoices and shipping documents, miscounting customer unit volume, inflating inventory, capitalizing expenses, and other age-old bookkeeping tricks. The late 1990s produced a series of accounting debacles, prompting the SEC, under Chairman Arthur Levitt, to enact a broad array of new rules, principally designed to enhance the independence of auditors and to separate them from the companies that they were auditing. The turn of the century exposed one of the largest accounting scandals to date, "Enron." Enron was a Texas-based energy company, which developed a staff of executives that, through the use of accounting loopholes, special purpose entities, and poor financial reporting, hid billions in debt from failed deals and projects. Chief Financial Officer Andrew Fastow and other executives misled Enron's board of directors and audit committee with regard to high-risk accounting issues and pressured the "independent" auditing firm, Arthur Andersen, to ignore the issues in its reports through the use of vague accounting standards that based many decisions on technicalities. These

---

7. Generally Accepted Accounting Principles.
8. Generally Accepted Auditing Standards.

---

technicalities allowed a company to achieve a more favorable and less accurate picture of its financial health in financial statements by giving internal accountants more leeway in deciding how to value assets and how to record changes in asset value (particularly with regard to those assets that had depreciated). The general corporate culture of deregulation at this time, coupled with the lack of accounting practices in this arena, also served as a disincentive for the independent auditor to challenge judgments made by a company's internal accounting department.[9]

On July 30, 2002, largely in response to the Enron scandal, President George W. Bush signed into law the *Sarbanes-Oxley Act of 2002*. The Act, which applies in general to publicly held companies and their audit firms, dramatically affects the accounting profession and impacts not just the largest accounting firms, but any CPA who is actively working as an auditor of, or for, a publicly traded company. The Act creates the *Public Company Accounting and Oversight Board* ("PCAOB") which is appointed and overseen by the SEC. The Board's charge is to oversee and investigate the audits and auditors of public companies. The Board is funded by public companies through mandatory fees and charged with issuing standards for audit firms and instituting quality control measures for the audits of public companies. The Sarbanes-Oxley Act and the PCAOB:

1. Require auditors to report directly to a company's audit committee, as opposed to management;

2. Prohibit auditors from providing certain non-audit services to audit clients, such as: bookkeeping, information systems design and implementation, appraisals and valuation services, actuarial services, internal audits, management or human resources services, or legal or expert services outside the scope of the audit;

3. Require the lead audit partner and the reviewing audit partner to rotate off the audit every 5 years;

4. Require the CEO and CFO of each company to prepare a statement to accompany the audit report to certify the "appropriateness of the financial statements and disclosures contained in the periodic report, and that those financial statements and disclosures fairly present, in all material respects, the operations and financial condition of the issuer";

5. Prohibit personal loans to executives;

6. Require directors, officers, and greater than 10% shareholders to report designated transactions with the company within two days of the transaction.

Even with the FASB in place and the existence of the PCAOB, accounting is still basically a common law discipline. A business often engages in some new transaction for which there is no customary accounting treatment. The in-house accountant, perhaps with management looking

---

9. www.chicagobooth.edu/pdf/weil_testimony.pdf

over his or her shoulder, uses judgment to record the transaction, frequently in the light best for the company. Outside auditors either accept the in-house characterization of the transaction or use their professional judgment to re-characterize it in a more accurate way. The SEC might require a different treatment the first time that the business files financial statements that reflect the new transaction with the agency. Then, similar businesses engage in analogous new transactions and record them similarly on the books. A custom or practice develops. Articles are written in professional journals. Litigation under federal securities laws or other relevant law might cause the accounting profession to modify its view. FASB (or the SEC) intervenes only if this process results in problematic financial statements.

Recently, the AICPA has reacted to public criticism regarding the role accounting practices have played in the onslaught of the sub-prime mortgage crisis by failing to identify toxic assets as such in the creation of corporate financial statements. Robert Herz, chairman of FASB, advocated for a review of current market accounting practices governing secured assets to reflect true value or liability to the corporation.[10] The ongoing dispute in this arena is the transparency (or lack thereof) of the "complex web of accounting and legal rules that govern mortgage loans that are pooled into mortgage-backed securities."[11] The prevalence of debt financing and the presence of complex financial instruments such as credit swaps, derivatives, and options shorting further highlight the need for an organized and detailed method of looking at an entity's range of financial positions. AICPA has also sought to implement financial education programs in both the workplace and the community to improve individuals' understanding of their own financial health.[12]

In financial, intermediate, and advanced accounting, the student is exposed to the double entry accounting method and GAAP, as well as the more sophisticated and subtle nuances of the practice of accounting, and the techniques of applying the rules and principles to the operations of a business. During this educational process, accounting students learn that the practice of accounting requires a surprising amount of creativity and judgment by the professional accountant. The novice seems to believe that accounting is a rote science, a mere application of rules to situations, but nothing could be farther from reality. When Generally Accepted Accounting Principles are applied with the proper exercise of judgment by practitioners in the field, the result is that investors and management are provided with critical information that enables the business system to move forward successfully. When the opposite occurs and poor judgment or deliberate manipulation is employed, the results can be perverse: not only is the market and its investors deprived of accurate information, but such inaccuracies can trigger large-scale financial crises as inflated (or deflated) numbers misrepresent the true financial condition of an industry.

Equally as important as the generation of initial accounting reports is the related science of auditing. In fact, there is a large body of accounting literature, Generally Accepted Auditing Standards (GAAS), that governs this important field. Auditing is the critical examination of a company's

---

10. www.reuters.com/article/idUSN0740608620080207
11. www.reuters.com/article/idUSN0923680720070810
12. www.aicpa.org/News/FeaturedNews/Pages/AICPASpringCouncilMay232010Summary.aspx

accounting records by an outside objective party to determine if they accurately and fairly present the results of operations of the entity. During the course of performing an audit, the certified public accountant performs a number of tests and techniques that could be considered investigative. This process serves as a reliability check on financial statements prepared by in-house accountants, who might otherwise seek to present an overly rosy picture to the outside world.

The culmination of the accounting process is the presentation of the financial results of the operation of a business entity in the form of financial statements. Merriam-Webster defines this process as "a system of recording and summarizing business and financial transactions and analyzing, reporting and verifying the result." Business Dictionary further elaborates: [accounting is] "the practice and body of knowledge concerned primarily with (1) methods for recording transactions, (2) keeping financial records, (3) performing internal audits, (4) reporting and analyzing financial information to the management, and (5) advising on taxation matters. It is a systematic process of identifying, recording, measuring, classifying, verifying, summarizing, interpreting and communicating financial information. It reveals profit or loss for a given period, and the value and nature of a firm's assets, liabilities and owners' equity. More succinctly, accounting provides the public with information on the (1) resources available to a firm, (2) the means employed to finance those resources, and (3) the results achieved through their use."

Introduction to Finance

Finance is the science of funds management.[13] Much of this science deals with analyzing accounting information to determine the interrelation of time, money and risk, frequently referred to as the time value of money. The time value of money is a concept that accounts for the change in relative value of money between points in time. Stakeholders use this information to decide between alternative outcomes and in the valuation of assets.

Although financial information has been recorded and analyzed since the invention of accounting, it was not until the late 1800s and the introduction and exploitation of the corporate form that financial analysis grew into the role that it plays today. With the advent of corporations there was a need for outside investors to compare opportunities and make judgments based on relative financial performance. Many investors looked to financial statements published by corporations to aid in this process. The use of this information as an objective indicator of performance led to the need for regulation. New York was the first state to monitor the publishing of this information and other states soon followed. The dawn of the 20th Century and financial debacles of the 1920s led to further regulation and reporting requirements, including mandatory external auditing of self-generated financial health reports.

---

13. *Webster's Third New International Dictionary of the English Language, Unabridged.* Springfield, Massachusetts: G. & C. Merriam Company.

In the 1950s, influenced by economics, modern finance theory began to develop. Finance evolved into the study and creation of risk models designed to predict both investor behavior and beneficial outcomes. Modern finance theory departed from the singular reliance on company produced documentation of financial health and began to incorporate market indices as well (sometimes exclusively). Modern finance theory was skeptical about the role of traditional accounting information in accurately capturing value, as opposed to accounting only for historical costs and historical operating performance.

A comparison of the disciplines of accounting and finance will highlight some of the weaknesses inherent in both bodies of knowledge. It is important to understand what we can learn from each of the endeavors, but it is also necessary to know the limitations of each field. Accounting is precise and fairly objective, but it is generally limited to an historical study of the monetary transactions of the particular business enterprise. Finance is more economically based than accounting, but it involves many more subjective judgments, estimates and projections about the entity. In combination, use of the two disciplines is highly informative about financial issues; however it is important to understand the strengths, weaknesses and limitations of each discipline to solve problems.

Finance, Accounting and the Law

The importance of finance and accounting is not limited to the corporate sphere; much of the practice of law relates to financial matters. Examples include:

1. contracts

2. corporate law

3. business and securities litigation

4. taxation (income, loss, valuation)

5. partnership law

6. tort law – calculation of damages

7. transactional law – mergers and acquisitions, IPOs

8. divorce law – division of assets

9. bankruptcy law

Money is a constant undercurrent of the U.S. legal system. At the outset of a new matter, a lawyer's realistic, important first question may be: "Is this case worth taking?" Unfortunately, the analysis is often determined by the extent to which financial remuneration may be available. Although, there are seminal cases seeking to rid the world of injustice or develop constitutional principles, the practicality of most "Main Street" legal matters boils down to the expectancy of some type of financial recovery for the client. If that prospect is slight, the client is usually ill-advised to proceed with the matter in light of the most basic cost-benefit analysis. Because, institutionally, our legal system realizes this reality, some cases, deemed to be of a higher societal importance that would not otherwise have enough financial incentive to entice counsel to represent clients, are awarded legal fees paid by the losing party or by the government to ensure that these causes, too, have their day in court.

Damages are an important part of the civil litigation process. Outside of the realm of criminal cases, where personal liberty is at stake, the purpose of most litigation (and settlement) is financial compensation for the wronged party. Although some cases are resolved through injunctions or specific performance, the vast majority hinge on finding the proper dollar amount of compensation to the harmed party. Even some criminal offenses carry a financial penalty, in addition to, or in lieu of, incarceration. Damages serve a variety of purposes. They can be compensatory (meant to compensate for some type of loss or breach of contract); they can be nominal (in name only); or they can be punitive (meant to punish and usually awarded for egregious, intentional, or reckless violations).

The system of awarding money damages is imperfect. Not all losses or wrongs can be quantified. Although one can estimate the amount needed to cover medical care for a coma victim, there is no amount of money that can return her to the functioning person she was before her injury. Despite the many issues and imperfections associated with the system of awarding financial damages for harm that was not directly financial, in many cases, that is often the only way to compensate a plaintiff.

There is no question that the accurate measurement of financial activity is critical to the stakeholders of the American business system. In the same way that investors and managers rely on competent accounting to make business and investment decisions, judges, lawyers and the public rely on accurate accounting and financial information to make reliable legal decisions. Our system thrives on the accuracy of this information, and lawyers operating within the system need to be knowledgeable about the subtleties of accounting principles and the economics of finance. These disciplines are essential to the competent practice of law in the United States.

The purpose of *Finance & Accounting for Lawyers* is to provide the reader with a technical overview of accounting principles and methods so the knowledge can be applied in the practice of law. In the finance and valuation sections of the textbook, the reader is introduced to the principles of finance and valuation that underlie all monetary transactions that are the subject of contracts, tax matters, disputes and litigation. The text proceeds in Chapters 10, 11 and 12 to deal with damages calculations and, finally, in Chapter 13, the importance of opinion evidence is presented.

Chapter 2

Accounting: An Introduction

Introduction

Accounting is a method of accumulating and measuring economic data about an entity and communicating that data to various stakeholders. Accounting's primary functions are to record, summarize and classify financial transactions, culminating in the preparation of financial statements. Financial statements report the historical results of the entity's operations to management, investors, lenders, regulators and other stakeholders.

This chapter introduces the two basic financial statements, the balance sheet and the income statement. The elements of these statements are assets, liabilities, equity, revenue and expense, and these elements are the fundamental categories of accounting data that comprise financial reporting. Each of the two statements reports on a different aspect of business operations that is important to know in order to understand the status of a business organization. Through accounting, all of the transactions of business are measured and summarized into a meaningful reporting structure that can be used by any person who possesses the basic knowledge of financial statements.

In this chapter, the reader is also introduced to the fundamental principles of accounting that form the foundation of the universe of financial reporting. These principles are accepted by the governing body of financial reporting in the United States and by the international regulators.

Overview

A Fundamental Principle. The ***entity concept***[1] is a fundamental accounting principle that identifies and separates an organization from its owner(s) or managers. The individual entity stands alone and its financial activity is measured independently. The entity concept applies even though the law may not draw complete distinctions between certain types of business organizations and their owners, like proprietorships and partnerships. Under the entity concept, even those entities will be accounted for separately.

The Transaction. An entity financially interacts with the world through ***transactions***. A transaction usually indicates some exchange of financial resources between the entity and an outsider; it can be a sale, the payment of an expense, a borrowing, a repayment, receipt of an investment, or other financial activity. It is an event that effects some change in the assets, liabilities, or capital

---

1. An "entity" can be any identifiable subject that exists: a business, a person, a nonprofit organization, a government, a division of a larger business, a partnership, etc. I will often casually describe an entity as a "business," although the term "entity" should not be so limited.

of a business. Most transactions are conducted with outsiders, although some can be internal. A transaction is the original trigger that sets the accounting process in motion. Accounting transactions are events that are recorded in the books of account of the business.

The Primary Financial Concerns. Financially, two items of measurement are critically important: 1) the financial status of the entity at a point in time (measured by the balance sheet); and 2) changes in the entity over a period of time (primarily measured by the income statement).

The Accounting Process

Balance Sheet: The Status of the Entity. The financial status of a business at a point in time is extremely relevant information. In accounting, this status is shown on a financial statement called the *Balance Sheet*. A balance sheet presents the assets, liabilities and equity of a business at a point in time, usually at the end of an accounting period. To understand a balance sheet, we will address each of its three major elements: assets, liabilities and equity.

Assets. Assets are economic resources owned by a business entity. In theoretical accounting literature, there are more sophisticated definitions of assets,[2] but, for now, the basic description as an economic resource will suffice. Assets can be tangible physical items, or they can be intangible economic resources. Here is a list of some examples of business assets, but the list is far from exclusive:

Tangible assets:

1. Cash
2. Marketable securities
3. Inventory
4. Accounts or notes receivable (technically an intangible asset, but often considered tangible)
5. Prepaid items, such as insurance or utilities
6. Land
7. Buildings
8. Leasehold improvements, such as remodeling or renovations that increase value
9. Machinery and equipment
10. Rolling stock (vehicles)
11. Furniture and fixtures
12. Security deposits
13. Investments

---

2. The International Accounting Standards Board defines an asset of an entity as "a present right, or other access, to an existing economic resource with the ability to generate economic benefits to the entity." The American Institute of Certified Public Accountants defines assets as follows: "Assets are probable future economic benefits obtained or controlled by a particular entity as a result of past transactions or events." Also, assets are "unexpired costs" of a business entity—something that has been purchased, but hasn't yet been used up.

Intangible assets:

1. Patents
2. Trademarks
3. Copyrights
4. Goodwill
5. Contractual rights
6. Certain financial assets (stocks, bonds, notes and accounts receivable)

Classification of Assets. There are three broad sub-categories of assets for balance sheet purposes: *current assets; fixed assets*[3]: and *other assets. Current assets* include cash and other assets that are expected to be converted into cash, sold or consumed within one year or the normal operating cycle[4] of the business. Current assets generally include cash, short-term investments, accounts receivable, inventory and prepaid items. Current assets are the most liquid of a business's assets, the very definition of liquidity being cash or ease of conversion to cash.

Fixed assets are those that are purchased for long term use in furtherance of the activities of the business. They consist of things such as factory buildings and land, machinery and equipment, vehicles, furniture and fixtures, etc. Fixed assets are not bought and sold in the normal course of business operations; they are held to be used in the production of revenue over long periods of time. *Other assets* are neither current nor fixed; they are comprised of intangible assets (patents, copyrights, etc.) as well as investments in assets not used in operations (lease deposits or fixed assets held for sale).

Introduction to the Balance Sheet. The assets of the business constitute the resources or the "things"[5] that the business owns. Assume that the following list (with cost amounts) is the complete list of the assets of AAA Company at December 31, 2010:

Assets:		
Cash	$	8,000
Inventory		12,000
Vehicle		15,000
Equipment		20,000
Building		45,000
Total Assets	$	100,000

---

3. "Fixed assets" are also often called "Long-term assets," "Property, plant & equipment" or "Long-lived assets." The differences in nomenclature are not important.

4. The operating cycle of a business is the "normal" period of time during which the assets of the business are converted from cash, through the cycle of the business, and back to cash. For example, a merchandising business buys inventory, holds it for a while, sells it, obtains an account receivable, and receives payment on the account receivable. The operating cycle is complete.

5. Using the term loosely.

The above assets are the economic resources of AAA Company at December 31, 2010, but the information is insufficient to make any judgment or decision about the business entity at that date. Yes, you know that the business owns assets "worth"[6] $100,000, but there is other information that is critical to understanding the status of the company. For instance, would you think differently about AAA if you were told that AAA Company owed the bank $100,000? Or, that AAA Company had no debt whatsoever? Those two situations highlight the fact that we need to know more about AAA to understand much of anything about it.

Liabilities and Equity. Liabilities are debts owed to outsiders.[7] They constitute present obligations of the business, and they are a claim on the assets of the business. (If the debts were paid off today, they would be paid from the existing assets of the business; if the business does not pay its debts, the creditors can make a claim against the assets.) Liabilities can be short-term obligations (those due in less than one year, classified as *current liabilities*) or *long term* (those due in more than one year). Let's assume that AAA Company owes the following amounts at December 31, 2010:

Liabilities:		
Accounts Payable	$	4,500
Notes payable		50,000
Total Liabilities	$	54,500

So, AAA Company may have assets equaling $100,000 (at cost), but we have just learned that the company has debts of $54,500. Whatever the amount of liabilities, it is a fact of consequence to our understanding of the financial condition of AAA at December 31, 2010.

The *equity* of a business is the owner's residual claim on the assets of the business, after the creditors' claims have been satisfied. Equity is also called capital, stockholders' equity or net worth. It is important to recognize that equity is not a "thing," but rather it is the owner's *claim* on the assets of the business, after all the creditors' claims have been paid. If we think about AAA Company, it has assets of $100,000 and liabilities of $54,500. That means, in concept, if the assets were liquidated into cash and the liabilities were paid off, there would be $45,500 remaining as the *owner's residual claim—the equity—*on the assets of the business.

The concept of equity is the same, regardless of whether the business is a proprietorship, partnership or corporation. The details of the accounting for equity are different in these different forms of business organizations, but there is no difference in the ultimate residual claim by the owners.

---

6. The term "worth" is used very loosely here. In subsequent chapters, we will discuss the difference between **cost** and **value**, and it is significant.

7. More precisely, a liability is a present obligation of the enterprise arising from past events, the settlement of which is expected to result in an outflow from the enterprise's resources, i.e., assets.

In summary, the status of a business at a point in time is reflected on the company's balance sheet. The balance sheet lists the total economic resources (assets) of the business and the total of the claims (liabilities and equity) on the assets of the business. The total claims are represented by the claims of the creditors (which take priority over the owner's claims) and the residual claims of the owners. Following is the balance sheet of AAA Company based on the previous facts:

The AAA Company					
Balance Sheet					
December 30, 2010					
Assets:			**Liabilities:**		
Cash	$	8,000	Accounts Payable	$	4,500
Inventory		12,000	Notes payable		50,000
Vehicle		15,000	Total Liabs	$	54,500
Equipment		20,000	**Equity:**		
Building		45,000	Owner's Equity	$	45,500
Total	**$ 100,000**		**Total**	**$ 100,000**	

The Fundamental Accounting Equation. The fundamental underlying truth of accounting, which is perfectly logical, is the fact that the total of the resources of a business is exactly equal to the total of the claims on the resources of the business. This truth is the basis for the accounting financial statement, the balance sheet, and it is expressed in the fundamental accounting equation:

$$Assets = Liabilities + Owner's\ Equity$$

Some authors suggest that the rationale for the logic of the fundamental accounting equation is the double entry bookkeeping system while others believe that "for every action there is a reaction." Neither of those explanations is wrong, but both are too simplistic. The fact is that one side of the balance sheet states the resources of the business and the other side shows the total of the claims against the resources. You can't have more (or less) claims than resources. Whatever is owned by the business is either claimed by the creditors or claimed by the ultimate owners of the enterprise.

The evolution of the creation of a balance sheet. The easiest way to understand the concepts underlying the balance sheet is to go through some simple, hypothetical steps of creating a new business, The BBB Company (a proprietorship). The following six transactions show the relationship of resources and claims in a very simple business situation, starting at the inception of the business. Two balance sheets—a simple one and a more detailed one—are shown for each example. Please forgive the fact that the business logic of some of these examples leaves something to be desired; they are only used for illustrative purposes.

1. Billy B. Best, the proprietor of BBB, invests $10,000 in his new business venture on January 1, 2010. The following balance sheet shows that the assets of the business (cash) go up by $10,000. The owner's equity also goes up by $10,000, indicating that Billy has a claim on the assets of the business in the amount of $10,000. At this point, since the $10,000 is the total of the economic resources of the business, and no other outsider has a claim on any of them, the entire claim rests with the owner. This claim is the concept of equity, specifically "owner's equity." If BBB was a corporation, it would have issued stock, and the equity section of the balance sheet would show the account, "Common Stock - $10,000," instead of Owner's Equity - $10,000.

	The BBB Company Balance Sheet - Simple January 1, 2010	
(resources)		*(claims)*
Assets: $ 10,000	Owner's Equity	$ 10,000
Total $ 10,000	Total	$ 10,000

	The BBB Company Balance Sheet - More Detail January 1, 2010	
(resources)		*(claims)*
Assets:		Equity:
Cash $10,000	Owner's Equity	$10,000
Total $10,000	Total	$10,000

2. On January 5, Billy's second transaction is to borrow $5,000 from Neighborhood Bank. The result of this transaction is for BBB to obtain $5,000 more cash as well as a liability to the bank of $5,000. Although most businesses normally prepare balance sheets at the end of accounting periods (usually a month or a year), we will prepare one after each of these initial transactions in order to illustrate the effect of each transaction on the balance sheet. Following is the balance sheet of The BBB Company on January 5, right after the loan transaction is completed:

	The BBB Company Balance Sheet - Simple January 5, 2010	
(resources)		*(claims)*
Assets: $ 15,000	Liabilities:	$ 5,000
	Owner's Equity	$ 10,000
Total $ 15,000	Total	$ 15,000

	The BBB Company Balance Sheet - More Detail January 5, 2010	
(resources)		*(claims)*
Assets:	Liabilities:	
	Bank Loan	$ 5,000
Cash $15,000	Total Liabs	$ 5,000
	Equity:	
	Owner's Equity	$10,000
Total $15,000	Total	$15,000

At this point in the life of The BBB Company, we can see that the business has economic resources (cash) of $15,000. The source of the economic resources is twofold: $10,000 of the cash was given to the business by its owner, and consequently, the owner has a claim on the assets for $10,000; an additional $5,000 was lent to the business by the bank, and consequently, the bank has a claim on the assets (a debt of the business to the bank) in the amount of $5,000. Note that the total of the claims (liabilities plus equity) equals exactly the total of the economic resources (assets) of the business.

3. On January 8, Billy borrows an additional $1,000 from Neighborhood Bank. Following is The BBB Company's balance sheet after the additional loan is made:

The BBB Company			
Balance Sheet - Simple			
January 8, 2010			
(resources)		*(claims)*	
Assets:	$ 16,000	Liabilities:	$ 6,000
		Owner's Equity	$ 10,000
Total	$ 16,000	Total	$ 16,000

The BBB Company			
Balance Sheet - More Detail			
January 8, 2010			
(resources)		*(claims)*	
Assets:		Liabilities:	
		Bank Loan	$ 6,000
Cash	$16,000	Total Liabs	$ 6,000
		Equity:	
		Owner's	
		Equity	$10,000
Total	$16,000	Total	$16,000

Note the status of the balance sheet at this point. The business has total assets of $16,000, liabilities of $6,000, and owner's equity of $10,000. If the business were to be liquidated at this moment in time, the bank would require its debt to be repaid, effectively "claiming" $6,000 of the total assets of the business, and Billy would be entitled to a "residual claim" on the assets in the amount of $10,000. The total resources of the business, $16,000, would be claimed first by the creditors and then residually by the owner.

This concept of business equity is exactly the same as the concept of the equity that a person has in his house. If your house is worth $500,000 and the mortgage loan on the house is $325,000, the owner is said to have "equity" in the house of $175,000. This means that if the house is sold and the bank is paid off, the owner has a residual claim on the value of the house, which is the asset in the example. If the value of the house increases (all other things being equal), the owner's equity increases, and vice versa. Note, however, that the house is the *asset*; the *equity* is the owner's *claim* on the asset, not the asset itself. This is a subtle distinction.

4. On January 15, Billy pays back $2,500 of debt to the bank. The following balance sheet shows the status of the business after the loan repayment. Note that the assets of the business decrease and the liabilities decrease, but the equity of the business does not change when The BBB Company repays debt:

The BBB Company			
Balance Sheet - Simple			
January 15, 2010			
(resources)		*(claims)*	
Assets:	$ 13,500	Liabilities:	$ 3,500
		Owner's Equity	$ 10,000
Total	$ 13,500	Total	$ 13,500

The BBB Company			
Balance Sheet - More Detail			
January 15, 2010			
(resources)		*(claims)*	
Assets:		Liabilities:	
		Bank Loan	$ 3,500
Cash	$13,500	Total Liabs	$ 3,500
		Equity:	
		Owner's	
		Equity	$10,000
Total	$13,500	Total	$13,500

When you pay off a debt, you feel like your net worth just went down, because you just sent $200 to the credit card company, and you have $200 less in your bank account. In fact, the repayment of a debt does not decrease a person's equity—it does not change equity at all. The repayment of debt reduces a person's assets but it also reduces a person's debt by an equal amount, causing no change in equity. So it may be true that your credit card payment is money gone out of your bank account, but the credit card company has less of a claim on your assets than it had before you made the payment. Think about this concept (the fact that the repayment of a debt does not reduce your equity) before you move forward. Also reflect on the fact that "getting" a loan from the bank does not increase your equity—yes, you "gain" some cash, but you also "gain" a debt to the bank. You are no further ahead than you were before the loan.

5. On January 20, Billy decides to invest an additional $4,000 in his new enterprise. When Billy invests the money, the business's cash will increase and so will Billy's claim on the assets of the business, measured by owner's equity. Following is the balance sheet after the additional investment:

The BBB Company
Balance Sheet - Simple
January 20, 2010

(resources)		*(claims)*	
Assets:	$ 17,500	Liabilities:	$ 3,500
		Owner's Equity	$ 14,000
Total	$ 17,500	Total	$ 17,500

The BBB Company
Balance Sheet - More Detail
January 20, 2010

(resources)		*(claims)*	
Assets:		Liabilities:	
		Bank Loan	$ 3,500
Cash	$17,500	Total Liabs	$ 3,500
		Equity:	
		Owner's Equity	$14,000
Total	$17,500	Total	$17,500

6. On January 25, Billy decides that the business is in a position to return $2,000 of his capital to him—the accounting term for a return of capital to an owner is a draw. (In a corporation, a payment to shareholders that signifies a return of the original capital investment is called a dividend, but in a proprietorship, it is called a draw.) The following balance sheet shows the condition of The BBB Company after the draw to Billy:

The BBB Company
Balance Sheet - Simple
January 25, 2010

(resources)		*(claims)*	
Assets:	$ 15,500	Liabilities:	$ 3,500
		Owner's Equity	$ 12,000
Total	$ 15,500	Total	$ 15,500

The BBB Company
Balance Sheet - More Detail
January 25, 2010

(resources)		*(claims)*	
Assets:		Liabilities:	
		Bank Loan	$ 3,500
Cash	$15,500	Total Liabs	$ 3,500
		Equity:	
		Owner's Equity	$12,000
Total	$15,500	Total	$15,500

These simple transactions illustrate some of the basic transactions of a business that can be seen in its balance sheet. Understand that we have not yet ventured into the actual operations of the business (revenues and expenses), but it is important to understand investments into a business and returns of those investments (examples 1, 5 and 6) and borrowing and loan repayment transactions (examples 2, 3 and 4).

Summary. A *balance sheet* lists assets, liabilities and equity of a business at a single point in time. Assets are the economic resources of the business and they can take many forms (see earlier list). Liabilities and equity represent the claims on the assets of the business and they are either the claims of outsiders (creditors) or the owners. Although a balance sheet only measures assets and claims at a moment in time, it is the accumulation of everything that has happened to the business up to that moment. It is important to recognize that the balance sheet is a static financial statement: it doesn't show anything about the flows or trends of business activity. Notwithstanding its importance as a relevant financial statement, a balance sheet has other limitations that will be discussed subsequently.

Income Statement. The *income statement*[8] is the primary financial statement that measures the changes in the status of the entity over a period of time. The income statement measures the flow of business activity by comparing revenues (assets or cash[9] coming into the business) to the expenses (assets or cash[10] going out of the business) over a period of time, as opposed to the momentary status of the business at a point in time. Because an income statement is a flow statement, it will always be identified in relation to a period of time, for example: "Income Statement *for the year ended* December 31, 2010," or "Income Statement *for the month ended* March 31, 2009." The period of time can be any defined accounting period that is relevant for the particular business; most businesses break up a year into months and quarters and some businesses even track revenues and expenses by week or other relevant period.[11]

The income statement's "comparison" of revenues and expenses means that expenses are subtracted from revenues to determine if the business achieved *net income* or a *net loss* for the period. Simply stated, net income means that the business had revenues greater than expenses; a net loss means that the expenses were greater than the revenues. Net income does not necessarily mean that the business had a net increase in cash during the period, because both revenues and expenses can be made up of things other than cash. For instance, a business can

---

8. The income statement is also called "Statement of Income," "Profit & Loss" statement, "P&L," "Statement of Earnings," or "Statement of Revenues and Expenses." All of these names describe the same financial statement.

9. REVENUES ARE MORE THAN JUST CASH COMING IN. For introductory purposes only, we are presently limited to discussing the cash method of accounting; you will soon learn that revenues can occur from other "assets" coming into the business, such as accounts receivable.

10. EXPENSES ARE MORE THAN JUST CASH GOING OUT. Again, we are only talking about the cash method. Expenses can occur without the payment of cash, but save that complication for later.

11. It would be logical, for instance, for a music group to summarize its business activity into relevant time periods identified by the dates of a concert tour, or concert season. A fruit packing house might have an accounting period that was the cherry packing season or apple packing season. In this text, when I refer to an accounting "period," I will always be referring to either a month or a year unless otherwise specified.

have revenue by gaining an account receivable from a client or it can incur an expense without immediately paying out cash. (Instead of an immediate cash payment, an account payable can be accrued.) So net income does not necessarily mean positive cash, and net loss does not necessarily mean negative cash.

Revenue. Revenue is the gross increase in assets that flows into an entity as a result of business operations. Simply stated, revenue is the measure of the business's sales of goods and services to its customers. (Importantly, note that revenue is not limited to *cash* flowing into a business; it could be other types of assets as well.[12]) In merchandising operations, revenues are usually called "sales," and in service businesses they are usually called "fees earned" or just "revenues." The critical part of the definition of revenues is that the inflow must be the result of business operations, or operating activities, as opposed to financing or investing activities. There are many reasons why assets could flow into a business that would not be revenue—proceeds from a loan, investment from investors, or the receipt of money in exchange for another asset. When assets flow into a business, they are only revenue if they are the direct result of the sale of the business's goods or services in the marketplace.

Depending on the nature of particular businesses, there are a handful of different types of revenue. Some examples are:

Sales—revenues obtained from the sale of goods

Fees earned—revenues earned from the performance of services

Revenues—a general term for revenue that can be used for most situations

Interest income—revenue from interest earned

Other income—revenue from miscellaneous activities that generate income

When revenue flows into a business, the equity of the business increases. However, the accounting measure of this increase occurs somewhat indirectly, by measuring the revenue as part of the business's income statement during the entire accounting period. Then, at the end of the accounting period, the income statement will summarize the net change in equity that results from the operations of the business for the entire period, rather than increasing equity every time a revenue transaction occurs. (Expenses, as you will see, have the opposite effect on the equity of the business, and are also handled within the income statement.)

---

12. Yes, revenue can result from assets flowing into the business other than cash. But 99 percent of the time, the ONLY other asset flowing into the business that constitutes revenue is an Account Receivable. Customers "pay" for goods and services with cash or accounts receivable; they do not ordinarily "pay" with cars, trucks, machines or the forgiveness of debt. These scenarios are possibilities within the meaning of revenue, but they are rare exceptions. Therefore, our discussion of non-cash revenues will always be limited to accounts receivable.

Expenses. The formal definition of expenses is "the costs that expire during the creation of revenue." This concept can be a little difficult to understand. A cost is the amount of money or property paid for a good or service. A cost can be unexpired, meaning that the business hasn't used up the thing that it purchased, or it can be expired, meaning that it is presently being used up. The concept of expenses is more complicated than just the spending of money, but that is a good place to start to understand expenses. The following example will explain.

During the course of its operations, a business purchases goods and services to further its objective of generating revenue. Let's take a simple case and gradually build more complexity.

Carl C. Clark's Landscaping Service ("CCC") pays wages to its employees and buys gasoline to run its lawn mowers in January. Since CCC pays wages at the end of every work week and it only buys enough gas to operate for one day at a time, the cost of those wages and gasoline are used up immediately in the production of revenue, so those costs expire. When those wages and gas costs are paid, they are treated as expenses of the business. In this simplest level of expense, CCC expenses those costs when they are paid because there is no future benefit of the costs to the business—they are being used up currently in the production of revenue.

Next level of complication: If Carl decided to start selling fruit trees to his customers, he might go to the nursery and buy 20 or 30 trees (inventory) to show to his customers for possible sale to them. When CCC's Landscaping buys those trees (assume in February), the company acquires inventory, an asset (an economic resource that it holds on its balance sheet—it is an unexpired cost). CCC will show those trees on its balance sheet at the end of the month because they are an asset of the business and not YET an expense. When CCC sells a tree (assume in March), the cost of that tree will expire and the company will expense the cost of that tree because that is the period in which the cost is used up in the production of revenue. If CCC only sold one tree in March, it would "expense" the cost of one item of inventory in March, and at the end of the month, the remaining trees would be shown on the company's balance sheet because those trees are still an economic resource of the business.

Next level of complication: CCC buys a new truck for $20,000 on April 1 to use in the business. Does CCC expense $20,000 in April? Of course not, because the $20,000 truck is not "used up" in April, but it will be used up over the course of a few years in the operation of the business. For the truck, CCC will adopt some method of depreciation (discussed in Chapter 5), which is a methodology to allocate the cost of a business asset as an expense over its expected useful life. But CCC will not "expense" $20,000 in April, even though it spent the money, because the cost of the truck is not expired (used up) in April.

A final complication to consider at the outset of understanding expenses is the expense that is not "paid" with cash. It is very possible to have an expense by incurring a liability, rather than immediately paying cash. Take the example of "purchasing" goods and services with credit (debt), as opposed to cash. The character of these costs (expired or unexpired) is not changed by the method of acquiring them (cash or debt). For example, if CCC's payroll is one week delayed (meaning that this Friday's paychecks are for work performed a week earlier), the cost of the wages for the last week of April is expired and the wages are owed (wages payable), even though the cash doesn't leave the business until May 7. CCC would have wages expense for the last week of April measured by the amount of payroll owed at the end of that week.

Creating the Income Statement. The income statement is the financial statement that summarizes the *flow* of the operations of the business for the period, and it does it through its presentation of revenues and expenses. At the end of the accounting period, all of the revenues and expenses that occurred during the period are summarized in the income statement for the period, resulting in a calculation of net income or net loss. If the business was successful during the period, the revenues will be greater than the expenses, resulting in net income for the period; if the expenses exceeded the revenues, a net loss will result. Either way, the net result of the income statement will affect the equity of the business, increasing equity if it is net income, or decreasing equity if it is a net loss. Here is a sample income statement for The CCC Company for the six months ended June 30, 2010:

The CCC Company
Income Statement
For the Six Months Ended June 30, 2010

Revenues

Landscaping fees		$ 78,425

Expenses:

Advertising Expense	$ 2,925	
Gas & Oil Expense	4,050	
Salaries Expense	36,500	
Payroll Tax Expense	3,650	
Depreciation Expense	3,800	
Equipment Repair Expense	1,475	
Supplies Expense	1,900	
Total Expenses		54,300

Net Income   **$ 24,125**

Completing the Process. At the end of the accounting period, all of the accounting transactions that occurred during the period are summarized into financial statements. The balance sheet shows the *status* of the business on the last day of the period by showing the company's assets, liabilities and equity. The income statement summarizes the *flow* of the operations of the business through its presentation of revenues, expenses and net income. By observing and analyzing both the balance sheet and income statement of the business, the user can understand the present financial status of the organization and see the flows of activity that have occurred in the past. While the financial history of the business may not be the only measure of the success of the company, most observers would agree that the historical and present financial health of the organization is among the most significant of the relevant facts about the company.

The preceding discussion is a simplified, introductory overview of the accounting process that will be expanded in subsequent chapters. For now, this overview will suffice.

Generally Accepted Accounting Principles

> The overarching objective of financial reporting is to provide useful information to investors, creditors, management and other interested parties. To accountants, the two most important characteristics of useful information are relevance and reliability. Information is relevant to the extent that it can potentially alter a decision. Reliable information is verifiable, representationally faithful, and neutral. The hallmark of neutrality is its demand that accounting information not be selected to benefit one class of users to the neglect of others.[13]

> In addition to being relevant and reliable, accounting information should be comparable and consistent. Comparability refers to the ability to make relevant comparisons between two or more companies in the same industry at a point in time. Consistency refers to the ability to make relevant comparisons within the same company over a period of time.[14]

Generally Accepted Accounting Principles ("GAAP") are defined as "the conventions, rules, and procedures that define accepted accounting practice at a particular time."[15] GAAP includes not only broad guidelines of general application but also detailed practices and procedures that provide a standard by which to measure financial presentations. GAAP is the combination of authoritative standards (set by policy boards) and the conglomeration of commonly accepted ways of recording and reporting accounting information. In the aggregate, GAAP is the "common law" of accounting, and GAAP has worked reasonably well over the last 75 years.

Beginning in the 1990s, there has been an international trend toward the adoption of the International Financial Reporting Standards (IFRS) promulgated by the International Accounting Standards Board (IASB). In fact, the U.S. Government has acknowledged the need for a single set of high quality global accounting standards—in addition to the continuing globalization of the capital markets—and the SEC's thoughtful approach to assessing IFRS adoption point to the inevitability of IFRS as the global standard.

---

13. Brittanica.com.
14. Id.
15. Accounting Principles Board (APB) Statement No. 4, *Basic Concepts and Accounting Principles Underlying Financial Statement of Business Enterprise.*

At a technical level, there are significant differences between GAAP and IFRS, but at the introductory level of basic concepts and conventions, the two sets of principles are essentially the same. The objectives of both GAAP and IFRS are the fair presentation of financial information of organizations so that the users of the information can be properly informed about decisions regarding the information.

Under both GAAP and IFRS, certain fundamental concepts have evolved as foundational to the accumulation of accounting information and preparation of financial statements. Whether the concepts are called standards, principles, conventions or other terms is not important; what is important is that the concepts are the foundation of modern accounting.

A. **Entity Concept.** The individual entity stands alone and its financial activity is measured independently. The entity concept applies even though the law may not draw complete distinctions between certain types of business organizations and their owners, like proprietorships and partnerships. Under the entity concept, even those entities will be accounted for separately.

B. **Time period.** To provide timely information about a company's progress, it is necessary to prepare periodic performance reports. The accounting process is therefore divided into time periods, most commonly months, quarters or years.

It is well understood that the life cycle of a business operation is continuous and any attempt to divide it into specific time periods is somewhat arbitrary. Nevertheless, it is only logical that business activity be reported in relation to time periods. Interestingly, the element of periodicity creates many of the problems of accountancy, requiring a high degree of precision and accuracy in time period cutoffs for the recording of revenue and expenses of the business.

C. **Going Concern.** A company is assumed to be in business indefinitely unless there is evidence to the contrary. The adoption of this assumption has significant consequences for accounting information, particularly the use of the historical cost concept for accounting for fixed assets and the recognition of prepaid items as assets of the business. It should be noted that the going concern assumption should be abandoned if there is evidence that the business has reason to believe that its future operations are in doubt. In that case, a liquidation assumption should be adopted for the preparation of financial statements. However, absent contrary information, the business is assumed to be ongoing, and this underlying assumption has significant consequences for the financial reporting of the entity.

D. **Historical cost.** Under the historical cost assumption, assets are recorded at the amount of cash or cash equivalents paid or the fair value of the consideration given to acquire them at the time of their acquisition. Liabilities are recorded at the amount of proceeds received in exchange for the obligation, or in some circumstances (for example, income taxes), at the amounts of cash or cash equivalents expected to be paid to satisfy the liability in the normal course of business. The underlying logic for the cost principle is twofold: first, historical cost is an objective measure in that it is derived from an arm's length transaction of purchase or other transaction; and second, since the going concern principle applies generally, it is presumed that the current fair market value of the particular asset is not primarily relevant because the entity is not in the business of selling the asset in the normal course of operation, but rather it uses the asset in the operation of the enterprise.

In recent years there has been a departure from the rigid application of the cost principle for certain types of assets, particularly financial instruments and intangible assets acquired in business acquisitions. At the elementary level of accounting, the only significance of this trend is its existence, not its effect on rudimentary accounting issues. But any departure from the long-established cost principle is noteworthy.

E. **Conservatism.** The conservatism principle applies to accounting judgments made in uncertain situations; if alternative values are possible and the accountant is uncertain about which to choose, the conservatism principle supports the choice of the option least likely to overstate assets and profits.

F. **Consistency.** The principle of consistency requires that accounting reports be prepared using methods and estimates that are consistent with those of prior periods. Financial statements are most useful when information about a company is measured and disclosed in the same manner from one accounting period to the next. Consistency does not preclude changing from one accounting method to another, but if such a change is made, the company must disclose the nature of and reason for the change, and its dollar effect, in the financial statements and the related footnotes.

G. **Materiality.** The concept of materiality is a backdrop to the reporting of all financial information about an enterprise. Materiality usually relates to the importance of a particular dollar amount, although it can also relate to the characterization of a transaction. The best definition of materiality is: would a reasonable user of the financial information about this company consider this amount significant in relation to the entire situation of the financial statement? If the amount or characterization is considered significant, then it should be specifically reported as part of the accounting process and in the preparation of financial statements.

There is a great reluctance by accountants to define materiality as a percentage or an absolute dollar amount. The concept is much broader than a simple mathematical definition. A judgment regarding materiality requires consideration of the magnitude of the amount, the nature of the item, and the surrounding circumstances in which the materiality judgment is made. Materiality judgments require both quantitative and qualitative considerations.

The concept of materiality controls the practicality of accounting for many types of transactions. For instance, it may be true that a law office purchases office supplies that it does not use up for several months—probably even extending into the next accounting year—but it is simply not practical (or material) to account for the office supplies as inventory, and then expense the supplies as they are used up. This type of exercise would be absurd: would someone have to take an inventory of pencils, paper clips and stationery at the end of the year and then determine how much was used up during the period? There is no need for this level of immaterial precision.

The materiality concept also arises when dealing with an adjustment or correction to a financial statement. If a $10,000 adjustment should be made to correct a financial statement, that adjustment would likely be material in the financial statements of a brand new law proprietorship, but it would be insignificant to the financial statements of a company listed on the New York Stock Exchange. The same $10,000 adjustment must be made in one situation to fairly present the financial statements, but it would not have to be made in the other.

H. **Objectivity.** The principle of objectivity requires that accounting data be unbiased and based on objectively verifiable information. There are many occasions in accounting where judgments, estimates and other subjective factors must be taken into account, but the objectivity principle requires that the most objective evidence should be relied on.

I. **Money Measurement.** The money measurement concept recognizes that accounting data only records transactions that are capable of being expressed in monetary terms. This concept also assumes the stability of the unit of measure—the dollar—even though it is understood that there has been an historical level of inflation embedded in the currency.

It should be noted that IFRS approaches the money measurement concept more aggressively than GAAP, but IFRS deals with many international currencies, some of which experience significant inflation. Under IFRS, accountants consider changes in the purchasing power of the functional currency up to but excluding 26% per annum for three years in a row (which would be 100% cumulative inflation over three years or hyperinflation as defined in IFRS) as immaterial. If inflation above this level is experienced, the implementation of units of constant purchasing power is employed for financial reporting.

As a brief side note, anyone can readily see the arbitrary nature of the IFRS's attempt to deal with the reality of significant inflation. It is easy to understand that something should be done to adjust financial statements for significant inflation, but as soon as an attempt is made to quantify a correction to the known problem, it is apparent that the solution does not fit all situations.

J. **Realization Principle.** The realization principle relates to the timing of revenue recognition, a critical issue in the determination of net income during an accounting period. The realization principle holds that items of revenue should be recognized when the entity has completed or virtually completed the exchange and it can reasonably estimate the probability of payment. The realization principle implicitly looks to the contract of the buyer and seller to determine if the steps of the exchange have taken place. If so, revenue is realized, whether or not cash has changed hands.

The underlying concept of the realization principle is relatively straightforward at the introductory level, but the application of the principle to complicated factual situations is difficult. Complex questions about revenue recognition arise in accounting for long term contracts, software development contracts and installment sales. Chapter 4 discusses the realization principle in detail.

K. **Matching**. The matching principle states that when specific revenues are recognized in a period, the expenses incurred to generate those revenues should also be assigned to that period. The matching principle is fundamental to the proper determination of net income, a critical objective of the accounting system. The matching principle is also covered in Chapter 4.

L. **Full Disclosure**. The principle of full disclosure requires that all facts needed to make the financial statements not misleading be disclosed. This principle is practically implemented by the requirement that financial statements include footnotes that disclose this relevant information.

Limitations of Accounting Information

Accounting information and financial statements report the historical financial activity of a business. This information is extremely important to the users of it, but there are many limitations to accounting information that must be considered. First, accounting only reports activity that can be measured in dollars, and businesses are much more dynamic than mere finances. Accounting information does not directly deal with a company's business plan, the strength of its management team, the quality of its workforce, the enforceability of its legal contracts and many other relevant business considerations. Of course, it can be suggested that the accumulation of all the qualities of a business organization are embodied in its historical financial performance, and there is some truth to that. In theory, a business that possesses great ideas, people and systems should produce strong financial results, and vice versa. Regardless of the theory, however, understand that accounting information only provides historical financial results.

Analyzing Financial Statements. When reviewing a company's financial statements, it is important to realize the limitations of a singularly accounting-based approach to analyzing the company. The recent financial performance of a company may be the most important fact of the company for some purposes, but that fact alone is not the entirety of the organization. Many times, historical financial statements are used as the best indicator of a company's expected near-term future performance, and this assumption may be well founded, but historical financial activity is not a guarantor of future performance. Obviously, myriad factors can affect a business's future performance, and history is only one fact of consequence in the assessment.

The sophisticated analysis of historical financial statements and their individual elements can provide extensive knowledge about the financial and management success of the organization, even given the limitations of accounting information. The "numbers" in the accounting data of a company can be quite meaningful when they are analyzed in relation to each other, other companies and the industry in which the organization operates. Chapter 7 shows the reader the financial analytic techniques that can be used to obtain very helpful information from a company's financial statements, relating to liquidity, leverage, profitability and management efficiency. So it is true that accounting information has significant limitations that the users must be aware of, but it is pretty difficult to argue against the success (or failure) of a particular business enterprise as shown in its properly prepared financial statements.

Conclusion

This introductory chapter lays the groundwork for an understanding of the accounting process and the development of the two basic financial statements, the balance sheet and the income statement. The elements of these statements are the fundamental categories of accounting data that comprise financial reporting. We learn the Generally Accepted Accounting Principles that provide the foundation for accumulating, measuring, summarizing and reporting the results of the financial activity of business organizations. Finally, the limitations of accounting information are identified.

Double Entry Accounting System

Introduction

Bookkeeping is the aspect of the accounting process that focuses on recording and summarizing a firm's daily financial activities. In an accounting system, all activity begins with a financial transaction, an economic event between the business and an outsider.[1] A bookkeeping system initially records each transaction individually and then summarizes groups of similar transactions in the accounts of the business. At the end of an accounting period, each account of the business is totaled to equal its account balance, and the account balances are used to prepare financial statements.

Today, virtually all businesses use software to implement accounting systems. Nevertheless, whether the bookkeeping system is computerized or manual, it summarizes the same basic flow of information:

Transactions occur. *The transaction is translated into debits and credits, the basic language of accounting. Debits and credits are the mechanism by which the accounting system is able to summarize and process the transaction.*

JOURNAL **Transactions are listed in a Journal.** *The Journal is the book of **original entry** of the accounting system, and transactions are listed in the journal as debits and credits.*

GENERAL LEDGER **The Journal entries (debits and credits) are posted to the individual accounts of the business that are contained in the General Ledger.** *The General Ledger is the book of **final entry**.*

The accounts in the General Ledger are each totaled to an account balance.

The account balances are used to create financial statements.

The revenue and expense account balances are "closed" at the end of the accounting period so the accounting process can begin again in the next period.

---

1.   Some transactions are internal, but these will be discussed later.

This chapter introduces the reader to a basic accounting system. The discussion should demystify some of the common misunderstandings about accounting information and take the reader through some simple examples. These examples demonstrate how information flows through an accounting system and is converted into relevant financial statements that can be used to evaluate the health of a business enterprise.

Although all modern accounting systems are computerized, it is very helpful to the reader's understanding of accounting systems to learn a basic manual system of bookkeeping. Through this process, the reader will understand the flow of money and capital through a business organization and the resulting financial statements that are produced. A basic understanding of debits and credits is essential to the understanding of accounting systems as a whole and should, therefore, not be overlooked.

One essential clarification about learning a manual accounting system: Recognize that in such an accounting system, transactions are first recorded in chronological series in the appropriate accounting journals before they are summarized and "posted" to the summary accounting record, the general ledger. The general ledger is then used as the basis for the preparation of financial statements. For example, in a manual accounting system, individual checks (payments) would be recorded serially in a cash disbursements journal during the month. At the end of the accounting period (the month), the cash disbursements journal would be summarized and "posted" to the general ledger. To understand a manual system, we will go through the transactions chronologically.

In contrast to a manual accounting system, a computerized system has the capability of running one individual transaction completely through the entire system instantaneously, so there is no "serial posting" of transactions as there is in old fashioned accounting journals. Obviously, a computerized system can process one transaction or a million transactions, from the date of transaction through to the final financial statement. In a manual system, there is no practical way to trace one transaction (a check written on the 10th of the month, for instance) through to the financial statements without summarizing the entire cash disbursements journal. This chapter will introduce the reader to a manual accounting system, complete with the delay of "running a transaction through the system" discussed in this paragraph.

The Transaction

As explained in Chapter 2, an entity financially interacts with the world through *transactions*. In accounting, a transaction is any event or condition recorded in the book of accounts.[2] It is an event that effects a change in the assets, liabilities, or equity of a business. A transaction usually indicates some exchange of financial resources between the entity and an outsider; it can be a sale, the payment of an expense, a borrowing, a repayment, receipt of an investment, or another financial activity. A transaction is the original trigger that sets the accounting process in motion, and each transaction is recorded individually in a company's accounting system.

---

2.   InvestorWords.com

Most transactions are external transactions, executed with outsiders, as, for example, those described in the preceding paragraph. Businesses also account for internal transactions, defined as those that reapportion costs within the business organization. Examples of internal transactions are the depreciation of fixed assets or the consumption of supplies and raw materials in the production process of the business. Whether internal or external, a transaction is the event that begins the accounting process.

In Chapter 2, we introduced some very basic transactions (initial investment in the business; borrowing money; repaying money to the bank; returning some capital to the owner). In this chapter, we will expand our knowledge of transactions to go to the next level of sophistication. Here are some examples of more complicated, external transactions that will be incorporated into the accounting for Pete's Proprietorship, our example in this chapter:

1. The company purchases some office equipment for $3,300.

2. The company pays various expenses, such as rent, salaries and travel expenses.

3. The company records fees collected from clients totaling $21,500 for work performed during the month of January.

4. The firm applies for, and obtains, a line of credit. It takes an initial advance of $2,500 on the line of credit.

These transactions will be recorded as journal entries, posted to a general ledger, and used to prepare financial statements in this chapter.

The Account

The basic component of the formal accounting system is the *account*, which is an individual record of increases and decreases in specific assets, liabilities, equity, revenues and expenses. It is the device used to accumulate increases and decreases in a specific item; the simplest form of account is called a "T account," and it looks like this:

Title

(Left side) | (Right side)

A simple T-account has three parts: 1) a title; 2) a left side; and 3) a right side. In a T-account, all increases to the account are listed on one side, and all decreases to the account are listed on the other side. It is important to note that some types of accounts are increased by entries on the left side, and other types of accounts are increased by entries on the right side. (See "Debits and Credits," discussed subsequently.)

A T-account accumulates increases and decreases in an account over a period of time, culminating in the calculation of a *balance* in the account. Here is an example of a handwritten T-account for cash for an accounting period:

	Cash	
	(increases)	*(decreases)*
Beginning Balance	10,000	3,000
	4,000	500
	3,000	350
	200	1,400
	1,350	
	425	
	18,975	5,250
New Balance	13,725	

In this T-account, the total of the entries on the left-hand side is $18,975 and the total of the entries on the right-hand side is $5,250. Mechanically, the summation of these entries results in a net *"balance"* of $13,725 that is "left sided." The "balance" simply means that the left side exceeds the right side by $13,725.

In actual practice, most accounting systems will have T-accounts that contain more information than the elementary examples shown. Regardless of the complexity of a particular T-account, keep in mind that it is fundamentally a "T." Here is an example of a more complicated account:

Account: Cash   Account No. 001-01

Date	Item	PR	Debit	Date	Item	PR	Credit
1/1/2010	Capital Investment		10,000	1/3/2010	January Rent Expense		1,750
1/10/2010	Loan from Neighborhood bank		2,500	1/16/2010	Office Furniture		3,300
1/29/2010	Fees Earned		21,500	1/20/2010	Pay back loan		1,500
				1/22/2010	Travel Expense		1,875
				1/31/2010	Salary Expense		8,200
			34,000				16,625
Balance			17,375				

There are three types of accounts: *permanent accounts, temporary accounts and nominal accounts.* *Permanent accounts* are maintained for asset, liability and equity accounts of the business. These accounts contain balances that change over time based on the activity posted to them, but permanent accounts remain open after the books of the business have been *closed* at the end of the accounting period. Permanent accounts are never "zeroed out," or closed, for the purpose of starting over in a new accounting period.

By contrast, *temporary accounts* record revenue and expense activity *for a period of time*, and then they are *closed* at the end of the accounting period, meaning they are adjusted to zero. For example, the revenue of a business is tracked for a period of time, and at the end of the period, the account is adjusted to zero so the revenue can start at zero for the next period. The same is true for expenses. The relevant accounting information contained in temporary accounts is "what is the amount of this item of revenue or expense for the accounting period," not "what is the total amount of this item since the inception of the business." Consequently, revenue and expense accounts are temporary accounts. They are accumulated for the entire accounting period; then they are "closed" (adjusted to zero) so the books and records can be summarized and prepared for the next accounting period.

Nominal accounts are T-accounts that are only used at the very end of an accounting period, in the mechanical process of closing the books. They are opened and closed during the closing process. Their function is to accumulate debits and credits in the process of closing out the temporary accounts, and they are finally closed when the net income or loss is posted to the equity accounts of the business. (This process is moderately complicated and typically understood more fully through an example.)

All accounts of a business are maintained in one accounting record, the *general ledger.* This document is discussed in detail subsequently.

At first, the possible list of accounts for a business entity can seem endless, but it usually is not. Every business will have a *Chart of Accounts*, a listing of the accounts that are used for the enterprise. Because the activities of most businesses become somewhat routine after an initial startup period, the chart of accounts doesn't change significantly from month to month or year to year. It is somewhat unusual—but not improbable—to require a new account. Here are two examples of "typical" charts of accounts, first for a small services proprietorship (Pete's), and then for a small, more complicated retailing corporation.

Examples of charts of account:

```
        Pete's Proprietorship
        Chart of Accounts

Cash
Furniture & Equipment
Loan Payable
Proprietor's Equity
Fees Earned
Salary Expense
Rent Expense
Travel Expense
Income Summary (*)

(*) "Income Summary" is a nominal account that is
    only used for closing the books.
```

Chart of Accounts
(more complicated)

Cash	Sales
Marketable Securities	Sales Discounts
Accounts Receivable	Purchases
Inventory	Advertising Expense
Prepaid Items	Amortization Expense
Land	Automobile Expense
Buildings	Depreciation Expense
Accumulated Depreciation - Bldgs.	Insurance Expense
Machinery & Equipment	Interest Expense
Accumulated Depreciation - M & E	Legal & Professional Fees
Vehicles	Pension & Profit Sharing Expense
Accumulated Depreciation - Vehicles	Rent Expense
Patents	Repairs & Maintenance Expense
Accounts Payable	Salaries Expense
Accrued Expenses	Sales Commissions Expense
Taxes Payable Notes Payable	Taxes
Common Stock	Travel & Entertainment Expense
Additional Paid In Capital	Utilities & Telephone Expense
Retained Earnings	Income Summary

Debits and Credits

In a T-account, the left-hand side is arbitrarily called the *debit* side and the right-hand side is arbitrarily called the *credit* side.[3] Amounts entered on the left-hand side are called debits and amounts entered on the right-hand side, credits. Accountants also use the words debit and credit as verbs, indicating that an account has been *debited* or *credited* for a particular amount.

The words *debit* and *credit* are very much the basic language of accounting because they are used to describe, define and explain every accounting transaction. When a transaction occurs, the way that it is translated into accounting language is to describe it as, for example, "debit Cash, credit Loans Payable," or, "debit Machinery & Equipment, credit Cash." The first step of the accounting process is to convert a transaction into the form of a debit and a credit. The transaction will then be entered into the books of original entry of the business.

The rules of debit and credit dictate increases and decreases in the different types of accounts in the accounting equation. In short, the rules dictate which account types are increased or decreased by debits or credits. Initially, there appears to be no apparent logic to these rules, so the best advice is to simply memorize the rules. The logic of the system will become apparent with repeated application. The following chart sets forth the basic rules of debits and credits and how each type of account is changed by debiting or crediting the account:

Account	To Increase	To Decrease
Asset	Debit	Credit
Liability	Credit	Debit
Owner's Equity	Credit	Debit
Revenue	Credit	Debit
Expense	Debit	Credit

Another way to visualize the same rules of Debit and Credit is:

Asset		Liability		Owner's Equity		Revenue		Expense	
(Dr.)	(Cr.)	(Dr.)	(Cr.)	(Dr.)	(Cr.)	(Dr.)	(Cr.)	(Dr.)	(Cr.)
+	−	−	+	−	+	−	+	+	−

---

3.   The terms debit and credit are abbreviated "Dr." and "Cr." The terms do not necessarily mean decrease or increase; debit does not have a negative connotation and credit does not have a positive connotation. They ONLY mean left-hand sided entry and right-hand sided entry.

As we will learn shortly, every transaction in the accounting system is stated in terms of debits and credits. Debits affect different types of accounts differently, causing increases and decreases in account balances, and the same can be said about credits. Accounts will be summarized into account balances at the end of the accounting period, and the account balances will be used to prepare financial statements.

A little bit of logic. At the risk of contradicting myself, I will attempt to infuse a little logic to the discussion of debits and credits. Keep in mind, if you have any difficulty understanding the rationale of debits and credits, just practice doing them and you will figure them out pretty quickly. For assets, liabilities and equity accounts, the rules are just what they are: assets are increased with debits (and decreased with credits[4]); liabilities and equity are increased with credits (decreased with debits). That is the starting place: there is no rationale to that order.

However, the theory of debit and credit in its application to revenue and expense accounts is based on the relationship of these accounts to equity. Revenue increases equity, and just as increases to equity are recorded as credits, increases in revenue during an accounting period are recorded as credits. Expenses, on the other hand, have the effect of decreasing equity. The more one spends, the more equity decreases. Just as decreases in equity are recorded as debits, increases in expense accounts are recorded as debits. Although debits to expense accounts signify decreases in equity, they may also be referred to as increases in expense. Again, this attempt at logic is nice, but not terribly necessary at this juncture.

Returning to a simple T-account, after the month's postings have been made to the account, the difference in dollars between the total debits and the total credits in the account is called the **account balance.** If the debits exceed the credits, the account has a **debit balance**; if the credits exceed the debits, the account has a **credit balance.**

All asset accounts normally have a debit balance, because increases to asset accounts are recorded with debits and it is hard to imagine a credit balance, or negative balance, in an asset account, absent some error. All liability accounts normally have a credit balance because liability accounts are increased with credits, and it is unlikely to have a negative liability. Such a condition would indicate overpayment to a creditor of the business, meaning that the liability has been paid down below zero. Continuing this logic, equity accounts normally have credit balances because the account would logically be positive. Finally, revenue accounts' "normal" balance is a credit and expense accounts' "normal" balance is debit.

Following is a table that summarizes the "normal" account balances for each type of account:

---

4. Of course, this inverse relationship is always true (if debits increase an account, credits decrease it, and vice versa). This relationship will not be restated every time.

Account	Normal Balance
Asset	Debit
Liability	Credit
Owner's Equity	Credit
Revenue	Credit
Expense	Debit

Double Entry Accounting System

Double entry is the method of bookkeeping in which every financial transaction is entered as a debit to one account and as a credit to another account, so that the totals of the debits and credits for every transaction are always equal. Every financial transaction affects at least two accounts, with more complicated transactions affecting more than two. Regardless of the complexity of a transaction or the number of accounts affected, the sum of the debits is always equal to the sum of the credits for every transaction entered into the books of original entry.

The double entry system ensures that all of the accounts of the business remain "in balance," with total assets equaling the sum of the liabilities plus the equity of the business at all times.

Recording a Transaction

The initial recording of a transaction in the accounting records of a business is called *"journalizing the transaction."* Here are the *necessary questions* that must be answered to journalize a transaction in the records of the business:

Is this an accounting event?

Which specific accounts are affected?

Are the effects to each account increases or decreases (debits or credits)?

What are the corresponding dollar amounts of each debit and credit?

When these questions have been answered, the transaction can be stated in terms of debits and credits and then entered in one of the *journals* of the business. Journals of the business are known as the *books of original entry,* and the form of the initial entry of the transaction to the books is a *journal entry.* A journal entry is the statement of a transaction in the form of debits and credits. Following are some examples of very simple transactions for our new business enterprise, Pete's Proprietorship, stated in the form of journal entries.

Chapter 3: Double Entry Accounting System

1. Pete, the proprietor, invests $10,000 into his new law practice venture on January 1, 2010:

Necessary Questions:

Is this an accounting event? Yes—it is a transaction that affects the accounts of the business.

Which specific accounts are affected? The cash of the business increases and the proprietor's equity increases.

Are the effects to each account increases or decreases (debits or credits)? Cash is an asset; assets increase with debits. Proprietor's Equity is an equity account; equity accounts increase with credits.

What are the corresponding dollar amounts of each debit and credit? $10,000 to each account.

Journal Entry:

Ref.	Date	Description	Dr.	Cr.
1.	Jan. 1	Cash	10,000	
		Proprietor's Equity		10,000
		To record initial investment in business		

2. The business pays rent for the month of January in the amount of $1,750 on January 3, 2010.

Necessary Questions:

Is this an accounting event? Yes—it is a transaction that affects the accounts of the business.

Which specific accounts are affected? The cash of the business decreases and the expenses of the business increase.

Are the effects to each account increases or decreases (debits or credits)? Cash is an asset; assets decrease with credits. Rent expense is an expense; expenses increase with debits.

What are the corresponding dollar amounts of each debit and credit? $1,750 to each account.

Journal Entry:

Ref.	Date	Description	Dr.	Cr.
2.	Jan. 3	Rent expense	1,750	
		Cash		1,750
		To record payment of rent expense		

3. The business borrows $2,500 from Neighborhood Bank on January 10, 2010.

Necessary Questions:

Is this an accounting event? Yes—it is a transaction that affects the accounts of the business.

Which specific accounts are affected? The cash of the business increases and the liabilities (to the bank) increase.

Are the effects to each account increases or decreases (debits or credits)? Cash is an asset; assets increase with debits. Loan Payable is a liability account; liabilities increase with credits.

What are the corresponding dollar amounts of each debit and credit? $2,500 to each account.

Journal Entry:

Ref.	Date	Description		Dr.	Cr.
3.	Jan. 10	Cash		2,500	
		Loan Payable			2,500
		To record receipt of loan proceeds from bank			

Query: Ignoring the $2,500 loan just discussed, would there be a journal entry if the bank approved a new line of credit (loan) in the amount of $1,500? Answer: No; the approval of a loan is *not* a transaction. There is no change to the assets, liabilities or equity of the business as a result of the bank's mere approval of the loan; no transaction has occurred until money is advanced to the business.

4. The business purchases $3,300 of office furniture on January 16, 2010.

Necessary Questions:

Is this an accounting event? Yes—it is a transaction that affects the accounts of the business.

Which specific accounts are affected? The cash of the business decreases and the Office Equipment account increases.

Are the effects to each account increases or decreases (debits or credits)? Cash is an asset; assets decrease with credits. Office Equipment is an asset; assets increase with debits.

What are the corresponding dollar amounts of each debit and credit? $3,300 to each account.

Journal Entry:

Ref.	Date	Description	Dr.	Cr.
4.	Jan. 16	Furniture & Equipment	3,300	
		Cash		3,300
		To record the purchase of office furniture		

5. The business repays $1,500 of its loan to the bank on January 20, 2010.

Necessary Questions:

Is this an accounting event? Yes—it is a transaction that affects the accounts of the business.

Which specific accounts are affected? The cash of the business decreases and the liabilities (to the bank) also decrease.

Are the effects to each account increases or decreases (debits or credits)? Cash is an asset; assets decrease with credits. Loan Payable is a liability account; liabilities decrease with debits.

What are the corresponding dollar amounts of each debit and credit? $1,500 to each account.

Journal Entry:

Ref.	Date	Description	Dr.	Cr.
5.	Jan. 20	Loan Payable	1,500	
		Cash		1,500
		To record loan repayment to bank		

6. On January 22, the business pays $1,875 of travel expense for Pete's client related trip to London in January.

Necessary Questions:

Is this an accounting event? Yes—it is a transaction that affects the accounts of the business.

Which specific accounts are affected? The cash of the business decreases and the expenses (travel) increase.

Are the effects to each account increases or decreases (debits or credits)? Cash is an asset; assets decrease with credits. Travel expense is an expense; expenses increase with debits.

What are the corresponding dollar amounts of each debit and credit? $1,875 to each account.

Journal Entry:

Ref.	Date	Description	Dr.	Cr.
6.	Jan. 22	Travel expense	1,875	
		Cash		1,875
		To record payment of travel expense		

7. On January 29, Pete's only client, Mr. Gil Bates, drops by the office to pay Pete for services rendered during January, leaving a check in the amount of $21,500.

Necessary Questions:

Is this an accounting event? Yes—it is a transaction that affects the accounts of the business.

Which specific accounts are affected? The cash of the business increases and the revenue (Fees Earned) increases.

Are the effects to each account increases or decreases (debits or credits)? Cash is an asset; assets increase with debits. Fees Earned is a revenue account; revenue accounts increase with credits.

What are the corresponding dollar amounts of each debit and credit? $21,500 to each account.

Journal Entry:

Ref.	Date	Description	Dr.	Cr.
7.	Jan. 29	Cash	21,500	
		Fees Earned		21,500
		To record fee revenues for the month		

8. On January 31, Pete pays his employees their monthly salaries of a total of $8,200.

Necessary Questions:

Is this an accounting event? Yes—it is a transaction that affects the accounts of the business.

Which specific accounts are affected? The cash account decreases and the salaries expense account increases.

Are the effects to each account increases or decreases (debits or credits)? Cash is an asset; assets decrease with credits; Salaries expense is an expense; expense accounts increase with debits.

What are the corresponding dollar amounts of each debit and credit? $8,200 to each account.

Journal Entry:

Ref.	Date	Description	Dr.	Cr.
8.	Jan. 31	Salaries expense	8,200	
		Cash		8,200
		To record payment of salaries expense for the month		

The foregoing are examples of transactions, all of which can be stated in the form of debits and credits, or journal entries.

General Journal and Special Journals. The *general journal* of a business is called the book of original entry. In concept (with significant exception to follow), it is the accounting record where each transaction of the business is initially recorded in the books of the business. It is essentially a list of every transaction undertaken by the business, with each transaction stated in the form of a debit and credit. An example of the general journal for Pete's Proprietorship is on the adjacent page, complete with the journal entries that we have discussed.

		Pete's Proprietorship General Journal		
Ref	Date	Account	Dr.	Cr.
1	1/1/2010	Cash	$ 10,000	
		Proprietor's Equity		$ 10,000
		To record initial cash investment in business.		
2	1/3/2010	Rent Expense	$ 1,750	
		Cash		$ 1,750
		To record rent expense for January.		
3	1/10/2010	Cash	$ 2,500	
		Loan Payable		$ 2,500
		To record receipt of loan from Neighborhood Bank.		
4	1/16/2010	Furniture & Equipment	$ 3,300	
		Cash		$ 3,300
		To record the purchase of office furniture with cash.		
5	1/20/2010	Loan Payable	$ 1,500	
		Cash		$ 1,500
		To record loan repayment to the bank.		
6	1/22/2010	Travel Expense	$ 1,875	
		Cash		$ 1,875
		To record travel expense.		
7	1/29/2010	Cash	$ 21,500	
		Fees Earned		$ 21,500
		To record fee revenues for the month.		
8	1/31/2010	Salary Expense	$ 8,200	
		Cash		$ 8,200
		To record payment of salaries expense for the month.		

Here is the major exception to the concept of the general journal. Because of the repetitive nature of most transactions, businesses create subsets of the general journal, called *special journals*, which are used to enter repetitive journal entries. For all practical purposes, these special journals become the books of original entry and the general journal is relegated to be used for non-repetitive transactions. At the end of an accounting period, each special journal is summarized into a compound journal entry[5] to avoid the necessity of posting every single transaction to the general ledger. So the details of every transaction are listed in the special journals and the totals of the special journals are posted to the general ledger. If there is an unusual transaction, or a necessary adjustment to the books, that transaction or adjustment is entered into the general journal, and subsequently posted to the general ledger.

An example of a special journal is the cash disbursements journal, the journal that is used to record the many checks that a business writes in a given month. Spend a few minutes studying the example of a special journal below. Note that the column for cash is a credit (because this journal summarizes disbursements of cash (decreases) which are recorded as credits to cash. For each disbursement of cash (credit), there is an offsetting debit to some other account. For ease of use, a special journal is set up with columns that include the accounts most often debited. So, for example, if the business was a law firm, it is likely that the regular disbursements of the law firm would be for accounts such as wages expense, client costs (expenses incurred on behalf of clients), office supplies expense, outside research expense, and so forth. It is not likely that the firm would regularly be purchasing office equipment or computers, even though at the beginning of the law practice, these costs might be frequent. So, the design of a cash disbursements journal for a particular business will consider what classifications of expenses are normally used in the operation of the particular business, and the journal will be set up accordingly. Consequently, cash disbursements journals for different businesses will be a little different, although the concept will be the same (numerous credits to cash, with offsetting debits to different expenses and other accounts, that will vary from business to business).

Pete's Proprietorship
Cash Disbursements Journal
January 2010
[Note: Every transaction affects two accounts.]

Date	Check #	Payee	Cash (Cr) (paid out)	Office Supplies (Dr)	Wages (Dr)	Travel Expense (Dr)	Rent Expense (Dr)	Other Acct. (Dr)	Other Account Name
3-Jan	1001	Larry Landlord	$ 1,750				$ 1,750		
16-Jan	1002	Staples	$ 3,300					$ 3,300	Office Furniture and Equipment
20-Jan	1003	Neighborhood Bank	$ 1,500					$ 1,500	Notes Payable
22-Jan	1004	British Airways	$ 1,875			$ 1,875			
31-Jan	1005	Eddie Employee	$ 8,200		$ 8,200				
			$ 16,625	$ -	$ 8,200	$ 1,875	$ 1,750	$ 4,800	

For the purpose of our introduction to the accounting system, in the next section, we will post journal entries to the general ledger directly from the general journal, not the special journals. In the Workbook, there are exercises that will illustrate how to use the special journals.

---

5. A journal entry that affects more than two accounts, although the total of the debits will still equal the total of the credits.

Posting to the General Ledger

The *general ledger* is the accounting document that contains all of the accounts of the business—the assets, liabilities, equity, revenues and expenses. It is the record of final entry: the place where all of the accounts of the business are located. The general ledger is the last stop in the internal accounting system of a business, and the balances of the accounts in the general ledger at the end of the accounting period are used to prepare the financial statements of the business. In a manual accounting system, the general ledger is a large book that contains one page per account. In computerized systems, the general ledger is a printout that includes a T-account for each account of the business.

Recall that we are learning about the process of accounting in a manual system, and therefore there is a chronology to the process of entering transactions, summarizing them, accumulating them in a logical fashion, and using the accumulated information to prepare financial statements. Assume that we are nearing the end of the accounting period, one month for purposes of our discussion, and that all of the transactions have been journalized through the general journal.[6] Every transaction that occurred in the month has been stated in the form of a journal entry, a balancing debit and credit. We are now ready to *post* all of the month's transactions to the company's general ledger. *Posting* is the process of transferring the debits and credits from the journals (general journal or special journals) to the proper ledger account.

In our example up to this point, Pete's Proprietorship's general ledger contains only eight accounts. In a small business, the general ledger might contain twenty to twenty-five accounts, but in a large entity, it is very possible that the general ledger could have thousands of accounts. In a manual system, each account will have its own page with some form of T-account, although most general ledgers are more complicated than a simple T-account.

The eight journal entries for Pete's Proprietorship can now be posted to the general ledger at the end of the accounting period. In order to post a journal entry to the ledger, the following steps must be taken:

1. Proceeding in the order of the journal entries in the general journal, find the corresponding T-account in the general ledger for each debit and credit of the journal entries.

2. Post (record) the amount of the debit of Journal entry #1 in the debit column of the appropriate general ledger account, identifying the general ledger entry with the reference number from the journal entry. Record the credit amount of journal entry #1 in the appropriate general ledger account.

3. Repeat the process for all journal entries in the general journal.

---

6. In the real world, the business would have special journals for repetitive transactions.

After each journal entry has been posted to the proper account in the general ledger, each account's balance is determined by "netting" the total of the debits and the credits. Total each side of the account's entries, and determine whether the account has a *debit balance* or a *credit balance*. The following table shows the general ledger posting of all of the transactions from the journal entries to the general ledger, and then calculates a balance for each account.

GENERAL LEDGER (before closing)

Cash

[1]	10,000	1,750	[2]
[3]	2,500	3,300	[4]
[7]	21,500	1,500	[5]
		1,875	[6]
		8,200	[8]
	34,000	16,625	
Balance	17,375		

Furniture & Equipment

[4]	3,300	
Balance	3,300	

Loan Payable

[5]	1,500	2,500	[3]
Balance		1,000	

Proprietor's Equity

		10,000 [1]
	-	10,000
Balance		10,000

Fees Earned

		21,500 [7]
Balance		21,500

Rent Expense

[2]	1,750	
Balance	1,750	

Salary Expense

[8]	8,200	
Balance	8,200	

Travel Expense

[6]	1,875	
Balance	1,875	

Income Summary

Balance	-	

[1] [2...] reference numbers correspond to general journal entries on page 43

Preparing the Trial Balance

At the end of the accounting period, when all the transactions have been posted to the general ledger, the next step in the process is to prepare a *trial balance*. The *trial balance* is a listing of all of the account balances of the business in columnar form, listed in the order in which they appear in the general ledger. The trial balance is essentially a worksheet that serves as a convenient basis for the preparation of the balance sheet and income statement. It is also an arithmetic proof that the total of the debits equals the total of the credits posted to the general ledger. This fact alone does not ensure that no errors have been made in the bookkeeping process, but it does show that the accounts are in balance and it eliminates some of the possible erroneous postings that could have been made.

Here are some errors that the preparation of a trial balance *will* disclose:

1. Posting a wrong amount

2. Posting an amount as a debit, as opposed to a credit, or vice versa

3. Omitting a posting

4. Double posting an amount

Here are some possible errors that a trial balance *will not* disclose:

1. A correct amount posted to the wrong account (the total of all the accounts' debits and credits will still balance).

2. An incorrect amount posted to the account if the incorrect amount is posted twice, meaning as both a debit and a credit (totals will still balance).

3. The omission of a complete journal entry (both the debit and credit are missing).

The preparation of the trial balance is the beginning of the financial statement preparation phase of the accounting process. Following is the trial balance for our example problem:

Pete's Proprietorship
Trial Balance
January 31, 2010

Account	Dr.	Cr.
Cash	17,375	
Furniture & Equipment	3,300	
Loan Payable		1,000
Proprietor's Equity		10,000
Fees Earned		21,500
Rent Expense	1,750	
Salary Expense	8,200	
Travel Expense	1,875	
Totals	32,500	32,500

Finalizing the Bookkeeping Process and Preparing Financial Statements

After the trial balance has been prepared, there is a step that occurs that will only be discussed briefly here. In an operating accounting system, there are *adjusting journal entries* that are made and posted at the end of the accounting period to adjust accounts *internally* within the business enterprise. (For now, we will omit the step of adjusting journal entries in our accounting system.) Adjusting journal entries are used to account for the changes in business resources that occur as a result of internal activity within the business, as opposed to external transactions. An example of such an internal transaction would be the using up of part of a fixed asset of the business through *depreciation expense*, which is adjusted internally at the end of the accounting period with an adjusting journal entry. For now, these types of internal transactions will be ignored. The example focuses only on the normal, external transactions of the business entity.

Preparing Financial Statements

The trial balance lists all the accounts of the business in the order that they appear in the general ledger, which is also the approximate order in which they appear in the balance sheet and income statement. To prepare financial statements, it is easiest to focus on the income statement accounts (revenue and expense) and first create the income statement for the period ending on the date of the trial balance. Using the trial balance for Pete's Proprietorship, take the account balances for the revenue and expense accounts and place them in the form of an income statement.

As previously noted, an income statement is a flow statement that summarizes revenues and expenses *for the period ended* on the last date of the accounting period. After the revenues and expenses have been totaled on the income statement, the subtraction of the total expenses from the total revenues results in the net income (or net loss) for the period. At this point, the income statement is complete. Following is the income statement for Pete's Proprietorship:

```
                    Pete's Proprietorship
                      Income Statement
              For the period ending January 31, 2010


    Revenues                                  $  21,500

    Expenses:
        Salary Expense           $   8,200
        Rent Expense                 1,750
        Travel Expense               1,875
            Total Expenses                       11,825

            Net Income                         $  9,675
```

The next step in the financial statement process is the preparation of the balance sheet. From the trial balance, select each of the asset, liability and equity accounts and place the account balances in the form of a balance sheet. Total the assets on the left side of the balance sheet. Then prepare a subtotal of the liabilities on the right side of the balance sheet.

Regarding the equity account(s), the final balance of the Proprietor's Equity account must be adjusted by adding the net income (or subtracting the net loss) in order for the balance sheet to balance. (Remember, we earlier learned that revenues and expenses are really a temporary subset of equity and, at the end of the accounting period, the net income or net loss must be "adjusted" to equity for the balance sheet to balance.) Since our income statement for Pete's Proprietorship resulted in a calculation of net income of $9,675, that amount must be added to the trial balance amount of Proprietor's Equity for the balance sheet to balance. Following is the balance sheet of Pete's Proprietorship:

Pete's Proprietorship
Balance Sheet
January 31, 2010

Assets:			Liabilities:	
			Loan Payable	$ 1,000
			Total Liabilities	1,000
Cash	$ 17,375			
Furniture & Equipment	3,300			
			Equity:	
			Proprietor's Equity	19,675
			Total Equity	19,675
Total Assets	$ 20,675		Total Liabilities & Equity	$ 20,675

Closing the Books

This is one of the most difficult bookkeeping exercises to explain, but the practice of doing it explains it. Working through the problems in the Workbook will facilitate the understanding of the process of *closing*.

Recall that there are three types of T-accounts: permanent, temporary and nominal. The temporary accounts (revenue and expense) accumulate information for a *period of time,* and then they are adjusted back to zero so they can accumulate accounting information for the *next* period of time. The term, "closing the books," describes the process of zeroing out the temporary accounts at the end of the accounting period. Also, recall that revenue and expenses are effectively a subset of equity, so the net difference in revenues and expenses for the period (net income or net loss) has to be added to or subtracted from equity so the balance sheet will balance after the temporary accounts are closed. So, the "zeroing out" of the temporary accounts and the final adjusting of the net income or net loss to equity is the process of closing the books of the business at the end of the accounting period. Again, the examples in the workbook will assist in better understanding this process.

In order to close the temporary accounts, one compound closing journal entry will be prepared that includes a debit for the total balance of each revenue account and a credit for the total balance of each expense account. After the closing journal entry has been partially prepared (debit all revenues and credit all expenses), calculate the debit or credit amount to make the journal entry balance. That balancing amount (which is a credit of $9,675 in the present example) is credited to a *nominal account* called **Income Summary**.[7] The effect of this closing journal entry is to zero out all of the revenue and expense accounts, leaving a credit in the income summary account.[8] Here is the closing journal entry for Pete's Proprietorship:

Ref.	Date	Description	Dr.	Cr.
9.	Jan. 31	Fees Earned	21,500	
		Rent expense		1,750
		Travel expense		1,875
		Salaries expense		8,200
		Income Summary		9,675
		To close the revenue and expense accounts to Income Summary		

The result of posting the closing entry is to "zero out" each of the temporary accounts, the revenue and expense accounts. However, this process has created a credit balance in the nominal account, Income Summary. The final act in the accounting process is to prepare a journal entry that closes the Income Summary account with a necessary debit or a credit, the other side of which is an off-setting debit or credit that will be posted to the Proprietor's Equity account. These closing journal entries must then be posted to the general ledger as the final step in the accounting process. Here is the final closing entry:

Ref.	Date	Description	Dr.	Cr.
10.	Jan. 31	Income Summary	9,675	
		Proprietor's Equity		9,675
		To close Income Summary to Equity		

---

7. The Income Summary account is a nominal account that is only used for this closing exercise. At the end of the closing process, the Income Summary account will be completely closed out.

8. If the net effect of the revenue and expense accounts was a loss, the Income Summary account would have a debit balance.

The closing journal entries are posted to the general ledger as shown below.

				Debit	Credit
Following are closing journal entries:					
9	1/31/2010	*Revenue*		$ 21,500	
		Rent Expense			$ 1,750
		Travel Expense			$ 1,875
		Salary Expense			$ 8,200
		Income Summary			$ 9,675
		To close the temporary accounts (revenue and expense) to the nominal account, Income Summary.			
10	1/31/2010	*Income Summary*		$ 9,675	
		Proprietor's Equity			$ 9,675
		To close Income Summary to the equity account.			

GENERAL LEDGER (after closing)

Cash

[1]	10,000	1,750	[2]
[3]	2,500	3,300	[4]
[7]	21,500	1,500	[5]
		1,875	[6]
		8,200	[8]
	34,000	16,625	
Balance	17,375		

Furniture & Equipment

[4]	3,300	
Balance	3,300	

Loan Payable

[5]	1,500	2,500	[3]
Balance		1,000	

Proprietor's Equity

	-	10,000	[1]
		9,675	[10]
	-	19,675	
Balance		19,675	

Fees Earned

[9]	21,500	21,500	[7]
	21,500	21,500	
Balance	-		

Rent Expense

[2]	1,750	1,750	[9]
	1,750	1,750	
Balance	-		

Salary Expense

[8]	8,200	8,200	[9]
	8,200	8,200	
Balance	-		

Travel Expense

[6]	1,875	1,875	[9]
	1,875	1,875	
Balance	-		

Income Summary

[10]	9,675	9,675	[9]
	9,675	9,675	
Balance	-		

[1] [2...] reference numbers correspond to general journal entries on page 43 and 50

In summary, the closing process does the following things:

1. It zeroes out all of the revenue and expense accounts, temporary accounts that need to be adjusted back to zero to begin the next accounting period.

2. It temporarily accumulates the net difference in the revenue and expense accounts in the nominal account, Income Summary. (Note that the difference in revenues and expenses will be the business's net income or net loss for the period.)

3. By closing the "Income Summary account to Proprietor's Equity,"[9] the net income or net loss of the business is properly added to or subtracted from Proprietor's Equity.

Further Discussion

The accounting cycle is now complete. We started with transactions and translated them into the language of debits and credits, creating a journal entry for each transaction. The journal entry of each transaction was then posted to the company's general ledger, where T-accounts for each account of the business are maintained. We then summarized the balances of each T-account and prepared a trial balance, the document that lists the debit or credit balance of each account of the business. From the trial balance, we were able to prepare an income statement and a balance sheet. (Note that we effectively "closed the books" when we took the Net Income of the business and added it to Proprietor's Equity on the balance sheet.) Finally, we prepared and posted the closing journal entries to the general ledger, enabling the balance sheet accounts (the permanent accounts) to be in balance and zeroing out the temporary accounts (the income statement accounts). Moving into the next accounting period, the income statement accounts (revenue and expense) will start with zero balances and the permanent accounts (assets, liabilities and equity) will have the proper balances at the beginning of the new accounting period.

Proprietorships versus Corporations

In this chapter, we worked through the accounting system with a simple proprietorship, Pete's Proprietorship. If Pete had incorporated, all of the transactions would be the same, but the equity section of Pete's Corporation's balance sheet would have two different categories: Common Stock and Retained Earnings. The overall concept of equity is the same for both types of entities, but the accounting in the equity section is slightly different. When Pete's Corporation issues its initial stock, the transaction would be journalized as follows (in place of the previous proprietor journal entry #1):

---

9. By using the language "closing the Income Summary to Proprietor's Equity," I mean that the offsetting debit or credit to the journal entry that closes the Income Summary account is Proprietor's Equity. This closing of the Income Summary account has the effect of adding Net Income to Proprietor's Equity or subtracting Net Loss from Proprietor's Equity.

Journal Entry:

Ref.	Date	Description	Dr.	Cr.
1.	Jan. 1	Cash	10,000	
		Common Stock		10,000
		To record initial issuance of common stock		

When the accounting cycle was completed and the books were closed, the income for the period would be added to the equity account, Retained Earnings, with the following journal entry (in place of the previous proprietor journal entry #10):

Journal Entry:

Ref.	Date	Description	Dr.	Cr.
10.	Jan. 31	Income Summary	9,675	
		Retained Earnings		9,675
		To close Income Summary to Retained Earnings		

The balance sheet of Pete's Corporation would be quite similar to that of Pete's Proprietorship, with the exception of the equity section, which would look like the following:

Pete's Corporation
Balance Sheet
January 31, 2010

Assets:			Liabilities:	
			Loan Payable	$ 1,000
Cash	$	17,375	Total Liabilities	1,000
Furniture & Equipment		3,300		
			Equity:	
			Common Stock	10,000
			Retained Earnings	9,675
			Total Equity	19,675
Total Assets	**$ 20,675**		**Total Liabilities & Equity**	**$ 20,675**

The Relationship between the Balance Sheet and the Income Statement

The elements of the balance sheet and the income statement are completely intertwined. The temporary accounts of the income statement measure the flow of assets in and out of the entity, and the permanent accounts of the balance sheet measure the status of the assets (and liabilities and equity) in the entity at a point in time. In accounting, the interrelation between the real/permanent accounts contained in the balance sheet and the temporary accounts contained in the income statement is called articulation. The articulation relationship stems from the fact that the elements of the balance sheet are affected by the changes in the elements of the income statement. At any point in time, the real accounts contain the cumulative effect of the changes in the temporary accounts.

A loose analogy illustrates the concept of accounting articulation between the income statement and the balance sheet. Assume there is a swimming pool being simultaneously filled up by a green hose (revenue) and drained by a red hose (expense). If we put a flow meter on the two hoses and measured the **net** inflow (or outflow) of water into the pool, we would know the net increase (or decrease) of water into the pool in a day, or any other defined period. At the end of the day, we could measure the amount of water in the pool, representative of the total assets in a business. To carry this analogy a little too far (to incorporate the concept of liabilities), suppose that the pool owner borrowed an additional 110 gallons of water from his neighbor and poured them into the pool. Yes, there would be an increase in the assets of the pool, but that increase didn't come from the green hose of revenue, it came from the neighbor pouring two 55 gallon drums of water into the pool and the pool owner owes the neighbor back the 110 gallons of borrowed water.

The end result of the accounting articulation relationship is that net income flows to the equity of the business. In a corporation, the equity account that shows the accumulated net income (or net loss) of the entity is Retained Earnings. In proprietorships and partnerships, the amount of net income (or net loss) in a period is simply added to the proprietor's or partners' equity accounts.

Conclusion

In this chapter, we have gone through the complete accounting process from initial transactions, through the preparation of financial statements, to closing journal entries. Although the transactions have been simple, the concepts are the full spectrum of the accounting process. In sophisticated legal matters that involve financial issues, these basic accounting concepts are essential. The Workbook problems will assist in the understanding of these basic accounting concepts. Doing the problems is the best way to learn the concepts.

Chapter 4

Accrual Accounting

Introduction

This chapter introduces accrual accounting, the embodiment of the foundational concept that measures the performance and position of a company by recognizing events based on true economic activity regardless of when cash transactions occur. Accrual accounting is all about the timing of revenue and expense recognition and the separation of that recognition from the related cash transactions. The objective of accrual accounting is to credit the income statement with all of the revenue earned in the accounting period regardless of when the related cash is received, and to burden the income statement with all of the expenses of the period regardless of when the cash is paid. We will learn about the effect of the timing of revenue and expense recognition as it relates to the accuracy of a company's net income. The significant differences between accrual basis accounting and cash basis accounting will be explored, and we will see the advantages and disadvantages of using either method.

The accounting principles underlying accrual basis accounting are the Realization Principle and the Matching Principle. The proper application of these principles will determine the accounting period in which items of revenue and expense are recognized. The mechanics of implementing accrual basis accounting consist of two mirror-image concepts: the concept of *accrual* and the concept of *deferral*. Accountants use the concept of accrual when the revenue or expense recognition occurs before the cash transaction; in that situation, an account receivable or account payable is "accrued" on the balance sheet and the corresponding entry is a revenue or expense transaction on the income statement. Conversely, when the related cash transaction occurs before the revenue or expense recognition should occur, accountants "defer" the revenue or expense recognition by creating a prepaid asset or a deferred revenue liability on the balance sheet, waiting until a later time to recognize the revenue or expense on the income statement. The concepts of accrual and deferral will become clear when they are explained later in the chapter with some straightforward examples.

Concurrent with the concept of the timing of the recognition of revenue and expense, we will be introduced to accounts receivable and accounts payable, the balance sheet accounts that are the complementary components of the accrual of revenue and expense. The discussion of accounts receivable includes consideration of uncollectible accounts receivable, aging of accounts receivable and the two common methods of bad debt accounting. The chapter also covers prepaid assets and deferred revenue,[1] the balance sheet accounts that are the complements to the deferral of revenue and expense.

---

1.   Unfortunately, the name of the liability account "Deferred Revenue" is confusing because the word "revenue" is in the account title. The account is a liability (not a revenue account) and it represents the amount of money that is owed back to the customer/client until the services are performed and the related revenue is earned. A perfectly explanatory title for the account would be something like "Money Owed Back to Client."

The conversion of cash basis accounting to accrual basis accounting shows the distortions that exist when only the cash method is relied upon. Generally Accepted Accounting Principles mandate the use of the accrual method for financial statement purposes, but small businesses and individuals most often use the cash basis because of its simplicity. It is important to realize that significant adjustments may be required to make the conversion to the accrual basis, and any serious analysis of financial statements should be done with accrual basis statements.

Accrual Basis Accounting

The Financial Accounting Standards Board Concept Statement 6, *Elements of Financial Statements*, discusses assets under a heading "Recognition, Matching, and Allocation." In paragraph 145, it states:

> Accrual accounting uses accrual, deferral, and allocation procedures whose [*sic*] goal is to relate revenues, expenses, gains, and losses to periods to reflect an entity's performance during a period instead of merely listing its cash receipts and outlays ... the goal of accrual accounting is to account, in the periods in which they occur, for the effects on an entity of transactions and other events and circumstances, to the extent that those financial effects are recognizable and measurable. [*Commas are added to the original to make the text more understandable.*]

A fundamental objective of accounting is to properly measure and report the net income of an organization during the accounting period. Net income is a critical measure of a business's activity over a defined time period.[2] The income statement is the financial statement that presents the measure of the flow of business activity during the period, so both the *amount* and the *timing* of its components (revenue and expense) must be accurate to properly calculate net income.

Net income is defined as revenue minus expenses, and it shows the net change in the equity of the business during the accounting period as the result of business operations. The determination of net income is entirely dependent on the accurate recording of both revenue and expenses during the accounting period. In this regard, the timing of the recognition of these component elements is as important as the amount of the item. If a proper amount of revenue or expense is reported too early or too late, the effect on the income statement is the same as reporting an erroneous amount.

Accrual basis accounting is a method of accounting that deals with the *timing* of the recognition of revenue and expense, and therefore the amount of net income reported in a period. *Accrual accounting recognizes revenue when it is earned and expenses when they are incurred, regardless of when the related cash is exchanged.* Accrual accounting *ignores* the receipt or payment of cash as the indicator of the proper timing of the revenue or expense. Accrual accounting follows both the Realization Principle and the Matching Principle of GAAP.

---

2.   For example, it is meaningless to say, "Joe's income is $100,000." Is that $100,000 a week? ... A month? ... A year? ... or every 4½ years? The concept of net income is only relevant in relation to time.

There are two fundamental methodologies used to separate the exchange of cash transaction from the revenue or expense recognition transaction under accrual basis accounting: *accrual* and *deferral*. Accrual is used when the revenue or expense recognition occurs *before* the cash transaction; deferral is used when the revenue or expense recognition occurs *after* the related cash transaction.

Accrual. When the revenue or expense recognition should happen before the exchange of cash occurs,[3] the methodology of accrual is used. Two simple examples are used to explain the concept of accrual, one for the accrual of revenue and the other for the accrual of an expense. 1) The accrual of revenue occurs when services are performed for the client in the accounting period and the client is billed for the services, creating an account receivable. The journal entry to record this transaction is: debit Accounts Receivable; credit Revenue. An asset is created and revenue is recognized, but no cash has changed hands. 2) For expenses, a second example of the concept of accrual is: Expenses are recognized in the accounting period by purchasing supplies or services and "paying" for them with an account payable. The journal entry to record this transaction would be: debit Supplies Expense; credit Accounts Payable. In both of these examples, the revenue or expense recognition will occur, offset by an account receivable (for revenue) or an account payable (for expense), and the cash receipt or payment does not occur until later, presumably in a later accounting period. These two examples show the concept of the "accrual of an account receivable or account payable," resulting in the recognition of either revenue or expense.

Deferral. The methodology of deferral is used when the cash activity occurs before the revenue or expense is recognized. Deferral is a little more confusing than accrual, but it is really a mirror image of accrual. Two examples will explain the concept of deferral, one for the deferral of revenue and the other for the deferral of expenses. 1) Deferred revenue occurs when a client pays a retainer to the firm in advance of the services being performed. The firm records an asset, cash, and also a liability called "Deferred Revenue," because the firm owes the client the value of the services. At the time of this transaction, no revenue is recognized, only the receipt of cash (an asset) and a corresponding liability. Conceptually, this example is similar to borrowing money from the bank: the company gets cash and they owe the bank a liability—the amount of the cash that was borrowed. It is only later, when the services are performed (and truly earned), that revenue is recognized. 2) Deferred expenses are assets that are called prepaid items. When a firm pays money, in advance, for a service that will be used up in the future, it records an asset called a prepaid item.[4] The prepaid item is an unexpired cost, and the firm has not incurred any expense until the cost actually expires. As the prepaid asset is used up, the firm "expenses" or writes off the asset and recognizes the expense in the period in which the cost is used up.

Both the concept of accrual and deferral will be explained in more detail in subsequent sections of this chapter.

---

3. The deciding factor for recognition will be the Realization Principle and the Matching Principle, not the receipt or payment of cash.
4. The actual account name of the prepaid item is usually related to the type of expense it will become: "Prepaid Insurance," "Prepaid Rent" or "Prepaid Taxes," for example.

The Realization Principle—the theory behind revenue recognition

The *Realization Principle* holds that items of revenue should be recognized when the entity has completed or virtually completed the exchange of goods or services and it can reasonably estimate the probability of payment. The focus of the Realization Principle is to determine the moment that revenue is *earned*, or the moment that the *revenue transaction* occurs. Depending on the nature of the business enterprise, there are several acceptable criteria for the timing of revenue recognition. Generally, however, the two key conditions that must be met in order to recognize revenue are that the seller must have no significant remaining obligation to the customer and the seller must be able to reasonably estimate the probability that it will be paid for the goods or services. Given those general conditions, different approaches to revenue recognition may be applied to different types of businesses.

Point of Sale Recognition. In most cases, revenue is recognized at the time of sale (defined as the moment when the title of the goods or services is transferred to the buyer). Measuring revenues at this point is logical because the firm has essentially completed the earning process and the realized value of the goods or services sold can be objectively measured in terms of the billed price. The only remaining step of the accounting process is collecting the payment, and the probability of this step can usually be reasonably estimated.

It should be noted that the exchange of title that triggers revenue recognition is different from the passing of consideration in a legal contract. Mutual promises are not sufficient for the accounting recognition of revenue, although the parties may be contractually obligated to one another. For accounting revenue recognition under the point of sale method, the seller must have no significant remaining obligation to the customer.

Percentage of Completion. For a firm involved in long-term contracting, the point of sale approach does not provide the most relevant information to management and investors; it is more relevant to measure revenue *during* the production process. Consider companies like Boeing or Morrison Knudson—companies that produce products (airplanes or power plants) that may take several years to manufacture. It is not particularly relevant to wait until the completion of their projects (the point of completion of the sale) to recognize all the dollars of revenue that the projects generated. For these types of companies, GAAP allows a percentage of completion method to be used for revenue recognition, assuming that two requirements are met. First, a long-term enforceable contract for the sale of the product must be in place, and, second, it must be possible to estimate the percentage of the contract that is completed to date. Under the percentage of completion method, the accountant will measure the percentage of the contract that has been completed to date (usually based on the percentage of the total costs that have been incurred to date), and he will then use that percentage to recognize a portion of the total revenue of the project in the current accounting period. The percentage of completion method requires that a number of accounting estimates be made, but this method is an example of the need to balance the principle of objectivity against the principle of relevance to produce meaningful financial statements. The details of the percentage of completion method of accounting are beyond the scope of this text; it is simply important to note that the methodology exists and it is used for companies engaged in long-term contracting projects.

Installment Sales Method. An installment sale is a sale of property at a *gain* where at least one payment is to be received in a later tax year. Federal tax regulations allow the seller to include in taxable income only a proportionate amount of the gain, plus the interest, that is received, or considered to be received, each tax year. GAAP only allows the installment sales method of revenue recognition in exceptional circumstances, where the collectability of the account receivable cannot be reasonably estimated or assured. The installment sales method might be appropriate for a company involved in the sale of consumer products that are financed over long periods of time, such as appliances or furniture on long-term seller financing plans. The doubtfulness of collectability can be caused by the length of an extended collection period or because no basis of estimation can be established.

Receipt of Payment (Cash Basis). Under the cash basis method of accounting (discussed subsequently), revenue is recognized at the time payment is made. The cash basis is not accepted under GAAP, but it is used for income taxes purposes for individuals and many small businesses. For most small businesses, the simplicity of the cash basis outweighs its theoretical weaknesses.

The Matching Principle—the theory behind expense recognition

The *Matching Principle* states that when specific revenues are recognized in a period, the expenses incurred to generate those revenues must also be assigned to that period. The concept of the Matching Principle is quite simple, but the application of it is one of the complexities of modern accounting. In order to properly determine net income, it only seems logical to match expenses with the revenue that they are used to produce. If a car dealer sells a Lexus 460 in March, it is obvious that it would be wrong to expense the cost of the Lexus in January, when the dealer bought the car. The net income of the dealership in March should consider both the selling price of the car as revenue and the cost of the car as expense, regardless of the date of purchase of the car.

The theory of determining net income is to properly compare revenue and expenses; by comparing the price received from selling something with the cost of making or buying it, you can determine the gain (net income) that you made from selling it. The difficulties in the application of the Matching Principle are:

1. Quantification: determining the proper amount of costs that relate to the item sold; and

2. Timing: expensing the proper amount of the costs of the item sold in the same period as the sale.

Violating the Realization Principle and the Matching Principle

The failure to apply the Realization Principle or the Matching Principle can lead to distortions (high or low) in reporting net income. Some examples of violating the Realization Principle would be:

a. Accelerating the recognition of revenue in the accounting period will overstate revenues, and therefore net income.

1. Receiving payment in the accounting period and recording it as revenue when the services have not been performed or the goods have not been produced and/or delivered. (Effect: overstate net income.)

2. Under a percentage of completion methodology, overestimating the percentage of the contract that has been completed and recognizing that revenue in the period. (Effect: overstate net income.)

3. (Not a timing issue, but . . .) Treating the receipt of some money or other assets as revenue when they are either loan proceeds, capital infusion, or trade-out of another asset (like receipt of cash on account). (Effect: overstate net income.)

b. Delaying the recognition of revenue to the next accounting period will understate net income.

1. Sliding a sale into the next period—deferring it for some reason—with the result being improperly understating revenue in the period for some reason. (Effect: understate net income.)

Violating the Matching Principle:

a. Failing to recognize an expense or delaying the recognition of an expense to a later period will overstate net income because not enough expenses will be matched against revenue in the period.

1. Selling goods in the current period but failing to expense the cost of the goods until a later period. (Effect: overstate net income.)

2. Expensing inventory to cost of goods sold when the inventory is purchased (as opposed to capitalizing it as inventory and holding it until sold). (Effect: understate net income.)

b. Improperly calculating the cost of an item of inventory by excluding portions of the cost (or or including erroneous costs in the calculation). (Effect: over- or understating net income.)

c. (Not a violation of the Matching Principle, but . . .) Capitalizing costs that should be expensed. This concept will become clear after we study fixed asset accounting in Chapter 5. Recognize that one definition of expenses is the costs that have expired during the accounting period and, if you capitalize a cost (make it an asset), you don't expire it. The failure to expire all the proper costs is an understatement of expenses (therefore overstating net income).

Cash Basis vs. Accrual Basis

Cash basis accounting relies entirely on the receipt or payment of cash as the indicator or trigger for the recognition of revenue or expense. Under cash basis accounting, the recognition of revenue occurs at the moment that cash changes hands, and expenses are incurred at the moment that they are paid. The attraction of the cash method of accounting is its simplicity; there is no judgment involved. The cash method is allowed for federal income tax purposes for individuals and certain small businesses, but cash basis accounting is not allowed under GAAP. Cash basis accounting does not accurately account for the true economic activities of the business during the accounting period.

Consider an accounting proprietorship, for example. A new client comes in December and hires the accounting firm to perform services for it in a major matter that is expected to extend over many months. The client advances a retainer of $25,000 to the firm on December 27, 2010. Under the cash method of accounting, the firm would recognize revenue at the time the cash is received, because that is the triggering event for revenue recognition. But, has the firm really *earned* any revenue at the time the cash is advanced to it? It's true, it has received the money, but has the *exchange* actually taken place? The only thing that has occurred is the receipt of cash; the accounting firm hasn't really done anything, except bring in the client. The reality of the transaction, which is correctly captured under the principles of accrual accounting, is that the firm owes the client the future services and it doesn't earn any revenue until it performs them.

Accrual basis accounting recognizes revenue when it is earned and expenses when they are incurred, regardless of when the related cash is exchanged. Accrual accounting applies the Realization Principle to determine the timing of the recognition of revenue and the Matching Principle to determine the timing of expense. Because it disregards cash transactions as the primary trigger for revenue and expense recognition, accrual accounting requires the understanding of accounts receivable and accounts payable, the balance sheet accounts that are the complements of revenue and expense under accrual accounting.

Accounts Receivable and Revenue Recognition

Accounts receivable, a current asset, are the expected receipts that are created by the sale of goods and services on credit. An account receivable is the asset created by a customer's promise to pay, and it is usually created by an invoice, the ancillary accounting document that contains the details of the sale transaction (date, items sold, price, delivery charges, sales tax, etc.). An invoice also shows the customer the terms of the sale: the requirements for the timing of payment and the allowance of discounts if payment is made early. Here is an example of a typical invoice:

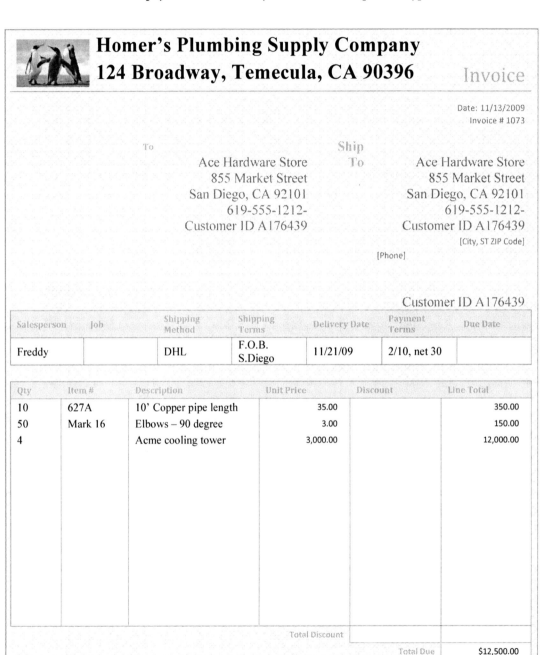

Homer's Plumbing Supply Company
124 Broadway, Temecula, CA 90396   Invoice

Date: 11/13/2009
Invoice # 1073

To	Ship To
Ace Hardware Store	Ace Hardware Store
855 Market Street	855 Market Street
San Diego, CA 92101	San Diego, CA 92101
619-555-1212-	619-555-1212-
Customer ID A176439	Customer ID A176439
	[City, ST ZIP Code]
	[Phone]

Customer ID A176439

Salesperson	Job	Shipping Method	Shipping Terms	Delivery Date	Payment Terms	Due Date
Freddy		DHL	F.O.B. S.Diego	11/21/09	2/10, net 30	

Qty	Item #	Description	Unit Price	Discount	Line Total
10	627A	10' Copper pipe length	35.00		350.00
50	Mark 16	Elbows – 90 degree	3.00		150.00
4		Acme cooling tower	3,000.00		12,000.00

Total Discount		
Total Due		$12,500.00
Sales Tax		resale
Total		$12,500.00

In a credit sale, the business sells goods or services in exchange for the customer's promise to pay, and the measure of the revenue is the amount of the promise to pay, or the account receivable. Under the accrual method of accounting, the revenue transaction is complete at the time the goods are delivered or the services are performed and the customer's promise to pay is materialized into an account receivable. At that time, the journal entry to record a completed sale that results in an accounts receivable of $12,500 is:

Ref.	*Date*	*Description*	*Dr.*	*Cr.*
XX.	*Jan. YZ*	*Accounts receivable*	*12,500*	
		Sales (or Fees Earned[5])		*12,500*
		To record credit sale.		

Note that an accrual revenue transaction affects two accounts: the flow of the asset into the business is recorded as a credit to a revenue account and the asset itself (the account receivable) ends up on the company's books. This is a classic example of the dual nature of the accounting system: the revenue account measures the *flow* of the asset coming into the business; and the asset account (accounts receivable) shows the *status* of the business—complete with its additional account receivable—immediately after the flow has come in. Question: When the customer pays the account receivable, presumably in the next accounting period, does the business have revenue? Answer: No; in the next accounting period when the customer pays his bill, the business is merely exchanging one asset (account receivable) for another asset (cash). No revenue occurs when the account receivable is paid. The journal entry to record payment is:

Ref.	*Date*	*Description*	*Dr.*	*Cr.*
XX.	*Feb. YZ*	*Cash*	*12,500*	
		Accounts Receivable		*12,500*
		To record receipt of payment on account.		

Also, if you think about it, the same $12,500 transaction is not going to be revenue two times—once when it is accrued and another time when it is paid. The business only has one "gross increase in assets as a result of the sale of goods or services," and that is when it accrues the account receivable. There is no increase in assets when the account is paid; the business is "exchanging" its account receivable for cash.

Aging of Accounts Receivable. One of the realities of a company's aggregate accounts receivable is that they are not 100 percent collectible. To properly state total accounts receivable on the balance sheet, it is necessary to estimate the uncollectible portion of the accounts receivable. The most common method of estimating the portion of uncollectible accounts receivable is to prepare an *aging* of accounts receivable at the end of the accounting period. Aging the receivables is a process of listing all of the company's accounts receivable by customer, outstanding balance amount and

---

5. "Fees earned" is a better description of the revenue account in a service business. "Sales" is normally the title of the account in a merchandising business.

date of invoice, and then identifying the age of the outstanding balance in categories, usually zero to 30 days, 31 to 60 days, 61 to 90 days, 91 to 120 days, and over 120 days. For each category of accounts receivable age, it is typical for the company to assign an estimated uncollectible percentage based on the firm's historical experience. Obviously, the percentage of uncollectible accounts in the zero to 30 day category is much lower than the uncollectible percentage in the over 120 day category. Here is an example of an Accounts Receivable Aging:

XYZ Company, Inc.
Accounts Receivable Aging
As of: December 31, 2010

Date of Invoice	Account Name	Total Balance	< 30 Days	31-60 Days	61-90 Days	91-120 Days	> 120 Days
12/10/10	Anthony's Production Co.	$ 100	$ 100				
12/12/10	Brian's Bakery	200	200				
12/20/10	Coby's Computers	300	300				
12/27/10	David's Donuts	400	400				
12/5/10	Emily's Dairy	500	500				
9/5/10	Frankie's Factory	150				150	
10/12/10	Gina's Gymnasium	150			150		
12/6/10	Hal's Heating & Air	200	200				
12/11/10	Ingrid's Ice Company	600	600				
11/20/10	Joshua's Juice	200		200			
10/7/10	Kelly's Keys	170			170		
11/6/10	Lisa's Luxury Goods	240		240			
3/10/10	Mike's Milkshakes	75					75
11/25/10	Nick's Network Support	240		240			
10/17/10	Olivia's Olives	160			160		
6/25/10	Paul's Pet Store	190					190
12/13/10	Raul's Roofing Company	175	175				
Totals		$ 4,050	$ 2,475	$ 680	$ 480	$ 150	$ 265

Accounts receivable are shown on the balance sheet at "cost," meaning the price of the sales transaction. If some of the total amount of the accounts receivable are later determined to be uncollectible by aging the accounts receivable, a contra asset account, Allowance for Doubtful Accounts, is created to show the uncollectible allowance. Since the Matching Principle requires that all of the costs incurred in order to produce revenue must be matched against the revenue, the fact that some of the accounts receivable that created the revenue will ultimately be uncollectible must be matched against the related revenue in the period in which the revenue was created.

Uncollectible Receivables. There are two methods to match uncollectible receivables with the revenue that produced them: the direct write-off method and the allowance method. The accounting details of these two methods are beyond the scope of our study, but a quick overview is appropriate. The direct write-off method simply expenses the bad account receivable in the period in which it is determined to be uncollectible, which may be a year or two after the related revenue was recorded. The allowance method more correctly applies the Matching Principle by estimating the amount of accounts receivable that will be uncollectible and charging that amount as bad debt expense in the period in which the related revenue is recorded. The allowance method is the better of the two because it conforms to the Matching Principle.

From a critical perspective, accounts receivable are an asset that is easily capable of misstatement in a company's financial records. The consequences of the overstatement are doubly significant because accounts receivable affects both the income statement and the balance sheet by increasing revenue with the creation of the receivable asset. The observer should be mindful of the risks and consequences of the overstatement of accounts receivable by considering the following facts and areas of inquiry about a company's accounts receivable:

1. The overstatement of accounts receivable has the related effect of increasing revenue (and therefore net income).

2. Does the company maintain a detailed ledger of its individual accounts receivable, and does the detailed ledger agree with the total accounts receivable reported on the balance sheet?

3. Does the company regularly prepare an aging of its accounts receivable? Based on the aging, are the uncollectible accounts written off to bad debt expense and the total accounts receivable balance reduced accordingly?

4. Does the company have adequate credit policies to ensure that customers are creditworthy? Do the policies provide for different levels of credit for different levels of customers?

5. Does the company have proper monthly billing and collection procedures? Are customers billed monthly? Are delinquent accounts handled quickly and appropriately?

6. Does the company have a clean cutoff at the end of the accounting period to ensure that the proper amount of sales is recorded in the period, the goods are shipped (not included in inventory) and that all of the expenses related to the sales are recorded?

Discounts and Early Payment Terms. In commercial transactions, offering discounts to customers for early payment is a common practice to speed up the collection of accounts receivable, a critical aspect of cash management in a business. Typically, the common terms for the collection of a routine account are 30 days. If payment is not received within the 30 day period, a late charge of some percentage of the outstanding balance is assessed. A vendor who offers a discount for early payment would typically offer a term such as a two percent discount to the balance due if paid within ten days of the date of the invoice. Such an arrangement is referred to as "2/10, net 30." The consequence of these discounts is very significant and a customer is very wise to partake of the discount offered. Consider the following example to demonstrate the financial benefit of this type of discount:

Facts: Balance due: $12,500
Credit terms: 2%/10, net 30 days

Discussion:
Discount obtainable: $250 (2% of the balance)
Time period: To obtain the discount, the customer has to advance the funds 20 days sooner than he otherwise would have to pay them. Therefore, the customer is effectively "earning" the $250 discount (2% of the balance) by advancing the funds for a 20 day period.

Financial issue: If 2% can be earned on a total amount in 20 days, what is the effective annual percentage rate of earnings on the principal balance?

> Financial Analysis:
> Percent "earned": 2%
> Time period: 20 days
> Number of "20 day periods" per year: 18 [365 ÷ 20 ≈ 18]
> Effective annual percentage rate: 36% [2% × 18 = 36%]

By paying the discounted amount, the debtor effectively earns 36% annual interest on the principal balance because a 2% discount can be obtained for advancing the money for 20 days. The converse of this is true: this is why credit card companies are thrilled with their customers who are just a few days late on their balances and are therefore charged a late fee, which is effectively a percentage of the balance due. From the card company's perspective, they "earn" a few percentage points on the outstanding balance by "advancing" the balance for only a few extra days. In the aggregate, the amount of interest earned on these slightly delinquent accounts is colossal.

Converting from Cash to Accrual and from Accrual to Cash

Under the cash basis of accounting, revenue is recognized when the cash is received, but under the accrual method, revenue is recognized when it is earned, and that is normally the time that the account receivable is booked. There is obviously a difference in the amount of revenue that is reported under the two methods and it is often necessary to be able to calculate that difference.

Under the cash method of accounting, cash received from sales activity equals revenue; end of story. Accounts receivable are not "booked" as a fundamental part of the accounting process; there is no general ledger account for accounts receivable. Even under the cash basis, however, the business will still keep track of its accounts receivable because, of course, the business wants to know how much its customers owe. So a small law proprietorship, for example, will maintain its accounting records on a cash basis, recording revenue in its general journal when the cash is received and recording expenses when the cash is paid. However, the business will keep track of its accounts receivable in a separate, "off book" accounts receivable ledger that will show the name of the client/customer, the balance due, the date of the invoice, etc. So, even though the business is on a cash basis, it will know the balance of its accounts receivable at any point in time.

So, if we know a cash basis business's cash receipts (revenue) during a year, and we know the accounts receivable balance at both the beginning of the year and the end of the year, can we determine the accrual revenue for the year? Before we delve into some calculations, let's consider why we care:

1. Assume in the first year of your cash basis law proprietorship (called "Jimmy's Law Firm" for later reference), you collect $100,000 in cash receipts. Therefore, your revenue will be $100,000 under the cash basis. At the beginning of the year, your accounts receivable balance was zero (you just opened your law firm), but at the end of the year, your total accounts receivable are $425,000 (all due from very creditworthy clients, of course). Is that significant to you? How much is your cash revenue for the year? (Answer: $100,000.) How much is your accrual revenue for the year? (Answer: ???) Does it matter?

   Answer: Your cash revenue is $100,000, but your accrual revenue is $525,000. You have to add the ending accounts receivable to your cash receipts from your first year to determine your complete, accrual revenue. At the end of the year, you have *earned* an additional $425,000 of income—it just hasn't turned into cash yet, but you expect it will shortly. Now, you can't run a business on accounts receivable, so my example might be a little "overly accountant," but it makes the point about the difference between cash revenue and accrual revenue.

2. Now assume it's your second year of operation in your law practice and you begin the year with $425,000 of accounts receivable. During this year, you collect $500,000 of cash, and your ending accounts receivable balance is $125,000. What is your cash revenue in year 2? (Answer: easy . . . $500,000.) What is your accrual revenue in year 2? (It's not your cash received *plus* your ending accounts receivable—you have to consider the fact that the beginning accounts receivable were collected in the $500K that you received.[6])

   Think about it. In a minute, you're going to realize that this law practice has a little problem in year 2 that the cash to accrual conversion is going to highlight.

---

6. Accrual revenue = cash receipts + ending accounts receivable – beginning accounts receivable.

The formula to convert cash basis revenue into accrual basis revenue is:

Accrual Basis Revenue

> Cash Receipts
> Plus: Ending Accounts Receivable
> Minus: Beginning Accounts Receivable
> Equals: Accrual Basis Revenue

The formula to convert accrual basis revenue to cash basis revenue is:

Cash Basis Revenue

> Accrual Basis Revenue
> Plus: Beginning Accounts Receivable
> Minus: Ending Accounts Receivable
> Equals: Cash Basis Revenue

The conversion from cash to accrual is often necessary to understand the reality of small business activity. Take the example of Jimmy's Law Firm above. In the first year of operation the cash revenue was only $100,000, which is not a whole lot if you have to cover significant expenses, but Jimmy was working on a large case and earning revenue, even though the revenue was in the form of an account receivable. His second year of practice is more problematic: although he is collecting a lot of cash from his previous year's revenue, his accrual revenue in year 2 is substantially lower than his accrual revenue in year 1. If Jimmy needs accrual revenues in the range of 500K+ to adequately cover expenses and make a reasonable profit, he is in pretty serious trouble in year 2, although a superficial look at his cash receipts might show otherwise.

There are sample problems dealing with conversion from cash to accrual and accrual to cash in Chapter 4 of the Workbook.

Accounts Payable and Expenses

Accounts payable is the balance sheet liability that is usually related to the payment of expenses, when expenses are incurred in the present but not actually paid in cash until later.[7] For this discussion, we should first separate the liability account, accounts payable, from any expense that the liability might be related to. We will then come back to the relationship between the liability and the expense.

Accounts payable is a current liability of a business, representing a short-term obligation to trade creditors for the purchase of goods and services, usually in the ordinary course of business operations. It is a form of credit that suppliers offer to creditworthy customers to facilitate ordinary business transactions when the goods or services are provided to the customer before the payment of cash is made. At the time of the purchase transaction, the business ("Mary's Wholesale," for this discussion) will record a debit to the asset or expense account, and a credit to Accounts Payable. For introductory purposes, we will consider that Mary's is incurring an account payable in order to purchase some miscellaneous office supplies that she will expense as "office expense" at the time of the purchase. So, at the time of the purchase, Mary will record the following journal entry:

Ref.	*Date*	*Description*	*Dr.*	*Cr.*
XX.	Jan. YZ	*Office expense*	*187.50*	
		Accounts Payable		*187.50*
		To record purchase of office supplies on account		

Even though the business has not "spent" any cash, it has accrued a debt, the account payable, and it has incurred an expense.[8] The accrual of the expense is not dependent on the payment of the bill; the expense is recognized when the liability is incurred. At the time that the account payable is paid (presumably in a subsequent accounting period), the transaction to record payment does not include any expense. It is simply the payment of an existing debt of the business and the journal entry to record the event is:

Ref.	*Date*	*Description*	*Dr.*	*Cr.*
XX.	Feb. YZ	*Account Payable*	*187.50*	
		Cash		*187.50*
		To record payment of account payable		

---

7. An account payable isn't always directly related to an expense, although it usually is. A business can accrue an account payable for the purchase of inventory, for example, and the inventory will not be expensed until it is sold (according the Matching Principle), which may be many accounting periods after it is acquired.

8. This transaction also involves the Materiality Principle in the following way. It could be suggested that Mary has purchased supplies that will not be used up, or "expired," until a later time and that the supplies should be shown as an asset of the business until they are used, following the Matching Principle. This argument is technically correct, but the Materiality Principle dictates that it is not important to precisely account for an immaterial amount that would not affect the financial reporting of Mary's overall financial statements. Consequently, the expense will be taken when the account payable is accrued.

Prepaid Items and Deferred Revenue

General Discussion. At the beginning of this chapter we were introduced to the foundational concepts that are used to implement accrual basis accounting: the concepts of *accrual* and *deferral*. Accrual is used when the revenue or expense recognition occurs before the related cash transaction. As we have seen in previous sections of the chapter, revenue is "accrued" when a related account receivable is "accrued." Similarly, expenses are "accrued" when a related accounts payable is "accrued." So, *accrual* is what happens when the revenue and expense recognition comes first and the related cash comes later.

The concept of *deferral* is applied when the cash happens first, before the related revenue or expense should be recognized. When this situation occurs, the accounting system uses an asset account called a "Prepaid," and a liability account called "Deferred Revenue." The prepaid asset account is used when the current cash payment paid from the company relates to a future expense; the deferred revenue account is used when the current cash receipt into the company relates to future revenue. These concepts will become clearer in the subsequent paragraphs.

Prepaid Items. A prepaid asset (or item) is best described as a purchased economic resource that will be used up in the near term future operations of the business. A prepaid item is an asset—an unexpired cost—that will soon be expensed (expired) in the operations of the business. At the outset, understand that the terminology surrounding prepaid items is confusing: a prepaid item is an asset but, because it is quickly converted into an expense, the asset is frequently referred to as a "prepaid expense" and the use of the word "expense" to describe the asset confuses the discussion. To simplify the terminology, the asset should be called a prepaid item; when the prepaid item is expensed, an expense is created. The best way to understand prepaid items is to use a common example, an insurance policy.

Assume that a business purchases an insurance policy for one year on January 1, paying the full amount of the annual premium, $12,000, on that date. At the time of the purchase, the business acquires an asset, called "Prepaid Insurance,"[9] an economic resource of the business expected to be used up in the near term future operations of the business. At the time of the purchase, has the business incurred an expense of $12,000? No, the business has acquired an asset (an unexpired cost) that will be used up in the future operations of the business.[10] The journal entry to record the purchase of the insurance policy is:

Ref.	Date	Description	Dr.	Cr.
XX.	Jan. 1	Prepaid Insurance	12,000	
		Cash		12,000
		To record purchase of insurance policy		

---

9. Sometimes confusingly called "Prepaid Insurance *Expense*." Sorry.
10. Another way to think about this is to assume that the company went out of business the day after it acquired the insurance policy. Theoretically, the company would get a full refund from the insurance company because it had not used up any of the policy—the unexpired cost.

What happens to the prepaid item, Prepaid Insurance, as the months of operation of the business pass by? Logically, the best way to "expense" the prepaid insurance asset is to recognize 1/12 of the prepaid annual cost as expense in each month of the year. Consequently, the adjusting journal entry at the end of each month would be:

Ref.	Date	Description	Dr.	Cr.
XX.	Jan. 31	Insurance Expense	1,000	
		Prepaid Insurance		1,000
		To record insurance expense for January		

As the months of the year go by, each month will include a proportionate amount of the entire year's insurance premium as insurance expense to be charged against that month's revenue. Concurrently, the Prepaid Insurance asset will be written down every month by the amount of the asset that has expired. Another common prepaid item that is similar to prepaid insurance is Prepaid Rent: a prepaid rent asset is normally written off evenly over time, the same way that prepaid insurance is. Note, however, that the expensing of some types of prepaid items might not occur evenly over time, the way that insurance policies or prepaid rent expire. Other possible prepaid items could include prepaid advertising, prepaid consulting fees, prepaid taxes, or others, and the expensing of these prepaid assets would occur as the assets expire, which may not be evenly over time.

Many expenses of a business could be prepaid, resulting in the creation of an asset. In most cases, the Materiality Principle applies, and the business does not "capitalize" every purchase of something that is soon going to be expensed, such as office supplies, dues and subscriptions, small tools, miscellaneous supplies, etc. In those cases, the business simply expenses the item when it is purchased, whether purchased by cash or account payable.

In summary, prepaid assets are slowly written down as their historical cost expires, and the ongoing expiration of the historical cost is expensed to the income statement through the related category of expense (insurance expense, rent expense, etc.). At the end of subsequent accounting periods, the unexpired cost of the asset is reduced on the balance sheet and the periodic reduction is measured by the related expense, which has the effect of ultimately reducing the equity of the business by the same amount. When the prepaid asset has been completely written off, the unexpired cost has completely expired and the business does not have any future benefit available to it from the used-up asset. For the prepaid item, the accounting process is complete: originally the business acquired an asset (an unexpired cost); the asset was recorded as an asset; the asset was subsequently used up, and the business systematically expired the cost of the asset by expensing it through the income statement; and finally, the asset is completely used up and the cost has completely expired.

Deferred Revenue.[11] Deferred revenue is a liability that results from the receipt of cash from a customer or client before the related services or goods are provided.[12] When the money is received, it isn't revenue because the services haven't been performed. In normal circumstances, the recipient "owes" the advance deposit back to the customer if the services are never performed or the goods aren't delivered. The best simple example of a deferred revenue item would be an advance retainer received from a client. At the time of the receipt, the firm hasn't earned any revenue, and the firm "owes" the client the value of the retainer in the form of services (or repayment of money if the services are never performed).

Upon receipt of a cash payment of an item of deferred revenue, the journal entry should be:

Ref.	*Date*	*Description*	*Dr.*	*Cr.*
XX.	Jan. 1	Cash	5,000	
		Deferred Revenue		5,000
		To record receipt of retainer		

After the advance cash payment that creates the deferred item is received and recorded above, the business continues to operate and the revenue is recognized under the Realization Principle. When services are performed pursuant to the agreement between the client and the business, the business will recognize revenue in the amount that is earned, in the period that it is earned. Assuming that $2,800 of services was performed in February, the journal entry to recognize the revenue is:

Ref.	*Date*	*Description*	*Dr.*	*Cr.*
XX.	Feb. 28	Deferred Revenue	2,800	
		Revenue (Fees Earned)		2,800
		To recognize revenue from previous advance payments		

As the deferred revenue liability is being earned by the firm, the liability will be written down (debited) to zero, and, correspondingly, revenue will be recognized (credited) over the period that the liability is written off. For the deferral, the accounting process is complete: originally the business received an advance of cash (an asset, offset by a liability, deferred revenue). As the advanced cash was earned by performing services, the deferred revenue liability was essentially "converted" into revenue (by debiting the deferred revenue liability and crediting revenue).

---

11. There is confusing terminology regarding deferred revenue; it is a liability account, even though its name includes the term "revenue."

12. It is possible, but unlikely, that a customer could make an advance payment with some form of property other than cash. For simplicity, I will assume the advance payment is made in cash.

Another Deferred Item—Taxes

Deferred Taxes. Deferred taxes can be an asset or liability account, depending on circumstances. A deferred tax liability usually results from the company's ability to defer or delay the payment of some amount of taxes on its income because of some beneficial tax treatment that it takes advantage of in its tax accounting, but not in its financial statement reporting. (See Chapter 5.) The best example of this situation is depreciation expense in a company that uses accelerated depreciation for tax purposes, but straight line depreciation for accounting purposes. Assume, for example, that the company has $100,000 of depreciation expense for the year under GAAP, using the straight line method. The result of that straight line depreciation deduction will reduce the company's net income by $100,000, resulting in a net income amount on which taxes are owed. The company, however, is able to use accelerated depreciation for income tax purposes, resulting in a higher depreciation expense (say $150,000) and ultimately resulting in a lower taxable net income on which taxes are calculated. (Assume 40% taxes in this example.) Therefore, the company is able to defer $20,000 of income tax that it should be paying on its financial statement net income to a later period of time because of some aggressive tax planning. The company's financial statements will show the tax expense based on the financial statement net income, but the IRS only requires current payment of the amount of taxes due. The deferred tax liability will reflect that $20,000 of income tax is ultimately owed, but not due until a later period.

Conversely, deferred taxes can be an asset of a company. Assume, for example, that a company experiences a net loss during a year and it is able to qualify for a net operating loss for tax purposes. There are provisions of the Internal Revenue Code that allow a company to "carry over" a net operating loss and use it as a deduction in a later year when the company has taxable income. As a result of this tax provision, the company has a present "benefit" that it owns that can be used to offset some taxes that it might otherwise owe in the future. This benefit can be a "Deferred Tax Asset" because it will be used to offset taxes that are owed for income in the future.

Conclusion

Accrual accounting measures the performance of a company by recognizing events based on true economic activity regardless of when cash transactions occur. Accrual accounting differs significantly from cash basis accounting and is the only method acceptable under GAAP. Although simplistic, the cash method accounting does not properly recognize all the revenue earned in the accounting period and it does not properly account for all of the expenses of the period. In order to accurately report the net income of an entity, it is necessary to effectuate the true economic reality of the timing of revenue and expense recognition based on the Realization Principle and the Matching Principle. The proper application of these principles will determine the accounting period in which items of revenue and expense are recognized. The Exercises & Practice Problems in the workbook will help you understand the concepts of deferral and accrual.

Chapter 5

Fixed Assets and Depreciation

Introduction

Fixed assets[1] are a separate class of business assets that require specialized accounting procedures. Fixed assets, also called capital assets, do not include items that are normally consumed or used up in the regular course of business operations or production. They are long-term assets such as vehicles, heavy equipment, machinery, real estate, building improvements and similar assets that contribute to business operations over many accounting periods.

Accounting for fixed assets involves the proper recording of the initial purchase of the asset, which requires the identification of the asset and all of the costs associated with its acquisition and installation. Then, the Matching Principle requires that the cost of the fixed asset be matched with the revenue that it is used to generate, and this matching is achieved through the mechanism of depreciation, a concept that is unique to fixed asset accounting. The disposition of fixed assets will usually create a gain or loss to the entity that must be accounted for, causing the recognition of the gain or loss in the company's income statement.

Depreciation is the mechanism for allocating the cost of a fixed asset to the operations of the business over the estimated useful life of the asset. There are several methods of depreciation that are acceptable for accounting purposes, each based on different types of accounting estimates and each based on different theories of asset utilization. This chapter will introduce all of the generally recognized methods.

The chapter also introduces accounting for natural resources and intangible assets. These types of long-term assets involve the concepts of depletion and amortization, concepts that are quite similar to depreciation.

Accounting for Fixed Assets

Fixed assets are tangible capital assets that are used in the long-term operations of a business, but are not consumed or converted into cash during the normal operating cycle of the business. Fixed assets are not assets that are held as financial investments or assets held for resale to customers. Fixed assets include assets like: land, buildings, machinery, equipment, furniture and fixtures, leasehold improvements, vehicles and computer equipment. The benefits that a business realizes from a particular fixed asset extend over several years, and this long-term utility of the asset causes the business to have to match the cost of the fixed asset to the periods in which it generates revenue for the business.

---

1. Fixed assets are also referred to as "Property Plant and Equipment," "Long-term Assets," "Machinery & Equipment" or other descriptive terms identifying the entire group of capital assets.

Initial Acquisition. Upon acquisition, a fixed asset is accounted for at its cost. The cost of a fixed asset includes all amounts incurred to acquire the asset and any amounts that can be directly attributed to bringing the asset into working condition. For instance, "cost" would include sales taxes paid, transportation and delivery expenses, and costs incurred to install the asset. If, for example, the installation of a machine requires some site preparation or leasehold renovation, those costs could be considered part of the cost of the fixed asset.

Despite the fact that historical cost may not be an accurate reflection of a fixed asset's current value, GAAP still requires booking the asset at historical cost because it is the most objective measure of the asset's value for purposes of initial financial statement presentation. Accounting for a fixed asset at its historical cost (less accumulated depreciation) also comports with the parallel concept that an entity is a going concern and therefore the fixed asset's current selling price or market value is irrelevant. Under GAAP, the cost of the asset and its depreciation are considered more relevant, and objective, than its current fair market value.

A distinction between capital expenditures and revenue expenditures can be drawn in relation to fixed assets. A capital expenditure is the purchase of an asset that is expected to benefit the company for a period longer than one year. For tax purposes, capital expenditures are costs that cannot be deducted in the year in which they are paid or incurred and must be *capitalized*, or made into an asset, as opposed to being *expensed,* or written off during the present accounting period. Revenue expenditures, on the other hand, are outlays that benefit the business currently, and are therefore treated as an expense to be matched against revenue in the current accounting period.

Additions to Fixed Assets. Significant repairs or renovations to fixed assets that extend the life, increase the capability, or increase the efficiency of the asset should be capitalized at the time they are incurred. This capitalization (addition of cost to the existing fixed asset) occurs during the life of the fixed asset by increasing its cost basis and recalculating depreciation from that date forward. Normal expenditures for repairs, maintenance or replacement of component parts that do not extend the asset's original life or significantly enhance its value are considered non-capital expenditures and are expensed in the period in which they are made.

The Concept of Depreciation

Under the Matching Principle, the cost of a fixed asset must be matched with the revenue that it is used to produce. This matching allocation is done through depreciation, a systematic write-off of the cost of the asset against (or matched to) the revenue that the asset is used to produce. Depreciation is a mechanism of allocating the cost of the fixed asset over its estimated useful life, with the objective being to match the total cost of the asset to the periods in which it is used to produce revenue. Depreciation applies to all fixed assets that are used in the revenue production process, if they are exhausted over an estimated useful life. The concept of depreciation does not apply to land, however, because land does not have a useful life—it is a perpetual resource. Depreciation does apply to other types of real property, such as buildings and lease-hold improvements, because they have useful lives and they wear out over time.

Two aspects of depreciation merit special comment here. First, depreciation is not a reduction in the fair market value of a fixed asset, although there may be some coincidental relationship between market value and an asset's accounting *net book value*.[2] Since fixed assets are initially accounted for at cost, and depreciation is an allocation of an asset's cost over its estimated useful life, the depreciated amount of an asset on the books of a company is nothing more than the depreciated cost of the asset. The concept of depreciation is not directly related to a decrease in the value of an asset. Second, one of the things that makes depreciation expense unique is that it is not tied to a current outlay of cash, like most expenses. For example, in the tenth year of the ownership of a building that has long since been paid for, a company is able to take a significant, non-cash deduction for depreciation expense from its income. The consequence of this deduction is to lower the company's net income and, if the company pays taxes, to lower the current taxes that the company will pay. The unsophisticated observer of this phenomenon may think that depreciation expense is a phony expense because it doesn't require a current cash outlay and it lowers taxes.

Both the theory and practice of depreciation accounting are sound, but the application of the concept of depreciation requires that a number of accounting estimates be made. Also, there are different methods of computing depreciation that have different conceptual bases, and different effects on the financial statements of a business. The methods, which are discussed subsequently, may result in different calculations of current depreciation expense, but they all have the same objective: to allocate the cost of the fixed asset to the revenue production of the business over the life of the asset. Depreciation is demonstrative of accounting's Matching Principle.

The Mechanics of Depreciation Accounting

Fixed assets are recorded on the balance sheet at cost, and depreciation expense allocates the cost of the asset to the income statement over its estimated useful life. Fixed assets can be thought of as unexpired costs (one of the definitions of an asset) and depreciation expense reflects the current accounting period's expiration of part of that unexpired cost. In layman's terms, depreciation expense records the current "using up" of the fixed asset and charging that use against the revenue of the business.

Accumulated Depreciation—A Contra Account. Accumulated depreciation is a contra asset account that is used to accomplish one-half of the two goals of depreciation, those goals being to "expire" the cost of the asset against revenue on an ongoing basis, and to show the reduction in the cost of the asset on the balance sheet over the same period of time. The current expiration of the cost is shown on the income statement through depreciation expense. The reduction in the cost

---

2. The difference between an asset's original cost and its accumulated depreciation is referred to as the "net book value" or the "book value" of the asset. Net book value = cost of fixed asset minus accumulated depreciation.

of the asset on the balance sheet is shown by the contra asset account, Accumulated Depreciation. The Accumulated Depreciation account records the accumulation of the total depreciation taken on a fixed asset since its acquisition. The fixed asset continues to be shown on the balance sheet at its original cost, but that cost is offset—reduced—by all of the past depreciation that has been taken on the asset that is summarized in the Accumulated Depreciation account. As its name indicates, a contra asset account "goes against" the asset that it is attached to, and when taken with its corresponding asset, the accumulated depreciation effectively reduces the "net" balance of the asset shown on the balance sheet, called the "net book value" or "book value" of the asset.

A contra asset account's normal balance is a credit. It is increased with a credit and reduced by a debit, the exact opposite of an asset account. The journal entry to record depreciation expense for a period is as follows:

Ref.	Date	Description	Dr.	Cr.
XX	Dec. 31	Depreciation Expense	7,500	
		Accumulated Depreciation		7,500
		To record depreciation expense for the period.		

On the balance sheet, the contra asset account, Accumulated Depreciation, is presented along with its related fixed asset account, as follows:

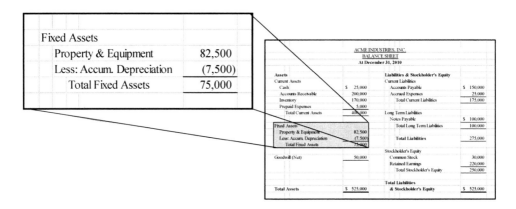

Methods of Depreciation

There are a number of acceptable methods for calculating depreciation under GAAP as well as for income tax reporting purposes.[3] Some companies use different methods for financial statement reporting purposes and for tax purposes, but these differences are not germane to this introductory discussion. Some methods of calculating depreciation are based on time (straight line, declining balance and sum of the year's digits) and others are based on activity (units of production). A second conceptual difference in depreciation methods is whether the method calculates a

---

3.   Depreciation is a "hot" tax issue, particularly for capital intensive businesses, because some of the methods of accelerated depreciation enable the company to artificially reduce net income in earlier years, consequently reducing income taxes.

constant amount of depreciation expense (straight-line calculation) or a higher amount of expense in earlier periods (accelerated depreciation).

Straight-Line Depreciation. The straight-line method of depreciation is a method of allocating the cost of the asset evenly over the estimated useful life of the asset. It is the simplest and most commonly used method for calculating depreciation. Under the straight-line depreciation method, the depreciable base[4] of the asset is written off evenly over the useful life of the asset; the same amount of depreciation expense is taken each year. The calculation of straight-line depreciation begins with the cost of the asset, and then it subtracts the salvage value from the cost of acquisition, and divides the resulting "depreciable base" by the useful life of the asset. The formula for calculating straight-line depreciation is:

$$\text{Depreciation Expense} = \frac{\text{Cost} - \text{Estimated Salvage Value}}{\text{Estimated Useful Life}}$$

The following three things have to be determined or estimated in order to calculate straight-line depreciation for an asset:

1. Acquisition cost—as previously noted, the original cost of an asset includes the acquisition cost, taxes, delivery charges, set up charges, and all other costs that are required to place the asset in service to the company.

2. Salvage value—the estimated value that the fixed asset will have at the end of its useful life. Salvage value is also called residual value or scrap value. Estimating an asset's salvage value obviously requires estimating a future market value in light of the anticipated useful life of the asset as well as the wear and tear on the asset.

3. Useful life—the period of time that it will be economically feasible to use the fixed asset. It should be noted that the Internal Revenue Service has tables that estimate reasonable useful lives for different classes of assets, and, while these tables are not controlling for GAAP, they certainly are helpful for making a reasonable estimate.

Let's take a simple example of straight-line depreciation here, and there are additional exercises and problems in the Workbook. Assume that ABC Company acquires a new plastic injection molding machine on January 1, 2009. The invoice price of the machine is $25,800, and sales tax of 8% ($2,064) was charged. ABC Company hired Freddy's hauling and installation company to get the machine in place, and Freddy's charge was $1,850. The machine has an estimated useful life of 8 years and a salvage value of $4,000. Calculate depreciation expense under the straight-line method for the complete year of service, 2009.

---

4.   An asset's "depreciable base" = acquisition cost minus salvage value.

Straight-Line Depreciation Calculation

Acquisition Cost:

Machine Price	$25,800
Tax	2,064
Delivery & Installation	1,850
Total Acquisition Cost	$29,714

Full year straight-line depreciation:

$$\text{Annual Depreciation Expense} = \frac{\text{Cost} - \text{Estimated Salvage Value}}{\text{Estimated Useful Life}}$$

$$\text{Depreciation Expense} = \frac{\$29,714 - 4,000}{8 \text{ years}}$$

$$\text{Depreciation Expense} = \underline{\$3,214.25}$$

The journal entry to record ABC's depreciation expense for this machine for 2009 is:

Ref.	Date	Description	Dr.	Cr.
XX	Dec. 31	Depreciation Expense	3,214.25	
		Accumulated Depreciation		3,214.25
		To record depreciation expense for 2009		

The fixed asset section of ABC's balance sheet, assuming that this was the only item on it, would appear as follows at December 31, 2009:

Fixed Assets	
Machinery & Equipment	$ 29,714
Less: Accum. Depreciation	(3,214)
Total Fixed Assets	26,500

Date of Service. Depreciation should begin when the asset in first placed in service, which, of course, is rarely at the beginning of an accounting period. Consequently, various reasonable conventions for estimating the starting date for depreciation have evolved. One convention is to assume that the asset was purchased exactly in the middle of the accounting period, say July 1, therefore allowing one-half of one year's depreciation in the first year of service ("half-year convention"). Another convention is to break the year into months and assume that the asset is placed in service on the first day of the month if it is placed in service during the first half of the month, or if it is purchased in the second half of the month, assume that the asset is placed in service on the first of the next month ("monthly convention"). Following the concept of materiality, logic dictates that these types of approximations are reasonable, as long as they are applied consistently throughout the business entity.

Using the example of ABC Company's new plastic injection molding machine discussed previously, what would the 2009 depreciation expense be if the machine was purchased on March 19, 2009 using the "monthly convention" described in the preceding paragraph.

Full year depreciation expense	$\underline{\$3,214.25}$
Monthly convention:	
Asset placed in service:	March 19, 2009
Assumed start date:	April 1, 2009
Fraction of year after acquisition:	$^9/_{12}$
Full year depreciation expense	$\$3,214.25$
	$\times \quad ^9/_{12}$
2009 Depreciation Expense	$\underline{\$2,410.69}$

The detailed accounting for each fixed asset of a business is different, and it requires maintaining a fixed asset register that records all of the details of the accounting for each fixed asset. The fixed asset register is often called a depreciation schedule, and it records the acquisition date, cost, depreciation method, current period depreciation expense and the accumulated depreciation for each asset. The depreciation schedule will agree to the total cost of all the fixed assets and total Accumulated Depreciation as set forth on the balance sheet of the business. Here is an example of a typical depreciation schedule for a small business.

ABC Company, Inc.
Depreciation Schedule
12/31/2009

No.	Class	Description	Date Acquired	Date Sold	Cost	Salvage Value	Prior Depr	Method	Useful Life	Rate	Current Yr. Depr
	Improvements										
8		Leasehold Improvements	6/30/2008		$ 62,500.00	$ -	$ 3,906.25	S/L	8		$ 7,812.50
	Furniture & Fixtures										
11		Office Furniture	3/1/2007		$ 32,500.00	$ 6,000.00	$4,858.33	S/L	10		$ 2,650.00
12		Conference Table	3/2/2007		$ 10,000.00	$ 2,000.00	$ 6,000.00	DDB	5	2.0	$ 1,333.33
	Office Equipment										
21		Copy Machine	3/19/2007		$ 22,000.00	$ 1,800.00	$12,032.00	DDB	5	2.0	$ 1,346.67
28		Computer Equipment	1/1/2009		$ 10,000.00	$ -	$ -	DDB	3	2.0	$ 6,666.67
	Vehicles										
4		2003 GMC Sierra Pickup Truck	12/17/2005		$ 17,350.00	$ 2,500.00	$ 6,364.29	S/L	7		$ 2,121.43
38		2006 Porsche 911 Carrera	9/1/2009		$ 85,000.00	$21,000.00	$ -	S/L	7		$3,047.62
		Total			$ 239,350.00	$ 33,300.00	$ 33,160.87				$ 24,978.22

Remember that the depreciation expense taken by a business has a direct effect on the reported net income of the business.[5] The greater the depreciation expense, the greater the reduction to net income as a result of depreciation. And, under a straight-line methodology, the depreciation for a particular asset is evenly allocated over the useful life of the asset, effectively assuming that the asset is "used up" ratably over its estimated useful life. Ask yourself: Is that a reasonable assumption? Better yet, is that the only reasonable assumption for the "using up" of a fixed asset?

Accelerated Depreciation Methods. In contrast to straight-line depreciation, accelerated depreciation methods seek to recover (or expense) more of the cost of the asset through depreciation expense in the earlier years of the asset's useful life than in the later years. The conceptual theory underlying accelerated depreciation is that the direct cost of a fixed asset expires more in the early years of its useful life than in the later years, as evidenced by the fact that a capital asset usually requires more repair and maintenance expense as it gets older. In the aggregate, accelerated depreciation still writes off the total cost of the asset over its expected useful life, but the timing of the write-off is hastened by allocating more cost of the asset in the earlier years and less cost of the asset in the later years. It is also worth noting that the financial reporting of many smaller businesses is motivated by tax considerations and the use of accelerated depreciation allows a higher depreciation expense, and lower current net income, in the earlier years, thereby reducing taxable income to the business. It is true that, over the entire life of the fixed asset, the total depreciation deductions will be the same, but most business owners would rather reduce their taxable income presently, save the taxes, and deal with the deferral later.

Declining Balance Method. The declining balance method is one of the most popular methods of accelerated depreciation. Initially, understand that the declining balance method can be calculated at different percentages of the straight-line rate ("double" declining balance = 200% of the straight-line rate; one and one-half declining balance = 150% of the S/L rate; and 1.25 declining balance = 125% of the S/L rate) and these different percentages are used for different types of assets in the Internal Revenue Code. Regardless of the multiple of the straight-line rate, the concept is the same. We will limit our discussion to the "double" declining balance method for our purposes, understanding that the other declining balance multiples are just math differences, not conceptual differences.

The double declining balance ("DDB") method is first calculated as a 200% multiple[6] of the straight-line rate. To determine the percentage straight-line rate, you divide 100% by the number of years of estimated useful life of the asset. (If the useful life is 8 years, the straight-line rate is 12½%: 100% ÷ 8 = 12½%.) Assuming an 8 year useful life, the double declining balance rate would be 25% (12½ % × 2 = 25%). Then, the DDB rate is applied to the net book value of the

---

5.   Everyone cares about the amount of a company's net income for one reason or another. Public companies usually want to show the highest net income possible to impress shareholders. Small firms, on the other hand, are conscious that taxes must be paid on net income, so they would usually like to minimize reported net income, particularly if the minimization is the result of an artificial accounting convention. We are about to discuss accelerated depreciation methods that artificially increase depreciation expense and reduce net income.

6.   The calculation would be 150% for 1.5 declining balance depreciation or 125% for 1.25 declining balance depreciation.

asset at the beginning of the period to determine the amount of depreciation for the period. Note that the DDB rate is not applied to "cost minus salvage value" as in the straight-line calculation, but it is applied to the net book value of the asset at the beginning of the period. To summarize, the simple steps to determine depreciation expense under the DDB method are:

1. Determine straight-line rate (divide 100% by the useful life of the asset).

2. Multiply the straight-line rate by 2 (= DDB rate).

3. Apply DDB rate to the net book value at the beginning of the period (ignore salvage value in the calculation) (= depreciation expense for the period).

Let's use the same example that was previously used for the straight-line depreciation calculation to compare the results. To repeat the facts in a truncated fashion: ABC Company's new plastic injection molding machine was acquired on January 1, 2009; price = $25,800; sales tax = 8% ($2,064); hauling and installation costs = $1,850; therefore, total installed cost = $29,714. The machine has an estimated useful life of 8 years and a salvage value of $4,000. Calculate the DDB depreciation for a complete year of service, and also calculate the DDB depreciation for 2009 using the "monthly convention" described in the straight-line section.

---

1. Straight-line rate: $100\% \div 8 = 12\,\frac{1}{2}\,\%$
2. Double Declining Balance rate: $12\,\frac{1}{2}\,\% \times 2 = 25\,\%$
3. Calculate full year Double Declining Balance Expense: $\$29,714 \times 25\% = \underline{\$7,428.50}$

If we complicate the example and assume that the machine was acquired on March 19, 2009, the DDB depreciation for 2009 would be calculated as follows:

4. Apply monthly convention for 2009: $\$7,428.50 \times \frac{3}{4} = \underline{\$5,571.38}$

As the name implies, the double declining balance method of depreciation does two things differently than the straight-line method: first, it doubles the straight line rate; and second, it applies its doubled rate to a decreasing balance of the net book value of the fixed asset. (Remember, the net book value of an asset is calculated by subtracting the accumulated depreciation from the cost of the fixed asset.)

Two other interesting aspects of DDB depreciation become evident when the method is applied to the entire useful life of a fixed asset. First, although the DDB method results in higher depreciation expense in earlier years, there is a point where the mathematics of the calculation cause the annual depreciation expense to become lower than the straight-line rate for the same asset. Second, if the DDB method is blindly applied for the entire useful life of an asset, the method never completely depreciates the asset. You would be applying a rate of, say, 25% to a decreasing balance, and you would never get to zero. Because of these two phenomena, both GAAP and the IRS allow a one-time switch from DDB to straight-line depreciation during the life of the asset.

This switch is logically made in the period in which the calculated DDB depreciation will result in a depreciation expense that is less than the straight-line rate. At that time, the net book value of the asset is calculated, and that net book value is straight-line depreciated over the remaining useful life. Although salvage value is not considered in determining the annual depreciation expense under the DDB method, the asset is never depreciated below its salvage value.

Using our example from ABC Company, let's examine the comparative results of depreciating the injection molding machine for its entire life:

Injection Molding Machine Depreciation Schedule				
Useful Life (years)		8		
Cost		$ 29,714		
Salvage Value		$ 4,000		
DDB Factor		2		
	Straight-line Method		Double Declining Balance	
Year	Annual Depreciation Expense	Adj. Book Value at 12/31	Annual Depreciation Expense	Adj. Book Value at 12/31
0		$29,714.00		$29,714.00
1	$ 3,214.25	$26,499.75	$ 7,428.50	$22,285.50
2	$ 3,214.25	$23,285.50	$ 5,571.38	$16,714.13
3	$ 3,214.25	$20,071.25	$ 4,178.53	$12,535.59
4	$ 3,214.25	$16,857.00	$ 2,507.12	$10,028.47
5	$ 3,214.25	$13,642.75	$ 2,507.12	$ 7,521.35
6	$ 3,214.25	$10,428.50	$ 2,507.12	$ 5,014.23
7	$ 3,214.25	$ 7,214.25	$ 1,014.23	$ 4,000.00
8	$ 3,214.25	$ 4,000.00	$ -	$ 4,000.00

In the above example of the double declining balance method, in the fourth year, the declining balance depreciation calculation ($2,507.12) resulted in a lower amount than the same year's straight-line depreciation expense ($3,214.25). When this "switch" occurs, GAAP allows a one-time change from DDB depreciation to straight-line depreciation for the remaining life of the asset. Remember, however, even though the DDB method doesn't factor in salvage value in its calculation, the adjusted book value is never reduced below estimated salvage value. Therefore, the seventh year of DDB depreciation expense is limited to $1,014.23 in this example.

Sum of the Years' Digits Method. The "SYD" method of depreciation is an accelerated method that results in a more accelerated write-off than straight line depreciation, but less than the DDB method. Under this method, the annual depreciation expense is calculated by multiplying the depreciable base by a schedule of fractions that are determined by the sum of the total years of the asset's useful life. The numerator of the fraction is the number of years left to be depreciated and the denominator is the sum of the total years of the useful life. Following are the steps to apply the SYD method to an asset with an original cost of $10,000, a salvage value of $1,000, and an estimated useful life of 5 years. To apply the SYD method

1. Determine the years' digits. Since the asset has a useful life of 5 years, the years' digits are 5, 4, 3, 2 and 1.

2. Calculate the sum of the digits (5 + 4 + 3 + 2 + 1 = 15)

3. Calculate annual depreciation by multiplying the depreciable base by:

   a. First year – 5/15 X $9,000 = $3,000

   b. Second year – 4/15 X $9,000 = $2,400

   c. Third year – 3/15 X $9,000 = $1,800

   d. Fourth year – 2/15 X $9,000 = $1,200

   e. Fifth year – 1/15 X $9,000 = $ 600

Activity Methods of Depreciation. Activity methods of depreciation are based on the level of activity or usage of the particular fixed asset. Activity depreciation is ideal for machinery and equipment whose useful life is dependent on usage, such as an aircraft (flying hours), a vehicle (miles), or a machine whose usage is not directly related to time. When the asset is acquired, its useful life is estimated in terms of the total activity or usage that is anticipated. Then the per-usage depreciation rate is calculated by dividing the depreciable base by the total activity life, resulting in a depreciation expense amount per unit of activity.

Units of Production Method. The most common activity method of depreciation is the units of production method. To calculate depreciation under this method, first determine the depreciation per unit as follows:

$$\text{Depreciation per Unit} = \frac{\text{Cost} - \text{Salvage Value}}{\text{Useful Life (in units: hours, miles, machine cycles, etc.)}}$$

Then determine depreciation for the period by multiplying the depreciation per unit by the number of units used in the accounting period.

Let's consider the following example. Your firm took delivery of its new CNC (computer numeric control) power lathe on April 11, 2009. The cost of the machine (including all taxes, delivery and set up charges) was $112,500. The operator's manual states that the life of the machine is estimated to be 16,200 hours. The salvage value of the lathe at the end of its life is $18,500 because it will need significant rebuilding at that point. From the time of its installation in April until the end of the year, the machine logged 1,163 hours. Calculate the depreciation expense for 2009 based on the units of production method.

$$\text{Depreciation Per Unit} = \frac{\$112,500 - 18,500}{16,200 \text{ hours}}$$

$$= \$5.8025 \text{ per hour}$$

$$\text{Depreciation Expense} = \$5.8025 \times 1,163 \text{ hours}$$

$$= \underline{\$6,748.31}$$

Gains and Losses on the Sale of Fixed Assets

During the life of a fixed asset, the company will depreciate the asset, record accumulated depreciation, and determine the net book value of the asset at the end of each accounting period. Consequently, the asset will be shown on the books at the net value of its cost minus its accumulated depreciation. Upon the sale or other disposition of the asset, it is necessary to remove both the asset and its related accumulated depreciation from the books. Unless the asset is sold for the exact amount of its book value, which is very unlikely, there will be a gain or loss on sale.

In order to record a sale transaction, it is necessary to record the consideration received for the sale of the asset (debit cash, probably[7]), then to credit the asset for its cost to remove it from the accounts, and to debit accumulated depreciation to remove it from the accounts. Assuming an asset (machine) with an original cost of $8,500, accumulated depreciation of $7,500, and a selling price of $1,850 cash on December 15, 2009, the following journal entry will record its sale:

Ref.	Date	Description	Dr.	Cr.
x.	Dec. 15	Cash	1,850	
		Accumulated depreciation	7,500	
		Machinery & Equipment		8,500
		Gain on sale of Asset		850
		To record gain on sale of machine		

---

7. It is possible that the business might receive some asset other than cash in the sale.

Note that the debits and credits will effectively calculate the gain or loss by requiring the journal entry to balance with a credit (gain) or a debit (loss).

If an asset is sold in the middle of an accounting period, it is necessary to first update the depreciation expense to the time of the sale, and then calculate the gain or loss on the sale of the asset. In order to accomplish this, the accountant will follow the same rules that are used when the asset is purchased. If the company follows the monthly convention, the annual depreciation expense will be calculated up to the month of the sale, based on the convention used at the time of the acquisition. If the company uses the annual convention, one-half year's depreciation will be taken in the year of the sale, regardless of the date of the sale.

Natural Resources and Depletion

Natural resources[8] are long-term capital assets that can be owned by a business and "used up," or depleted, during the course of the operations of the business. They are conceptually similar to fixed assets because a business incurs significant costs to acquire or otherwise obtain the resources, and then that cost must be allocated to the revenues that the costs produce. Natural resources are different from depreciable assets because they are wasting assets, physically extracted from the earth through business operations and they are only replaceable through natural processes. Accounting for natural resources is a complicated area that involves many industry-specific accounting measurements that are beyond the scope of this introduction to the subject. Basically, however, the cost of natural resources is determined by the direct cost of the resource plus related costs such as exploration and development costs, as well as consideration of the costs to restore the property to its original condition.

Depletion is the process of allocating the depletable cost of natural resources to expense as individual units of the resource are extracted. Depletable cost is similar to depreciable base; it is the total cost of the natural resource plus any restoration cost less any salvage value remaining after the resources are extracted. Depletion expense is usually calculated by an activity method of depletion, such as units of production. Under this method, a per-unit cost of depletion is calculated by dividing the depletable cost by the estimated number of units the resource contains. The per-unit depletion times the actual number of units extracted and sold during the accounting period equals the amount of depletion expense recorded for the asset during the period.

Assume that the Ticonderoga Mining Company paid $14,000,000 for an existing copper mine that is expected to produce 32,000,000 pounds of copper. The company anticipates incurring $3,500,000 (in present value dollars) of costs to restore the property at the end of its life. What is the per-unit depletion expense for Ticonderoga?

---

8. Examples of natural resources are: oil and gas reserves, standing timber and mineral deposits.

Calculating Units-of-Activity Depletion. Assuming that the mine sold 1,375,000 pounds of copper during 2009, what is the depletion expense for 2009?

$$\text{Per-Unit Depletion} = \frac{\text{Depletable Cost}}{\text{Units of Resource}}$$

$$= \frac{\$14,000,000 + 3,500,000}{32,000,000 \text{ pounds}}$$

$$= \$0.546875 \text{ per pound}$$

$$\text{Annual Depletion Expense} = \text{Per-Unit Depletion} \times \text{Units During Year}$$

$$= \$0.546875 \text{ per pound} \times 1,375,000 \text{ pounds}$$

$$= \$\underline{751,950}$$

Unlike fixed assets, for natural resources, the depletion expense can either be accumulated in a contra asset, accumulated depletion, or it can be directly credited to the natural resource asset, thereby lowering the cost of the asset on the balance sheet. Therefore, either of the following journal entries could be used to record the depletion expense for 2009:

Ref.	Date	Description	Dr.	Cr.
X.	Dec. 31	Depletion expense	751,950	
		Accumulated Depletion		751,950
		To record depletion expense for 2009		

Ref.	Date	Description	Dr.	Cr.
X.	Dec. 31	Depletion expense	751,950	
		Copper Mine		751,950
		To record depletion expense for 2009		

There are many subtleties of accounting for both fixed assets and natural resources that create significant differences between the two categories of assets. For our introductory purposes, however, the accounting for them is fairly similar. Both types of assets are long-term capital assets that have a benefit to the business entity over many accounting periods and their cost must be allocated to periods of revenue production through either depreciation or depletion.

Intangible Assets and Amortization

Intangible assets are identifiable nonphysical economic resources that have been acquired or created through time and effort and are identifiable as a separate asset. Intangible assets exclude monetary assets such as stocks, securities, accounts and notes receivable. Intangible assets are only booked as assets if they are purchased.[9] Intangible assets can cover a wide range of economic resources that have probable future value to an entity, but, practically, accountants are only accounting for a relatively short list of items.

Intellectual property is a generic term that describes the form of intangible asset that exists because it is legally defined and gives its owner legal rights against infringers. Examples of intellectual property are patents, copyrights, trademarks, trade secrets and goodwill. If these assets are created by a business through its normal operations, the costs associated with them are not capitalized, they are expensed when incurred. When these assets are purchased, however, the cost of acquisition must be amortized (allocated as expense to the income statement) over the identifiable finite life of the asset. Patents are exclusive rights for the manufacture, use and sale of a particular product, granted in the United States for a period of 20 years. A copyright is the exclusive legal right to reproduce, publish, sell, or distribute the matter and form of something (as a literary, musical, or artistic work), and its life is for 50 or 70 years after the death of its owner. These assets are (according to US GAAP) amortized to expense over 5 to 40 years with the exception of goodwill.

Amortization is the method of allocating the cost of an intangible asset over its estimated useful life. Amortization is done following a straight-line method and the reduction in the asset can be accounted for using a contra asset account, Accumulated Amortization, or the asset can be directly written down when the period expense is recorded. So, the methodology for straight line depreciation is essentially followed to calculate amortization for intangible assets, culminating in a determination of amortization expense for the period. Like depreciation, amortization is a non-cash expense that doesn't require an outlay of cash during the current period, but it reduces net income (and therefore income taxes).

Conclusion

In this chapter, we have seen the specialized accounting procedures surrounding fixed assets. Those procedures include the proper recording of the initial purchase of the asset and the application of different depreciation methods to allocate the cost of the fixed asset over its estimated useful life. At the end of the fixed asset's useful life, the disposition of the asset will create a gain or loss to the entity that is accounted for and recognized in the company's income statement. Accounting for natural resources is quite similar to fixed asset accounting, but the cost allocation mechanism is depletion, not depreciation. Finally, the accounting for intangible assets and the concept of amortization was introduced.

---

9. In other words, even though a business may accumulate nonphysical economic resources over time (like start-up costs, systems, processes, procedures, etc.), these intangibles are not booked as assets unless they are specifically purchased. Under GAAP, all research and development costs are charged to expense when incurred (as opposed to being capitalized), but this is one of the areas where GAAP differs from International Financial Reporting Standards.

Chapter 6

Inventory Accounting and Cost of Goods Sold

Introduction

Inventory is one of the most significant assets in merchandising or manufacturing businesses. Accounting for inventory involves questions of the amount of product on hand, its cost, the timing of its sale, and its valuation. Because the sale of inventory is both a revenue transaction (dollars coming into the business) and a cost transaction (assets going out of the business), accounting for inventory affects both the balance sheet and the income statement. An error in the amount of inventory at the end of an accounting period affects the balance sheet, of course, but it also directly affects the company's income statement for the period.

This chapter will discuss the concepts surrounding inventory, the mechanics of inventory accounting and the differences between perpetual inventory accounting and periodic inventory accounting. Our primary focus will be on merchandise inventory, as opposed to manufacturing inventory, although the distinction between inventory accounting for manufacturing concerns and merchandising businesses will be shown. We will learn to apply the different inventory costing assumptions of first-in, first-out (FIFO), last-in, first-out (LIFO), and weighted average costing. The different inventory cost assumptions have significant effects on a company's financial statements, and the observer must understand the significance of these alternatives.

Finally, we will briefly discuss the inventory accounting issues involved in manufacturing concerns. Manufacturing companies have three types of inventory: raw materials, work in process and finished goods. Raw materials and finished goods inventory accounting is quite similar to inventory accounting in merchandising operations, but work in process accounting is much more complex.

The Business Cycle as It Relates to Inventory

A business buys inventory to hold for resale to its customers. Inventory is recorded at cost on the books of the business,[1] not at its market value or selling price, so the balance sheet of the business shows the inventory at cost (debit inventory, credit cash or account payable) when it is purchased. At a later time, customers buy inventory at a selling price that, hopefully, is higher than the cost of the inventory. When the inventory is sold to the customer, two things have to happen, each of which affects both the balance sheet and the income statement. First, the sale has to be recorded to show the selling price/revenue coming into the business (debit cash or accounts receivable;

---

1. This is generally true, but there are significant exceptions to the rule of cost for inventory that will be addressed later.

credit sales). Second, the balance sheet has to be "relieved" of the inventory asset and the income statement will show the expiration (expense) of the cost of the inventory (debit cost of goods sold[2]; credit inventory).

Recognize the close relationship that the asset—inventory—has with the income statement. When inventory is sold to a customer, the asset "leaves" the company, and its "leaving" is accounted for as an expense in the income statement. The expense category is called "cost of goods sold," although CGS is usually calculated as a combination of several accounts (to be explained in the next section).

Inventory—The Basics

Inventory is stock in trade that is owned by a company and held for resale, or materials held to be used in the manufacture of goods for sale. It exists in merchandising companies (retail, wholesale and some service businesses like restaurants) and manufacturing companies. Companies acquire large amounts of inventory, over long periods of time, and it is sold to customers over several accounting periods, or used in the manufacturing process over several accounting periods. The fact that different quantities of inventory are acquired over several accounting periods in which other quantities of the same inventory are sold (or used in manufacturing) creates a significant accounting problem. The fundamental problem of inventory accounting is twofold: 1) properly accounting for the quantity and cost of inventory on hand at the end of the accounting period, the balance sheet date; and 2) appropriately matching the cost of the inventory sold (or used) during the period with the revenue received from the sale of the inventory in the period. Our discussion of inventory will focus on these problems, and, from this point forward, we will limit our discussion to merchandise inventory and not manufacturing inventory.[3]

Balance Sheet Presentation. Inventory is a current asset of the business and must be presented on the balance sheet. The task is difficult because of the constantly changing quantity of inventory on hand and the fact that it is impractical to maintain records of each individual item of inventory and its specific cost. The quantity of inventory on hand can be determined by physical count and there are several inventory costing conventions[4] that are used to estimate its balance sheet carrying amount.

Cost of Goods Sold ("CGS"). When inventory is sold, the income statement must be charged with an expense that recognizes the cost of the inventory sold. Until the time of the sale of the inventory, the balance sheet will include the item of inventory as an asset; when it is sold, the cost of the

---

2. The debiting of cost of goods sold is usually accomplished through a several-step process involving an account called "Purchases," but those steps will be explained later.

3. There is a large body of accounting theory surrounding manufacturing inventory that is beyond the scope of our introductory inquiry. However, the general concepts and issues relating to manufacturing inventory are introduced at the end of the chapter and the concepts are similar to those relating to merchandise inventory.

4. FIFO, LIFO and weighted average cost, explained subsequently.

---

inventory is "expired" through an expense called "cost of goods sold." Cost of goods sold is often the largest expense on the income statement in a merchandising organization, and its computation is somewhat complicated. CGS is the result of a calculation that incorporates the purchases of inventory that were made during the year as well as the change in the amount of inventory held by the business from the beginning to the end of the year.

The top part of the income statement is composed of three critically important accounts: Sales, Cost of Goods Sold,[5] and Gross Profit. Gross profit is the profit that a company earns directly from the sale of its merchandise, before consideration of the expenses of operating the business. It is a very important financial statistic that shows the performance of a company with respect to its industry, its pricing and its cost structure.

Let's digress for a moment to understand the concept of gross profit and gross profit margin.[6] Consider these three companies: Tiffany & Company, Nordstrom and Costco. Following are the top parts of their income statements on a percentage basis, with sales equaling 100%:

	Tiffany & Company	Nordstrom	Costco
Sales	100%	100%	100%
Less: Cost of Goods Sold	-43%	-62%	-87%
Gross Profit	57%	38%	13%

The dramatically different gross profit margins of these three companies are indicative of the different types of business that each company is in. Tiffany & Company is a high-end jewelry retailer that has a relatively high gross profit margin.[7] It is the type of company that buys its very expensive merchandise and holds it in very nice retail locations with significant markups, waiting for the right customer to pay a high price in relation to Tiffany's cost for the product. At the other end of the spectrum is a company like Costco that prides itself in carrying a relatively small number of inventory items[8] of high quality and very low price relative to its costs. Its gross profit margins bear that out. Anyone who has shopped at Costco knows that it is a warehouse setting that offers a limited selection of items and no traditional customer service. Nordstrom is somewhere in the middle—high quality, intense customer service, and pretty full retail prices. Now, these three companies are in different segments of the retail market, so their numbers aren't really comparable, but think what could be learned by comparing one company's gross profit margin to

---

5. As we will shortly see, CGS is actually made up of several accounts.
6. "Gross profit margin," or "gross margin," is simply stating a company's gross profit as a percentage of the company's sales.
7. A fairly minor explanatory point: The use of the term "margin" indicates that we are referring to a financial statistic in percentage terms, as opposed to absolute terms.
8. Interestingly, relative to other retailers, Costco carries a small number of items in its inventory—about 4,000. Compare that to the number of items in Target's or Wal-Mart's inventories—about 40,000 items. This quantitative difference just shows one of the business differences of the companies.

other companies in the same market segment. For instance, if you learned that Nordstrom had a 38% gross profit margin and all of its competitors (Saks, Lord & Taylor, Macy's, etc.) had lower gross profit margins, that is financial information that would indicate some positive things about Nordstrom. (For example, it is able to maximize its prices in relation to its costs; it is efficient in converting merchandise into sales; its buying practices are meeting its target market; and, generally, it is running a "tight ship" in its line functions.) A company's gross profit margin is a critically important statistic about the firm.

In order to understand the relationship between inventory and cost of goods sold, we will examine an income statement that is more complicated than the ones that we dealt with in Chapters 3 and 4. The 2009 income statement for Doug's Hardware Store is on the adjacent page. Our focus will be the Cost of Goods Sold section.

The Cost of Goods Sold is the total of the direct costs of the products that compose a company's sales. In a merchandising operation, CGS represents the total cost of the inventory that has been sold in the period. The total cost of inventory includes its original cost and all the costs to get it in place to sell. Those additional costs would include things like freight and delivery charges. The cost of inventory does not include the carrying costs of holding the inventory for sale, such as interest or rent, nor does CGS include the other ongoing operating expenses of the business. As you can see from Doug's income statement, all of the company's ordinary operating expenses are deducted "below the line"[9] in the income statement.

Referring to the income statement for Doug's Hardware Store, we see that the Cost of Goods Sold is a calculation that incorporates several line items. The first component of CGS is the Cost of Goods Available for Sale, and its formula is as follows:

$$CGAS = BI + P \ [\text{Purchases}^{10}]$$

To understand the CGAS formula, think about what items a business has "available" for sale during a year. It has all the products that are on its shelves at the beginning of the year (Beginning Inventory, or "BI") plus all of the products that it purchases ("P") during the year. In total, that is the universe of inventory that Doug's has available to sell to its customers during the year. Nothing more could be sold from Doug's Hardware Store. Now that we know how many products Doug had available to sell, let's explore how many products Doug actually sold. The formula for Cost of Goods Sold is:

$$CGS = CGAS - EI$$

---

9.   This term is often used to indicate that certain expenses are considered below the Gross Profit "line" of the income statement.

10. Abbreviated as "P." Purchases is an expense account in which all of a company's purchases are accumulated. It is a temporary account, so it is closed out at the end of the period along with other expense accounts and revenue accounts.

Doug's Hardware Store
Income Statement
For the period ended December 31, 2009

Sales		$ 3,647,500	100.0%
Cost of Goods Sold:			
Beginning Inventory	$ 543,200		
Plus: Purchases	2,128,950		
Equals: Cost of goods			
Available for Sale	2,672,150		
Less: Ending Inventory	(556,600)		
Equals: Cost of Goods Sold		2,115,550	58.0%
Gross Profit		1,531,950	42.0%
Expenses:			
Advertising	127,000		3.5%
Auto & Truck	37,200		1.0%
Bank Charges	5,120		0.1%
Commissions	36,475		1.0%
Depreciation	46,500		1.3%
Employee Benefits	46,608		1.3%
Freight	34,500		0.9%
Insurance	31,700		0.9%
Interest	51,300		1.4%
Legal & professional	22,300		0.6%
Maintenance	11,400		0.3%
Officer's Salaries	120,000		3.3%
Payroll tax expense	31,072		0.9%
Postage & printing	31,350		0.9%
Rent	141,300		3.9%
Salaries	268,400		7.4%
Travel & entertainment	6,350		0.2%
Utilities & telephone	7,850		0.2%
Total expenses		1,056,425	29.0%
Net Income before taxes		475,525	13.0%
Income taxes		(166,434)	-4.56%
Net Income		$ 309,091	8.5%

Or, to state the formula completely, from beginning to end:

$$CGS = BI + P - EI$$

These formulas are among the easiest to understand in all of accounting. In plain English, the inventory that you had available to sell (CGAS) consists of what you had at the beginning of the year (BI) plus what you purchased during the year (Purchases). The inventory that you sold (CGS) consists of what was available to sell (CGAS) minus what you had left over at the end of the year (EI).

The Relationship of Inventory to Cost of Goods Sold. If you understand the formula to determine Cost of Goods Sold, you should understand the relationship between inventory and CGS. In simple terms, the items that a business sells during the year are "taken from" the beginning inventory plus the items purchased during the year. What is left over—what wasn't sold—is the ending inventory. Therefore, if you subtract the ending inventory from the beginning inventory plus the purchases, you end up with how much you sold during the year. So, to key up the importance of the next part of the discussion, understand that both the *physical quantity* and the *method of costing* of the ending inventory is a critical part of the equation.

Two Types of Inventory Accounting

Physical inventory is accounted for either on a perpetual method or on a periodic method.

Perpetual Method. Under the *perpetual method* of inventory accounting, every item of inventory is specifically identified in the inventory accounting records, its cost is recorded, and it is specifically accounted for during the time that it is held by the business. When the item is sold, the exact cost of the specific item is removed from the asset account, inventory, and the expiration of that cost is recorded in the income statement as a cost of goods sold. The perpetual inventory method is generally used by companies that deal in larger, more expensive items of inventory, such as jewelry, machinery and equipment or similar items. The perpetual method of inventory accounting is precise in its tracking of inventory costs, and it does not require any estimates or approximations to be made in its application. When an item is sold, there are two journal entries that are required to be made by a business that uses the perpetual method: one entry to record the sale and another entry to relieve the balance sheet of the inventory item and expense it to the income statement. Assuming the sale of a Piaget watch for $14,500 that cost the jeweler $9,600, the two entries would be as follows:

Ref.	Date	Description	Dr.	Cr.
XX.	Feb. YZ	Cash	14,500	
		Sales		14,500
		To record sale of Piaget watch.		

Ref.	Date	Description	Dr.	Cr.
XX.	Feb. YZ	Cost of Goods Sold	9,600	
		Inventory		9,600
		To record cost of sale of Piaget watch.		

The effect of these two journal entries is to record both the revenue from the sale and the expense related to the sale. Because the perpetual inventory method is used, the company knows the exact cost of the specific item of inventory that was sold. No judgment or estimating is required to make these entries, given the perpetual method of inventory accounting. The perpetual method is impractical for many businesses, however, because they deal with inventory that is made up of many small items.[11]

Periodic Method. The periodic method of inventory accounting is more practical for most businesses, but it is less precise than the perpetual method. Under the periodic method, the amount of inventory on hand is determined by a physical count of the inventory at the end of the accounting period. To determine the cost of the inventory in the accounting records, different inventory costing assumptions are applied (LIFO, FIFO and average cost), resulting in an estimate of the cost of the physical inventory on hand. That process takes care of accounting for the inventory at the end of the accounting period for balance sheet purposes. Finally, the amount of inventory sold during the accounting period is estimated by comparing the amount on hand at the beginning of the period, adding the amount of purchases during the period, and then subtracting the amount on hand at the end of the period (the same formula previously discussed: BI + P − EI). The difference between the beginning inventory plus the purchases minus the ending inventory is the amount of product that has been sold during the period.

A business's accumulation of its inventory occurs over a period of time as a result of many, many purchases of goods; it does not acquire the inventory all at once. Furthermore, during the normal operations of the business, customers purchase the inventory from the business every day, resulting in reductions to the accumulated inventory. Although modern computerization continues to change the technology of inventory accounting, it has not been historically practical to account for each and every item of inventory on a perpetual basis. Consequently, under a periodic system of inventory accounting, the company records its purchases of goods in bulk, in the Purchases account, and the cost of the items sold during the year is determined by the formula, BI + P − EI. While it is practical to account for every purchase made by a business and every sale made by the business, it is not usually practical to account for each item of inventory held by the business on an ongoing basis, unless the business deals with high-priced, individualized items.

---

11. Interesting point: Even though computerization has made it much more possible to account for every item of inventory in a mass retail business, businesses still generally use the periodic method of inventory accounting.

Methods of Costing Ending Inventory under the Periodic Method

The challenge of inventory accounting is to properly state the cost of inventory on the balance sheet, and, as a result of that proper accounting, to accurately record cost of goods sold on the income statement. Under the perpetual method of inventory accounting, this challenge is relatively easy: the business has a perpetual record of the cost of every item in inventory; when an item sells, the cost of goods sold can be charged with the cost of the specific item, and that item can be removed from the company's inventory. We saw this previously in the Perpetual Method section.

The periodic method of inventory accounting is used in situations where it is not practical to account for each item of inventory because the items are too small, fungible or impractical to specifically identify. In these situations—which amount to the majority of business entities—the business keeps track of its total purchases during the accounting period, and then physically counts the inventory at the end of the period. Now, it's one thing to determine that a company has 1,000,000 items on hand on December 31, but it's another thing to determine the *cost* of the 1,000,000 items, particularly when the items on hand are the result of a series of purchases at different prices during the year, as well as some holdover items from the inventory at the beginning of the year. Accounting has resolved this problem by applying alternative methods of estimating the cost of ending inventory, based on different, artificial assumptions of the flow of goods through an enterprise. As we begin the discussion of inventory costing methods, remember the importance of the dollar amount assigned to ending inventory—that will be the amount that will be presented on the balance sheet and the dollar amount of ending inventory is also used as a subtraction in the cost of goods sold formula (CGS = BI + P − EI). Because ending inventory is subtracted to determine CGS, the higher the amount of ending inventory, the lower the cost of goods sold; and the lower the amount of ending inventory, the higher the amount of goods of goods sold.

*[Some thinking person's questions before we proceed . . . Why do you care about this? If you are a small-business person **and a taxpayer**, would you rather report higher, or lower, net income? If one method of inventory costing will artificially alter your taxable income, are you interested in that? All other things being equal, which artificial distortion (higher or lower?) would you like to have in your **ending inventory**? Think about how **the formulas**[12] **to determine net income work** as you answer these questions. Alternatively, if you are the Chief Financial Officer of a publicly traded company, would you like your reported net income to be higher or lower, all other things being equal? As you read on, think about the simple formula for calculating cost of goods sold and how it is affected by the amount of ending inventory. In the context of inventory accounting, also ask yourself which financial statement is more important to you: the balance sheet or the income statement?]*

Three Methods of Inventory Costing. We are going to learn three different methods to estimate the cost of ending inventory. The methods are based on different assumptions about the physical flow of goods through the business organization. At the outset, however, note that

---

12. Net income = revenues minus expenses. CGS is an expense. CGS = BI + P − EI. Do you want CGS to be higher or lower?

the terminology is somewhat confusing: we are talking about a method for costing the ending inventory, but the *description* of the method (FIFO, LIFO or weighted average cost) doesn't describe the ending inventory, it describes the flow of the cost of goods sold through the organization. Remember this inconsistent terminology when you are trying to understand each of the methods.

The different methods of inventory costing are easiest to understand with a simple example. Let's assume the following facts for the 2007 year of operations of Sammy's Soccer Ball Store:

1. Sammy has only one product in his sporting goods store: soccer balls.

2. Sammy follows the periodic method of inventory accounting because it is very difficult to differentiate the hundreds of soccer balls that Sammy has in his store.

3. Following is a schedule of the purchases of soccer balls that Sammy has made during the year:

Sammy's Soccer Ball Store Summary of Purchases - 2007			
	# items	Price	Extension
Beginning inventory	900	$ 14.40	$ 12,960
Purchases:			
10-Feb	100	$ 14.60	$ 1,460
15-Mar	150	14.70	2,205
7-Apr	640	14.85	9,504
28-May	495	14.90	7,376
20-Jun	770	15.05	11,589
29-Jul	580	15.20	8,816
15-Sep	630	15.30	9,639
24-Oct	400	15.45	6,180
20-Nov	380	15.60	5,928
21-Dec	375	15.75	5,906
Total Purchases	4,520	*calculated*	$ 68,602
C/G/A/S	5,420	$ 15.05	$ 81,562

4. There are 1,220 soccer balls in ending inventory, based on a physical count of the inventory in the store at December 31, 2007.

The challenge is to determine the proper cost of ending inventory to use for accounting purposes, recognizing that the amount used has dramatic consequences on the income statement. We also enter this discussion knowing that these different inventory costing assumptions are theoretical constructs, and not precise assignments of actual cost. The company has a determinable quantity of inventory in its warehouse (physical count = 1,220 soccer balls) and the costing of that inventory requires some arbitrary allocations of historical purchase costs. The next sections will discuss the three alternative methods of inventory costing: FIFO, LIFO and weighted average cost.

First-In, First-Out: "FIFO." One assumption a business may make in determining the cost of goods sold is that the first goods purchased are the first to be sold. This method of determining the cost of ending inventory is called First-In, First-Out, or FIFO. This methodology is analogous to the physical flow of merchandise in a bakery or the dairy section of the grocery store. The newest inventory is put on the back of the shelf and the older inventory is pushed forward to the front of the shelf, presumably encouraging the customer to buy the older inventory (the "first-in" inventory). If a merchant purchased inventory on Monday, Tuesday, and Wednesday and made one sale on Thursday, it is assumed that the item bought on Monday was the one sold (for cost purposes) whether or not this is actually the case. Since we are using this inventory costing assumption to "cost" the ending inventory, it is logically assumed that the ending inventory consists of the last items purchased (because the first ones purchased have been sold).

At Sammy's Soccer Store, the physical count of the items of inventory on December 31, 2007 shows that there are 1,220 soccer balls on hand. The only accounting records that exist are for the beginning inventory (900 balls at a cost of $12,960) and a number of purchases during the year as shown on the previous schedule. If the FIFO method of inventory costing is to be used, it can be assumed that the first balls purchased have been sold ("FIFO"), leaving the ending inventory to be populated with the most recent purchases. To determine the cost of ending inventory under FIFO, proceed backwards through the purchase layers until 1,220 balls have been accounted for through purchases. The calculation is as follows:

	FIFO Ending Inventory		
	# items	**Price**	**Extension**
21-Dec	375	$ 15.75	$ 5,906
20-Nov	380	15.60	5,928
24-Oct	400	15.45	6,180
15-Sep	65	15.30	995
Totals	1,220		$ 19,009

Under FIFO, the assumed cost of Sammy's ending inventory is $19,009 based on the assumption that the 1,220 soccer balls in ending inventory are the last 1,220 balls that Sammy purchased. Sammy will never really know which 1,220 balls he has, and which groups of purchases they actually came from, but the FIFO method of inventory costing will make the determination for him. This fact will forever be: the 1,220 soccer balls in Sammy's ending inventory "cost" $19,009.

Last-In, First-Out: "LIFO." A business may also make the opposite cost flow assumption, that the most recently purchased goods are the first to be sold. This method of determining cost is called Last-In, First-Out, or LIFO. This method can be thought of as a barrel of nails or a pile of gravel, where new goods are placed on top of the old goods, and the customer reaches in and grabs the merchandise, taking the most recent purchases of inventory. Under LIFO, if a merchant purchased inventory on Monday, Tuesday, and Wednesday and made one sale on Thursday, the merchant would assume that the Thursday sale was of the items added to inventory on Wednesday. The last items purchased are the first ones sold, so the remaining inventory is composed of earlier purchases—the nails that remain in the bottom of the barrel.

Returning to Sammy's Soccer Store, the challenge is to "cost" the 1,220 soccer balls on hand at the end of the year under LIFO. Again, the only accounting records that exist are for the beginning inventory (900 balls at a cost of $12,960) and a number of purchases during the year as shown on the previous schedule. If the LIFO method of inventory costing is to be used, it can be assumed that the last balls purchased have already been sold ("LIFO"), leaving the ending inventory to be populated with the earliest purchases, including the beginning inventory. To determine the cost of ending inventory under LIFO, proceed from the beginning inventory through the next earliest purchase layers until 1,220 balls have been accounted for through purchases. The calculation is as follows:

LIFO Ending Inventory			
	# items	Price	Extension
Beg. Inv.	900	$ 14.40	$ 12,960
10-Feb	100	14.60	1,460
15-Mar	150	14.70	2,205
7-Apr	70	14.85	1,040
Totals	1,220		$ 17,665

Under LIFO, the assumed cost of Sammy's ending inventory is $17,665 based on the assumption that the 1,220 soccer balls in ending inventory are the first 1,220 balls that Sammy purchased. Notice how much lower the "cost" of ending inventory is under LIFO than it is under FIFO because of the makeup of the layers of the ending inventory. Remember, this example is presented in an environment of significant inflation, and that definitely affects the calculation.

Weighted Average Cost. The weighted average cost method for valuing ending inventory is based on the weighted average of all the goods that comprise the cost of goods available for sale, those being the beginning inventory and the purchases for the entire year. To calculate the weighted average method, simply take the total cost of the beginning inventory plus the cost of all the purchases ($12,960 + $68,602 = $81,562) and divide by the total number of units purchased plus the units in beginning inventory (4,520 + 900 = 5,420). This quotient is the weighted average cost of an individual item in ending inventory ($81,562 ÷ 5,420 = $15.05).

The following calculation shows the weighted average cost for Sammy's inventory at December 31, 2007:

Weighted Avg. Cost. Ending Inventory			
	# items	**Price**	**Extension**
Totals	1,220	$ 15.05	$ 18,359

Comparison of the Differences in Methodologies

The discussion of the comparison of FIFO and LIFO assumes that we are operating in an inflationary economy. Under FIFO, since the ending inventory is "costed" at the most recent purchase prices, the value presented on the balance sheet will be higher, and the cost of goods sold will be lower, because the inventory sold is valued at earlier, cheaper prices. Under LIFO, the exact opposite is true: the ending inventory will be lower (it is valued at earlier layers of cost) and the cost of goods sold will be higher because the goods sold are priced at the most recent (higher) purchases.

Why does this matter? Again, to the extent that the financial statements can be skewed higher or lower using Generally Accepted Accounting Principles, certain stakeholders may have a bias to choose one method over another. Remember, the Consistency Principle will not allow methods to be changed from year to year, so the dramatic effect of the difference between LIFO and FIFO cannot be applied to a business in the short term, but a slight bias (lower income or higher income) can be effectuated by selecting one method over another.

Let's look at the results of the inventory costing methods on the financial statements, specifically the Cost of Goods Sold section of the income statement, of Sammy's Soccer Ball Store for 2007.

	# of units	**Cost of Goods Sold**		
		FIFO	**Avg Cost**	**LIFO**
Beg. Inv.	900	$ 12,960	$ 12,960	$ 12,960
Purch's	4,520	$ 68,602	$ 68,602	$ 68,602
C/G/A/S	5,420	81,562	81,562	81,562
End. Inv.	(1,220)	(19,009)	(18,359)	(17,665)
CGS	4,200	$ 62,554	$ 63,203	$ 63,898

The use of LIFO versus FIFO results in a higher Cost of Goods Sold calculation on the income statement. Why? Because the last items purchased (at the higher inflation prices) are the ones that are assumed to be sold, leaving the lower priced goods in ending inventory. If you subtract a lower ending inventory amount from Cost of Goods Available for Sale, the result is a higher Cost of Goods Sold. The opposite of all of this discussion is true for FIFO. So, what is the result of this inventory costing difference on the income statement of Sammy's? Following is a hypothetical income statement for 2007 for Sammy's. Every item of revenue and expense is the same; the only difference in the comparative statements is the method of inventory costing—FIFO, LIFO or weighted average cost. Look at the differences in cost of goods sold, gross profit and net income caused only by the difference in the inventory costing assumptions.

Sammy's Soccer Ball Store
Income Statement
For the period ended December 31, 2007

	FIFO	Wtd. Avg. Cost	LIFO
Sales	$ 120,000	$ 120,000	$ 120,000
Cost of Goods Sold:			
Beginning Inventory	12,960	12,960	12,960
Plus: Purchases	68,602	68,602	68,602
Equals: C/G/A/S	81,562	81,562	81,562
Less: Ending Inventory	*(19,009)*	*(18,359)*	*(17,665)*
Equals: Cost of Goods Sold	*62,554*	*63,203*	*63,898*
Gross Profit	*57,447*	*56,797*	*56,102*
Less: Total expenses	(47,400)	(47,400)	(47,400)
Net Income	$ 10,047	$ 9,397	$ 8,702

Finally, think about the probable next step of the income statement reality: paying income taxes. From our discussion of FIFO, LIFO and weighted average costing, we realize that the company: A) has the same amount of inventory in its warehouse at the end of the year; and B) sold the same amount of "stuff" during the year. The only factual difference in the alternative inventory costing scenarios is the way in which costs are allocated to ending inventory and, resultantly, to cost of goods sold. But the choice of the inventory costing method affects the "bottom line" of the business in two ways: the assets are higher or lower depending on the method selected, and the net income is higher or lower also. If your net income is lower, what happens to your taxes?

Errors in Inventory Accounting

Inventory accounting frequently requires a physical count of thousands of items at many locations under circumstances that are less than ideal. It is logical to expect that mistakes are sometimes made in this area of accounting. Inventory errors tend to be counterbalancing, however, because one year's ending inventory becomes the next year's beginning inventory. Let's consider an example. Here, the base case correctly includes ending inventory in Year 1 at $2,400, resulting in net income of $2,200 in Year 1 and $2,650 in Year 2.

Ending Inventory Error Example
Base Case
Correct Ending Inventory

	Year 1	Year 2	Total Both Years
Sales	$ 10,000	$11,000	$ 21,000
Cost of Goods Sold:			
Beginning Inventory	$ 2,000	$ 2,400	
Plus: Purchases	4,700	5,100	
Equals: C/G/A/S	6,700	7,500	
Less: Ending Inventory (correct)	(2,400)	(2,750)	
Equals: Cost of Goods Sold	4,300	4,750	9,050
Gross Profit	5,700	6,250	11,950
Expenses: Total expenses	3,500	3,600	7,100
Net Income	$ 2,200	$ 2,650	$ 4,850

At the end of Year 1, assume there is some mistake in the physical inventory, resulting in an overstatement of ending inventory of $350. There is a consequence of this error in both Year 1 and Year 2, but the overall effect of the error is corrected after the second year. The income statement, assuming the error, is on the adjacent page.

The general rule is that overstatements of ending inventory cause that year's income to be overstated, while understatements of ending inventory cause understatements of income. The reciprocal is true for beginning inventory: overstatements of beginning inventory cause net income to be understated; understatements of beginning inventory cause net income to be overstated. [Hint: Rather than try to memorize the confusing formulas that are set forth in this paragraph, I find it much easier to know the formula for cost of goods sold (BI + P – EI = CGS), and then just apply it with a simple mathematical model to any situation to see what effect an over- or understatement has on the income statement. Of course, you also have to know the formula for an income statement (Sales – CGS = Gross profit – Expenses = Net Income.)]

	Incorrect Ending Inventory Overstated by $350		
	Year 1	Year 2	Total Both Years
Sales	$ 10,000	$11,000	$ 21,000
Cost of Goods Sold:			
Beginning Inventory	$ 2,000	$ 2,750	
Plus: Purchases	4,700	5,100	
Equals: C/G/A/S	6,700	7,850	
Less: Ending Inventory (wrong)	(2,750)	(2,750)	
Equals: Cost of Goods Sold	3,950	5,100	9,050
Gross Profit	6,050	5,900	11,950
Expenses: Total expenses	3,500	3,600	7,100
Net Income	$ 2,550	$ 2,300	$ 4,850

Inventory in Manufacturing Companies

The concepts of inventory accounting are essentially the same in a manufacturing business as they are in a merchandising organization, but the details of the accounting are more complicated because there are more types of inventory. This section covers an overview of inventory accounting for manufacturing entities.

Manufacturing is the process of producing finished goods from raw materials by fabricating or assembling the materials, adding labor and performing the activity in an organized process. From the perspective of inventory accounting, the manufacturing process is divided into three distinct parts, each of which has its own type of inventory. The three types of manufacturing inventory are raw materials, work in process and finished goods. Each type of inventory has distinct accounting considerations.

Raw Materials. Accounting for raw materials inventory is quite similar to merchandise inventory accounting. The company purchases raw materials inventory to hold until it is needed for the production process. The inventory is accounted for at cost, and, during any accounting period, an amount of the inventory is consumed or "contributed" to the production process. (The using up of raw materials inventory is similar to cost of goods sold accounting in a merchandising company—what is the cost of the raw materials that were transferred into the production process during this accounting period?) At the end of an accounting period, the company has an ending inventory of raw materials that must be counted and accounted for in the same way as merchandise inventory. In fact, all of the same kinds of issues that we dealt with in periodic inventory in merchandising organizations apply to raw materials inventory: physical count, costing method of ending inventory, and determining the "cost" of goods placed into production. An additional complexity, though, is that in the manufacturing company, the raw materials inventory is only a part of the company's total inventory.

Work in Process. The manufacturing process is a process by which a company takes raw materials, combines them in various ways, adds labor, adds other components (proprietary or patented processes), and converts them into finished goods for sale to its customers. Accounting for manufacturing processes is the substance of the entire subject of cost accounting, the details of which are far beyond the scope of this text. Accounting for work in process inventory is much more complex than accounting for merchandising or raw materials inventory; however, many of the same conceptual issues that we have already discussed apply to work in process accounting.

During the process of manufacturing, the economic factors that are contributed to the creation of work in process inventory are raw materials, direct labor and overhead. Each of these factors is accounted for, is added to, and becomes part of the cost of the company's work in process inventory. The accounting issues for work in process revolve around the proper cost of beginning inventory, the costing of the factors that are added to the production process (which are capitalized into inventory and not expensed until the inventory is sold), and the transfer of work in process to finished goods. (This last stage is somewhat analogous to "selling" the inventory in a merchandising company, except the "sale" here is a transfer to the finished goods "department.")

Cost accounting is the process of identifying, recording and analyzing the costs of production and distribution. In cost accounting, there are many sophisticated methods for allocating different cost components to manufactured goods. Some of the methodologies involve temporary allocations of costs with adjustments for variances from "standard" costs, and other methodologies involve the concept of process costing for determining the cost of fungible type products such as chemicals or gasoline. Here, we will touch on the major components of cost accounting because the components are relevant to damages calculations.

In the manufacturing process, the costs that are added to work in process are raw materials, direct labor and overhead. Raw materials are added at their cost, and the primary issue in cost accounting is the allocation of the cost of materials to the units that are manufactured. Direct labor consists of the labor that can be directly traced to the manufactured goods, like assembly line labor. Direct labor would usually exclude labor costs of supervision or management because these costs are considered to be indirect. Overhead is a grouping of expenses that are *indirectly* related to the manufacturing process. Examples of overhead expenses would be factory supervision expenses, factory utilities, factory insurance, factory rent and other expenses of operating the manufacturing process that cannot be directly tied to the products that are manufactured. The challenge of accounting for overhead is adopting a reasonable method of allocation of the overhead to the units of production.

Work in process inventory is the most complicated of the inventory accounting issues. In short, it is important to know that the cost issues are complex and they involve direct labor and overhead allocation issues. Some of the components of work in process accounting involve costs that are directly traceable to the finished products but others are assigned to work in process on a more arbitrary allocation basis. When inventory accounting relates to damages calculations (Chapters 10 and 11), cost allocation issues must be considered.

Finished Goods. Finished goods inventory represents the amount of manufactured product on hand that awaits sale to customers. Finished goods inventory represents a current asset in the balance sheet, and its "cost" is determined from the accumulation of costs in the manufacturing stage of production. Once the "cost" of finished goods inventory is established, the accounting for finished goods is identical to accounting for merchandise inventory.

Conclusion

In this chapter, we have reviewed the effects of inventory transactions on the balance sheet and income statement, focusing on the components of cost of goods sold, often the largest item on a company's income statement. We have seen how an error in the amount of inventory at the end of an accounting period affects both the balance sheet and the income statement, but the effect on the income statement is self-correcting over two years.

The chapter presented the mechanics of inventory accounting and the differences between perpetual inventory accounting and periodic inventory accounting, and introduced the different inventory costing assumptions of first-in, first-out; last-in, first-out; and weighted average costing. We analyzed the significant consequences of alternative inventory cost assumptions on a company's financial statements. Finally, we touched on the complex accounting issues involved in manufacturing concerns, but we will leave the details of work in process accounting to the cost accountants.

Chapter 7

Financial Statement Analysis

Introduction

Financial statement analysis is the quantitative analysis of financial information of a company with a view toward determining important facts about the firm—liquidity, solvency, profitability, leverage and certain aspects of management effectiveness. Through the analysis of a firm's financial statements, the analyst uses the accounting information to make judgments about the company's operations and its management's performance. Investors call this type of analysis "fundamental analysis,"[1] and it is the basis for an entire investment philosophy.

Financial statement analysis is used to determine the financial health and stability of a firm at the present time, and it is also often used as the basis for projections of the anticipated performance of the company in the future. Financial statement analysis is both an end and a means. The results of financial analysis—the numbers—are important in and of themselves as a quantitative conclusion of business activity, but they also should be used as a diagnostic tool to evaluate a company's performance and provide management with relevant consulting advice.

Concepts for This Chapter

Profitability. A firm's profitability is its ability to earn income and, as a result, sustain growth in both the short and long term. A company's degree of profitability is usually based on the income statement, but analysis of the firm's financial statements will show that the amount of assets and equity are relevant to understanding the company's profitability. For example, a firm would be considered to be profitable if it earned $100,000 in a year, but what if the firm had $10,000,000 of owner's equity invested in it? It would still be "profitable," but $100,000 is a woefully inadequate return on a $10 million investment.

Solvency. A firm's solvency is its ability to pay its obligation to creditors and other third parties in the short term. Insolvency, the opposite of solvency, is the condition in which the firm's liabilities exceed its assets. We will see that insolvency can exist in several different forms, and, in addition to its obvious financial ramifications, insolvency can be legally relevant in a number of different contexts, one of those contexts being bankruptcy law.

---

1. Fundamental analysis is the investment philosophy that is based on the financial strength and profitability of the individual company, as opposed to technical analysis, which is based on statistical analysis of stock price trends.

Liquidity. The ability of a company to easily convert assets into cash is its liquidity. The ultimate liquid asset is cash, and a firm's liquidity is a measure of the current status of the firm's cash and its ability to convert other assets into cash in the short term without discount or penalty. A firm's ability to satisfy its immediate obligations is a critically important condition of the company because without liquidity, every business will die.

Leverage. Leverage measures the amount of a firm's capital that is provided by lenders as opposed to the amount provided by equity investors, or owners. The degree to which a company is leveraged is an element of the firm's financial risk. The more capital that is provided by creditors, the higher the risk of being unable to respond to exigent circumstances such as lower profitability or other unanticipated difficulties encountered in the operation of the company. The proper amount of a company's leverage is a balancing act between the high risk of overleveraging and underutilization of available resources (underleveraging and not using some appropriate level of debt).

Management Effectiveness. Certain activities of the business can be evaluated through financial statement analysis. For instance, you can see the effectiveness of the company's credit management (collection of accounts receivable) or the utilization of the amount of the company's inventory through financial analysis.

Fixed Costs. Fixed costs are those costs that do not vary with the level of sales over a relevant range of production. A typical, simple example of a fixed cost is rent; a company's rent expense does not change if sales goes up or down by five or ten percent.

Variable Costs. Variable costs are costs that vary with the level of production. Examples of variable costs are cost of goods sold, sales commissions or possibly utilities expense in a manufacturing company. In the long run, all costs are variable.

Semifixed and Semivariable Costs. These are costs that are partially fixed and partially variable. An example of this type of cost is one that has a base cost and a usage cost, such as the rental of a machine with a usage factor, like a photocopy machine.

Methods of Financial Statement Analysis

Ratio Analysis. This type of analysis compares different accounts, categories or elements of a firm's financial statements to one another to derive meaningful information about the financial health of the organization. Ratio analysis is probably the most common form of financial analysis. It provides relative measures of a firm's financial condition and performance.

Trend Analysis or Comparative Analysis. Analyzing portions of historical financial statements of a firm to determine relevant historical trends of activity, such as growth (or decline) in revenues, costs and expenses, and net income. The comparison of significant financial statistics of a business to those of other businesses or composites of relevant industry information can provide useful additional information regarding a firm's overall performance.

Common Size Technique. This analysis restates the financial statements of a business into percent-ages to facilitate comparison to other accounts and categories within the financial statement as well as to other companies in the relevant industry. After a financial statement has been reduced to percentages, it is easy to perform vertical and horizontal analysis. *Vertical analysis* is reviewing the statement vertically to view the percentages of the accounts to one another, for example, to assess the amount of cost of goods sold as a percentage of gross revenue. *Horizontal analysis* is analyzing the annual percentages horizontally, meaning in relation to the same accounts in other years as the statements are placed next to one another in a trend analysis. One of the benefits of using common size financial statements is the ability to compare companies of different sizes to one another on a percentage basis, rather than on an absolute basis, because the absolute basis comparison is often difficult to do. (How do you compare the gross profit of a small specialty clothing store to Nordstrom without doing it by percentages? The absolute numbers are dramati-cally different, but the percentages in relation to the respective company's sales might be similar.)

Analysis of Financial Statements

To perform a competent, basic financial analysis of a company, the first step is to take the historical financial statements (balance sheets and income statements) and "spread" them in a spreadsheet program so they can be viewed in a comparative fashion. Typically, a thorough financial analysis of a company includes at least 5 years of financial data, allowing the analyst to view a representa-tive long-term operating cycle of the business. In addition to viewing the absolute amounts of the accounts, the statements should also be "common sized," or reduced to percentages for further analysis. In the income statements, gross revenues should be set to 100% and each item on the statement should be related to revenues as a percentage. In the balance sheets, total assets should be set to 100% and all other items stated as a percent of the total assets.

Following are the "spread" balance sheets (Table 1) and income statements (Table 2) for ACME Industries, Inc. for the years 2005 through 2009. ACME is a hypothetical company that will initially be the base case for our financial analysis.[2] In the Workbook for Chapter 7, the success of ACME will vary (ACME Industries, Inc. will be changed into BETA2 Industries, Inc. and also into Charlie Industries, Inc.), so you will see the difference between a healthy company and a sick one. For now, ... well, you decide: is ACME healthy or not?

---

2. ACME Industries, Inc. is a small metal fabricating company that was formed as a California C Corporation in 1995. It operates from leased premises in San Marcos, California and it employs 14 to 18 people. The company makes metal parts for a number of customers, both on an individual order basis and several exclusive supply contracts. No customer amounts to over 15% of ACME's business. As you can see from the financial history, ACME's business has been quite consistent in the last 5 years.

Table 1
ACME INDUSTRIES, INC.
Balance Sheet Spreads

	12/31/2005		12/31/2006		12/31/2007		12/31/2008		12/31/2009	
Assets										
Current Assets										
Cash	$ 8,100	2.3%	$ 19,425	4.9%	$ 26,625	5.6%	$ 31,900	6.4%	$ 25,000	5.0%
Accounts Receivable	97,600	28.0%	120,300	30.1%	169,500	36.0%	187,500	37.8%	200,000	40.0%
Inventory	92,375	26.5%	113,600	28.4%	137,650	29.2%	159,600	32.1%	170,000	34.0%
Prepaid Expenses	5,600	1.6%	4,150	1.0%	2,800	0.6%	4,750	1.0%	5,000	1.0%
Total Current Assets	203,675	58.4%	257,475	64.4%	336,575	71.4%	383,750	77.3%	400,000	80.0%
Fixed Assets										
Property & Equipment	110,800	31.8%	126,500	31.6%	143,700	30.5%	143,700	28.9%	150,000	30.0%
Less: Accum. Depreciation	(32,000)	-9.2%	(46,000)	-11.5%	(67,000)	-14.2%	(85,000)	-17.1%	(100,000)	-20.0%
Total Fixed Assets	78,800	22.6%	80,500	20.1%	76,700	16.3%	58,700	11.8%	50,000	10.0%
Goodwill (Net)	66,000	18.9%	62,000	15.5%	58,000	12.3%	54,000	10.9%	50,000	10.0%
Total Assets	$ 348,475	100.0%	$ 399,975	100.0%	$ 471,275	100.0%	$ 496,450	100.0%	$ 500,000	100%
Liabilities & Stockholder's Equity										
Current Liabilities										
Accounts Payable	$ 91,850	26%	$ 109,450	27%	$ 145,600	31%	$ 162,500	33%	$ 150,000	30.0%
Accrued Expenses	14,500	4%	8,650	2%	21,300	5%	19,300	4%	25,000	5.0%
Total Current Liabilities	106,350	31%	118,100	30%	166,900	35%	181,800	37%	175,000	35.0%
Long Term Liabilities										
Notes Payable	$ 93,500	27%	$ 113,750	28%	$ 120,000	25%	$ 112,400	23%	$ 100,000	20.0%
Total Long Term Liabilities	93,500	27%	113,750	28%	120,000	25%	112,400	23%	100,000	20.0%
Total Liabilities	199,850	57%	231,850	58%	286,900	61%	294,200	59%	275,000	55.0%
Stockholder's Equity										
Common Stock	5,000	1%	5,000	1%	5,000	1%	5,000	1%	5,000	1.0%
Retained Earnings	143,625	41%	163,125	41%	179,375	38%	197,250	40%	220,000	44.0%
Total Stockholder's Equity	148,625	43%	168,125	42%	184,375	39%	202,250	41%	225,000	45.0%
Total Liabilities & Stockholder's Equity	$ 348,475	100%	$ 399,975	100%	$ 471,275	100%	$ 496,450	100%	$ 500,000	100.0%

Analyzing the income statement. Because it is the flow statement, the income statement is the logical place to begin the financial analysis of a company. After the statement has been "spread" into worksheet format, the analyst should focus on the categories of accounts, their absolute amounts, and their relationship to one another. Let's take the simple analysis of ACME Industries, Inc. The most productive approach is to first perform a **horizontal analysis** by comparing each year to the others. Let's begin.

1. *Gross Revenue.* Review the historical trend of gross revenue. Is it increasing, and by how much? Decreasing? Flat? Sporadic? Volatile? Cyclical? Predictable? Unpredictable? How does it compare with industry trends? How does it compare with economic trends? Are the trends normal? Abnormal? Think about the "numbers" as an indicator of financial activity and performance, not just a bunch of digits; think about the absolute amount of a particular year's revenue and its relationship to the year before and after it. Here are some specific steps that a financial analyst should perform regarding ACME's gross revenues:

		Table 2 ACME INDUSTRIES, INC. COMPARATIVE INCOME STATEMENTS							
	December 31, 2005		**December 31, 2006**		**December 31, 2007**		**December 31, 2008**		**December 31, 2009**	
Income										
Sales	$ 966,900	100.2%	$ 1,244,200	100.3%	$ 1,206,600	100.5%	$ 1,373,050	100.5%	$ 1,367,700	100.4%
Less: Returns	(2,400)		(4,200)		(5,600)		(7,150)		(6,100)	
Total Income	**964,500**	100.0%	**1,240,000**	100.0%	**1,201,000**	100.0%	**1,365,900**	100.0%	**1,361,600**	100.0%
Cost of Sales										
Materials	197,500	20.5%	210,000	16.9%	200,000	16.7%	230,000	16.8%	230,000	16.9%
Cost of Labor	388,500	40.3%	425,000	34.3%	410,000	34.1%	475,000	34.8%	475,000	34.9%
Overhead	104,600	10.8%	115,000	9.3%	120,000	10.0%	125,000	9.2%	125,000	9.2%
Total Cost of Sales	690,600	71.6%	750,000	60.5%	730,000	60.8%	830,000	60.8%	830,000	61.0%
Gross Profit	**273,900**	28.4%	**490,000**	39.5%	**471,000**	39.2%	**535,900**	39.2%	**531,600**	39.0%
Operating Expenses										
Compensation of Officers	100,000	10.4%	221,000	17.8%	206,000	17.2%	246,000	18.0%	228,000	16.7%
Salaries and Wages	68,500	7.1%	73,500	5.9%	69,400	5.8%	76,000	5.6%	81,000	5.9%
Sales Commissions	9,650	1.0%	13,000	1.0%	12,000	1.0%	15,000	1.1%	14,000	1.0%
Repairs and Maintenance	6,100	0.6%	10,000	0.8%	9,000	0.7%	11,000	0.8%	12,500	0.9%
Rents	52,800	5.5%	60,000	4.8%	59,000	4.9%	65,000	4.8%	66,000	4.8%
Taxes and Licenses	2,000	0.2%	2,000	0.2%	2,000	0.2%	2,400	0.2%	2,600	0.2%
Amortization	4,000	0.4%	4,000	0.3%	4,000	0.3%	4,000	0.3%	4,000	0.3%
Depreciation	16,000	1.7%	14,000	1.1%	21,000	1.7%	18,000	1.3%	15,000	1.1%
Advertising	5,000	0.5%	5,000	0.4%	5,000	0.4%	6,700	0.5%	5,500	0.4%
Pension Plan Expense	0	0.0%	10,000	0.8%	10,000	0.8%	12,500	0.9%	13,500	1.0%
Other Deductions										0.0%
Auto Expenses	2,250	0.2%	3,500	0.3%	6,500	0.5%	7,500	0.5%	6,500	0.5%
Insurance	12,900	1.3%	18,800	1.5%	18,000	1.5%	21,000	1.5%	22,000	1.6%
Legal and Professional	16,500	1.7%	8,000	0.6%	7,000	0.6%	7,000	0.5%	8,000	0.6%
Office Expense	3,000	0.3%	3,000	0.2%	2,500	0.2%	3,000	0.2%	4,000	0.3%
Telephone	500	0.1%	500	0.0%	700	0.1%	1,000	0.1%	1,500	0.1%
Travel & Entertainment	950	0.1%	1,500	0.1%	1,300	0.1%	2,500	0.2%	3,000	0.2%
Utilities	8,500	0.9%	8,500	0.7%	7,500	0.6%	8,000	0.6%	7,500	0.6%
Total Operating Expenses	**308,650**	32.0%	**456,300**	36.8%	**440,900**	36.7%	**506,600**	37.1%	**494,600**	36.3%
Net Operating Income (EBIT)	(34,750)	-3.6%	**33,700**	2.7%	**30,100**	2.5%	**29,300**	2.1%	**37,000**	2.7%
Other Income (Expense):										
Interest Income	0	0.0%	2,500	0.2%	2,000	0.2%	5,500	0.4%	4,500	0.3%
Interest Expense	(8,220)	-0.9%	(6,200)	-0.5%	(7,100)	-0.6%	(7,300)	-0.5%	(6,500)	-0.5%
Net Income Before Taxes	(42,970)		**30,000**		**25,000**		**27,500**		**35,000**	
Tax Provision (35%)	0	0.0%	10,500	0.8%	8,750	0.7%	9,625	0.7%	12,250	0.9%
Net Income	**$ (42,970)**	-4.5%	**$ 19,500**	1.6%	**$ 16,250**	1.4%	**$ 17,875**	1.3%	**$ 22,750**	1.7%

Calculate the percentage increase or decrease in revenues for each year:

2005 to 2006 _____

2006 to 2007 _____

2007 to 2008 _____

2008 to 2009 _____

Calculate the compound average growth rate from 2005 to 2009[3]:

2005 to 2009 _____

---

3. The algorithm for this calculation is covered in the upcoming finance chapter.

Discussion. The company's revenues seem to be growing quite consistently in an economic environment that has been difficult for most businesses.[4] Discuss the strength of the business with management. Why is it going against the trend of the economy? Does it have some specific reason that its revenues are able to steadily increase, like an exclusive supply contract with a large customer? Ask about the fairly sharp spike in revenues from 2005 to 2006. Recognize that the most recent years' activity is more important to the financial analyst than the earlier years.

2. *Gross Profit.* Look at the historical trend of gross profit, especially as it is characterized by its percentage of sales. Gross profit is a statistic that is most significantly measured and evaluated as a percentage of sales, as opposed to its absolute amount. Is it consistent, and increasing, and by how much? Or is it erratic? Decreasing? Flat? Sporadic? Volatile? Cyclical? Predictable? Unpredictable? How does it compare with industry trends? How does it compare with economic trends? Are the trends normal? Abnormal? Here are some specific steps that a financial analyst should perform regarding ACME's gross profit margin:

Identify the gross profit margin (gross profit divided by sales) for each year under consideration:

2005 _____

2006 _____

2007 _____

2008 _____

2009_____

Note significant fluctuations (there only seems to be one) in the overall gross profit margin and inquire about that year with management. Also, analyze the components of cost of sales to see if there are any unusual fluctuations in the components.

Discussion. The company's gross profit margin seems quite consistent, except for the 2005 year. Obviously, something was going on during 2005 that must be investigated. This is an example where the "numbers" can't answer the question, but they certainly can identify the question/problem. Again, the most recent years' activity is more important to the financial analyst than the earlier years.

---

4. It is generally acknowledged that the "Great Recession" of the 21st Century started on the second to third quarter of 2008.

3. *Net Income.* In the final analysis, a company's net income is the most important element of the income statement. Obviously, net income is entirely driven by revenues and expenses, so the analysis of those categories is important, but achieving net income is the fundamental goal of every profit-oriented enterprise. Look at the historical trend of net income and study it with the same questions that have been previously discussed: trends, consistency, volatility, stability. Ultimately, the characteristics of a healthy firm are the amount, consistency and stability of net income. It is true that a financial analysis of a company is entirely historical, but a solid history is probably the best indicator of the future, absent some significant external factor affecting the company.

Discussion. ACME Industries is a very consistent company, based on the review of its historical income statements. One noteworthy observation is that it doesn't earn a very significant amount of profit, but it is quite stable. Yes, there was some problem in 2005—five years ago—but since that time the performance of ACME has been very stable, with revenues growing at a moderate pace and net income remaining constant.

4. *Expenses.* A horizontal analysis of a company's expenses can be very telling to the financial analyst because it identifies fluctuations in the internal and external operations of the business. Looking at both the amount and percentage of the expense categories over the five years under consideration, the analyst observes a remarkable consistency for a small business. Again, the only aberrant year is 2005, where we see the compensation of officers lower than the other years, a fact that is perfectly explainable when one considers the relatively weak performance of the company in that year. It would be logical that the officers (who might be owners also) would take a smaller share in the form of compensation in a poor performance year. From the perspective of the common size percentages, one observes that the cost of goods sold, salaries and wages, and a few other expense categories are proportionately higher than in the other years, but that is also probably explainable because of the relatively low gross revenue in 2005 versus the later years. Note that this conclusionary discussion is not an excuse for ignoring the variances in discussions with management, but on the surface, the fluctuations seem logical.

A **vertical analysis** of ACME's income statements is a study of the items of expense in relation to the amount of the company's revenue. It is looking at the components of expense as a percentage of revenue and making an assessment of the propriety of those percentages. Vertical analysis is most informative when it is done on a comparative basis by relating the company to some external benchmark, usually some industry financial data. The typical approach is to identify the company by its NAICS[5] code and obtain industry information

---

5.   The North American Industry Classification System (NAICS) is the standard used by Federal statistical agencies in classifying business establishments for the purpose of collecting, analyzing, and publishing statistical data related to the U.S. business economy. NAICS was developed under the auspices of the Office of Management and Budget (OMB), and adopted in 1997 to replace the Standard Industrial Classification system (SIC). The official 2007 *U.S. NAICS Manual* includes definitions for each industry, background information, tables showing changes between 2002 and 2007, and a comprehensive index.

based on that classification. There are dozens of data collection firms[6] that provide industry research and financial statistics on companies in identified industries, and this information is what analysts use for comparative analysis.

By comparing the company's operating performance to an industry norm, the analyst can make judgments about the firm. Are the costs in line with what is expected in this industry? Are the components of cost of goods sold in the proper proportion for this industry? Are the company's expenses similar to those of other firms in the industry, or are there anomalies that need to be addressed. Is this company stronger or weaker than the typical firm in the industry? A vertical comparative analysis identifies the issues; it is the job of the competent financial analyst to answer the questions (or lawyer who is inquiring into the operations of the firm.)

Profitability Ratios

Income statement ratios are particularly useful for analyzing a company's performance relative to its industry. Analysts employ financial ratios because numbers in isolation have little value, but when stated in percentages or ratios, they can be compared to industry norms.

The most significant profitability financial ratios that can be determined from the income statement are the gross profit margin, the operating profit margin and the net profit margin. In combination with the balance sheet, the analyst can determine the company's profit return on assets and return on equity.

Gross profit margin. The gross profit margin is a measure of a company's ability to meet its selling, general and administrative expenses and to earn a profit. Changes in this ratio may indicate changes in sales prices, changes in unit costs for goods purchased or changes in the sale mix (the quantity of goods with low profit margins that is sold compared to the quantity of goods with high profit margins sold). Trends in a company's gross profit margin are significant, as is a comparison of a company's gross profit margin with that of other businesses in the industry. The formula for calculating gross profit margin is:

$$\text{Gross Profit Margin} \quad = \quad \frac{\text{Gross Profit}}{\text{Sales}}$$

---

6.   Some of the companies that provide this information are: Hoovers.com, Dun & Bradstreet, Valuation Resources.com, RMA Statement Studies, FirstResearch.com and Integra. Also, many industries have active trade associations that provide financial information (especially financial ratios) to subscribers and other consultants.

The gross profit margin is one of the most important metrics in evaluating a business operation because it is a direct measure of two of the most important aspects of the business: the price that the business can sell its goods for measured against the direct cost of obtaining the goods. The price is an indication of the external forces on the business—the business is constrained by its environment, the competition and the market's demand for the goods or services. The cost of goods sold is a measure of the efficiency of the business's management of its production and/or purchasing activities. The following table sets forth the gross profit margin for ACME for 2005 through 2009:

	2005	2006	2007	2008	2009
Gross Profit Margin =	273,900 / 964,500	490,000 / 1,240,000	471,000 / 1,201,000	535,900 / 1,365,900	531,600 / 1,361,600
Gross Profit Margin =	28.40%	39.52%	39.22%	39.23%	39.04%

Again, observing ACME's gross profit margin in isolation is a limited analysis. We can see a very tight consistency in the last four years, which is certainly a positive characteristic. However, it would also be useful to have an industry benchmark to compare with ACME.

Operating profit margin. Operating profit is also known as net income from operations, operating income, or earnings before interest and taxes (EBIT). This ratio is an extremely important measure of management's ability to control operating costs and raise productivity. Operating income is profit from continued operations before interest and taxes. If a company had irregular gains or losses, such as losses from a discontinued operation, these items would be excluded from the operating profit margin. A company's operating profit margin is often a better measure of management skill than is its net profit margin because net income is influenced by the amount of debt (interest expense) and by income taxes, which are not always within the control of management. The formula for calculating operating profit margin is:

$$\text{Operating Profit Margin} = \frac{\text{EBIT}}{\text{Sales}}$$

The following table sets forth the operating profit margin for ACME for 2005 through 2009:

	2005	2006	2007	2008	2009
Operating Profit Margin =	(34,750) / 964,500	33,700 / 1,240,000	30,100 / 1,201,000	29,300 / 1,365,900	37,000 / 1,361,600
Operating Profit Margin =	-3.6%	2.7%	2.5%	2.1%	2.7%

Net profit margin. Net profit margin is calculated after deducting all expenses—ordinary or extraordinary—from operating net income as well as income taxes. It is the final net gain (or net loss) experienced by the business for the accounting period. This ratio enables the analyst to compare a company's return on sales with the performance of other companies in the industry.

$$\text{Net Profit Margin} \quad = \quad \frac{\text{Net Income}}{\text{Sales}}$$

	2005	2006	2007	2008	2009
Net Profit Margin =	$\frac{(42,970)}{964,500}$	$\frac{19,500}{1,240,000}$	$\frac{16,250}{1,201,000}$	$\frac{17,875}{1,365,900}$	$\frac{22,750}{1,361,600}$
Net Profit Margin =	-4.5%	1.6%	1.4%	1.3%	1.7%

The two significant observations to draw from ACME's net profit margin are the consistency (in the last four years) and the small amount of the net profit. The problem with the small amount is that some slight misfortune or inefficiency could put the company into a loss position. But, as we will shortly see, ACME has a strong balance sheet that could help it weather a difficult financial time.

Return on Total Assets. This ratio measures how efficiently profits are being generated from the business's assets. It is calculated by dividing the current year's net income by the average of the total assets from the beginning of the year and the end of the year. The best comparison is with the ratios of companies in similar businesses or industries. A ratio that is low compared to the industry average indicates that business assets are being used inefficiently. Here is the ratio and the calculation for ACME for the last five years:

$$\text{Return on Total Assets} \quad = \quad \frac{\text{Net Income}}{\text{Average Total Assets}}$$

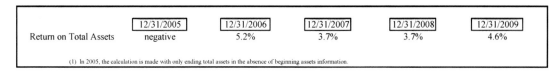

	12/31/2005	12/31/2006	12/31/2007	12/31/2008	12/31/2009
Return on Total Assets	negative	5.2%	3.7%	3.7%	4.6%

(1) In 2005, the calculation is made with only ending total assets in the absence of beginning assets information.

Return on Equity. This ratio gives the percentage return on funds invested in the business by its owners. If the ROE is less than the rate of return on a relatively risk free investment, such as a money market fund or savings account, the owner may be wise to sell his or her interest in the company. There is no question that an investment in a small firm is much more risky than many alternative investments and a small business investment should yield a return that is commensurate with its high level of financial risk. Here is the ratio and the calculations for ACME Industries, Inc.

$$\text{Return on Equity} \quad = \quad \frac{\text{Net Income}}{\text{Average Total Equity}}$$

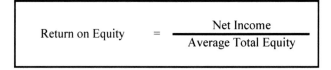

	12/31/2005	12/31/2006	12/31/2007	12/31/2008	12/31/2009
Return on Equity	negative (1)	12.3%	9.2%	9.2%	10.6%

(1) In 2005, the calculation is made with only ending total assets in the absence of beginning assets information.

As you can see, the return on equity is higher that the return on assets because the business has some debt, which is capital provided by creditors as opposed to owners. If the company's marginal rate of return on its assets (ROA) is higher than the rate of interest payable on its debt, then its return on equity (ROE) will be higher than if it did not borrow. Here, ACME's return on equity is higher than its return on assets.

Solvency, Liquidity and Leverage Ratios

Analyzing the balance sheet. Balance sheet ratios measure **solvency** (the condition of assets exceeding liabilities), **liquidity** (the ability of a firm to convert assets into cash and meet its current debts) and **leverage** (the extent to which the company is dependent upon the financing of creditors). These concepts are analyzed by ratios of the balance sheet and we will deal with each concept separately.

Solvency (and insolvency). Solvency is the financial condition in which the entity's assets exceed its liabilities; insolvency is the opposite condition. For accounting purposes, the concept of solvency considers assets and liabilities at their accounting book values. In many legal applications of the concept of solvency (or usually insolvency), the appropriate standard may be the fair market value of assets minus liabilities. The concept of insolvency has more extensive significance in bankruptcy law and fraudulent conveyance matters where more discrete legal definitions of the term should be considered.

In accounting, the determination of "balance sheet" solvency can be made by simply comparing the total assets of an enterprise to the total liabilities. If the result is that assets exceed liabilities, the enterprise is solvent; if liabilities exceed assets, the company is insolvent. The concept of "cash flow" or "income statement" insolvency exists when an enterprise cannot pay its debts when they become due, regardless of its overall solvency. This condition can exist when a firm doesn't possess sufficient liquidity to operate successfully, a subject that is covered next.

Liquidity. A firm's liquidity is its ability to easily convert assets into cash to meet its current obligations without having to dispose of fixed assets. All things being equal, greater liquidity is valuable and produces flexibility for a firm, but it tends to decrease profitability. Highly liquid assets are not usually the most profitable investments for a company, so management should be mindful that too much liquidity is inefficient. The three principal measures of a company's liquidity are: 1) working capital; 2) the current ratio; and the quick ratio. The following paragraphs discuss the measures and present the calculations for our example company, ACME Industries.

Working capital. Working capital is the amount by which a firm's current assets exceed its current liabilities, indicating the amount of liquidity available to satisfy maturing short-term debts and fund continued short-term operations. The management of working capital involves managing inventories, accounts receivable, accounts payable and cash. ACME Industries' working capital at December 31, 2005 through December 31, 2009 is calculated as follows:

	12/31/2005	12/31/2006	12/31/2007	12/31/2008	12/31/2009
Working Capital:					
Current assets	$ 203,675	$ 257,475	$ 336,575	$ 383,750	$ 400,000
Less: Current liabilities	(106,350)	(118,100)	(166,900)	(181,800)	(175,000)
Working Capital	$ 97,325	$ 139,375	$ 169,675	$ 201,950	$ 225,000

At each year end, ACME has very adequate working capital. In fact, it could be suggested that the amount is beginning to become inefficient in later years.

Current ratio. The current ratio is another representation of a firm's working capital, only the metric is stated in a ratio rather than an absolute number. The current ratio enables comparison of the subject company to industry norms because the status of the firm's liquidity is presented as the ratio of current assets to current liabilities, indicating how many times the current liabilities can be "covered" by the theoretical liquidation of all the current assets. By using a ratio, different sized firms can be compared to one another, and an individual firm can be compared to an industry average. The formula for calculating the current ratio is:

$$\text{Current Ratio} = \frac{\text{Current Assets}}{\text{Current Liabilities}}$$

The current ratio of ACME Industries for each of the last five year ends is:

	12/31/2005	12/31/2006	12/31/2007	12/31/2008	12/31/2009
Current Ratio	1.92	2.18	2.02	2.11	2.29

Although there is no absolute rule of thumb, it is logical that the minimum current ratio that a business should have is 1.0 (meaning that current assets are exactly one times current liabilities). The best indicator of a "standard" current ratio would be a median for many companies in the subject company's industry. ACME's current ratio is quite strong, indicating strong liquidity and possible overinvestment in current assets.

Quick ratio (also called the "acid test" ratio). Inventory is the least liquid of a company's current assets, and the quick ratio measures a company's liquidity without considering its inventory. It is a measure of highly liquid assets that are mostly composed of cash, short-term securities and accounts receivable. The quick ratio measures the firm's ability to meet its current obligations even if none of its inventory can be sold. The formula for the quick ratio is:

$$\text{Quick Ratio} = \frac{\text{Current Assets - Inventory}}{\text{Current Liabilities}}$$

ACME's quick ratio for the last five year ends is:

	12/31/2005	12/31/2006	12/31/2007	12/31/2008	12/31/2009
Quick Ratio	1.05	1.22	1.19	1.23	1.31

As with the current ratio, the best indicator of a healthy quick ratio would be a median for many companies in the subject company's industry.

Summary of liquidity ratios. Most financially healthy businesses have positive working capital. It is possible for a business to finance itself with negative working capital, but that situation is definitely the exception. Minimum working capital requirements are often stipulated in loan agreements and a company can be in breach of its covenants if its working capital (or other agreed-upon ratios) becomes deficient. For most business enterprises, liquidity is probably the most important financial status that can be achieved. Without liquidity, the very existence of the business is severely jeopardized.

Leverage. Leverage is a measure of the amount of a firm's capital that is provided by lenders as opposed to the amount that is provided by equity investors, or owners. Financial leverage refers to the use of debt to finance the assets of a company in addition to the use of equity capital. Companies use leverage to attempt to increase returns on equity capital. For the price of the debt (interest expense), a company can have more capital to invest in its assets to try to earn income. Leverage adds risk to the operation of the firm; if a firm does not generate enough income to pay the interest on its debt, its creditors can force it into bankruptcy. Two widely used financial ratios to measure leverage are the Debt Ratio and the Debt to Equity ratio. They are calculated as follows:

$$\text{Debt Ratio} = \frac{\text{Total Liabilities}}{\text{Total Assets}}$$

$$\text{Debt to Equity Ratio} = \frac{\text{Total Liabilities}}{\text{Total Equity}}$$

Following are the calculated ratios for ACME Industries for each year end from 2005 to 2009:

	12/31/2005	12/31/2006	12/31/2007	12/31/2008	12/31/2009
Debt Ratio (Debt to Assets)	0.57	0.58	0.61	0.59	0.55
Debt to Equity Ratio	1.34	1.38	1.56	1.45	1.22

The debt ratio simply measures the percentage of the total assets of the firm that are financed with debt, as opposed to equity. For example, ACME seems to have 55% to 61% of its total capital provided by lenders, rather than owners. If you think of that in terms of a typical home or automobile purchase, you will probably conclude that ACME operates at a relatively low leverage position in relation to the consumers of the world. The debt ratio (along with the debt to equity ratio) indicates to creditors how well protected they are in the event the firm becomes insolvent. A high ratio has a negative influence on a company's ability to obtain additional financing.

ACME's debt to equity ratio sets forth the relationship of its debt to its equity. It is just another mathematical expression of its leverage position. As with almost all of the ratios presented, the most meaningful use of the ratio is in relation to ratios of other companies within the same industry. Is it stronger or weaker than the average company in its same business environment? That is the ultimate determination that can be made from the financial ratio analysis we have undertaken so far.

Management and Activity Ratios

Management ratios are extremely important as a tool to evaluate management's performance in various areas of business operations. Usually, the ratios are derived from both the balance sheet and the income statement. Some of these ratios evaluate how effectively certain assets are converted into cash while others provide information on how efficiently the enterprise uses its assets. Other management ratios assist in evaluating how well the company has operated during the year. The following paragraphs discuss some key management ratios:

Inventory turnover ratio and average age of inventory. The inventory turnover ratio measures how rapidly a firm's inventory is sold. Generally, a firm's business cycle takes the following steps: cash is used to buy or produce inventory; inventory is sold in exchange for accounts receivable; and the accounts receivable are converted back into cash. Those are the general steps of the business cycle, and the efficiency with which those steps are implemented is a major management issue.

The inventory turnover ratio and its extension into the "average age of inventory" shows the analyst how quickly (efficiently) the company "turns" its inventory. If a firm earns profit by selling inventory, then the more times that the firm can turn its inventory, the more profitable it is. Let's identify the two relevant ratios and then discuss them. Following are the inventory activity ratios:

$$\text{Inventory Turnover Ratio} = \frac{\text{Cost of Goods Sold}}{\text{Average Inventory}}$$

$$\text{Average Age of Inventory} = \frac{365}{\text{Inv. Turnover Ratio}}$$

The inventory turnover ratio identifies how many times a company "turns over" its inventory in a year. The denominator of the formula is calculated by averaging the beginning and ending inventory of the particular year, and the numerator is the cost of goods sold. Cost of goods sold measures the cost of the inventory "going out the door," and the inventory turnover ratio indicates how many "warehouses full of inventory" go out the door during the year. In thinking about the components of the ratio, remember that both CGS and inventory are measured at cost[7]; CGS is the flow of inventory to the customer in exchange for the receipt of sales revenue, and the average of beginning inventory and ending inventory is the average amount of inventory on hand during the year. Consequently, the inventory turnover ratio measures the "turns" of inventory during the year. In the case of ACME Industries, the inventory turnover ratios are calculated as follows:

	12/31/2005	12/31/2006	12/31/2007	12/31/2008	12/31/2009
Inventory Turnover	7.48 (1)	7.28	5.81	5.58	5.04

(1) In 2005, the calculation is made with only ending inventory in the absence of beginning inventory information.

Even without comparing ACME's inventory turnover ratio with an industry benchmark, it is intuitively clear that the company is extremely efficient regarding its inventory management. The company is turning its inventory over 5 times per year, which seems like a very efficient rate. And specifically, the next calculation will tell us how many days (on average, of course) that it takes to "turn" ACME's inventory. Here is the average age, in days, of ACME's inventory:

	12/31/2005	12/31/2006	12/31/2007	12/31/2008	12/31/2009
Average age of inventory	48.82 (1)	50.12	62.81	65.36	72.47

(1) In 2005, the calculation is made with only ending inventory in the absence of beginning inventory information.

The inventory turnover ratio and average age of inventory calculation tell us that ACME has 50 to 70 days of inventory on hand. The most noteworthy aspect of this statistic is that ACME's quantity of inventory is increasing fairly significantly in relation to its sales. In other words, the relationship between inventory and CGS is not constant—it's increasing. This is not necessarily a problem, but the analyst can observe this fact through thoughtful ratio analysis and inquire about it with management.

Accounts receivable turnover ratio and the average age of receivables. These two metrics provide an indication of how successfully a company collects its receivables. Receivables should be collected in accordance with the company's terms and policies; if the company is slow in converting its receivables into cash, its liquidity may be seriously undermined. The accounts receivable turnover ratio measures the number of times a company "reinvests" its accounts receivable into sales and, as a result, the average collection period of accounts receivables can be determined.

---

7.   Recall that LIFO, FIFO and weighted average have some effect on the "cost" of inventory.

Here are the accounts receivable activity ratios:

$$\text{Accts. Rec. Turnover} = \frac{\text{Credit Sales}}{\text{Avg. Accts. Receivable}}$$

$$\text{Average Collection Period} = \frac{365}{\text{Accounts Receivable Turnover}}$$

For ACME Industries, here are the calculations of the accounts receivable ratios:

	12/31/2005	12/31/2006	12/31/2007	12/31/2008	12/31/2009
Accts. Receivable Turnover	9.9 (1)	11.4	8.3	7.7	7.0

(1) In 2005, the calculation is made with only ending accounts receivable in the absence of beginning A/R information.

	12/31/2005	12/31/2006	12/31/2007	12/31/2008	12/31/2009
Average Collection Period	36.9 (1)	32.1	44.0	47.7	51.9

(1) In 2005, the calculation is made with only ending accounts receivable in the absence of beginning A/R information.

The ratios show that ACME converts its accounts receivables into sales over 7 times a year, and, presently, the company has 51.9 days of sales in its accounts receivable. In a perfect world, a company would have 30 days of revenues in its accounts receivable, but this ideal goal is not realistically attainable. ACME has less than two months' sales in its accounts receivable, and that is a relatively healthy amount. As noted in the inventory turnover discussion, the analyst should be mindful of the continuously increasing average collection period.

Sales to working capital ratio. The sales to working capital ratio measures the efficiency with which working capital is employed. A low ratio may indicate inefficient use while a very high ratio may signify overtrading—a vulnerable position for creditors. Based on the ratio analysis and the strong cash and accounts receivable balance of ACME (totaling $395,000 at the recent balance sheet date), it appears that the company has excess working capital. Following is the ratio and the calculation:

$$\text{Sales to Working Capital} = \frac{\text{Total Sales}}{\text{Avg. Working Capital}}$$

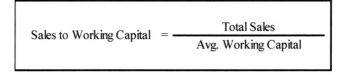

	12/31/2005	12/31/2006	12/31/2007	12/31/2008	12/31/2009
Sales to Working Capital	9.91 (1)	10.48	7.77	7.35	6.38

(1) In 2005, the calculation is made with only ending inventory in the absence of beginning inventory information.

This ratio shows how there can be different interpretations of most financial ratios. For example, ACME's sales to working capital ratio is decreasing in recent years. Simple logic would lead one to think that a higher ratio is better, meaning that a company is getting more sales from the same amount of working capital. What is causing ACME's ratio to decrease? Since the ratio is driven by two factors—sales and working capital—either one can affect the mathematics of the relationship. Here, ACME's average working capital is increasing quite significantly in recent years, and that fact is causing its sales to working capital ratio to decrease. In absolute dollars, more working capital is probably a good thing; however, the decreasing ratio might indicate a subtlety—that the company is not using its increased working capital to generate more sales as efficiently as it was in past periods.

Conclusion

Financial statement analysis is a process that gives meaning to accounting numbers and enables the analyst to draw important conclusions about the history of operations of the subject company. The process suffers the same limitations that burden most accounting information: it is historical and limited by the weaknesses of financial reporting standards. Financial ratios say little about a company's prospects or performance in an absolute sense. Most of the possible insights from financial statement analysis about the relative performance of the firm require a reference point from other time periods or similar firms.

One ratio holds little meaning. A ratio's values may be distorted because account balances change from the beginning to the end of an accounting period, or experience some other aberrant movement. As indicators, ratios can be logically interpreted several ways, and it is helpful to combine related ratios to develop a more comprehensive picture of the firm's performance.

Regardless of the limitations of financial statement analysis, it is an extremely valuable tool by which to apply accounting information to real business situations. Through the analysis of financial statements, we can understand the concepts of liquidity, solvency, profitability and leverage. The concepts can be studied and applied to evaluate the financial health of a business concern and to assist the company in its management efforts. The analyst must be mindful of the limitations of the underlying information as well as the inapplicability of historical information as a predictor of future events. But a thoughtful analysis of a company's historical financial statements along with a comparison of the firm to its industry will provide the analyst with invaluable information about the company.

Summary of Financial Ratios

Profitability:

Gross Profit Margin $= \dfrac{\text{Gross Profit}}{\text{Sales}}$

Net Profit Margin $= \dfrac{\text{Net Income}}{\text{Sales}}$

Operating Profit Margin $= \dfrac{\text{EBIT}}{\text{Sales}}$

Return on Total Assets $= \dfrac{\text{Net Income}}{\text{Average Total Assets}}$

Return on Equity $= \dfrac{\text{Net Income}}{\text{Average Total Equity}}$

Liquidity:

Working Capital $=$ Current Assets -- Current Liabilities

Current Ratio $= \dfrac{\text{Current Assets}}{\text{Current Liabilities}}$

Quick Ratio $= \dfrac{\text{Current Assets - Inventory}}{\text{Current Liabilities}}$

Leverage:

Debt Ratio $= \dfrac{\text{Total Liabilities}}{\text{Total Assets}}$

Debt to Equity Ratio $= \dfrac{\text{Total Liabilities}}{\text{Total Equity}}$

Activity Ratios:

Inventory Turnover Ratio $= \dfrac{\text{Cost of Goods Sold}}{\text{Average Inventory}}$

Average Age of Inventory $= \dfrac{365}{\text{Inv. Turnover Ratio}}$

Accts. Rec. Turnover $= \dfrac{\text{Credit Sales}}{\text{Avg. Accts. Receivable}}$

Average Collection Period $= \dfrac{365}{\text{Accounts Receivable Turnover}}$

Sales to Working Capital $= \dfrac{\text{Total Sales}}{\text{Avg. Working Capital}}$

Chapter 8

Introduction to Finance: The Time Value of Money

Introduction

Finance is the science of funds management, and it involves the interrelationships of money, interest, time and risk. There are two major branches to this field, corporate finance and monetary finance. Corporate finance deals with the task of providing the funds for a company's activities, called capitalization. Corporate finance also involves the competing policies of risk management and profitability maximization. Monetary finance addresses the time value of money, a concept that underlies all economic transactions.

Corporate finance deals with the allocation of the sources of capital (equity or debt) that are available to an entity, with a view toward optimizing the balance between the cost of the capital and the benefits received from using the capital. Monetary finance is the study of money and the relationship between its current purchasing power and its ability to earn interest. Other branches of finance include personal finance (an individual's personal financial planning), public finance (taxation, government spending and government financing issues), mergers and acquisitions. The focus of this chapter is monetary finance: money; interest; time; and risk.

As a general proposition, finance is the study of the allocation of scarce capital resources, measured by money, over time. As an academic discipline, finance seeks to weigh the relative cost of taking current action against the anticipated future benefit from forgoing the current action, to allow people to choose between the two alternatives. Financial analysis contains an element of uncertainty because it almost always deals with some comparison of the present to anticipated future events.

Basic finance underlies all monetary transactions, and knowledge of the principles of finance is critically important to understand transactions, analyze them and counsel clients about them. The time value of money, as applied through the concepts of present value and future value, exists in every transaction, and the value of the deal can change dramatically depending on the use of this concept. The time value of money is driven by the principle of compound interest, which is the addition of accumulated interest to the principal sum at the end of a period, before the interest is recalculated and added in the next compounding period. Our discussion of finance will center around measuring money as a unit of the measure of capital, recognizing that the concepts are different.

The chapter will explain all the concepts of basic finance, but there will be a focus on doing short problems to apply the concepts. The problems in the chapter are designed to teach the reader to use the Texas Instruments BA II PLUS financial calculator in order to apply the concepts. There are many other handheld calculators that will suffice, but it is important for the student of these concepts to learn how to apply them. For most of the concepts, it is easier to "do them" rather than "talk about them." Also, the practical application of the concepts of finance is what is needed to practice law, not a theoretical discussion of them.

Wealth, Capital and Money

Wealth is the totality of valuable resources or possessions under the ownership or control of a person or an entity. There are two common types of wealth: monetary wealth and non-monetary wealth. Monetary wealth is anything that can be bought and sold, and for which there is a market, and therefore a price. Non-monetary wealth is composed of things that depend on scarce resources, and for which there is a demand, but which are not bought and sold in a market and hence have no price.[1] Examples of non-monetary wealth are education, health and defense. In business, wealth is the total of all assets (net of liabilities[2]) of an economic unit that can be used in the further production of income.

Capital is a measure of the accumulated wealth of an individual or entity that has been created by sacrificing present consumption in favor of investment to generate future returns above investment costs.[3] Capital is slightly different from wealth; it is the *measure* of wealth, not the wealth itself. For our purposes, however, capital and wealth are the same.

Money, capital and wealth are interrelated concepts. Money is a medium of exchange, a unit of account, a measure of value and a standard of deferred payment. Money is a means of facilitating commercial transactions and allocating wealth; it has no inherent value. It is merely a means of measuring capital (human, natural, industrial). Wealth is the value that underlies money; it is the capital. Although money does not have inherent value, it does have the value assigned to it as a representative of underlying wealth or capital. Because it is a unit of account for wealth, it is used as the basic measure of wealth or of value.

The Time Value of Money: Interest

Money has both a current purchasing power and the ability to earn interest. The owner of money has a choice to spend it to satisfy current wants or needs, or to lend it to someone and receive interest on the money.[4] (The owner also has a choice to invest it with the hope of earning a return, but our present discussion will focus on lending to solidify the concept of the time value

---

1. BusinessDictionary.com
2. Sounds a lot like Owners' or Stockholders' Equity in accounting, doesn't it?
3. BusinessDictionary.com
4. The owner also has a choice to do nothing with his money—to store it under the mattress—and the economic analysis of that alternative is implicit in our discussion: it is the benefit that is forgone by not productively employing the money.

---

of money.[5]) Interest is the "rental value" of money and it is measured by a percentage rate on the principal amount in question. Interest measures the time value of money: to the owner of the money, it is the value of employing the money by lending it to someone else and collecting interest (income) on the principal sum over the time of the loan. To the borrower, interest is the cost of using someone else's money, presumably to satisfy a current need of the borrower like buying a house or a car. The concept of the time value of money is economically the same to both the lender and the borrower. To the lender, the time value of money is a benefit; to the borrower, it is a cost.

The mathematical components of an interest rate calculation are simple, but the complete application of the concept of interest is not. Mathematically, the amount of interest on a principal sum is:

(The Amount of) Interest = Principal x Interest Rate x Time Period

$$I \quad = \quad \text{"PV"} \quad x \quad \text{"I/Y"} \quad x \quad \text{"N"}^{[6]}$$

Theoretically, the interest rate[7] contains three components: the real rate of interest; an estimate of the anticipated inflation rate; and for loans that have any risk above risk-free,[8] an additional component for risk, called a risk premium.

The *real rate of interest* is the base rate for the rental of money, without consideration of inflation. In practice, however, this rate is not usually seen because it is only a theoretical part of the total market rate of interest, known as the nominal rate of interest. As part of the total interest rate, the real rate of interest does not include inflation; it is only the "non-inflation" price of money. The real rate of interest reflects the real cost of funds, and, in a world in which there was no inflation, the real rate of interest would equal the nominal, or market, rate of interest.

The real rate of interest for a U.S. government security can be estimated by taking the market rate of interest on the security and subtracting the current inflation rate. The real rate of interest is used in some debt instruments, such as Treasury Inflation-Protected Securities (TIPS) or inflation indexed bonds. These bonds pay a coupon amount of interest (approximately a real rate) and the principal is adjusted by changes in the Consumer Price Index. At the end of the term of the bond, the bondholder is repaid an inflation-adjusted principal amount, so the bondholder's possible loss due to inflation is protected.

---

5. To simplify our discussion, you can think of lending and investing as conceptually similar concepts. In both cases, the owner of the money puts it somewhere with the expectation of having it returned later, along with some additional receipt—either interest or profit—to compensate him for the use of the money. For instructional purposes, it is easier to talk about interest from lending money as the measure of the time value of money, rather than dividends or entrepreneurial profit resulting from investing the money. But, in broad concept, both lending and investing money are the same; the owner of the money is advancing it to someone else for a while expecting to get more back than what he advanced.

6. Also denoted as "T" in many presentations of this formula.

7. The market rate of interest is referred to as the "nominal" interest rate. The "real" interest rate is the nominal rate minus the inflation rate.

8. The accepted proxy for the interest rate for a risk-free investment is the present interest rate on U.S. government securities maturing in the short term.

The second component of the market interest rate is the *inflation rate.* It is only logical that, as part of the cost of money, the loss in purchasing power of the money is incorporated into the interest rate. If the marketplace presently perceives that inflation will be high, lenders will require a higher amount of interest to cover the anticipated loss in value of the money over the period of the loan. The converse is also true.

Finally, the interest rate contains a *risk premium* to compensate the lender for the risk of nonpayment. If the discussion is limited to U.S. Government Securities, those securities are considered "risk free" because they are backed by the full faith and credit of the United States government, an institution that has historically been considered the least risky (risk free) by the investment community. There is no risk premium on risk-free securities. On all other debt securities, the market interest rate includes a risk premium, a component that increases the "price" of the money to account for the possibility of the default of the debtor. The risk premium is the premium, above the risk-free rate, that the lender demands to be compensated for taking on the additional risk of the particular loan. In finance, there are sophisticated models that attempt to calculate the appropriate risk premium for particular securities, but those models are not significant here. It is only important to know that a third component of the interest rate exists for securities that are not risk-free.

Notwithstanding our conceptual discussion of the interest rate, the interest rate on a sum of money is determined by the marketplace, as a function of supply and demand. Borrowers want to borrow, and lenders want to lend, and the invisible hand of the marketplace brings the opposing sides to the transaction to a place of equilibrium, resulting in a marketplace interest rate for the transaction.[9] The millions of transactions aggregate into a marketplace, resulting in a "market" rate of interest for the particular type of loan (a home loan, a car loan, etc.). The market interest rate is a function of many intangible factors for a particular transaction that are difficult to rank, but the most significant ones are risk, the anticipated rate of inflation, the amount of the loan and the time for repayment.

Interest is a measure of the time value of money: the ability of money to earn income by being loaned to a borrower. This economic value of money is in addition to money's current purchasing power. The holder of money can use it now to satisfy wants or needs, or the holder can lend it to someone and earn interest. Consequently, money has the ability to earn interest over time; hence the "time value" of money.

In contemplating the time value of money, recall that there is no conceptual difference in the value of money between the lender and the borrower. Of course, any thinking person would prefer to be the one receiving the interest, rather than paying it, but the concept is exactly the same on both sides of the equation. One hundred dollars is one hundred dollars—whether Grandpa is giving it to Grandson, or Grandpa is receiving it from Grandson.

---

9.   Many would correctly suggest that the invisible hand of the marketplace is swayed by the U.S. government's monetary policy, but we will leave that discussion for another day.

In *Finance & Accounting for Lawyers*, the reader needs to understand the time value of money, to differentiate simple and compound interest, to know how to make interest calculations, and to apply the concepts of present value and future value. This chapter will proceed through all of these concepts, but it will do it by using lots of examples and problems. In the area of basic finance, it is easiest to learn the concepts by doing them as opposed to talking (or reading) about them.

Definition of Terms for This Chapter

The following terms and concepts are foundational for studying and understanding basic finance.

1. **Principal**—the present amount of a sum of money. In finance, this amount is called "Present Value" or "PV." This should not be confused with the term, "principle" which is a basic truth, law or assumption.

2. **Interest**—the percentage rate charged on a principal sum for lending or borrowing purposes. In finance, this rate is referred to as "I/Y" or sometimes "% *i*." The interest rate is generally quoted as a percentage per year. The dollar amount of interest calculated is referred to as "I."

3. **Time period**—the length of time for which an interest calculation will be made. In finance calculations, the time period is stated as "N," meaning the number of compounding periods in the calculation.

4. **Periods per year or Payments per year**—"P/Y"—the number of compounding periods per year is an important component of any interest calculation. Compounding periods are usually daily, monthly, quarterly, semi-annually or annually.

5. **Payment**—the amount of a regular payment (usually monthly) that will pay off a loan over a defined period of time. In finance, the payment is stated as "PMT." A constant stream of equal payments is an annuity, a concept that will be discussed later in the chapter.

6. **Future value**—"FV"—the future value of money is the total future accumulation of principal plus interest on a present sum of money. It is the amount to which an investment will grow at a point in the future, assuming it earns interest for a period of time.

7. These next terms will be explained throughout the chapter:

   a. Simple interest

   b. Compound interest

   c. Loan amortization

   d. Fixed rate loan

   e. Variable rate loan

   f. Annuities—ordinary and future value

Simple Interest

Simple interest is the easiest interest calculation to deal with, and get off the table, because it is not financially sound and it is not used in commercial financial transactions. Under the concept of simple interest, the interest rate is applied to the original principal balance (only), at the agreed-on rate and for the time period of the loan. There is never an adjustment to the principal balance for the accumulation of unpaid or accrued interest. The formula to calculate simple interest is:

(The Amount of) Interest = Principal × Interest Rate × Time Period

$$I \quad = \quad \text{``PV''} \quad \times \quad \text{``I/Y''} \quad \times \quad \text{``N''}$$

Now, let's assume we are going to calculate simple interest on a $100,000 loan at 6% annual interest[10] for 1 ½ years. The calculation would be:

$$I \quad = \quad \text{``PV''} \quad \times \quad \text{``I/Y''} \quad \times \quad \text{``N''}$$

$$I \quad = \$100,000 \quad \times \quad 6\% \quad \times \quad 1\tfrac{1}{2} \,{}^{*}$$

$$I \quad = \quad \$9,000$$

> * The time period is always stated in the same common denominator as the interest period. If the interest rate is 6% per year, then the time period in the calculation, N, is stated in years,

Understanding simple interest is important for two reasons. Sometimes, the law requires simple interest to be applied to a sum of money owed or determined to be owed, particularly when the debt is a prejudgment obligation. The second reason to understand simple interest is to understand the economic fallacy of its application. For a short lending period, simple interest can be the same as compound interest, but the concept quickly falls short of economic reality.

Take, for example, our basic factual problem of $100,000 at 6% annual interest. For 1½ years, the total interest due on the principal is $9,000 ($100,000 × 6% × 1.5 years = $9,000). Following the logic of the problem, if the length of the loan is changed to a total of ten years, the total interest due would be $60,000 ($100,000 × 6% × 10 years = $60,000). This calculation is mathematically correct, but does it make economic sense? If you are the lender, and you negotiate to collect 6% interest per year, but payments of interest are delayed until the end of the loan period, are you made whole by a simple interest calculation? Using these facts, and breaking the loan down into annual increments, isn't the lender owed $6,000 of interest at the end of the first year, not just the $100,000 of principal? At the end of year two, the lender is owed another $6,000 of unpaid

---

10. Interest rates are always stated on an annual basis unless specifically stated otherwise. Common usage of the term "5% interest" would imply 5% per year unless otherwise stated.

interest, right?[11] If the lender doesn't require interest payments as the term of the loan goes along, the lender is effectively lending the accumulated unpaid interest as well as the original principal. Given that dollars are the common measure of wealth, a dollar of interest owed to the lender has the same value as a dollar of principal owed to the lender, and both of those unpaid dollars have a time value. Because the initial loan amount is never changed in a simple interest calculation, a calculation of simple interest does not account for the time value of the unpaid interest on the principal amount of the loan. Simple interest does not conform to financial or economic logic.

The easiest way to calculate simple interest for any period of time is to reduce the annual interest rate calculation to a daily rate and multiply the daily rate times the number of days in the calculation. In Example #1, the daily interest amount is $16.43 ($100,000 × 6% = $6,000 per year, divided by 365 = $16.43). If the loan is outstanding for 1.5 years, that is 548 days, or total interest of $9,003.64 ($16.43 × 548 = $9,003.64). If the loan is outstanding for 10 years, that is 3,650 days, or total interest of $60,000 ($16.43 × 3,650 ≈ $60,000). (Ignore small rounding differences in the calculations.)

Before we leave the subject of simple interest, a short discussion of its history will shed light on the lingering existence of the concept. Historically, in many cultures, lending money and charging any type of interest was frowned upon. As the practice of lending money and charging interest became accepted, some cultures (and laws) held on to the traditional view and limited the legal interest rate of interest to simple interest, adopting the view that compound interest was a calculation of "interest on interest," and that there was something morally wrong with the practice. Consequently, the convention of simple interest remains in many situations.

Compound Interest and the Time Value of Money

Compound interest is the financial convention under which the original principal balance is increased by the amount of accumulated interest at the end of each compounding period; then, interest is computed on the new balance, which includes accumulated unpaid interest as well as the original principal. Under compound interest, the lender is compensated for lending the principal and also for "lending" the unpaid interest to the borrower. Compound interest is financially sound and is used in all modern-day financial transactions. The principle of compound interest incorporates the time value of money by recognizing that unpaid interest has the same economic value as unpaid principal.

A foundational principle of modern finance is the time value of money: a dollar today is worth more than one promised tomorrow. Given the choice to receive money now or defer the receipt of money, it is intuitive that a rational person would rather have the money now. Economically, there are four reasons why people recognize the fundamental concept of present value, and in fact do prefer a present receipt of money over a delayed payment.

---

11. Actually, if you think about it, the lender is owed $6,360 because the lender is owed interest on the $100,000 AND interest on the $6,000 of unpaid interest.

The first reason is utility: money in hand may be spent to satisfy immediate wants or needs whereas future dollars may not. The second reason is risk. Specifically, there is risk that the dollar promised tomorrow may not materialize. There is always a risk of non-payment with money promised in the future, and this also leads people to inherently prefer current receipt. Third, there is opportunity cost. Opportunity cost recognizes that some opportunities are mutually exclusive, i.e., the receipt of money tomorrow may cause the recipient to forgo opportunities today; the ability to take advantage of today's opportunities adds to the value of the dollar in hand. Finally, inflation may cause money to be worth less in the future, and this possibility is a risk of deferring receipt of the cash.

Calculating Compound Interest. Under the concept of compound interest, the interest that is earned on the original principal is accumulated and added to the principal balance for the next compounding period. Mathematically, the calculation of compound interest is very straightforward. At 6 % compound annual interest, a $100,000 present value sum grows like this for five years:

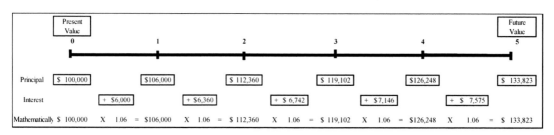

Take the initial principal amount, calculate interest at 6% for one compounding period (a year, in this problem), add the year's interest to the existing principal balance, and move into the next compounding period. As you can see, the original principal balance increases over time with the accumulated interest from each compounding period. In the above calculation, the future value of $100,000 at 6% (compounded annually) for five years is $133,823.

Solve for Future Value. Now we will do the same calculation with the Texas Instruments BA II PLUS calculator, using the finance mode of the calculator. To find the future value of any amount, the following factors must be known:

> PV – The initial principal amount.
> N – The number of compounding periods.
> I/Y – The interest rate per year.
> P/Y – The number of compounding **periods** per year.
> FV = ????

EXAMPLE 1

Your client invests **$100,000** in a certificate of deposit, at **6.0%** interest per year, compounded annually for 5 years. What amount will be on deposit at maturity?

Answer: _____

EXAMPLE 1 - CALCULATOR SOLUTION

PROCEDURE	PRESS				DISPLAY
1. Clear calculator	CE / C				0.00
2. Clear finance worksheet	2nd	CLR TVM			0.00
3. Enter number of compounding periods per year	2nd	P/Y	1	ENTER	P/Y = 1.00
4. Return to standard calculator mode	2nd	QUIT			0.00
5. Enter loan amount	100,000	PV			PV = 100,000.00
6. Enter interest rate per year	6	I/Y			I/Y = 6.00
7. Enter number of compounding periods	5	N			N = 5.00
8. Compute future value	CPT	FV			FV = − 133,822.56

THE AMOUNT ON DEPOSIT AT MATURITY IS $133,822.56

(Reminder: If you enter the PV as a positive, the FV will show up as a negative. One or the other of them must be a negative.)

Other compounding periods. Interest rates are (almost) always stated on an annual basis, but the compounding convention may vary significantly. Normally, compounding periods are daily, monthly, quarterly, semi-annually or annually. Because interest is recalculated at the end of every compounding period and added to principal, the more compounding periods in a calculation, the greater the future value, all other things being equal. Let's consider the same fact pattern, with the only change being quarterly compounding. First, here is the problem mathematically calculated:

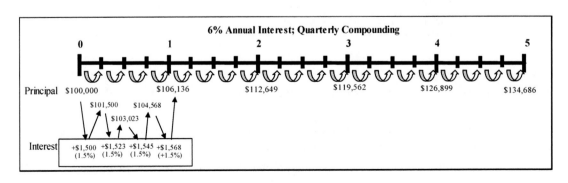

Conceptually, the quarterly compounding calculation is identical to the annual compounding calculation; the only difference is that now the periods are broken up into quarters, and the amount of interest per quarter is ¼ of one year's interest, or 1.5%. Mathematically, take the initial principal amount for one quarter of a year, calculate interest at 1.5%, add the quarter's interest to the existing principal balance, and move into the next compounding period. As you can see, the original principal balance increases over time with the accumulated interest from each compounding period. In the above calculation, the future value of $100,000 at 6% (compounded annually) for five years is $133,823; compounded quarterly, the future value is $134,686.

EXAMPLE 2

Your client invests **$100,000** in a certificate of deposit, at **6.0%** interest per year, compounded **quarterly** for five years. What amount will be on deposit at maturity?

Answer: _____

EXAMPLE 2 - CALCULATOR SOLUTION

PROCEDURE	PRESS				DISPLAY
1. Clear calculator	CE / C				0.00
2. Clear finance worksheet	2nd	CLR TVM			0.00
3. Enter number of compounding periods per year	2nd	P/Y	4	ENTER	P/Y = 4.00
4. Return to standard calculator mode	2nd	QUIT			0.00
5. Enter loan amount	100,000	PV			PV = 100,000.00
6. Enter interest rate per year	6	I/Y			I/Y = 6.00
7. Enter number of years	5	2nd		x P/Y	20.00
THEN	N				N = 20.00
8. Compute future value	CPT	FV			FV = – 134,685.50

THE AMOUNT ON DEPOSIT AT MATURITY IS $134,685.50

(Reminder: If you enter the PV as a positive, the FV will show up as a negative. One or the other of them must be a negative.)

Solving for Other Variables. In a time value of money problem, you can solve for any of the variables, present value (PV), interest rate (I/Y), time period (N), or future value (FV).

To solve for interest rate. You can compute the interest rate that makes the present value compound forward to equal a specified future value. Alternatively, you can compute a rate that makes a future value discount back to equal a specified present value. To compute the interest rate, you must know: "N," the total number of compounding periods; "P/Y," the number of compounding periods per year; "PV," the initial principal amount; and "FV," the desired amount at the end of N compounding periods.

EXAMPLE 3

Your client has **$150,000** and desires to build the amount to **$425,000** in **5 years**. Assuming semi-annual compounding of interest, what rate must the client obtain to achieve this goal?

Answer: _____

EXAMPLE 3 - CALCULATOR SOLUTION					
PROCEDURE	PRESS				DISPLAY
1. Clear calculator	CE / C				0.00
2. Clear finance worksheet	2nd	CLR TVM			0.00
3. Enter number of compounding periods per year	2nd	P/Y	2	ENTER	P/Y = 2.00
4. Return to standard calculator mode	2nd	QUIT			0.00
5. Enter loan amount	150,000	PV			PV = 150,000.00
6. Enter FV AS A NEGATIVE	425,000	+/−	=	FV	FV = − 425,000.00
7. Enter number of years	5	2nd		x P/Y	10.00
THEN	N				N = 10.00
8. Compute interest rate	CPT	I/Y			I/Y = 21.95

To solve for number of compounding periods. You can calculate the total number of compounding periods needed to make the present value compound forward to equal a specific future value. The input required to calculate the total number of compounding periods is: "PV," the beginning principal amount; "FV," the ending principal amount; "I/Y," the interest rate per year; and "P/Y," the number of compounding periods per year.

EXAMPLE 4

Your client has **$27,500** and wants to increase the amount to **$75,000**. At an **8%** annual interest rate, compounded semi-annually, how many years will it take for your client to achieve the goal?

Answer: _____

(**Caution:** Your calculator solution will state the number of compounding periods required, not the number of years. You must convert the solution to years by dividing the number of compounding periods (N) by the number of compounding periods per year (P/Y), or 2. Answer = 12.79 **years.**)

EXAMPLE 4 - CALCULATOR SOLUTION		
PROCEDURE	PRESS	DISPLAY
1. Clear calculator	CE / C	0.00
2. Clear finance worksheet	2nd CLR TVM	0.00
3. Enter number of compounding periods per year	2nd P/Y 2 ENTER	P/Y = 2.00
4. Return to standard calculator mode	2nd QUIT	0.00
5. Enter loan amount	27,500 PV	PV = 27,500.00
6. Enter FV AS A NEGATIVE	75,000 +/− = FV	FV = − 75,000.00
7. Enter interest rate per year	8 I/Y	I/Y = 8.00
8. Compute # of compounding periods	CPT N	N = 25.58

The Concept of Present Value

The concept of present value is an application of the concept of compound interest. Compound interest problems generally focus on the calculation of some accumulated amount of money in the future. In compound interest problems, we have a principal amount (present value), an interest rate, and a time period, and the question is what amount will be accumulated at the end of the time period being considered. In the previous section of this chapter, we have learned how to calculate this future value amount. In a pure present value problem, we know the existence of a sum certain at a point in the future. The question is, what is the present value of that amount of money?

A present value calculation is the simple reversal of a future value calculation. A future sum is said to be "discounted" to present value whereas a present amount is "compounded" forward into future value. The mathematics are exactly the same—one goes forward; the other goes backward. If you understand the basic concepts of compound interest, you understand present value.

The concept of present value is essential to all financial transactions. Because money has a time value (the ability to earn interest), the timing of a payment (or receipt) of money is economically important. The following simple example always demonstrates the point of present value. If you were offered a gift of $1,000 from a benefactor, and the choice was to take the $1,000 today or one year from today, every economically rational person would want the money today, not one year from today. Why? Well, the financial answer is that the $1,000 today is worth more than the $1,000 one year from today. If you get the money today, you can, of course, spend it to satisfy your immediate wants. But, let's deal with it economically. You could get the money today and invest it in an interest bearing account of, say, 6%, and in one year you will have $1,060.00. You can go to the bank and get your $1,060 while the unknowledgeable gift recipient who chose to take the $1,000 one year from tonight will be walking to pick up his $1,000 while you have $1,060 in your pocket. Here is a mathematical graphic of compound interest and present value:

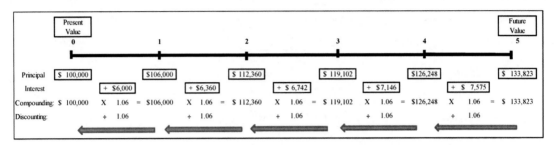

To be comparable, all sums of money must be compared at the same time. Generally, the present time (present value) is used to compare the economic value of sums of money at differing times. When analyzing a complicated financial problem, use a time line and place each future sum of money on the time line. Each amount can then be brought back to present value for and economically meaningful analysis. It does not matter whether you are dealing with a receipt, a payment, a loss or a gain, the concepts of compounding (to future value) and discounting (to present value) are applicable. The appropriate interest rate (for compounding or discounting) is often a subject of controversy. Note how significantly the amount of a future value or present value calculation can change when the interest rate is varied, particularly if the time period is great.

EXAMPLE 4 A

Your grandfather offers to give you **$1 million** on your twenty-first birthday, **7 years** from today. Assuming an **8%** annual interest rate (compounded annually), what is the present value of grandpa's gift?

Answer: _____

EXAMPLE 4 B

Your client will receive his retirement from XYZ Company in a lump sum. His date of retirement is **12 years** from today. Assume that he is completely vested and that no additional contributions by him are required. The client will receive **$100,000**, 12 years from today. Assuming a marketplace interest rate of **8%**, compounded annually, what is the present value of his retirement benefits for the purpose of community property division? (Use Example 4 A as a guideline.)

Answer: _____ ($39,711.38)

EXAMPLE 4 A - CALCULATOR SOLUTION

PROCEDURE	PRESS				DISPLAY
1. Clear calculator	CE / C				0.00
2. Clear finance worksheet	2nd	CLR TVM			0.00
3. Enter number of compounding periods per year	2nd	P/Y	1	ENTER	P/Y = 1.00
4. Return to standard calculator mode	2nd	QUIT			0.00
5. Enter future value amount	1,000,000	FV			FV = 1,000,000.00
6. Enter interest rate per year	8	I/Y			I/Y = 8.00
7. Enter number of years	7	2nd		x P/Y	7.00
THEN	N				N = 7.00
8. Compute present value	CPT	PV			PV = − 583,490.40

THE PRESENT VALUE IS $583,490.40.

(Reminder: If you enter the FV as a positive, the PV will show up as a negative. One or the other of them must be a negative.)

Regular Mortgage Loan Calculations

The traditional mortgage instrument has a fixed number of equal payments and a constant interest rate. Payments are made at the end of each payment period, which is normally a month. The following four variables affect a regular mortgage:

1. The amount borrowed (Present Value, or "PV");

2. The interest rate per year ("I/Y") and the number of compounding periods per year ("P/Y")—this is the same as the number of payments per year;

3. The life of the mortgage ("N" payment periods);

4. The equal payment ("PMT").

Any of the four variables—PV, I/Y, N or PMT—can be solved-for using the Texas Instruments calculator. It should be noted that regular mortgage calculations are identical to ordinary annuity calculations. This is discussed later in the chapter.

Solving for the Payment

EXAMPLE 5

Mr. F.T. Deed is borrowing **$145,000** at 5¾% annual interest. The loan is for **30 years**. What is the amount of the monthly payment?

	EXAMPLE 5 - CALCULATOR SOLUTION		
PROCEDURE		**PRESS**	**DISPLAY**
1. Clear calculator	CE / C		0.00
2. Clear finance worksheet	2nd · CLR TVM		0.00
3. Enter number of payments per year	2nd · P/Y · 12 · ENTER		P/Y =12.00
4. Return to standard calculator mode	2nd · QUIT		0.00
5. Enter loan amount	145,000 · PV		PV = 145,000.00
6. Enter interest rate per year	5.75 · I/Y		I/Y = 5.75
7. Enter number of years/payments	30 · 2nd · x P/Y		360.00
THEN	N		N = 360.00
8. Compute the monthly payment	CPT · PMT		PMT = − 846.18
	Note: Payments are shown as negatives.		

BA II Plus REMINDERS

1. Finance worksheet must be clear at beginning of problem

   2nd · CLR TVM · 2nd · QUIT

2. Payments are shown as negative numbers.

3. Enter "N" as number of years, then number of payments:

   30 · 2nd · x P/Y · N

EXAMPLE 6

Loan amount $82,500
Interest rate 8½% per year
Time period 5 years, monthly payments

Calculate the monthly payment.
(Follow procedure for Example 5.)

The monthly payment is **$1,692.61.**

EXAMPLE 7

Loan amount $212,750
Interest rate 6¼% per year
Time period 30 years, monthly payments

Calculate the monthly payment.
(Follow procedure for Example 5.)

The monthly payment is **$1,309.94.**

Solving for number of payments

EXAMPLE 8

As a result of division of community property, Husband owes Wife $22,000. Husband can afford to make payments of **$500 per month** and the annual interest rate is to be **9%**. For how many months must Husband make payments?

EXAMPLE 8 - CALCULATOR SOLUTION					
PROCEDURE	PRESS				DISPLAY
1. Clear calculator	CE / C				0.00
2. Clear finance worksheet	2nd	CLR TVM			0.00
3. Enter number of payments per year	2nd	P/Y	12	ENTER	P/Y =12.00
4. Return to standard calculator mode	2nd	QUIT			0.00
5. Enter loan amount	22,000	PV			PV = 22,000.00
6. Enter interest rate per year	9	I/Y			I/Y = 9.00
7. Enter payments as negative amount	500	+/ –	=	PMT	PMT = – 500.00
8. Compute the number of payments	CPT	N			N = 53.60
Husband must pay wife 53.6 payments of $500.00 per month					

EXAMPLE 9

Principal amount	$64,500
Interest rate	10½% per year
Monthly payment	$1,000

How many months to amortize loan?
(Follow procedure for Example 8.)

The answer is: **95.38 months**

Solving for Interest Rate

EXAMPLE 10

Your client knows only the following facts: His mortgage was **$125,000**; the time period was **30 years**; and the **monthly payment is $950.00**. What is the annual interest rate for your client's loan?

EXAMPLE 10 - CALCULATOR SOLUTION				
PROCEDURE	PRESS			DISPLAY
1. Clear calculator	CE / C			0.00
2. Clear finance worksheet	2nd	CLR TVM		0.00
3. Enter number of payments per year	2nd	P/Y	12 ENTER	P/Y =12.00
4. Return to standard calculator mode	2nd	QUIT		0.00
5. Enter loan amount	125,000	PV		PV = 125,000.00
6. Enter number of payments	360	N		N = 360.00
7. Enter payment amount as negative	950	+/ –	= PMT	PMT = - 950.00
8. Compute interest rate per year	CPT	I/Y		I/Y = 8.37
The interest rate per year is 8.37%.				

Solving for Mortgage Amount ("Present Value")

EXAMPLE 11

Your client wants to sell her house to her adult child. She is adamant about the following facts: She wants **$800 per month** for **10 years** with **no interest**. Client thinks she is selling the house for **$96,000**. How much is she really selling it for?

[This isn't a trick question, but all the variables are not in the problem. In order to solve Example 11, it is necessary to impute an interest rate into the calculation (even though the client says there is no interest in the problem, there is imputed interest).]

Answer:_____ (Assuming ____% interest/year.)

Advanced Mortgage Calculations

Discussion. The principal amount (PV, or loan amount) of a mortgage reduces to zero over the life of the loan. The principal amount does not decline on a straight line basis, rather it declines as the result of complicated mathematical equations that calculate a monthly interest amount, monthly principal reduction, and a constant payment. In the early months of a mortgage, the amount of principal reduction is small (relative to the monthly payment), and in the later months of the mortgage, the amount of principal reduction is large (relative to the monthly payment). Since the monthly payment is composed only of interest payments and principal reduction payments, the larger the principal portion of a payment (principal reduction), the smaller the interest portion, and vice versa. One reason this is particularly significant is that the interest portion of a payment is often a deductible business or tax expense, while the principal reduction part of a payment is never deductible. The principal portion of a mortgage payment is the repayment of a debt; it is not an expense. The interest portion is the ongoing expense of having borrowed the money.

An *amortization schedule* is the financial schedule that shows the ongoing loan balance, the amount of the monthly payment, and the portion of the monthly payment that comprises interest and principal reduction. The mortgage (or loan) is said to "amortize" according to the schedule. At any point during the loan's amortization schedule, there is a remaining unpaid principal balance that is owed. The unpaid principal balance is sometimes referred to as the "Balloon Payment" that would be required to repay the loan completely at any point in time.

The following sections will present calculations for:

1. Balloon payments (or the "unamortized" balance of the loan at any point in time);

2. The interest portion of a payment (or a series of payments);

3. The principal repayment portion of a payment (or series of payments); and

4. Variable interest rate loans.

Solving for Balloon Payments. A balloon payment is the remaining balance on a mortgage loan at some point during the life of the loan. Frequently, the situation of a balloon payment arises when a mortgage loan is amortized on, say, a 20-year amortization schedule with the full balance due at some earlier time, say, 10 years.

EXAMPLE 12

In the sale of his business, Seller finances **$285,000** at **10%** interest per year. The loan is to be amortized over **20 years** but the entire balance is due and payable in **10 years**.

  a. What are the monthly payments on the loan?

  b. What is the balance due at the end of the tenth year?

EXAMPLE 12 - CALCULATOR SOLUTION					
PROCEDURE	PRESS				DISPLAY
1. Clear calculator	CE / C				0.00
2. Clear finance worksheet	2nd	CLR TVM			0.00
3. Enter number of payments per year	2nd	P/Y	12	ENTER	P/Y =12.00
4. Return to standard calculator mode	2nd	QUIT			0.00
5. Enter loan amount	285,000	PV			PV = 285,000.00
6. Enter interest rate per year	10	I/Y			I/Y = 10.00
7. Enter number of payments	240	N			N = 240.00
OR 20	2nd	x P/Y		N	N = 240.00
8. Compute monthly payment	CPT	PMT			PMT = -2,750.31
9. To calculate balances, interest paid to date, and principal paid to date, go to the Amortization Worksheet	2nd	AMORT			P1 = 1.00
10. Scroll down using ↓ key					P2 = 1.00
11. Enter number of payments in P2	120	ENTER			P2 = 120.00
12. Scroll down to "Balance" using ↓ key	↓				BAL = 208,119.64
The balance after 10 years is $208,119.64					

The Amortization Worksheet (BAll Plus Guidebook, pages 21, 23, 25, 26)

The BA II Plus contains worksheets with embedded formulas to solve specific problems—we will only deal with the Amortization Worksheet in this course. (Think of this "worksheet" as a subset of the mortgage calculation. It is the place to go to find the loan amortization schedule—the schedule that contains the balloon payment (remaining principal balance), the interest portion of a payment (or series of payments) and the principal portion of a payment (or series of payments).)

After solving a mortgage problem, you can use the Amortization Worksheet to generate an amortization schedule that will tell you the balloon payment, and interest part of payments and principal reduction.

Using the Amortization Worksheet:
After you have entered all the variables in the calculator for a mortgage problem (PV, I/Y, N and PMT), you can use the Amortization Worksheet to compute an amortization schedule. Here's how:

1. Press 2nd AMORT . The current P1 value appears (that is the first payment in a range of payments that you will be inquiring about). Key in a value for P1 and press ENTER .

2. Press ↓. The current P2 value appears. (That is the last payment in a range that you will be inquiring about.) Key in a value for P2 and press ENTER .

3. Press ↓ to display each of the automatically computed values:

    BAL – The remaining balance AFTER payment P2.

    PRN – The total principal payments made between P1 and P2.

    INT – The total interest payments made between P1 and P2.

EXAMPLE 13

Loan amount	$48,500
Interest rate	9½% per year
Amortized over	8 years
Payment amount	= ??

Balloon payment due in 5 years = _____

Solving for Interest and Principal Portion of a Payment
To calculate interest portion of a payment:

EXAMPLE 14

Loan amount	$84,000
Interest rate	9¼%
Amortized over	30 years
Monthly payment	$691.05

What is the principal portion of the 24th payment?
The interest portion?

EXAMPLE 14 - CALCULATOR SOLUTION

PROCEDURE	PRESS	DISPLAY
First, enter the data for the mortgage problem. Solve for the payment.		
Then, use the Amortization Worksheet as follows:		
1. Enter the Amortization Worksheet	2nd AMORT	P1 = 1.00
2. Enter the payment # in P1.	24 ENTER	P1 = 24.00
3. Scroll down using ↓ key	↓	P2 = 1.00
4. Enter the payment # in P2.	24 ENTER	P2 = 24.00
5. Scroll down to "Balance" using ↓ key	↓	BAL = 82,856.71
6. Scroll down to "PRN" using ↓ key	↓	PRN = - 51.96
7. Scroll down to "INT" using ↓ key	↓	INT = -639.09

The principal portion of the 24th payment is $51.96.
The interest portion of the 24th payment is $639.09.

Discussion: In the Amortization Worksheet, "PRN" is designed to show the total principal paid *between two payments*, denoted as P1 and P2. "INT" is designed to show the total interest paid *between two payments*, denoted as P1 and P2. Therefore, if you only want to know the principal portion, or interest portion, *of one payment*, you must enter that payment number as *both* P1 and P2. Obviously, if you want to know the interest (or principal) paid for the first year, for example, enter P1 as "1" and P2 as "12," then scroll down to PRN and INT.

Variable Interest Rate Loans. A variable rate loan is nothing more than a series of fixed rate loans. Until the interest rate is changed, all the calculations are similar to those for fixed rate loans. When the interest rate is changed, compute the balance of the loan at that point (i.e., balloon payment). Then make new calculations using the new principal balance, the remaining time period, and the new interest rate.

EXAMPLE 15

Loan amount $484,000
Interest rate   3¾%
Amortized over 30 years
Monthly payment $2,241.48
New terms: After the first year, the interest rate is changed from the original 3 ¾% to 6 ¼%. Calculate the new payment as of the second year of the loan.

PROCEDURE	PRESS	DISPLAY
EXAMPLE 15 - CALCULATOR SOLUTION		
1. Clear calculator	CE / C	0.00
2. Clear finance worksheet	2nd CLR TVM	0.00
3. Enter number of payments per year	2nd P/Y 12 ENTER	P/Y = 12.00
4. Return to standard calculator mode	2nd QUIT	0.00
5. Enter loan amount	484,000 PV	PV = 484,000.00
6. Enter interest rate per year	3.75 I/Y	I/Y = 3.75
7. Enter number of payments	360 N	N = 360.00
OR 30	2nd x P/Y N	N = 360.00
8. Compute monthly payment	CPT PMT	PMT = -2,241.48
9. To calculate balances, interest paid to date, and principal paid to date, go to the Amortization Worksheet *(set P1 equal to 1)*	2nd AMORT	P1 = 1.00
10. Scroll down using [↓] key		P2 = 1.00
11. Enter payment # for end of first year	12 ENTER	P2 = 12.00
12. Scroll down to "Balance" using ↓ key	↓	BAL = 475,100.30
13. Enter balance in mortgatge problem	CE / C PV	PV = 475,100.30
14. Enter new interest rate	6.25 I/Y	I/Y = 6.25
15. Enter new time period 29	2nd x P/Y N	N = 348.00
16. Compute the monthly payment	CPT PMT	PMT = − 2,959.56

Ordinary Annuities (BA II Plus Guidebook, pages 21-43)

An annuity is a series of consecutive, equal cash flows occurring for N equal time periods with interest calculated at the end of each cash flow. (Does this sound like a mortgage?) The cash flows are usually called payments, even though they might actually represent an outflow (payment) or an inflow (receipt) of cash. The key concepts to remember about annuities are that all payments must be equal (excluding PV and FV), they must occur every time period (no missing payments), and all payments must be of the same nature (either receipts or payments).

Our discussion is limited to "ordinary annuities," which are annuities with payments occurring at the end of each period. This type of annuity is identical to traditional loan amortization and is the more frequent of the two types of annuities. (An annuity with payments occurring at the beginning of each time period is called an "annuity due." A practical example of an annuity due is rent, which is paid—or received—at the beginning of a month.)

An ordinary annuity having payments compounded forward to accumulate a future sum is often called a "future value annuity" or "compound sum of an annuity." When the payments are discounted back to a present value, the annuity is often called a "present value annuity." The terms used for both types of annuities are described below.

a. Future Value (FV)—The value at the *end* of the last payment period of a series of equal payments *compounded* forward at *x* % interest rate. This situation is exemplified by a regular monthly deposit into some type of interest-bearing account, assuming a fixed interest rate. The question is: how much will be on deposit at the end of the series of deposits, given that the money is accumulated with the interest rate.

b. Present Value (PV)—The value at the *beginning* of the first payment period of a series of equal payments *discounted* back at *x* % interest rate.

c. Interest Rate (I/Y)—The interest per year that makes the series of equal payments compound forward to a specified future value, or makes the series of equal payments discount back to a specified present value. Note that the BA II calculator requires you to enter the number of payments or compounding periods per year (P/Y), and this factor is calculated into the interest rate. (For your information, the annual interest rate is divided into an interest rate per payment period. The math is straight division—simply take the interest rate per year and divide by the number of compounding periods per year to get the interest rate per compounding period.)

d. Payments (PMT)—The equal amount paid or received each period for N periods. Payments for ordinary annuities occur at the end of each period. (Payments for "annuities due" occur at the beginning of the period.)

e. Number of Payments (N)—The total number of equal payments.

Future Value Ordinary Annuity

The future value of an ordinary annuity is the accumulation of principal and interest at the end of the annuity period. The first payment occurs at the *end* of the first payment period, and the final payment occurs at the *end* of the last payment period. The future value (FV) of an ordinary annuity is the accumulated value of a given number of equal payments (PMT), all compounded forward with interest to the end of the total period of all the payments. Each payment is made at the end of each payment period (N) and compounded forward to the end of the last payment period. To calculate the future value of an ordinary annuity, you must know: N, the total number of payments; I/Y, the interest rate per year; P/Y, the number of payment periods in a year; and PMT, the equal payment (or receipt) occurring at the *end* of each payment period.

EXAMPLE 16

Company X is depositing $10,000 in a bank account at the end of each quarter for **6 years.** Assuming the account pays **8½%** annual interest with quarterly compounding, what is the value at the end of 6 years?

EXAMPLE 16 - CALCULATOR SOLUTION

PROCEDURE	PRESS				DISPLAY
1. Clear calculator	CE / C				0.00
2. Clear finance worksheet	2nd	CLR TVM			0.00
3. Enter number of payments per year	2nd	P/Y	4	ENTER	P/Y = 4.00
4. Return to standard calculator mode	2nd	QUIT			0.00
5. Enter payment amount	10,000	PMT			PMT = 10,000.00
6. Enter interest rate per year	8.50	I/Y			I/Y = 8.50
7. Enter number of compounding periods					
EITHER 6	2nd	x P/Y		N	N = 24.00
OR 24	N				N = 24.00
8. Compute the future value	CPT	FV			FV = − 308,902.10

The future value is $308,902.10.
(Reminder: Either the PV or the FV must be a negative.)

EXAMPLE 17

You make an annual contribution of **$2,000** to an IRA account and you anticipate accumulating the money for **21 years**. The interest rate on your account is 7½ % compounded annually. What amount will you have at the end of the 21st year? (Follow procedure for Example 16.)

Answer: _____ ($95,105.06)

To Solve for Payment

The payment of an ordinary annuity is the amount paid or received at the end of each payment period for N periods that compounds forward to a specified future value. To compute the payment, you must know: N, the total number of payments; I/Y, the interest rate per year; P/Y, the number of payment periods per year; and FV, the future value of the payments.

EXAMPLE 18

Z Company must establish a fund to retire a **$1 million** bond issue at the end of **10 years**. The deposits are to be made at the end of each **6 month period**. If the **10%** annual interest rate is compounded semi-annually, what is the required amount of each deposit?

EXAMPLE 18 - CALCULATOR SOLUTION

PROCEDURE	PRESS				DISPLAY
1. Clear calculator	CE / C				0.00
2. Clear finance worksheet	2nd	CLR TVM			0.00
3. Enter number of payments per year	2nd	P/Y	2	ENTER	P/Y = 2.00
4. Return to standard calculator mode	2nd	QUIT			0.00
5. Enter future value	1,000,000	FV			FV = 1,000,000.00
6. Enter interest rate per year	10.00	I/Y			I/Y = 10.00
7. Enter number of compounding periods					
EITHER 10	2nd	x P/Y		N	N = 20.00
OR 20	N				N = 20.00
8. Compute the payment amount	CPT	PMT			PMT = – 30,242.59

The company must deposit $30,242.59 at the end of each 6 month period
to accumulate $1,000,000 after 10 years.

EXAMPLE 19

You will retire in **21 years**. Assuming an **8%** annual interest rate (compounded annually), how much will you have to deposit at the end of each year to retire with **$1 million**? (Follow procedure for Example 18, but change the number of payments per year.)

Answer: _____

To Solve for Interest Rate:
Enter FV, N, PMT, and CPT I/Y. (Remember to enter either the future value or the payment as a negative.)

To Solve for Total Number of Payments:
Enter FV, PMT, I/Y, and CPT N..

To Solve for Present Value:
The present value of an ordinary annuity is the present value of N payments occurring at the end of each payment period discounted back to the beginning of the first payment period. To compute the present value of an ordinary annuity, you must know: N, the total number of payments; I/Y, the interest rate per year; P/Y, the number of annuity payments in a year; and PMT, the equal payment amount.

EXAMPLE 20

Your client, the plaintiff, suffered a permanent loss of earnings of **$18,500** per year and it was anticipated that his working life expectancy was **27 years**. Assuming a **6%** discount rate (compounded annually), what is the present economic loss suffered by your client?

EXAMPLE 20 - CALCULATOR SOLUTION

PROCEDURE	PRESS				DISPLAY
1. Clear calculator	CE / C				0.00
2. Clear finance worksheet	2nd	CLR TVM			0.00
3. Enter number of payments per year	2nd	P/Y	1	ENTER	P/Y = 1.00
4. Return to standard calculator mode	2nd	QUIT			0.00
5. Enter payment (annual loss) amount	18,500	PMT			PMT = 18,500.00
6. Enter interest rate per year	6.00	I/Y			I/Y = 6.00
7. Enter total number of payments	27.00	N			N = 27.00
8. Compute the present value	CPT	PV			PV = – 244,394.88

The present value of your client's loss is $244,394.88.
Note: If you don't put payment in as a negative, the PV will be shown as a negative number.

EXAMPLE 21

Loss	$35,000 per year
Time Period	9 years
Interest Rate	8% per year

Compute present value. (Follow procedure for Example 20.)

Answer: _____

To Solve for Interest Rate:
Enter other variables and CPT I/Y

To Solve for Number of Payments:
Enter other variables and CPT N

Conclusion

The time value of money, as applied through the concepts of present value and future value, exists in every transaction. The time value of money is driven by the principle of compound interest, which is the addition of accumulated interest to the principal sum at the end of a period, before the interest is recalculated and added in the next compounding period. Basic finance underlies all monetary transactions, and knowledge of the principles of finance is critically important to understand transactions, analyze them and counsel clients about them.

This chapter has introduced the basic concepts of finance that relate to the practice of law. The problems in the chapter are designed to teach the reader to use the Texas Instruments BA II PLUS financial calculator in order to apply the concepts. The problems and exercises in the Workbook will add to the reader's understanding of these concepts. Our focus has been practical, not theoretical, and being able to apply these concepts of finance is essential to successfully counseling clients in a sophisticated law practice.

Chapter 9

General Principles of Appraisal and Valuation of Businesses

Introduction

This chapter introduces the principles that apply to the appraisal of all assets. The next few pages will briefly cover the general economic principles and methods used to determine value, recognizing that this effort is an attempt to summarize hundreds of pages of discussion into a brief overview. In the valuation of businesses section of the chapter, the capitalization of excess earnings method of business valuation is presented to help the reader understand the most often used method for valuing small businesses and professional practices.

General Principles of Appraisal

An appraisal is a professional opinion, usually written, of the market value of a property, such as a home, business, or other asset whose market price is not easily determined. It is usually required when a property is sold, taxed, insured, or financed.[1] The fair market value of property is often the subject of civil dispute, so expert appraisal opinion is often required in litigated matters. The need to determine the value of property is as old as human interaction. From the time of cave men fighting over food and territorial rights to modern day financial transactions, knowing the value of an item of property is an important part of all commercial activity.

There are a number of economic concepts that provide the foundation for the appraisal of property. Some of the most significant are:

1. *Principle of Substitution*—The appraisal principle that states that a buyer of property will pay no more for the property than the amount for which a property of like utility may be purchased; that a property's value tends to be limited by the cost of acquiring an equally desirable substitute.

2. *Principle of Contribution*—The appraisal principle that requires an appraiser to measure the value of any improvement to a property by the amount it contributes to the market value of the property, not by the cost of the improvement.

3. *Principle of Anticipation*—The appraisal principle that bases the value of property on the expectation of benefits to be derived in the future.

---

1. Investorwords.com

Approaches to Determining Value

Fundamentally, there are three approaches to determining the value of property, and the approaches are independent of one another. They are:

1. *Cost approach.* The cost approach is a method of determining value based on the summation of all of the costs required to reproduce the property in its present condition. It is most reliable when applied to newer properties and it is also used for special use properties. Its application to business appraisal focuses on the balance sheet.

2. *Sales comparison approach ("market approach").* Relying on the principle of substitution, the sales comparison is a method of estimating the fair market value of a property by comparing it to the sale of similar properties in the marketplace. The application of this method to real estate is common because of the availability of market data for the sale of other properties, including price, terms, description and other information that enables the appraiser to compare the subject to the marketplace. The method is also used in the appraisal of businesses, although its application in this context is more difficult because of comparability issues.

3. *Income approach.* The income approach to valuation is based on the assumption that the value of a property is the present value of all its future economic benefits. For businesses and investment properties, if the income of the property can be estimated, the income projection can be discounted to present value, resulting in an estimate of the present economic value of the property. The concept of discounting a future stream of income to present value is financially similar to capitalizing a current amount of income into present value. The income approach is frequently referred to as the "capitalization of earnings" method or, in public stock market parlance, the "price/earnings" approach. Under the concept of this methodology, the "earnings" used in the algorithm can be different measures of economic benefit such as Net Income, Earnings Before Interest and Taxes ("EBIT") or Earnings Before Interest Taxes Depreciation and Amortization ("EBITDA").

Standards of Value

A *standard of value* is a definition of the type of value being sought in an appraisal. The standard of value usually reflects an assumption as to who will be the buyer and who will be the seller in the hypothetical or actual transaction regarding the subject property of the appraisal. For many situations, the standard of value is legally mandated, either by statute or contract. The task of an appraisal is usually to determine the value of property under a particular standard of value. Following are the generally accepted standards of value for property.

1. *Fair market value*—the price at which the property will change hands between a willing seller and a willing buyer, neither party being under compulsion to buy or sell, and both having reasonable knowledge of the relevant facts.[2]

2. *Investment value*—the specific value of an investment to a particular investor or class of investors based on individual investment requirements; distinguished from market value, which is impersonal and detached.[3]

3. *Intrinsic* or *fundamental value*—differs from investment value in that it represents an analytical judgment of value based on the perceived characteristics inherent in the investment, not tempered by characteristics peculiar to any one investor, but rather tempered by how these perceived characteristics are interpreted by one analyst versus another.[4] The best example of intrinsic value is the value of a stock determined by a securities analyst based on fundamental analysis of the company's assets, earning power and other factors. In theory, that value will become the market value when other investors reach the same conclusion.

4. *Fair value*—a term that has a number of definitions, depending on the context of its use. For accounting and financial reporting purposes, fair value is defined by the Financial Accounting Standards Board as:

   > ...the exchange price in an orderly transaction between market participants to sell the asset or transfer the liability in the market in which the reporting entity would transact for the asset or liability, that is, the principal or most advantageous market for the asset or liability.[5]

   In most states, fair value is the statutory standard of value applicable in cases of dissenting stockholders' appraisal rights, minority oppression cases and corporate dissolution statutes. It must be noted, however, that there is no consensus definition of fair value, nor agreement on the appraisal approaches required to make the determination of fair value. In California, fair value is defined in the state's corporate dissolution statute somewhat ambiguously, as follows:

   > The fair value shall be determined on the basis of the liquidation value as of the valuation date but taking into account the possibility, if any, of sale of the entire business as a going concern in a liquidation.[6]

---

2. U.S. Treasury regulation 20.2031-6.
3. *The Dictionary of Real Estate Appraisal*, 4th ed. (Chicago; Appraisal Institute, 2002), p. 152.
4. Pratt, Shannon P., *Valuing a Business*, 5th ed. (New York: McGraw Hill, 2008), p. 44.
5. Statement of Financial Accounting Standards No. 157—Fair Value Measurements, paragraph 4.
6. California Corporations Code Section 2000(a).

---

5. *Replacement value*—the amount necessary to replace an asset (at its current level of utility) at current market prices. Replacement value is different from *reproduction value*, which refers to reproducing an exact replica of the asset.

6. *Fair market value, in continued use*—the present value of an item of property as part of a larger assemblage of assets. Generally, this standard of value is considered to be the depreciated replacement cost of the asset, giving consideration to the age and condition of the asset.

Premise of Value[7]

The premise of value is an assumption about the likely set of transactional circumstances that apply to the valuation process. Virtually all interests may be appraised under each of these following four alternative premises of value:

1. *Value as a going concern*—Value in continued use, as a mass assemblage of income-producing assets, and as a going-concern business enterprise.

2. *Value as an assemblage of assets*—Value in place, as part of a mass assemblage of assets, but not in current use in the production of income, and not as a going-concern business enterprise.

3. *Value as an orderly liquidation*—Value in exchange, on a piecemeal basis (not part of a mass assemblage of assets), as part of an orderly disposition; this premise contemplates that all of the assets of the business enterprise will be sold individually and that they will enjoy a normal exposure of their appropriate secondary market.

4. *Value as a forced liquidation*—Value in exchange, on a piecemeal basis (not part of a mass assemblage of assets), as part of a forced liquidation; this premise contemplates that the assets of the business enterprise will be sold individually and that they will experience less than normal exposure to their appropriate secondary market.

Valuing Small Businesses[8]

The valuation of a small business is a complex appraisal process. A competent valuation analysis requires a thorough understanding of the nature and history of the small business, the results of its financial operations, the marketplace for its sale, and the proper application of complex valuation

---

7. The discussion of "Premise of Value" is taken from Pratt, *op. cit.*, page 47-48.

8. "Valuing Small Business" is the update of an original article and eight-hour continuing education presentation by Brian P. Brinig, J.D., C.P.A., and S. Chris Summers, C.P.A., C.F.A., for the California Society of CPAs.

techniques to arrive at a credible, supportable valuation analysis. The result of the appraiser's efforts in this area can range from an informal oral consultation with a buyer, seller or interested party to the preparation of a full written appraisal report that incorporates all of the considerations and analysis undertaken.

The need for small business valuation arises primarily in two situations. First, potential buyers or sellers of small businesses or professional practices often require valuation services in preparing to negotiate transactions. These services can be marketplace related or litigation related, as in corporate or partnership dissolutions. Secondly, the issue of small business or professional practice valuation arises in the context of the division of community property, where one spouse is a business owner or a practicing professional with an ownership interest in an ongoing business or professional practice. In the context of marital dissolution, the appraiser's valuation role must be carefully integrated with the relevant community property statutes and case law so that a legally acceptable conclusion is reached.

Small business or professional practice valuation is an exciting and challenging area of accounting and appraisal practice. It is an area that requires careful analysis, broad knowledge of law and valuation theory, and intelligent judgments by the financial analyst. After a valuation analysis is completed and a report is issued, there is often another party in the matter (a buyer, seller, or opposing litigant) who will be glad to point out all the considerations that the appraiser has failed to incorporate into the analysis.

Overview of the Business Appraisal Process

In 1959, the Internal Revenue Service promulgated Revenue Ruling 59-60 that outlined and reviewed the approach, methods and factors to be considered in valuing the shares of closely-held corporations for estate and gift tax purposes. Revenue Ruling 59-60 remains the seminal treatise on the subject and it is quoted today as the fundamental basis for valuing privately held stock. It is set forth in its entirety at page 189 of this text. The Ruling sets forth the following eight factors that are considered fundamental and require careful consideration in each case:

1. The nature of the business and the history of the enterprise from its inception.

2. The economic outlook in general and the condition and outlook of the specific industry in particular.

3. The book value of the stock and the financial condition of the business.

4. The earning capacity of the company.

5. The dividend-paying capacity.

6. Whether or not the enterprise has goodwill or other intangible value.

7. Sales of the stock and the size of the block of stock to be valued.

8. The market price of stocks of corporations engaged in the same or a similar line of business having their stocks actively traded in a free and open market, either on an exchange or over-the-counter.

In 1968, the IRS published Revenue Ruling 68-609, stating a "formula" approach as follows:

> A percentage return on the average annual value of the tangible assets used in a business is determined, using a period of years (preferably not less than five) immediately prior to the valuation date. The amount of the percentage return on tangible assets, thus determined, is deducted from the average earnings of the business for such period and the remainder, if any, is considered to be the amount of the average annual earnings from the intangible assets of the business for the period. This amount (considered as the average annual earnings from intangibles), capitalized at a percentage of, say 15 to 20 percent, is the value of the intangible assets of the business determined under the "formula" approach.

In Revenue Ruling 68-609, the IRS stated that the "formula" approach may be used in determining the fair market value of intangible assets of a business only if there is no better basis available for making the determination. The Ruling is on page 197 of the text.

Over the last forty years, the business appraisal community has become professionalized. Leading scholars have synthesized and advanced the financial theories relating to the valuation of businesses, and volumes of literature have been published on the subject. The methodology of business valuation includes sophisticated valuation theories relating to financial projections, capitalization rate theory, and financial and data analysis. All of the modern valuation techniques stem from the general principles of appraisal (for any type of property) and fundamental business appraisal techniques articulated in Revenue Ruling 59-60.

Possible Methods of Valuing a Business

There are a number of financial ratios or metrics that can be applied to the value of a business. In some cases the metrics have a logical economic basis and they can be said to be methods of appraisal; in other cases the metrics are anecdotal or coincidental. Although there are many slight variations on the themes, following are the "generally accepted" methods of appraising a business.

Income approaches to value

Capitalization of earnings. Under this method, the value of the enterprise is estimated by capitalizing the representative earnings base at an appropriate capitalization rate that represents the required rate of return to an investor in consideration of the perceived risk of the expected earnings stream. The method is also referred to as the "price/earnings" method and it is a two-factor method to determine the value of the business. It is relatively easy to describe, but its application requires an appropriate estimate of the company's earnings base and the derivation of a capitalization rate that estimates a required rate of return for the particular investment. Also, in order to apply the method properly, the analyst must add or subtract any "excess" or "deficient" assets to the two-factor conclusion.

Capitalization of other benefit streams. The capitalization of earnings method may also be used for other measures of net economic benefit streams to the enterprise such as Debt-Free Cash Flow, Earnings Before Interest and Taxes (EBIT) or Earnings Before Interest Taxes Depreciation and Amortization (EBITDA). There is logic to capitalizing these benefit streams into value if the measure of the capitalization rate (or multiple) is determined from the same benefits stream.

Discounted future benefits stream. Under this methodology, the value of the enterprise is estimated by projecting the anticipated net income or cash flow into the future and discounting the projection to present value at an appropriate risk adjusted rate. The method is conceptually sound, but it requires a detailed future projection of business operations and the determination of an appropriate discount rate that considers the risk of achieving the projection.

Capitalization of gross revenues. This is the measure of the value of a business in relation to its annual gross revenue. It is the value of the business stated at a "multiple" of its annual revenue, such as "one times gross" or "one and one-half year's gross." As a method of valuation, it has questionable value, but it is often casually considered as a metric or measure of the value of a business. In some very limited circumstances, it can be used as a method, but only when there is sufficient data from market transactions of comparable information based on gross revenues. As in any two-factor methodology, if the capitalization of gross revenues is used, the conclusion must be adjusted for other assets and liabilities that are part of the valuation.

Market approaches to value. Generally, market approaches to business valuation are a variation of income approaches, but they rely on some market data for the determination of the capitalization rate, or multiple, to apply to the net income flow of the business to determine value.

Publicly traded comparables. Under this methodology, the analyst seeks price information about publicly traded stocks in the same or similar industries and draws comparisons about the publicly traded price in relation to earnings per share. This information is used to "price" the stock of the subject company. This methodology is held in high regard in valuation literature, but careful scrutiny of the method's application discloses that it is very difficult to overcome obvious comparability issues between privately held corporate investments and highly liquid publicly traded stocks.

Comparable business sales. Over the years, some private companies have developed databases that report the details of sales of businesses. The databases contain information about the types of business, location, date of sale, selling price and financial information about the operations of the business prior to its transfer. This information is helpful in understanding how the marketplace views particular types of businesses. There are two problems with an appraiser's ability to use this information in a meaningful way to determine the value of a subject. First, there are always issues of comparability of the subject business to the industry information. Individual businesses are unique and it is difficult to draw close comparisons among them, unlike real estate, where the characteristics are generally quite comparable: rental rate, vacancy rate, economic conditions of the area, operating expenses, etc. Second, the financial details of business sales are not publicly reported so the information obtained by the databases is generally self-reported, and this process calls into question the reliability of the information.

Cost approaches to value

Net book value. The net book value is the accounting summation of the total assets minus liabilities of a business at the date of the balance sheet. As an indicator of the total value of a business, net book value has a very limited application because it fails to consider the fair market value of the underlying assets and it gives no consideration to the historical earnings or earnings capacity of the business enterprise.

Adjusted book value. The adjusted book value of a business is the total of the assets, net of liabilities, with the assets adjusted to their realizable market value. Adjusted book value is relevant as a part of the total value of a business, but it fails to consider the earnings capacity of the enterprise.

Capitalization of excess earnings. The excess earnings method is considered a cost approach to valuation because, in addition to including the adjusted book value of the assets and liabilities of the business, it also includes an estimate of the intangible asset value of the enterprise, based on excess earnings generated by the business. It should be characterized as a "hybrid" approach because it includes a reproduction cost for tangible assets of the business and it uses income (excess earnings) to determine the value of intangibles. The method is discussed at length in the subsequent section of this chapter.

Capitalization of Excess Earnings Method

The focus of the example in the remainder of this chapter will be the method called the "formula" approach that was identified in Revenue Ruling 68-609. This approach, known as the *Capitalization of Excess Earnings* method, has been derided by the IRS as inappropriate unless there is no better method available. Notwithstanding the derision, it is the most often used method of business valuation, and it has great application to determine the value of small businesses and professional practices. The reason it is so valuable is that it is most applicable to very small businesses, and buyers, sellers and brokers of these businesses rely on an analysis of excess earnings to determine the value of the businesses in the real world. Although it is technically considered a cost approach to valuation, the method is really a hybrid of the cost approach and the income approach. It divides the value of a business enterprise into two components: the net tangible assets (assets minus liabilities) and intangible asset value (based on the income that the intangibles produce). The following sections discuss the application of the excess earnings method.

Balance Sheet Review (Determination of Net Tangible Assets)

The account balances stated on the balance sheet of the business will, of course, reflect the book value of the various accounts. For many small businesses or professional practices, the balance sheet will have been prepared for tax purposes using the cash basis of accounting. When that is the case, it is possible that some of the operating assets have been expended or depreciated far below their actual value. Also, some important assets and liabilities will not even appear on the statement.

To correct these inaccuracies,[9] the analyst must conduct a specific evaluation of the fair market value of the business's assets and liabilities. This requires adjustments to the book values in the following two general areas: 1) adjustments required to restate account balances from book value to actual economic value, and 2) adjustments necessary to reflect the value of assets and liabilities which are not included on the balance sheet. It will also be necessary to distinguish operating and non-operating items in this analysis. Non-operating assets and liabilities should be removed from the balance sheet and valued separately, if necessary.

Adjustments Generally Required in the Analysis

Cash & Equivalents—Typically, no adjustments to these items are required. In general, cash balances are not included in the sale of small businesses or professional practices. Typically, a sales price includes operating assets, intangible value and inventory. However, cash held by the business must be included in the determination of the total business value. Understand the distinction that is being made here. If the task is to determine the value of the entire business (proprietorship, partnership or corporation), all assets and liabilities must be included in the analysis. Sometimes, the task is to "value the business for sale." In the case of a sale, certain assets will usually be excluded. For instance, it is typical for a seller to retain all cash and the buyer to start his new business with his own cash. If the seller has some assets that are considered "personal," those assets will usually be excluded from the sale.

Accounts Receivable—This is often the most valuable asset owned by a small business or professional practice, but again, it is usually not included in the sales price. Rather, the buyer will typically agree to segregate the existing receivables and remit them to the seller as they are collected. Nevertheless, to determine the total business or professional practice value, it is necessary to estimate the present value of the collectible accounts. Accounts receivable will not appear on cash basis statements but must also be included in this analysis.

There are two general ways to approach the valuation of accounts receivable. The first method involves examining the historical collection patterns of the business or professional practice. The growing use of computer software programs specifically designed for professional practices has

---

9.   The accounting balance sheet isn't really inaccurate, it is simply a presentation of assets and liabilities based on accounting principles.

made this method more reliable. In many instances, the office administrator is able to calculate the business or practice's collection percentages in each of several billing classifications. For example, a medical practice may track collections on Medicare, Medi-Cal, Private Insurance, Champus, Workers Compensation and direct patient billings. The appraiser can apply these historical collection percentages to the outstanding balances of each receivable category to derive an estimate of the net collectible amount.

The second method uses an aging of the accounts receivable to estimate the net realizable value of the accounts. In this method, older accounts are assigned a lower probability of collection. For example, accounts less than 30 days old may be 80% collectible, while those greater than 180 days old may be only 20% collectible. In most cases, the appraiser must rely on the practitioner or the billing assistant for these percentages.

Work in Process—Certain types of professional practices can have a significant amount of unrecorded receivables in the form of work in process. This results from services which have been provided to clients but which have not yet been billed. The reason for the delayed billing may be simply the normal policy of the practice. The work in process records should be reviewed with the practitioner to determine the amount expected to ultimately be realized.

Similarly, many law practices provide services for which they will be compensated only upon successful resolution of a case. Estimating the value of these contingent fees is probably the most subjective calculation the appraiser will ever be asked to provide. When possible, it is most accurate to reserve judgment on the value of these contingent fees until the conclusion of each case. At that time, the fee actually received can be allocated based on the amount of time expended on the case before and after the date of valuation. When that is not possible, the appraiser must estimate the value based on some reasonable approach. One method is to assign a value based on the number of hours expended on each contingency case and the normal billing rates.

Inventory—Inventory can be the most significant asset in many small business operations, particularly those engaged in retail or distribution operations. Inventory should be carefully scrutinized for obsolescence, and it should be included in a valuation analysis at its current wholesale replacement cost. The appraiser should be careful to adjust the account balances for LIFO reserves or other accounting distortions that may affect the true value of inventory.

Supplies Inventory—Most businesses and professional practices expense their supplies purchases rather than carrying them in inventory. Therefore, this account will not appear on the balance sheet as an asset, and, in some businesses, the accumulated amount of supplies can be significant. Ideally, a physical inventory should be taken with values based on the current replacement cost. Where this is impossible, impractical, or immaterial, this adjustment can be estimated based on a percentage of the annual supplies expense.

Prepaid Expenses—If the recorded prepaid expenses will benefit future periods, no adjustment is necessary. More often than not, however, expenses that were prepaid will not be recorded as assets in the accounting of a small business. (Recall the bias of a small business owner for tax reporting purposes—to expense as much as possible in the current accounting period.) Prepaid items that will benefit future periods should also be included in the adjustments, meaning that they should be added to assets of the business. Common examples of expenses which may be prepaid include insurance, rent, and professional dues.

Furniture, Fixtures & Equipment—There are several possible values that can be assigned to these assets. These include liquidation value, replacement cost, fair market value in continued use, etc. For the viable small business, it is generally most appropriate to use the depreciated replacement cost (i.e., the current cost of a new asset less an allowance for the percentage of useful life that has transpired) of each asset unless specific information on the market value of comparable used equipment is available. For businesses or professional practices with a substantial investment in specialized equipment, such as dental practices, the services of an equipment appraiser may be necessary.

Leasehold Improvements—These should be valued in the same manner as Furniture, Fixtures & Equipment unless the lease will not be renewed prior to the end of their useful lives. In that case, their value can be estimated through straight line depreciation of the original cost over the period between the purchase date and the expiration of the lease.

Real Estate—The great majority of small businesses lease their facilities from third-party lessors. For those that own their facilities, it is usually best to classify the real estate as a non-operating asset and remove it from the balance sheet. In connection with this adjustment, it would also be necessary to remove real estate debt from the balance sheet and to replace expenses relating to the real estate on the income statement with a fair rent amount.

Intangible Assets—The balance sheet may include accounts such as Patient Records, Covenant not to Compete or Goodwill. These represent the unamortized balance of purchase price allocations which were made in connection with the purchase of the practice or a segment thereof. The book value of these assets should be removed from the balance sheet. The actual value of the practice's intangible assets will be separately determined.

Liabilities—Unless there is information to the contrary, no adjustment to the liability accounts is normally required. Certain liabilities, including Notes Payable to Shareholders, Deferred Taxes and Obligations under Leases may require adjustments based on the specific situation. The possible existence of unrecorded or contingent liabilities should also be investigated.

Tax Consequences of Making Adjustments

The tax consequences of making the adjustments described above should also be considered. If an asset sale is contemplated, the gross adjusted values should be used. If a sales price for the shares of stock in a corporation is needed, or if the net value to the seller (as in a divorce) is being determined, the preferred treatment is to make the adjustments net of tax.

For example, if the book value of a company's fixed assets is lower than their fair market value, taxes payable on the gain should be either deducted from the assigned value or included as a deferred liability. For some appraisals, it might be argued that the assets are not actually being sold, and consequently no gain will be realized for taxes paid. However, the practitioner's future depreciation expense will continue to be based on the book value, not the assigned fair market value. Taxes incurred by not receiving the depreciation shield which would have been provided by the "stepped up" fixed asset base are equivalent to taxes on gain.

A more controversial issue involves adjusting the cash basis accounts receivable for the effect of personal income taxes. This is a necessary adjustment in those instances where the buyer must retain the seller's zero basis in the receivables. The primary argument against this adjustment is that the accounts receivable will be offset by future expenses, and consequently taxation will be permanently deferred. This argument ignores the similar fact that as long as the practice continues, the receivable balance itself is also permanently deferred.

Income Statement Review

The objective of the income statement review is to determine the current earning capacity of the business or professional practice. This is accomplished, in part, through an examination of the income statements for several years prior to the date of valuation. As in the balance sheet analysis, adjustments must be made to the historical records to determine the true economic profit that was generated by the business. These adjustments correct distortions caused by items in the following general categories: 1) non-operating items, 2) non-recurring items, and 3) expected future deviations. After the appropriate adjustments are made, it is the general practice to use some averaging of historical results as a benchmark for the current earning capacity of the business. While history is often the most reliable indicator of the near-term future activities of the enterprise, the analyst must be aware that history is not the only indicator of the current earnings generating capacity of the business. There may be factual reasons to vary significantly from the historical operations of the business, and these should be explored.

Non-operating items include income and expenses which are not essential to the normal operations of the business or professional practice. Since the objective of income statement analysis is to determine the income from the operations of the business, unusual items should be removed from the analysis. Common examples of these items are interest and investment income, owner perquisites, and excess owner's compensation. If operating real estate was removed in the balance sheet analysis, it will be necessary to remove expenses relating to the real estate and substitute a fair rent expense. A similar adjustment may be necessary if the facilities are leased from a related party for something other than market rates. Also, many appraisers eliminate interest expense to keep the value of the business independent from its capital structure.

Non-recurring items include revenues or expenses which are either the result of unique events or outside of their normal ranges. Examples include gains or losses on the sale of assets, moving expenses, legal fees or judgments in lawsuits, and uninsured property losses.

Expected future deviations include anticipated changes from the historical level of revenue sources, access to new markets or changes in labor or other costs. These items are worthy of consideration because the objective is to estimate representative current earnings, and near-term changes are definitely relevant to the analysis.

Example: ACME Industries, Inc.

For an example of a small business valuation, we return to ACME Industries, Inc., the company that was introduced in Chapter 7. ACME Industries, Inc. is a small metal fabricating company that was formed as a California S Corporation in 1995. It operates from leased premises in San Marcos, California and it employs 14 to 18 people. The company makes metal parts for a number of customers, both on an individual order basis and several exclusive supply contracts. No customer amounts to over 15% of ACME's business. In our example, the analyst is charged with determining the fair market value of 100% of the common stock of ACME Industries at December 31, 2009 for the purpose of a community property division between the owners, Mr. and Mrs. Jones. Appendix A to this chapter is a sample appraisal report for ACME Industries along with the financial schedules and notes that present the analysis of the company at the date of valuation. Following are the "spread" balance sheets (Table 1) and income statements (Table 2) for ACME Industries, Inc. for the years 2005 through 2009.

The assigned date of valuation is December 31, 2009. In order to accomplish the appraisal task, the appraiser will begin with the balance sheet of ACME at December 31, 2009 and make the appropriate adjustments to the assets and liabilities of the business at that date. This schedule is presented as Schedule II in the appraisal report, page 182 of this text. Various adjustments are made to the tangible assets and liabilities that are presented in the corporation's balance sheet at December 31, 2009 as explained in the notes to Schedule II in the appraisal report. The result of the Net Tangible Asset analysis on Schedule II is a conclusion of "Adjusted Net Tangible Assets" of $180,000. This amount is the first component of the total value of the business, representing the "hard assets" (net of liabilities) of the business at the date of valuation.

The second part of the appraisal analysis under the Excess Earnings Method is an analysis of the company's net income to make a determination of the "representative" or "average" historical earnings to be used for valuation purposes. The Net Income Analysis is begun on Schedule III of the appraisal report, page 184, and it begins with the historical results of operations as set forth on the company's income statements. The Net Operating Income before Taxes (EBIT) is scheduled out historically from 2006 to 2009. Then, for valuation purposes, various adjustments are made to the reported amounts. Specifically, all Officer Compensation amounts are added back to the reported income because the appraisal analysis will analyze the total "net" income that is available to the owner as a step in the process. An allowance for the owner's fair compensation will be deducted in the next stage of this analysis. Second, depreciation expense, a non-cash item, is initially added back to net income as a step to determining the historical adjusted operating cash flow of the business. This permits the calculation of the total discretionary cash flow that is produced by the business. A true, economic depreciation allowance will be made after the historical income is analyzed.

Table 1 ACME INDUSTRIES, INC. Balance Sheet Spreads	12/31/2005		12/31/2006		12/31/2007		12/31/2008		12/31/2009	
Assets										
Current Assets										
Cash	$ 8,100	2.3%	$ 19,425	4.9%	$ 26,625	5.6%	$ 31,900	6.4%	$ 25,000	5.0%
Accounts Receivable	97,600	28.0%	120,300	30.1%	169,500	36.0%	187,500	37.8%	200,000	40.0%
Inventory	92,375	26.5%	113,600	28.4%	137,650	29.2%	159,600	32.1%	170,000	34.0%
Prepaid Expenses	5,600	1.6%	4,150	1.0%	2,800	0.6%	4,750	1.0%	5,000	1.0%
Total Current Assets	203,675	58.4%	257,475	64.4%	336,575	71.4%	383,750	77.3%	400,000	80.0%
Fixed Assets										
Property & Equipment	110,800	31.8%	126,500	31.6%	143,700	30.5%	143,700	28.9%	150,000	30.0%
Less: Accum. Depreciation	(32,000)	-9.2%	(46,000)	-11.5%	(67,000)	-14.2%	(85,000)	-17.1%	(100,000)	-20.0%
Total Fixed Assets	78,800	22.6%	80,500	20.1%	76,700	16.3%	58,700	11.8%	50,000	10.0%
Goodwill (Net)	66,000	18.9%	62,000	15.5%	58,000	12.3%	54,000	10.9%	50,000	10.0%
Total Assets	$ 348,475	100.0%	$ 399,975	100.0%	$471,275	100.0%	$496,450	100.0%	$ 500,000	100.0%
Liabilities & Stockholder's Equity										
Current Liabilities										
Accounts Payable	$ 91,850	26%	$ 109,450	27%	$145,600	31%	$162,500	33%	$ 150,000	30.0%
Accrued Expenses	14,500	4%	8,650	2%	21,300	5%	19,300	4%	25,000	5.0%
Total Current Liabilities	106,350	31%	118,100	30%	166,900	35%	181,800	37%	175,000	35.0%
Long Term Liabilities										
Notes Payable	$ 93,500	27%	$ 113,750	28%	$ 120,000	25%	$ 112,400	23%	$ 100,000	20.0%
Total Long Term Liabilities	93,500	27%	113,750	28%	120,000	25%	112,400	23%	100,000	20.0%
Total Liabilities	199,850	57%	231,850	58%	286,900	61%	294,200	59%	275,000	55.0%
Stockholder's Equity										
Common Stock	5,000	1%	5,000	1%	5,000	1%	5,000	1%	5,000	1.0%
Retained Earnings	143,625	41%	163,125	41%	179,375	38%	197,250	40%	220,000	44.0%
Total Stockholder's Equity	148,625	43%	168,125	42%	184,375	39%	202,250	41%	225,000	45.0%
Total Liabilities & Stockholder's Equity	$ 348,475	100%	$ 399,975	100%	$471,275	100%	$496,450	100%	$ 500,000	100.0%

It is also appropriate to neutralize the historical income statements for interest income and interest expense because these items are not operating income or expenses of the business; rather they are financing income and expense. To explain further, if the current owner is highly leveraged, he will have a high interest expense, but this expense doesn't relate to the operations of the business. Rather it relates to the financial strength (or weakness) of the present owner. In order to analyze the operating net income of the business for valuation purposes, the interest income/expense should be removed. In the case of ACME, no adjustment is necessary because the analysis begins with the company's EBIT, which is an income statement amount that is before consideration of interest income and expense. If the analysis started with ACME's final net income (after interest), an interest income/expense adjustment would be necessary.

When the historical Adjusted Operating Cash Flow of the business has been analyzed (Schedule III, page 184) for each relevant period, it is necessary to determine the Representative Operating Cash Flow to be used as the basis for the business valuation. This is the most probable level of net cash flow that the business will produce in the near future. There are various techniques which can be used for this calculation, depending on the specific situation. Trends and periods with unusually high or low levels of operating cash flow must be closely examined. In the example, the

Table 2
ACME INDUSTRIES, INC.
COMPARATIVE INCOME STATEMENTS

	December 31, 2005		December 31, 2006		December 31, 2007		December 31, 2008		December 31, 2009	
Income										
Sales	$ 966,900	100.2%	$ 1,244,200	100.3%	$1,206,600	100.5%	$ 1,373,050	100.5%	$1,367,700	100.4%
Less: Returns	(2,400)		(4,200)		(5,600)		(7,150)		(6,100)	
Total Income	964,500	100.0%	1,240,000	100.0%	1,201,000	100.0%	1,365,900	100.0%	1,361,600	100.0%
Cost of Sales										
Materials	197,500	20.5%	210,000	16.9%	200,000	16.7%	230,000	16.8%	230,000	16.9%
Cost of Labor	388,500	40.3%	425,000	34.3%	410,000	34.1%	475,000	34.8%	475,000	34.9%
Overhead	104,600	10.8%	115,000	9.3%	120,000	10.0%	125,000	9.2%	125,000	9.2%
Total Cost of Sales	690,600	71.6%	750,000	60.5%	730,000	60.8%	830,000	60.8%	830,000	61.0%
Gross Profit	273,900	28.4%	490,000	39.5%	471,000	39.2%	535,900	39.2%	531,600	39.0%
Operating Expenses										
Compensation of Officers	100,000	10.4%	221,000	17.8%	206,000	17.2%	246,000	18.0%	228,000	16.7%
Salaries and Wages	68,500	7.1%	73,500	5.9%	69,400	5.8%	76,000	5.6%	81,000	5.9%
Sales Commissions	9,650	1.0%	13,000	1.0%	12,000	1.0%	15,000	1.1%	14,000	1.0%
Repairs and Maintenance	6,100	0.6%	10,000	0.8%	9,000	0.7%	11,000	0.8%	12,500	0.9%
Rents	52,800	5.5%	60,000	4.8%	59,000	4.9%	65,000	4.8%	66,000	4.8%
Taxes and Licenses	2,000	0.2%	2,000	0.2%	2,000	0.2%	2,400	0.2%	2,600	0.2%
Amortization	4,000	0.4%	4,000	0.3%	4,000	0.3%	4,000	0.3%	4,000	0.3%
Depreciation	16,000	1.7%	14,000	1.1%	21,000	1.7%	18,000	1.3%	15,000	1.1%
Advertising	5,000	0.5%	5,000	0.4%	5,000	0.4%	6,700	0.5%	5,500	0.4%
Pension Plan Expense	0	0.0%	10,000	0.8%	10,000	0.8%	12,500	0.9%	13,500	1.0%
Other Deductions										0.0%
Auto Expenses	2,250	0.2%	3,500	0.3%	6,500	0.5%	7,500	0.5%	6,500	0.5%
Insurance	12,900	1.3%	18,800	1.5%	18,000	1.5%	21,000	1.5%	22,000	1.6%
Legal and Professional	16,500	1.7%	8,000	0.6%	7,000	0.6%	7,000	0.5%	8,000	0.6%
Office Expense	3,000	0.3%	3,000	0.2%	2,500	0.2%	3,000	0.2%	4,000	0.3%
Telephone	500	0.1%	500	0.0%	700	0.1%	1,000	0.1%	1,500	0.1%
Travel & Entertainment	950	0.1%	1,500	0.1%	1,300	0.1%	2,500	0.2%	3,000	0.2%
Utilities	8,500	0.9%	8,500	0.7%	7,500	0.6%	8,000	0.6%	7,500	0.6%
Total Operating Expenses	308,650	32.0%	456,300	36.8%	440,900	36.7%	506,600	37.1%	494,600	36.3%
Net Operating Income (EBIT)	(34,750)	-3.6%	33,700	2.7%	30,100	2.5%	29,300	2.1%	37,000	2.7%
Other Income (Expense):										
Interest Income	0	0.0%	2,500	0.2%	2,000	0.2%	5,500	0.4%	4,500	0.3%
Interest Expense	(8,220)	-0.9%	(6,200)	-0.5%	(7,100)	-0.6%	(7,300)	-0.5%	(6,500)	-0.5%
Net Income Before Taxes	(42,970)		30,000		25,000		27,500		35,000	
Tax Provision (35%)	0	0.0%	10,500	0.8%	8,750	0.7%	9,625	0.7%	12,250	0.9%
Net Income	$ (42,970)	-4.5%	$ 19,500	1.6%	$ 16,250	1.4%	$ 17,875	1.3%	$ 22,750	1.7%

adjusted operating cash flows were weight averaged. There is no absolute rule for determining this "representative" amount; it is a matter of subjective judgment, but the judgment must be reasonable in light of the facts and circumstances of the particular situation.

To reduce the Representative Operating Cash Flow to Representative Operating Net Income, an allowance for economic depreciation is subtracted. In the company's financial statements, an accounting depreciation expense was allowed, but in the valuation adjustments, that accounting depreciation was added back. At this point in the analysis, there is no provision for a real, economic depreciation of the fixed assets, and depreciation is a true cost of business operations. The depreciation adjustment should reflect future capital outlays required to maintain the tangible operating asset base. In the example, the $20,000 allowance for economic depreciation was based on an assumed average remaining asset life of five years of the fixed assets, which are valued at $100,000 on the balance sheet of the company, based on specific fixed asset appraisal. The result of this entire analysis is the estimate that the Representative Operating Net Income of ACME Industries, Inc. at December 31, 2009 is $264,000.

Excess Earnings Analysis

The Excess Earnings method, often called the formula approach, is probably the most commonly used technique for the valuation of small businesses and professional practices. When used correctly, the method provides a reliable evaluation of the tangible and intangible assets of the business. However, improper use of the method often leads to unreasonable conclusions. This has resulted in a great deal of criticism of the method.

The Excess Earnings method originated in 1920 with the publication of Appeals and Review Memorandum 34 by the U.S. Department of the Treasury. In 1968, the Internal Revenue Service updated the method in Revenue Ruling 68-609. In part the ruling states:

> The "formula" approach should not be used if there is better evidence available from which the value of intangibles can be determined. If the assets of a going business are sold upon the basis of a rate of capitalization that can be substantiated as being realistic, though it is not within the range of figures indicated here as the ones ordinarily to be adopted, the same rate of capitalization should be used in determining the value of the intangibles.

> Accordingly, the "formula" approach may be used for determining the fair market value of intangible assets of a business only if there is no better basis therefore available.

With such a guarded endorsement by the IRS, it is little wonder that valuation professionals have not always embraced the method. Still, various forms of the method are routinely employed by buyers and sellers of businesses, business brokers, accountants, and others involved in the valuation process.

The basic assumption underlying the Excess Earnings method is that profit, if any, in excess of a replacement salary for the owner and a "normal" rate of return on tangible assets is produced by intangible assets. If these "excess earnings" exist, they can be capitalized into intangible value or goodwill. The following are the general steps in the application of the Excess Earnings method.

1. Determine the value of the tangible operating assets and liabilities (Schedule II, page 182).

2. Determine the "representative" or normalized operating profit (Schedule III, page 184).

3. Determine the fair value of the owner/officer's services (Schedule IV, page 186).

4. Determine the required rates of return for the tangible operating assets. These rates are used to calculate a return on the tangible assets component which is subtracted from the representative operating profit to derive "Excess Earnings." (Schedule IV, page 186)

5. Determine the required rate of return for the intangible assets. This rate is used to calculate intangible asset value or "goodwill." (Schedule IV, page 186).

6. The total business value can then be found by combining the value of the goodwill with the Net Tangible Asset Value determined in step one (Schedule I, page 181).

The first two steps were accomplished in the review of the Balance Sheet and Income Statement presented earlier. The final steps will be explained in detail in the sections that follow.

The excess earnings method estimates the earnings of a business that are actually available to the owner and allocates them to the three factors used to produce the earnings: labor (value of owners' services), capital (return on investment), and intangible assets (goodwill). After allocating earnings to the measurable factors used to produce those earnings (labor and capital), the remainder, if any, is termed "excess earnings" and forms the basis for goodwill value. Excess earnings represent the amount of income earned by the business beyond the value of the owner's services and the capital employed in the business. Those earnings are attributable to intangible assets in the business and must be present for goodwill to exist. In the final analysis, excess earnings are capitalized to calculate the value of the intangible asset known as goodwill.

In Schedule IV (page 186) of the appraisal report, the final steps of the excess earnings analysis for ACME are performed. The Fair Value of Officer Services adjustment should be based on the fair market value of the services provided by the owner. Making this determination often becomes a subjective and controversial exercise. In some instances, the appropriate level should be based on an estimate of the compensation which would be forgone by the most probable buyer of the business. In other cases, it may be appropriate to use median compensation information obtained in surveys of owners or professional practitioners in similar circumstances. The allocation must ultimately be made in consideration of the nature of the specific business and the purpose of the appraisal.

The purpose of the fourth step in the excess earnings analysis is to determine the portion of the Representative Operating Net Income which was produced by the tangible investment in the business. The business cannot operate without a significant tangible asset investment and the opportunity cost of that investment must be charged against the Representative Operating Net Income. The Return on Tangible Assets is a function of the adjusted tangible asset value and the required rate of return on those assets.

A key issue in making this calculation concerns the appropriate asset base to use. Most descriptions of the Excess Earnings Method specify the use of Net Tangible Asset Value (NTAV), that is, total adjusted tangible assets less liabilities. However, using the NTAV inherently links the intangible value to the financial leverage employed in the firm. As mentioned earlier, a way to avoid this problem is to determine the Representative Operating Profit on a debt-free basis by adding back interest expense. When that is done, the appropriate asset base is the adjusted (tangible) capital value of the business where capital is defined as NTAV plus interest bearing debt. Alternatively, total capital can be restated as adjusted fixed assets plus working capital.

As with any required rate of return, the rate used to determine Return on Tangible Assets is dependent upon the relative risk of the investment. While it is possible to use a blended rate for the total capital investment, it is often helpful to divide the capital into two categories: first, the relatively liquid investment in working capital, and second, the investment in fixed assets. For this analysis, interest bearing debt should be removed from current liabilities prior to calculating working capital (defined as current assets minus current liabilities).

The investment in working capital is not generally subject to substantial risk. Therefore, the required rate of return for this capital should be relatively low. Yields on low-risk, fixed-income securities or the prime lending rate can be used as a proxy for this rate. The average level of working capital investment should be multiplied by the selected rate to determine the required return. If any components of working capital can be used to produce interest income, the required return should be lowered by a corresponding amount.

The investment in fixed assets is subject to a higher level of risk than working capital. The assets are usually not liquid, and their value in use is dependent upon the continued viability of the practice. Consequently, a premium above the rate for working capital is appropriate. The premium should be based on the specific nature of the fixed assets, but a range of 4% to 8% would probably encompass most situations.

Presented below is an example of the Excess Earnings Analysis, the allocation of the business's Representative Operating Net Income to the factors used to produce the income: the fair value of the officer's services and the tangible assets (capital). By subtracting the value of these factors from the net income, a determination of excess earnings is made.

Representative Operating Net Income (Schedule III)	$ 264,000
Allocations:	
Fair Value of Officer Services	(120,000)
Return on Capital	
Return on Working Capital [($360,000 - $180,000) × 10%]	(18,000)
Return on Fixed Assets [$100,000 × 15%]	(15,000)
Excess Earnings	$ 111,000

The final step in the process is to convert the "Excess Earnings" into intangible value. This requires the selection of a capitalization rate which is appropriate for the practice being valued. A common error is to blindly use the 15 to 20 percent range of rates suggested by Revenue Ruling 68-609 despite its admonition that these rates are only examples. A comprehensive evaluation of the quality, consistency, and expected duration of the excess earnings must be performed. A fair amount of subjective evaluation is necessary in this process, and, not surprisingly, a fair amount of difference exists among appraisers.

The Principle of Substitution is important in the development of this capitalization rate. That is, given the adjusted tangible operating asset value, how much more would a reasonable buyer be willing to pay to acquire the intangible assets of the business? This cannot exceed the cost of developing these assets independently. Shannon P. Pratt, in his text entitled *Valuing Small Businesses and Professional Practices*, comments: "In general, investors are not willing to pay cash up front for more than one to five years' worth of earnings from commercial goodwill, implying a range of rates from 20 percent to 100 percent to be applied to such earnings, depending on the perceived persistence of those earnings in the future, independent of further investment of time and effort to perpetuate them."[10]

These comments relate to investments in commercial businesses. Due to the various factors described earlier which limit their transferability, capitalization rates for smaller businesses and professional practices primarily fall into the highest part of this range. For highly specialized professional practices which rely heavily on referral networks or the personal reputation of the practitioner, capitalization rates of 100 percent or higher may be appropriate. The "Excess Earnings" are divided by the capitalization rate to calculate goodwill value. The goodwill value is then added to the Net Tangible Asset Value to determine the total value of the practice. This final step of the analysis can be seen in Schedule I of the ACME Industries, Inc. example, page 181 of the text.

Conclusion

This chapter introduced the principles that apply to the appraisal of all assets. We focused on small business valuation because the value of small businesses is frequently the subject of disputes between parties in the regular practice of law. Most practitioners have nowhere to look to determine this complicated problem, and a review of the excess earnings method is helpful to the practice of law. For larger business situations, the practitioner can seek the counsel of sophisticated financial consultants, but the small cases cannot afford that financial luxury. The practicing lawyer should be familiar with the basic approaches to small business valuation.

---

10.   Pratt, Shannon, *Valuing Small Businesses and Professional Practices* (Illinois: Dow Jones-Irwin, 1986).

Sample Appraisal Report

Smith & Company, Inc.
Valuation Consultants

ACME Industries, Inc.

Appraisal Report at

December 31, 2009

Smith & Company, Inc.
Valuation Consultants

February 28, 2010

John D. Black, Esq.
1000 Broadway
San Diego, CA 92101

Susan M. Green, Esq.
4000 "B" Street
San Diego, CA 92101

Dear Mr. Black and Ms. Green:

We have been asked to give our opinion of the fair market value of a 100% shareholder interest in ACME Industries, Inc. The purpose of this appraisal is to establish the fair market value of ACME Industries, Inc. at December 31, 2009 in order to assist in the division of the community assets of Mr. Jones and Ms. Jones.

In our opinion and based on recognized valuation techniques, the fair market value of ACME Industries, Inc. at December 31, 2009 is approximately $513,000. See Schedule I for valuation conclusions.

The accompanying Appraisal Report and financial analysis describes the facts and reasoning upon which our opinion is based. Our estimate of value is subject to the Assumptions and Limiting Conditions set forth in the report.

Respectfully submitted,

Smith & Company, Inc.

DESCRIPTION OF THE PROPERTY

Smith & Company, Inc. has been engaged to estimate the fair market value of a 100% shareholder interest in ACME Industries, Inc. at December 31, 2000. The business is a metal fabricating company engaged in the manufacture of steel machined parts for commercial customers in the Southern California area. The California Subchapter S corporation is operated from leased space located at 100 Main Street, San Marcos, California.

DEFINITION OF TERMS

As used in this report, "fair market value" is defined as the most probable price at which the property would change hands between a willing buyer and a willing seller, both having reasonable knowledge of the relevant facts, and neither being under any compulsion to buy or to sell.

ASSUMPTIONS AND LIMITING CONDITIONS

1. The opinion letter and accompanying text constitute our Appraisal Report. The report does not purport to be a comprehensive list of all of the considerations undertaken in order to arrive at our opinion of value.

2. This report is an appraisal report designed to give a conclusion of value. It is not an accounting report, and it should not be relied upon to disclose hidden assets or liabilities or to verify financial reporting. It is an opinion of value of the specific assets and liabilities considered by Smith & Company, Inc.

3. Smith & Company, Inc. has accepted the corporation's tax returns of ACME Industries for 2005 through 2009 and the financial statements for the same period. The financial statements have not been audited by Smith & Company, and the accuracy of the financial information is the sole responsibility of management.

4. Smith & Company, Inc. has relied on representations made by the officers of ACME Industries, Inc. about the nature and history of the entity. These representations are believed to be reliable; however, Smith & Company, Inc. assumes no responsibility for their accuracy.

5. This Appraisal Report was prepared for the use of Mr. Black and Ms. Green in connection with the community property division of Mr. Jones and Ms. Jones. No reproduction, publication, distribution, or other use of this Appraisal Report is authorized without the prior consent of Smith & Company, Inc.

6. All facts and data as set forth in this report are true and accurate to the best of the appraiser's knowledge and belief. No matters affecting the conclusions have knowingly been withheld or omitted.

7. The fee charged for this Appraisal Report is not contingent upon the conclusion of value set forth herein.

8. The appraisal and its conclusion are subject to review upon the presentation of data which may have been undisclosed or not available at this writing.

9. The text of this Appraisal Report is copyright ©2011 Smith & Company, Inc. All rights are reserved and further publication is prohibited.

10. This appraisal was prepared by and under the direction of John J. Smith. Mr. Smith is in full compliance with the requirements of the American Society of Appraisers' mandatory reaccreditation program.

STATEMENT OF DISINTEREST

Smith & Company, Inc. and its employees have no present or contemplated future interest in the subject properties of this Appraisal Report. We have no interest in or bias with respect to the subject property or the owners thereof.

OVERVIEW OF ACME INDUSTRIES, INC.

ACME Industries, Inc. was incorporated as a C Corporation on August 20, 1995 and was converted to a California Subchapter S Corporation on January 1, 1999. The entity is owned 100% by Mr. Jones and Ms. Jones. The entity operates as a metal fabricating company specializing in steel parts for the commercial trade in Southern California. The entity currently employs approximately eighteen staff members, growing from about ten employees in 1995. Presently, the firm operates from leased facilities located at 100 Main Street, San Marcos, California.

Financially, the firm's revenues have remained relatively consistent in the last few years, from $1,240,000 in 2006 to $1,361,600 in 2009. The firm's profitability has also remained relatively consistent, as shown in Schedule V.

APPRAISAL METHODS

The value of the corporation must be determined with a view toward the intrinsic value of its operating assets, the value of its income flow, and the fair market value of its saleable assets. This appraisal analysis has considered all of these elements of value in arriving at its ultimate conclusion.

Alternate valuation methods focus on different elements of value in arriving at an overall conclusion. Book value and adjusted book value are asset based methods that consider an entity's assets and liabilities as the basis for its value. Income methods, including the multiple of gross revenues, the capitalization of net income, discounted cash flow, and excess earnings methods focus on income flows as the determinant of value.

Smith & Company has considered the propriety of each of these methods in the present valuation assignment. While no single valuation method was solely relied upon to estimate the value of the entity, the Excess Earnings method was the primary analysis used and is presented in this report.

EXCESS EARNINGS ANALYSIS

Net Tangible Asset Analysis

The first component of value in the corporation is its tangible assets offset by liabilities. Schedule II presents a Statement of Assets and Liabilities for the corporation at December 31, 2009. Adjustments to the balance sheet accounts are often necessary to convert the reported Stockholder's Equity to the true economic value of the entity's net tangible assets.

As shown in Schedule II, adjustments were made to the book value of ACME Industries, Inc.'s balance sheet. The notes to Schedule II describe the information sources and the analyses used for the adjustments in detail. Our adjustments to the tangible assets at December 31, 2009 result in a conclusion of Adjusted Stockholder's Equity of $180,000, also referred to as Adjusted Net Tangible Asset Value.

Intangible Asset Analysis

The second step in applying the excess earnings model is to estimate the intangible or goodwill value of the company. Excess earnings represent the amount of income earned by the company beyond the value of the officer's services and the capital employed in the company. Those earnings are considered to be attributable to intangible assets in the company and must be present for goodwill to exist. To estimate the intangible or "goodwill" value of a business, this method allocates the earnings to the three factors used to produce them: labor (value of the officer's services), capital (return on investment), and intangible assets (goodwill). After allocating the earnings to the measurable factors used to produce those earnings (labor and capital), the remainder, if any, is termed "excess earnings," and forms the basis for goodwill.

In order to determine the possible existence of economically valuable goodwill in ACME Industries, Inc., we performed a Net Income Analysis (in Schedule III) and an Excess Earnings Analysis (in Schedule IV) for the years ended December 31, 2006 to December 31, 2009. In the Net Income Analysis, the Net Income Before Taxes (EBIT) is adjusted for various expenses to determine the true economic income earned by the corporation. The Notes to Schedule III explain the adjustments that were made to the corporation's reported income.

Schedule III then computes Representative Operating Cash Flow for the corporation as of the date of valuation. In this process the Adjusted Operating Cash Flow for the four years prior to the date of valuation was weight averaged giving the most effect to recent years, to determine Representative Operating Cash Flow of $284,000. This amount was reduced by an allowance for economic depreciation.

In Schedule IV we have undertaken an excess earnings analysis. The representative operating net income is allocated to the factors that produce that income: fair value of officer services, return on capital and excess earnings. The fair value of officer services is the amount considered necessary to replace the services performed by the owner and it is based on local compensation surveys dealing with sport manufacturing executives. A return on capital of $33,000 is allocated to the capital invested in the business. The result of the excess earnings analysis is a conclusion of excess earnings of $111,000.

The derived excess earnings are capitalized at a 33.3% capitalization rate into goodwill value of $333,000. The capitalization rate is determined based on our assessment of specific factors for ACME Industries, Inc., including the length of the establishment of the business, the trends and stability of the earnings and the transferability of the business in the marketplace. We also consulted published sources for the appropriate range of capitalization rates.

VALUATION CONCLUSIONS

The result or our analysis is a conclusion that the fair market value of a 100% shareholder interest in ACME Industries, Inc. is best represented by the sum of the Net Tangible Asset value (Adjusted Stockholder's Equity) and the Intangible Asset Value (goodwill) indicated by the excess earnings method. Therefore, in our opinion, the fair market value of 100% shareholder interest in ACME Industries, Inc. at December 31, 2009 is approximately $513,000.

Our valuation calculations are set forth in Schedules I through V, which follow:

> Schedule I   - Valuation Conclusions
> Schedule II   - Statement of Assets and Liabilities:
>   Adjusted Equity at December 31, 2009
> Schedule III   - Income Analysis
> Schedule IV   - Excess Earnings Analysis

SCHEDULE I
ACME INDUSTRIES, INC.
VALUATION CONCLUSIONS

At December 31, 2009

EXCESS EARNINGS METHOD:

Net Tangible Asset Value		
Adjusted Stockholder's Equity (Schedule II)	$	180,000
Intangible Asset Value		
Goodwill (Schedule IV)		333,000
Fair Market Value of ACME Industries, Inc.		
at December 31, 2009	$	513,000

SCHEDULE II
ACME INDUSTRIES, INC.
NET TANGIBLE ASSET ANALYSIS

	At December 31, 2009		
	Balance Sheet	Adjustments (See Notes)	Balance for Valuation
Assets			
Current Assets			
Cash	$ 25,000		$ 25,000
Accounts Receivable	200,000	(30,000) [1]	170,000
Inventory	170,000	(10,000) [2]	160,000
Prepaid Expenses	5,000		5,000
Total Current Assets	400,000		360,000
Fixed Assets			
Property & Equipment	150,000	(50,000) [3]	100,000
Less: Accum. Depreciation	(100,000)	100,000 [4]	-
Total Fixed Assets	50,000		100,000
Goodwill (Net)	50,000	(50,000) [5]	-
Total Assets	$ 500,000		$ 460,000
Liabilities & Stockholder's Equity			
Current Liabilities			
Accounts Payable	$ 150,000		$ 150,000
Accrued Expenses	25,000	5,000 [6]	30,000
Total Current Liabilities	175,000		180,000
Long Term Liabilities			
Notes Payable	$ 100,000		$ 100,000
Total Long Term Liabilities	100,000		100,000
Total Liabilities	275,000		280,000
Stockholder's Equity			
Common Stock	5,000		
Retained Earnings	220,000	Derived	
Total Stockholder's Equity	225,000		180,000
Total Liabilities			
& Stockholder's Equity	$ 500,000		$ 460,000
	Adjusted Net Tangible Asset Value:		$ 180,000

NOTES TO SCHEDULE II

1. The gross Accounts Receivable balance was reduced for estimated uncollectible accounts based on the collection experience of the business.

2. After visual inspection of the inventory, an adjustment was made to reduce the inventory value for obsolete items.

3. John Doe & Associates, Ltd. provided the fair market value in use of the Fixed Assets.

4. The accumulated depreciation has been removed in connection with the adjustment for the Fixed Assets to their estimated fair market values.

5. The purpose of Schedule II is to determine the Net Tangible Asset Value of the entity. Therefore, the book value of intangible assets has been removed. The fair market value of the intangible assets will be estimated in a later section of this report.

6. The represented amount was necessary to adjust for a liability that was previously not reported on the balance sheet.

SCHEDULE III
ACME INDUSTRIES, INC.
NET INCOME ANALYSIS

	Notes:	Fiscal Year Ending			
		12/31/06	12/31/07	12/31/08	12/31/09
Income Analysis:					
Total Income		$ 1,240,000	$ 1,201,000	$ 1,365,900	$ 1,361,600
Less: Cost of Sales		(750,000)	(730,000)	(830,000)	(830,000)
Gross Profit		490,000	471,000	535,900	531,600
Less: Total Operating Expenses		(456,300)	(440,900)	(506,600)	(494,600)
Net Operating Income before Taxes (EBIT)	[1]	33,700	30,100	29,300	37,000
Adjustments					
Officer Compensation	[2]	221,000	206,000	246,000	228,000
Depreciation	[3]	14,000	21,000	18,000	15,000
Interest Expense	[4]	-	-	-	-
Interest Income	[4]	-	-	-	-
Shareholder Perks	[5]	3,500	4,500	7,000	5,000
Total Adjustments		238,500	231,500	271,000	248,000
Adjusted Operating Cash Flow		$ 272,200	$ 261,600	$ 300,300	$ 285,000
% of Gross Sales		22.0%	21.8%	22.0%	20.9%

	Notes:	
Representative Operating Cash Flow	[6]	$ 284,000
Less: Economic Depreciation	[7]	(20,000)
Representative Operating Net Income		$ 264,000

NOTES TO SCHEDULE III

1. The source of the company's reported pre-tax income figures are the internal financial statements for the years ended December 31, 2006, 2007, 2008 and 2009. The documents are believed to be reliable but no responsibility for their accuracy is assumed by Smith & Company, Inc.

2. Based on recognized valuation techniques, Officer Compensation has been added back to reported pre-tax income. An allowance for replacing the services of the officer will be provided at a later point in the analysis.

3. 100% of the depreciation expense was added back to reported pre-tax income to determine Adjusted Operating Cash Flow. An estimate of future economic depreciation is deducted at a later point in the analysis.

4. Interest Income and Expense is considered to be a financing rather than an operating expense of the business. However, no adjustment is necessary for ACME because we have begun our analysis with Net Operating Income (EBIT). EBIT is calculated before interest income or expense, so no adjustment is required.

5. The represented amounts per year represents discretionary shareholder perks rather than operating expenses and have been added back to determine Adjusted Operating Cash Flow.

6. The Adjusted Operating Cash Flow for the four years prior to the date of valuation was weight averaged giving the most effect to recent years. In this analysis, a weighting of 1,2,3 and 4 was applied to the Adjusted Operating Cash Flow for the years 2006, 2007, 2008 and 2009, respectively. The result of the calculation is an estimate of Representative Operating Cash Flow of $284,000 (rounded).

7. Because 100% of the historical depreciation expense was added back in the Cash Flow Analysis, it is necessary to provide an allowance for the actual economic depreciation for the fixed assets. This allowance was based on an estimated average remaining useful life of five years.

SCHEDULE IV
ACME INDUSTRIES, INC.
EXCESS EARNINGS ANALYSIS

Representative Operating Net Income (Schedule III)	$	264,000
Allocations:		
Fair Value of Officer Services (Note 1)		(120,000)
Return on Capital (Note 2)		(33,000)
Excess Earnings	$	111,000
Capitalization Rate (Note 3)	÷	33.3%
Estimated Goodwill Value	$	333,000

NOTES TO SCHEDULE IV

1. In order to properly analyze the excess earnings of the entity, it is necessary to estimate the value of the owner's services that are rendered in exchange for the net income generated. Although this step in the analysis cannot be undertaken with exact precision, we have consulted several sources of compensation data for this industry. Based on the data we consulted reasonable compensation necessary to replace the services performed by the owner ranges from $100,000 to $140,000, therefore, we have used $120,000 for fair compensation for officer services.

2. Under the capitalization of excess earnings method, it is necessary to attribute part of the Representative Operating Net Income to a return on the capital employed in the business. A 10% return has been assigned to the working capital (current assets of $360,000 minus total current liabilities of $180,000) and a 15% return was assigned to the fixed assets. The total adjustment for Return on Capital is $33,000.

3. The capitalization rate is the rate by which excess earnings are converted into intangible asset value. The appropriate capitalization rates for the excess earnings of most businesses generally range from 20% (5.0 X) to 100.0% (1.0 X) of the measurable excess earnings stream (see Pratt, Valuing Small Businesses and Professional Practices, Business One Irwin, 1993). A capitalization rate of 33.3% (3.0 X) was considered appropriate for the excess earnings produced by ACME Industries, Inc. For ACME Industries, we considered the length of the establishment of the business, the trends and stability of the earnings, and the transferability of the business in the marketplace in arriving at a capitalization rate of 33.3%.

IRS Revenue Rulings

IRS Revenue Ruling 59-60

Rev. Rul. 59-60, 1959-1 CB 237 -- IRC Sec. 2031 (Also Section 2512.) (Also Part II, Sections 811(k), 1005, Regulations 105, Section 81.10.)

Reference(s): Code Sec. 2031 Reg § 20.2031-2

In valuing the stock of closely held corporations, or the stock of corporations where market quotations are not available, all other available financial data, as well as all relevant factors affecting the fair market value must be considered for estate tax and gift tax purposes. No general formula may be given that is applicable to the many different valuation situations arising in the valuation of such stock. However, the general approach, methods, and factors which must be considered in valuing such securities are outlined.

Revenue Ruling 54-77, C.B. 1954-1, 187, superseded.

Full Text:

Section 1. Purpose.

The purpose of this Revenue Ruling is to outline and review in general the approach, methods and factors to be considered in valuing shares of the capital stock of closely held corporations for estate tax and gift tax purposes. The methods discussed herein will apply likewise to the valuation of corporate stocks on which market quotations are either unavailable or are of such scarcity that they do not reflect the fair market value.

Sec. 2. Background and Definitions.

.01 All valuations must be made in accordance with the applicable provisions of the Internal Revenue Code of 1954 and the Federal Estate Tax and Gift Tax Regulations. Sections 2031(a), 2032 and 2512(a) of the 1954 Code (sections 811 and 1005 of the 1939 Code) require that the property to be included in the gross estate, or made the subject of a gift, shall be taxed on the basis of the value of the property at the time of death of the decedent, the alternate date if so elected, or the date of gift.

.02 Section 20.2031-1(b) of the Estate Tax Regulations (section 81.10 of the Estate Tax Regulations 105) and section 25.2512-1 of the Gift Tax Regulations (section 86.19 of Gift Tax Regulations

108) define fair market value, in effect, as the price at which the property would change hands between a willing buyer and a willing seller when the former is not under any compulsion to buy and the latter is not under any compulsion to sell, both parties having reasonable knowledge of relevant facts. Court decisions frequently state in addition that the hypothetical buyer and seller are assumed to be able, as well as willing, to trade and to be well informed about the property and concerning the market for such property.

.03 Closely held corporations are those corporations the shares of which are owned by a relatively limited number of stockholders. Often the entire stock issue is held by one family. The result of this situation is that little, if any, trading in the shares takes place. There is, therefore, no established market for the stock and such sales as occur at irregular intervals seldom reflect all of the elements of a representative transaction as defined by the term "fair market value."

Sec. 3. Approach to Valuation.

.01 A determination of fair market value, being a question of fact, will depend upon the circumstances in each case. No formula can be devised that will be generally applicable to the multitude of different valuation issues arising in estate and gift tax cases. Often, an appraiser will find wide differences of opinion as to the fair market value of a particular stock. In resolving such differences, he should maintain a reasonable attitude in recognition of the fact that valuation is not an exact science. A sound valuation will be based upon all the relevant facts, but the elements of common sense, informed judgment and reasonableness must enter into the process of weighing those facts and determining their aggregate significance.

.02 The fair market value of specific shares of stock will vary as general economic conditions change from "normal" to "boom" or "depression," that is, according to the degree of optimism or pessimism with which the investing public regards the future at the required date of appraisal. Uncertainty as to the stability or continuity of the future income from a property decreases its value by increasing the risk of loss of earnings and value in the future. The value of shares of stock of a company with very uncertain future prospects is highly speculative. The appraiser must exercise his judgment as to the degree of risk attaching to the business of the corporation which issued the stock, but that judgment must be related to all of the other factors affecting value.

.03 Valuation of securities is, in essence, a prophesy as to the future and must be based on facts available at the required date of appraisal. As a generalization, the prices of stocks which are traded in volume in a free and active market by informed persons best reflect the consensus of the investing public as to what the future holds for the corporations and industries represented. When a stock is closely held, is traded infrequently, or is traded in an erratic market, some other measure of value must be used. In many instances, the next best measure may be found in the prices at which the stocks of companies engaged in the same or a similar line of business are selling in a free and open market.

Sec. 4. Factors To Consider.

.01 It is advisable to emphasize that in the valuation of the stock of closely held corporations or the stock of corporations where market quotations are either lacking or too scarce to be recognized, all available financial data, as well as all relevant factors affecting the fair market value, should be considered. The following factors, although not all- inclusive are fundamental and require careful analysis in each case:

(a) The nature of the business and the history of the enterprise from its inception.

(b) The economic outlook in general and the condition and outlook of the specific industry in particular.

(c) The book value of the stock and the financial condition of the business.

(d) The earning capacity of the company.

(e) The dividend-paying capacity.

(f) Whether or not the enterprise has goodwill or other intangible value.

(g) Sales of the stock and the size of the block of stock to be valued.

(h) The market price of stocks of corporations engaged in the same or a similar line of business having their stocks actively traded in a free and open market, either on an exchange or over-the-counter.

.02 The following is a brief discussion of each of the foregoing factors:

(a) The history of a corporate enterprise will show its past stability or instability, its growth or lack of growth, the diversity or lack of diversity of its operations, and other facts needed to form an opinion of the degree of risk involved in the business. For an enterprise which changed its form of organization but carried on the same or closely similar operations of its predecessor, the history of the former enterprise should be considered. The detail to be considered should increase with approach to the required date of appraisal, since recent events are of greatest help in predicting the future; but a study of gross and net income, and of dividends covering a long prior period, is highly desirable. The history to be studied should include, but need not be limited to, the nature of the business, its products or services, its operating and investment assets, capital structure, plant facilities, sales records and management, all of which should be considered as of the date of the appraisal, with due regard for recent significant changes. Events of the past that are unlikely to recur in the future should be discounted, since value has a close relation to future expectancy.

(b) A sound appraisal of a closely held stock must consider current and prospective economic conditions as of the date of appraisal, both in the national economy and in the industry or industries with which the corporation is allied. It is important to know that the company is more or less successful than its competitors in the same industry, or that it is maintaining a stable position with respect to competitors.

Equal or even greater significance may attach to the ability of the industry with which the company is allied to compete with other industries. Prospective competition which has not been a factor in prior years should be given careful attention. For example, high profits due to the novelty of its product and the lack of competition often lead to increasing competition. The public's appraisal of the future prospects of competitive industries or of competitors within an industry may be indicated by price trends in the markets for commodities and for securities. The loss of the manager of a so-called "one-man" business may have a depressing effect upon the value of the stock of such business, particularly if there is a lack of trained personnel capable of succeeding to the management of the enterprise. In valuing the stock of this type of business, therefore, the effect of the loss of the manager on the future expectancy of the business, and the absence of management-succession potentialities are pertinent factors to be taken into consideration. On the other hand, there may be factors which offset, in whole or in part, the loss of the manager's services. For instance, the nature of the business and of its assets may be such that they will not be impaired by the loss of the manager. Furthermore, the loss may be adequately covered by life insurance, or competent management might be employed on the basis of the consideration paid for the former manager's services.

These, or other offsetting factors, if found to exist, should be carefully weighed against the loss of the manager's services in valuing the stock of the enterprise.

(c) Balance sheets should be obtained, preferably in the form of comparative annual statements for two or more years immediately preceding the date of appraisal, together with a balance sheet at the end of the month preceding that date, if corporate accounting will permit. Any balance sheet descriptions that are not self-explanatory, and balance sheet items comprehending diverse assets or liabilities, should be clarified in essential detail by supporting supplemental schedules. These statements usually will disclose to the appraiser (1) liquid position (ratio of current assets to current liabilities); (2) gross and net book value of principal classes of fixed assets; (3) working capital; (4) long-term indebtedness; (5) capital structure; and (6) net worth. Consideration also should be given to any assets not essential to the operation of the business, such as investments in securities, real estate, etc. In general, such nonoperating assets will command a lower rate of return than do the operating assets, although in exceptional cases the reverse may be true. In computing the book value per share of stock, assets of the investment type should be revalued on the basis of their market price and the book value adjusted accordingly. Comparison of the company's balance sheets over several years may reveal, among other facts, such developments as the acquisition of additional production facilities or subsidiary companies, improvement in financial position, and details as to recapitalizations and other changes in the capital structure of the corporation. If the corporation has more than one class of stock outstanding, the charter or certificate of incorporation should be examined to ascertain the explicit rights and privileges of the various stock issues including: (1) voting powers, (2) preference as to dividends, and (3) preference as to assets in the event of liquidation.

(d) Detailed profit-and-loss statements should be obtained and considered for a representative period immediately prior to the required date of appraisal, preferably five or more years. Such statements should show (1) gross income by principal items; (2) principal deductions from gross income including major prior items of operating expenses, interest and other expense on each item of long-term debt, depreciation and depletion if such deductions are made, officers' salaries, in total if they appear to be reasonable or in detail if they seem to be excessive, contributions (whether or not deductible for tax purposes) that the nature of its business and its community position require the corporation to make, and taxes by principal items, including income and excess profits taxes; (3) net income available for dividends; (4) rates and amounts of dividends paid on each class of stock; (5) remaining amount carried to surplus; and (6) adjustments to, and reconciliation with, surplus as stated on the balance sheet. With profit and loss statements of this character available, the appraiser should be able to separate recurrent from nonrecurrent items of income and expense, to distinguish between operating income and investment income, and to ascertain whether or not any line of business in which the company is engaged is operated consistently at a loss and might be abandoned with benefit to the company. The percentage of earnings retained for business expansion should be noted when dividend-paying capacity is considered. Potential future income is a major factor in many valuations of closely-held stocks, and all information concerning past income which will be helpful in predicting the future should be secured. Prior earnings records usually are the most reliable guide as to the future expectancy, but resort to arbitrary five-or-ten-year averages without regard to current trends or future prospects will not produce a realistic valuation. If, for instance, a record of progressively increasing or decreasing net income is found, then greater weight may be accorded the most recent years' profits in estimating earning power. It will be helpful, in judging risk and the extent to which a business is a marginal operator, to consider deductions from income and net income in terms of percentage of sales. Major categories of cost and expense to be so analyzed include the consumption of raw materials and supplies in the case of manufacturers, processors and fabricators; the cost of purchased merchandise in the case of merchants; utility services; insurance; taxes; depletion or depreciation; and interest.

(e) Primary consideration should be given to the dividend-paying capacity of the company rather than to dividends actually paid in the past. Recognition must be given to the necessity of retaining a reasonable portion of profits in a company to meet competition. Dividend-paying capacity is a factor that must be considered in an appraisal, but dividends actually paid in the past may not have any relation to dividend-paying capacity. Specifically, the dividends paid by a closely held family company may be measured by the income needs of the stockholders or by their desire to avoid taxes on dividend receipts, instead of by the ability of the company to pay dividends. Where an actual or effective controlling interest in a corporation is to be valued, the dividend factor is not a material element, since the payment of such dividends is discretionary with the controlling stockholders. The individual or group in control can substitute salaries and bonuses for dividends, thus reducing net income and understating the dividend-paying capacity of the company. It follows, therefore, that dividends are less reliable criteria of fair market value than other applicable factors.

(f) In the final analysis, goodwill is based upon earning capacity. The presence of goodwill and its value, therefore, rests upon the excess of net earnings over and above a fair return on the net tangible assets.

While the element of goodwill may be based primarily on earnings, such factors as the prestige and renown of the business, the ownership of a trade or brand name, and a record of successful operation over a prolonged period in a particular locality, also may furnish support for the inclusion of intangible value. In some instances it may not be possible to make a separate appraisal of the tangible and intangible assets of the business. The enterprise has a value as an entity. Whatever intangible value there is, which is supportable by the facts, may be measured by the amount by which the appraised value of the tangible assets exceeds the net book value of such assets.

(g) Sales of stock of a closely held corporation should be carefully investigated to determine whether they represent transactions at arm's length. Forced or distress sales do not ordinarily reflect fair market value nor do isolated sales in small amounts necessarily control as the measure of value. This is especially true in the valuation of a controlling interest in a corporation. Since, in the case of closely held stocks, no prevailing market prices are available, there is no basis for making an adjustment for blockage. It follows, therefore, that such stocks should be valued upon a consideration of all the evidence affecting the fair market value. The size of the block of stock itself is a relevant factor to be considered. Although it is true that a minority interest in an unlisted corporation's stock is more difficult to sell than a similar block of listed stock, it is equally true that control of a corporation, either actual or in effect, representing as it does an added element of value, may justify a higher value for a specific block of stock.

(h) Section 2031(b) of the Code states, in effect, that in valuing unlisted securities the value of stock or securities of corporations engaged in the same or a similar line of business which are listed on an exchange should be taken into consideration along with all other factors. An important consideration is that the corporations to be used for comparisons have capital stocks which are actively traded by the public. In accordance with section 2031(b) of the Code, stocks listed on an exchange are to be considered first. However, if sufficient comparable companies whose stocks are listed on an exchange cannot be found, other comparable companies which have stocks actively traded in on the over-the-counter market also may be used. The essential factor is that whether the stocks are sold on an exchange or over-the-counter there is evidence of an active, free public market for the stock as of the valuation date. In selecting corporations for comparative purposes, care should be taken to use only comparable companies. Although the only restrictive requirement as to comparable corporations specified in the statute is that their lines of business be the same or similar, yet it is obvious that consideration must be given to other relevant factors in order that the most valid comparison possible will be obtained. For illustration, a corporation having one or more issues of preferred stock, bonds or debentures in addition to its common stock should not be considered to be directly comparable to one having only common stock outstanding. In like manner, a company with a declining business and decreasing markets is not comparable to one with a record of current progress and market expansion.

Sec. 5. Weight To Be Accorded Various Factors.

The valuation of closely held corporate stock entails the consideration of all relevant factors as stated in section 4. Depending upon the circumstances in each case, certain factors may carry more weight than others because of the nature of the company's business. To illustrate:

(a) Earnings may be the most important criterion of value in some cases whereas asset value will receive primary consideration in others. In general, the appraiser will accord primary consideration to earnings when valuing stocks of companies which sell products or services to the public; conversely, in the investment or holding type of company, the appraiser may accord the greatest weight to the assets underlying the security to be valued.

(b) The value of the stock of a closely held investment or real estate holding company, whether or not family owned, is closely related to the value of the assets underlying the stock. For companies of this type the appraiser should determine the fair market values of the assets of the company. Operating expenses of such a company and the cost of liquidating it, if any, merit consideration when appraising the relative values of the stock and the underlying assets. The market values of the underlying assets give due weight to potential earnings and dividends of the particular items of property underlying the stock, capitalized at rates deemed proper by the investing public at the date of appraisal. A current appraisal by the investing public should be superior to the retrospective opinion of an individual. For these reasons, adjusted net worth should be accorded greater weight in valuing the stock of a closely held investment or real estate holding company, whether or not family owned, than any of the other customary yardsticks of appraisal, such as earnings and dividend paying capacity.

Sec. 6. Capitalization Rates.

In the application of certain fundamental valuation factors, such as earnings and dividends, it is necessary to capitalize the average or current results at some appropriate rate. A determination of the proper capitalization rate presents one of the most difficult problems in valuation. That there is no ready or simple solution will become apparent by a cursory check of the rates of return and dividend yields in terms of the selling prices of corporate shares listed on the major exchanges of the country. Wide variations will be found even for companies in the same industry. Moreover, the ratio will fluctuate from year to year depending upon economic conditions. Thus, no standard tables of capitalization rates applicable to closely held corporations can be formulated. Among the more important factors to be taken into consideration in deciding upon a capitalization rate in a particular case are: (1) the nature of the business; (2) the risk involved; and (3) the stability or irregularity of earnings.

Sec. 7. Average of Factors.

Because valuations cannot be made on the basis of a prescribed formula, there is no means whereby the various applicable factors in a particular case can be assigned mathematical weights in deriving the fair market value. For this reason, no useful purpose is served by taking an average of several factors (for example, book value, capitalized earnings and capitalized dividends) and basing the valuation on the result.

Such a process excludes active consideration of other pertinent factors, and the end result cannot be supported by a realistic application of the significant facts in the case except by mere chance.

Sec. 8. Restrictive Agreements.

Frequently, in the valuation of closely held stock for estate and gift tax purposes, it will be found that the stock is subject to an agreement restricting its sale or transfer. Where shares of stock were acquired by a decedent subject to an option reserved by the issuing corporation to repurchase at a certain price, the option price is usually accepted as the fair market value for estate tax purposes. See Rev. Rul. 54-76, C.B. 1954-1, 194. However, in such case the option price is not determinative of fair market value for gift tax purposes.

Where the option, or buy and sell agreement, is the result of voluntary action by the stockholders and is binding during the life as well as at the death of the stockholders, such agreement may or may not, depending upon the circumstances of each case, fix the value for estate tax purposes. However, such agreement is a factor to be considered, with other relevant factors, in determining fair market value. Where the stockholder is free to dispose of his shares during life and the option is to become effective only upon his death, the fair market value is not limited to the option price. It is always necessary to consider the relationship of the parties, the relative number of shares held by the decedent, and other material facts, to determine whether the agreement represents a bonafide business arrangement or is a device to pass the decedent's shares to the natural objects of his bounty for less than an adequate and full consideration in money or money's worth. In this connection see Rev. Rul. 157 C.B. 1953-2, 255, and Rev. Rul. 189, C.B. 1953-2, 294.

Sec. 9. Effect on Other Documents.

Revenue Ruling 54-77, C.B. 1954-1, 187, is hereby superseded.

Rev. Rul. 68-609

1968-2 C.B. 327

IRS Headnote

The `formula' approach may be used in determining the fair market value of intangible assets of a business only if there is no better basis available for making the determination; A.R.M. 34, A.R.M. 68, O.D. 937, and Revenue Ruling 65-192 superseded. Ruling is to update and restate, under the current statute and regulations, the currently outstanding portions the currently outstanding portions of A.R.M. 34, C.B. 2, 31 (1920), A.R.M. 68, C.B. 3, 43 (1920), and O.D. 937, C.B. 4, 43 (1921).

Full Text

Rev. Rul. 68-609 /1/

The question presented is whether the `formula' approach, the capitalization of earnings in excess of a fair rate of return on net tangible assets, may be used to determine the fair market value of the intangible assets of a business

The `formula' approach may be stated as follows:

A percentage return on the average annual value of the tangible assets used in a business is determined, using a period of years (preferably not less than five) immediately prior to the valuation date. The amount of the percentage return on tangible assets, thus determined, is deducted from the average earnings of the business for such period and the remainder, if any, is considered to be the amount of the average annual earnings from the intangible assets of the business for the period. This amount (considered as the average annual earnings from intangibles), capitalized at a percentage of, say, 15 to 20 percent, is the value of the intangible assets of the business determined under the `formula' approach.

The percentage of return on the average annual value of the tangible assets used should be the percentage prevailing in the industry involved at the date of valuation, or (when the industry percentage is not available) a percentage of 8 to 10 percent may be used.

The 8 percent rate of return and the 15 percent rate of capitalization are applied to tangibles and intangibles, respectively, of businesses with a small risk factor and stable and regular earnings; the 10 percent rate of return and 20 percent rate of capitalization are applied to businesses in which the hazards of business are relatively high.

The above rates are used as examples and are not appropriate in all cases. In applying the `formula' approach, the average earnings period and the capitalization rates are dependent upon the facts pertinent thereto in each case.

The past earnings to which the formula is applied should fairly reflect the probable future earnings. Ordinarily, the period should not be less than five years, and abnormal years, whether above or below the average, should be eliminated. If the business is a sole proprietorship or partnership, there should be deducted from the earnings of the business a reasonable amount for services performed by the owner or partners engaged in the business. See Lloyd B.

Sanderson Estate v. Commissioner , 42 F.2d 160 (1930). Further, only the tangible assets entering into net worth, including accounts and bills receivable in excess of accounts and bills payable, are used for determining earnings on the tangible assets. Factors that influence the capitalization rate include (1) the nature of the business, (2) the risk involved, and (3) the stability or irregularity of earnings.

The `formula' approach should not be used if there is better evidence available from which the value of intangibles can be determined. If the assets of a going business are sold upon the basis of a rate of capitalization that can be substantiated as being realistic, though it is not within the range of figures indicated here as the ones ordinarily to be adopted, the same rate of capitalization should be used in determining the value of intangibles.

Accordingly, the `formula' approach may be used for determining the fair market value of intangible assets of a business only if there is no better basis therefor available.

See also Revenue Ruling 59-60, C.B. 1959-1, 237, as modified by Revenue Ruling 65-193, C.B. 1965-2, 370, which sets forth the proper approach to use in the valuation of closely-held corporate stocks for estate and gift tax purposes. The general approach, methods, and factors, outlined in Revenue Ruling 59-60, as modified, are equally applicable to valuations of corporate stocks for income and other tax purposes as well as for estate and gift tax purposes. They apply also to problems involving the determination of the fair market value of business interests of any type, including partnerships and proprietorships, and of intangible assets for all tax purposes.

A.R.M. 34, A.R.M. 68, and O.D. 937 are superseded, since the positions set forth therein are restated to the extent applicable under current law in this Revenue Ruling. Revenue Ruling 65-192, C.B. 1965-2, 259, which contained restatements of A.R.M. 34 and A.R.M. 68, is also superseded.

/1/ Prepared pursuant to Rev. Proc. 67-6, C.B. 1967-1, 576.

Chapter 10

Damages

Introduction

Monetary damages are one of the remedies that a court may award to a plaintiff to compensate him or her for the wrongful conduct of the defendant. Monetary damages, or simply "damages," are financial compensation claimed by or paid to the plaintiff to attempt to make him whole, after the wrong committed by the defendant or to return him to the *status quo ante*, the way he was before the wrong occurred. Damages, especially the calculation of damages, are one of the most contentious areas of the litigation process and represent the area in which accounting and financial judgment is most frequently required to be involved.

Damages are a remedy available to a plaintiff as a result of a defendant's commission of a tort or a breach of contract. In tort, a plaintiff is entitled to be compensated for all damages proximately caused by a defendant's wrongful conduct. In contract, the plaintiff is entitled to recover everything that he anticipated to receive under the contract, as well as any additional damages that could have reasonably been foreseen. These concepts are very understandable in the abstract, but it is the application of the concepts that presents significant difficulty. There are thousands of pages of cases and scholarly treatises that discuss the nuances of the concepts of damages and proximate cause, but a relatively small amount of this literature is clearly dedicated to the details of calculating damages. Unfortunately, the damages analyst is forced to rely on legal abstractions as the highest authority for guidance on damages calculations, with limited direction from the accounting or finance communities.

Damages are only one of the remedies to which a plaintiff may be entitled in a particular case. Other remedies, which are not discussed in this chapter except to define them, include rescission, restitution and specific performance. Rescission is the remedy that places both parties back in the same situation that they were in before the wrongful act. Restitution requires a defendant to restore all of his ill-gotten gains to the plaintiff. Specific performance, a contract remedy, requires that the defendant do exactly what was promised in the contract, for instance, transferring the title to a promised parcel of land, rather than just paying money (damages) for the breach of the contract. There is no question that accounting analysis may be required to effectuate any or all of the other civil remedies, but the focus of this section of study will be damages.

Definition of Damages

In law, damages are money claimed by, or ordered to be paid to, a person as compensation for loss or injury.[1] Damages are the financial compensation that is awarded to a plaintiff as a result of a defendant's misconduct. Damages are the monetary amount that is intended to "make the plaintiff whole" after suffering the harm caused by the defendant.

---

1. *Black's Law Dictionary.*

By definition, damages are only a monetary measure; sometimes they are used to measure a financial harm, and other times they must be used to measure a problem that has both a financial and a nonfinancial component (a bodily injury or a wrongful death). Because the concept of damages is so broad, it is easy to see that there are many aspects of damages that cannot be handled with simple formulae or rote calculations. Damages analysis is the "thinking person's" accounting, and it involves a blending of financial and legal theory. In some situations, the marriage of the theories is a happy one, while in others it is tumultuous.

Legal Concepts Underlying Damages[2]

In tort law, the fundamental legal principle underlying damages is to "make the plaintiff whole" after suffering the wrongful conduct of the defendant. The plaintiff is entitled to be compensated for all damages proximately caused by a defendant's wrongful conduct. **In contract,** the law attempts to give the plaintiff exactly what was promised in the breached contract plus additional foreseen damages. Where damages are economic, as opposed to noneconomic, a damages analysis compares the difference between plaintiff's economic position if the harmful event had not occurred with the plaintiff's actual economic position, given that the harmful event did occur. The first part of the damages calculation is often called the "but-for" analysis or projection; it is an estimate of the plaintiff's situation assuming the wrongful conduct had not occurred. The second part of the calculation compares the but-for projection to the plaintiff's actual situation given the occurrence of the harmful event. Ultimately, damages are the net economic loss suffered by the plaintiff resulting from the difference between the plaintiff's but-for situation and the plaintiff's actual situation.

The intention of the legal principles underlying damages is certainly noble, but the application of them can be very challenging due to the degree of estimation required and the uncertainty of future events that could alter eventual outcomes. The number of ways in which a plaintiff can be harmed from a defendant's misconduct is countless, and it soon becomes obvious that there are many, many ways to approach a financial measurement of the damages resulting from the harmful act. The focus of the damages chapters of this textbook will be to cover the more conventional, acceptable methods of calculating damages. Damage calculations must conform to the law of the particular jurisdiction as well as recognized financial and economic principles.

Proximate Cause. Recovery of damages is subject to the legal principle that damages must be proximately caused by the wrongful conduct of the defendant. This principle governs the recovery of all compensatory damages, whether the underlying claim is based on contract, tort or both. It is fair to say that there is no absolute definition of proximate cause that will dictate a hard and fast rule to define the connection between the damages and the wrongful conduct, or a clear ending point to a damage calculation; the application of this principle to a particular situation must be addressed on a case-by-case basis.

---

2. Dunn, Robert L., *Recovery of Damages for Lost Profits*, 6th Ed. (Westport, CT: Lawpress Corporation, 2005). Mr. Dunn's treatise on damages is comprehensive and authoritative; it is a "must read" for all students of damages. In the discussion of the legal concepts of damages, I have summarized certain legal aspects from Mr. Dunn's fine work.

In practical terms, the concept of proximate cause requires that the harm suffered, for which damages compensate, be logically connected—and relatively closely connected—to the defendant's act. If a defendant damages a plaintiff's car, it is very logical that costs to repair the car are damages proximately caused by the defendant's conduct. The logic of proximate cause could also be easily extended to damages for the cost of renting a replacement vehicle while the damaged car is being repaired. Possibly, the plaintiff could claim lost wages for a day or two because he could not get to work while the car was being repaired, before he could rent a replacement. But what if the plaintiff claims that he couldn't get to work and, as a result, he lost the commission on a sale that he could have made to a major customer? Further, because he didn't make the commission that he expected to make, he was not able to invest in a stock that his broker wanted him to buy, and the stock went up 100% since the day he missed work because his car was being repaired.

Do you get the picture? There is no absolute rule that defines where proximate cause ends, but the loss must be "proximately caused" by the wrongful conduct of the defendant. Lawyers will argue what constitutes proximate cause and what is outside of proximate cause, but the financial expert should be mindful that there must be a reasonable nexus between the damages as calculated and the wrongful act of the defendant.

Reasonable Certainty. A second legal principle that governs the calculation of damages is the general requirement that damages be proven with "reasonable certainty." As a general statement, however, most courts have recognized that the rule applies only to the fact of damages, not to the amount of damages. Courts seem to hold an injured plaintiff to a lower standard for showing the *precision* of a damage calculation, as long as the plaintiff can show that damages have actually occurred. As a practical matter, this lessens the burden on the plaintiff to show exact or precise measures of harm; it appears that reasonable estimates or approximations will suffice. The allowance of a lower standard of precision should not be interpreted to mean that damages may be speculative, because speculation is always below a legally permissible standard.

Duty to Mitigate. All plaintiffs have a duty to mitigate their damages, although the exact extent of the duty is vaguely defined in the law. In general, the responsibility to mitigate, or minimize, damages means that the aggrieved party cannot passively sit back and allow damages to accumulate without undertaking some responsibility to lessen them. If a person is injured and cannot perform the functions of his job post-injury, the law assigns him the responsibility of seeking and attempting to perform a lesser job based on his current capacity as opposed to not working and claiming his entire loss from the defendants. A business that is harmed by a breach of contract cannot claim continuing lost profits without attempting to cover those losses by other, alternative activities. The effect of the duty to mitigate is to limit a plaintiff's damages to the amount of his total loss of earnings minus his mitigating earnings.

Collateral Source Rule. In contrast to the concept of mitigation, there are some circumstances where a plaintiff is entitled to recover the full measure of his damages from the defendant, regardless of the fact that the plaintiff may have been compensated for his loss from another source. The collateral source rule is a rule of evidence that prohibits the defendant from showing that the plaintiff has been compensated for his loss from another source, usually insurance. This rule is supported by public policy: the law seeks to encourage citizens to adequately insure themselves, and limiting a plaintiff's recovery based on his prudence would unfairly benefit the defendant and also provide a disincentive to insure against risk. In most circumstances, the damages analyst should calculate and opine to all of the plaintiff's damages, regardless of the fact that the plaintiff may have been compensated elsewhere. Sometimes the effect of the collateral source rule is to allow a plaintiff double compensation for his or her loss, but most insurance contracts provide for the right of subrogation, meaning that the insurance carrier has the right to recover the amount of the paid claim from the plaintiff if the plaintiff prevails against the defendant.

General Classifications of Damages

There are two overarching classifications of damages: general (noneconomic) damages and special (economic) damages. There are other sub-categories of damages that blur the lines between general and special damages because some of the sub-categories of damages can be both economic and noneconomic.

General damages compensate the plaintiff for the aspects of the specific harm suffered that are not objectively quantifiable. They are considered noneconomic damages, despite the fact that they are ultimately reduced to a money award, and they include compensation for pain and suffering, emotional distress, loss of care and companionship, loss of consortium and punitive damages.[3] Although general damages must be reduced to a monetary value, they are considered to be noneconomic because they are not objectively verifiable. As such, they are not normally the subject of the forensic accountant's analysis or other types of economic expert testimony. They are usually an amount that is subjectively awarded to a plaintiff based on the conclusion of a jury (or a judge) without specific financial or economic analysis. General damages are based on the fact finder's opinion of the amount of money that will financially compensate the plaintiff for some noneconomic harm. Some general damages fall under the sub-category of compensatory while others fall into the categories of punitive, nominal or hedonic (see list on page 204).

Special damages are specifically identifiable economic losses that a plaintiff has suffered as a proximate result of the defendant's conduct, and they compensate the plaintiff for the quantifiable losses suffered. Special damages may be the direct result[4] of the defendant's conduct (property damage, extra costs incurred, loss of income) or they may result as a more indirect consequence[5]

---

3. The list of "harms" for which general damages could be awarded is long. Additional examples of possible claims would include: loss of reputation, loss of quality of life, emotional distress, disfigurement, loss or impairment of mental or physical capacity.

4. "Direct" damages are direct losses suffered by the plaintiff as a result of defendant's conduct, and the list of possible direct losses is virtually endless depending on the case.

5. "Consequential" damages are indirect losses suffered by the plaintiff as a consequence of the defendant's wrongful conduct. The list of possible indirect losses is also extensive and is ultimately only limited by the legal principle of proximate cause. The list could include: loss of earnings capacity, loss of household services, retraining costs, increased business or personal expenses, legal fees, administrative expenses, etc.

of the claimed wrongful conduct. (Example: Because of the plaintiff's injury and resulting loss of income, the plaintiff had to liquidate his retirement plan and suffer some adverse tax consequences.) The primary legal requirement for the existence of special damages is that they be proximately caused by the actions of the defendant. Thousands of legal cases have addressed the issue of proximate cause and there is simply no litmus test that can be applied to every situation to determine whether the claimed loss was proximately caused by the defendant. Suffice it to say, however, that the damages must be related to the defendant's conduct. The more directly related the damages are, the more "proximately caused" they are, and vice versa. All special damages fall under the sub-category of compensatory.

Specific Sub-Categories of Damages

Compensatory damages, also called **actual damages**, are paid to compensate the claimant for loss, injury, or harm suffered by another's wrongful conduct. Compensatory damages can be both special (economic) or general (noneconomic) because they compensate the plaintiff for harm suffered, whether or not the harm is economic. For example, damages paid to a plaintiff for pain and suffering would *compensate* the plaintiff for his loss, but they would not be considered economic damages because they are not economically verifiable.

Punitive damages, also called exemplary damages, are charged against a defendant to punish the defendant for egregious conduct. An award of punitive damages is generally limited to cases in which the defendant has committed an intentional tort that involves some type of malicious conduct like fraud, libel or slander. Punitive damages fall under the category of general damages because they are not economically verifiable. The forensic accountant or financial expert witness is not asked to ultimately determine punitive damages because they are a judgment call of the fact finder, but the accountant may be involved in some foundational aspects of punitive damages. Specifically, the net worth and income of the defendant are considered relevant issues for determining punitive damages, and the accountant would likely be involved in determining those amounts.

Nominal damages are awarded to a plaintiff as a result of proving that some right of the plaintiff was violated by the defendant, but the actual damage was slight. For instance, the minor violation of someone's civil rights might give rise to an award of nominal damages. It is unlikely that an accountant or financial expert would be involved in this noneconomic issue.

Hedonic damages are only allowed in a minority of jurisdictions, and their acceptance is quite controversial. They are damages that seek to objectively measure the loss of the quality of a person's life as a result of suffering some injury. The controversy arises for two reasons. First, there is no question that a person's quality of life may be diminished as a result of a serious injury, but the financial amount of that diminution has historically been within the province of the jury. There is a very legitimate argument that the attempt to make this question an objective calculation takes this issue away from the jury, and the courts are generally reluctant to do so.

Second, the approaches that have been proffered by economists to quantify hedonic damages are very controversial. They are filled with broad assumptions and their direct connection to an individual's injury are very questionable. Most forensic accountants reject the notion that hedonic damages are calculable.

Classifications and Categories of Damages

General Damages (Non-Economic) (Not objectively verifiable)	Special Damages (Economic) (Objectively verifiable)
Pain and suffering (C)	Property damage (C)
Emotional distress (C)	Diminution in value of property (C)
Loss of care and comfort (C)	Loss of earnings (C)
Loss of consortium (C)	Loss of earning capacity (C)
Loss of reputation (C)	Loss of employment benefits (C)
Punitive damages	(medical, dental, retirement, etc.)
Nominal damages	Medical expenses (C)
Hedonic damages	Lost household services (C)
	Vocational rehabilitation costs (C)
	Life care expenses (C)
	Extra costs (C) (special transportation costs, special residential costs, etc.)
	Lost profits (business) (C)
	Extra expenses (business) (C)

(C) means compensatory; some general damages are compensatory

Spectrum of Damages Calculations

In its simplest form, a damage amount may be very easy to calculate. If the defendant owes the plaintiff $10,000 due and payable on December 31, 2008, and the defendant refused to pay the plaintiff, calculating the amount of damages suffered by the plaintiff is straightforward. Of course, there may be many legal arguments about whether the defendant really owes the money or the exact date on which it is owed, but those arguments are not within the province of the damages analyst. The facts relevant to the damages calculation are the principal sum of money, the date from which it is owed and the date to which it is owed. Finally, it may be proper to calculate an accrual of interest on the sum that is owed, but the proper rate and the compounding convention (simple, compound, and number of compounding periods per year) are most likely legal questions that the damages analyst will be instructed on. Regardless of the details, calculating damages from the failure to pay a sum certain is probably the simplest damages calculation possible. In some jurisdictions, such a basic calculation is not even within the province of expert opinion or calculation; some courts may allow it as a matter of lay testimony and take judicial notice of a basic interest calculation.

Damages analyses quickly become more complicated for a number of reasons. The first complicating problem is that many types of wrongful conduct do not logically reduce themselves to economic measurement, but oftentimes the only remedy is money. Most everyone would agree that there is no amount of money that can adequately compensate someone for the loss of a limb or some other human attribute, like sight or hearing, but when such a loss occurs, there is no method of compensation available to the plaintiff other than money damages. It is only logical that reasonable minds can disagree on the proper amount of compensation for these types of human losses.

Even when a wrong can be reduced to some monetary or financial calculation, there are many different perspectives on the economics of every situation. Consider a simple example of property damage, for instance. Assume that the defendant damaged the plaintiff's expensive car by backing into it in a parking lot. There are no injuries, other than property damage to the vehicle. Let's consider some of the possible property damage arguments, given the following assumptions (that are not contradicted):

1. The Plaintiff purchased the car—a 2010 Porsche Turbo Cabriolet—one month earlier for $146,500. Because the car has been "driven off the lot," its fair market value at the date of the accident is $110,000.

2. An average of three estimates to repair the vehicle is $32,500.

The plaintiff may make any of the following arguments,[6] all of which have some degree of reasonableness. You can quickly see that there is no perfect answer to any of the damages issues.

1. Because the car is so new, its real economic value is higher than the depreciated "fair market value," because everyone knows that cars don't really depreciate that much when you drive them off the lot. The plaintiff would like to be given a one-month-old vehicle to replace his damaged car.

2. Because this car is so special (there aren't many $146,000 Porches around), the repairs will not adequately restore the car to its pre-accident value. It will suffer a reduction in its value because of the stigma it will carry due to the fact that it has previously been damaged. Therefore, the cost to repair the vehicle is not adequate compensation. The real argument here is that the cost to repair does not adequately restore the car to its fair market value.

---

6. Don't confuse any of these arguments with the issue of insurance. If the defendant has insurance, it is exactly like the defendant "paying" the amount of the damage. If the plaintiff is forced to collect from his own insurance company, that is a matter of the insurance company's contract with the plaintiff, and the amount that the plaintiff collects may be less than the damages suffered, limited by the insurance contract.

3. In addition to the cost of repairs, the plaintiff wants to be compensated for a rental vehicle during the time that the car is being repaired. Furthermore, he wants the rental car to be a Porsche Turbo Cabriolet which is (or was) available at an exotic car rental agency for $625 per day. (What if the plaintiff demands $625 per day, but decides to rent a Toyota Corolla while his Porsche is in the shop?)

4. The plaintiff would like the repairs to be made by the most expensive repair shop of the three estimates because that repair shop specializes in repairing exotic vehicles.

5. The plaintiff used the vehicle in his business and was unable to make certain appointments because the car was unavailable. Consequently, the plaintiff lost some sales and the resulting income that he believes he would have earned. (This extension of the damages argument is a question of proximate cause. At what point in the chain of harms to the plaintiff does the causal connection become too attenuated to allow for damages?)

Furthermore, consider some more attenuated damages arguments:

6. During the time that the car was being repaired, the plaintiff had to use a rental car of lesser quality. Consequently, his clients were less impressed with him and his business position, and he suffered some lost opportunities as a result.

7. A friend of the plaintiff's wanted to rent the Porsche for a weekend to impress his girlfriend, and the plaintiff was sure that the friend would give him $1,500 for the rental. Because the car was in the shop, the rental didn't occur.

8. Assume that the damage to the car was so significant that the car is considered to be "totaled." Consequently, the defendant wants to pay the plaintiff $110,000 but the plaintiff claims that he can't replace the one-month old car for $110,000.

Let's continue to complicate the spectrum of damages calculations from the perspective of the date of the harmful act versus the date of the damages estimate. The wrongful conduct of the defendant occurred on a particular date. However, the estimate of damages from the conduct does not occur until sometime later. Is it proper to use information learned after the date of the wrong to estimate damages? This question highlights the difference in the possible damages amount simply based on the date of the analysis. A brilliant hypothetical illustration of the significance of the date of the analysis was created by Franklin M. Fisher and R. Craig Romaine in *Janis Joplin's Yearbook and the Theory of Damages*.[7] Here's the summary of the hypothetical:

---

7. Fisher, F.M. and Romaine, R.C., "Janis Joplin's Yearbook and the Theory of Damages," *Journal of Accounting, Auditing & Finance*, Vol. 5, Number 1, Winter 1990.

Assume that Janis Joplin's[8] autographed high school yearbook was stolen shortly after it was published and distributed to the seniors at her high school in Port Arthur, Texas. At that time, Janis was just another high school senior who had received and written some typical comments in the book and it was worth a nominal amount of money, say $5. The legal proceedings surrounding the theft took a long time and by the time damages were calculated, Janis had experienced her meteoric rise to rock star fame, become a household name among her constituency, overdosed on heroin and died. Setting aside any personal feelings about the tragic death of a young star, the hypothetical illustrates the significance of the timing of a damages question. If the stolen yearbook's value is determined at the time that it was taken, its value is nominal. If, on the other hand, the value of the stolen yearbook is determined at the time the theft is discovered, the value of the yearbook is enormous. The events that occurred after the theft of the yearbook have dramatically affected its value. Is there a financial answer to this question?

Janis Joplin's story shows the very legitimate differences in conclusions that are arrived at based on the information available at the date of the damages analysis versus information that is available after the date. If after-acquired information can be considered in the damages analysis, it is very possible that the conclusion will be dramatically different from the conclusion based only on information available at the time of the wrongful conduct. A calculation of damages on the day of the wrongful conduct is called *ex ante*; a calculation at a later date—usually the date of trial—is called *ex post*. The date of valuation issue is discussed further in Chapter 12, Commercial Damages.

Another complication encountered in damages calculations is determining the point at which the consequence of the loss ends. The law generally provides for the plaintiff to be compensated for "all damages proximately caused" by the defendant, but the law is often understandably vague about defining the stopping point of damages. The legal principle of proximate cause controls this continuum; it is not subject to a bright line accounting answer.

Finally, even if the theory of damages is quite clear, there can be many arguments about the proper calculation of damages in a particular situation. Assume that the plaintiff's business is harmed by some wrongful conduct of the defendant and the plaintiff loses some customers. There are myriad facts, assumptions and calculations that must be undertaken to estimate the plaintiff's losses. The but-for situation must be reasonably established and compared to the plaintiff's actual, historical situation. Numerous estimates of fixed and variable costs must be made and the length of time of the anticipated loss must be estimated. Future loss projections must be discounted to present value at an appropriate discount rate for the total economic loss to be determined. Finally, the calculated losses must be causally connected to the defendant's wrongful conduct and they must be separated from other possible macroeconomic causes.

---

8.   I assume everybody knows this, but Janis Joplin was a famous rock star of the 1960s who skyrocketed to fame in a relatively short period of time, going from an unknown lounge singer to a household name because of her incredible talent, and culminating in her appearance at Woodstock in 1969.

The spectrum of damages calculations varies from so simple that an expert is not needed, to so complex that several experts are needed to perform various aspects of the analysis. It is important to recognize that a competent damages analysis is a blend of the relevant law of the jurisdiction and appropriate accounting and financial methods to properly estimate the losses suffered by a plaintiff. Given the broad spectrum of the different types of claims that can give rise to damages and the complexity of the calculations themselves, it is reasonable that differing opinions can result.

Damages in Contracts

There are two alternative theories of contract damages: the *out of pocket rule* and the *benefit of the bargain rule*. Under the out of pocket rule, the aggrieved party will receive as damages the amount that he paid under the contract, or the amount that he is "out of pocket." Under the benefit of the bargain rule, the non-breaching party is entitled to everything that he would have received, including profits, if the breach had not occurred. A comparative example will illustrate the difference. Assume a contract to buy a used car for $10,000 is breached by the seller. The out of pocket rule would allow the buyer to recover the amount of money that he paid, up to $10,000, but no more. Under the benefit of the bargain rule, the buyer could recover the value of what he was promised in the contract as well as other benefits that were foreseeable at the time of the contract. So, if the buyer had a good deal in the contract (i.e., the fair market value of the car was $12,500), his claim would be for $12,500; if it was foreseen that the buyer would use the car in his business, the buyer could claim lost profits for the time that he didn't have the car, subject to his duty to mitigate his losses.

Recall that there are remedies other than damages for breach of contract. Specific performance is the remedy that requires each party to do what was promised under the contract. Specific performance is called for when the subject of the contract is unique, like the promised transfer of a parcel of real estate. If the land cannot be replaced with another parcel—as is usually the case because of the unique nature of real property—then the appropriate remedy is to force the non-performing party to transfer the promised parcel to the plaintiff. Rescission is the remedy that places each party to the breached contract back into the exact position that they were in before the breach. Rescission is an equitable remedy invoked at the discretion of the court, usually when a contract was based on mutual factual error of the parties or for other good cause such as a contract that is contrary to public policy. Restitution is the remedy that forces a defendant to repay ill-gotten gains to a harmed party. It is frequently employed when one party is unjustly enriched to the detriment of the other party and especially when the profit realized as a result of the defendant's action does not parallel the loss suffered by the plaintiff.

It is likely that a forensic accountant or financial expert will be involved in the financial aspects of all of the remedies available to the plaintiff, but it is certain that the expert will determine and estimate the amount of monetary damages in cases in which money damages are claimed as a remedy. An award of damages is based on the calculation of a qualified financial expert using recognized principles of finance and law. The forensic accountant is often the most knowledgeable and qualified individual to analyze the plaintiff's damages.

Financial Concepts Underlying Damages Analyses

Damages calculations for economic losses[9] attempt to measure the financial harm suffered by a plaintiff as a result of a defendant's legally impermissible conduct, usually the commission of a tort or the breach of a contract. Damages are an estimate of the monetary compensation to which the plaintiff is entitled in order to be made whole. A damages analysis is a specific financial calculation that is intended to implement a series of abstract legal principles. By definition, damages analyses are a melding of financial theory, precise financial analysis and abstract legal principles.

The simplest form of damages to estimate are direct damages, or those damages directly stemming from the defendant's unlawful conduct. Although there can always be an argument about the attenuation of direct damages, simple examples of direct damages are: property damage, additional costs incurred, clean-up expenses, temporary replacement of property, etc. Setting aside the proximate cause argument, direct damages are most often measured by estimating the cost to repair or replace the damaged property, or reimburse the plaintiff for extra expenses incurred resulting from the defendant's conduct. There is no question that the estimation of direct damages can become complicated, but it isn't possible in the abstract to contemplate the spectrum of complexities that this type of loss could involve. Each component of direct damages is subject to measurement based on the best evidence available to compensate the plaintiff for the harm suffered.

Generally, more complicated damages analyses involve consequential damages, or those damages that result as a consequence of the defendant's conduct. A damages analysis is an estimate of the financial gain that the plaintiff would have realized, but for the wrongful conduct of the defendant, minus what the plaintiff actually received. The plaintiff is entitled to receive what he would have gotten in the but-for world versus what he did (or will) get in the actual world. To calculate these damages, the financial expert will project the extent of the plaintiff's loss into the foreseeable (and actuarially calculated) future. For legal purposes, the trial must resolve the plaintiff's claim and provide finality to both parties, and because of this need for finality, many types of ongoing damages such as lost wages or cost of medical care must be projected far into the future. In the final damages estimate, the future losses will be discounted to present value.

The focus of the next two chapters is personal economic loss and commercial damages. While there are many possible components to each of these types of losses, our concentration will be the plaintiff's loss of earnings (in the case of personal economic losses) and lost profits (in commercial settings). To calculate damages in either situation, the first step in the analysis is to project "but-for" earnings, or the earnings that would have occurred, but for the conduct of the defendant.

---

9. This discussion is limited to economic losses, as opposed to noneconomic losses. The discussion does not deal with the types of losses that are not objectively quantifiable. Examples of noneconomic losses are listed on page 204 under General Damages.

The algorithm for estimating loss of earnings or profits is quite simple, but its application is complicated. Although there can be variations depending on specific facts and circumstances of each case, the typical approach to a lost earnings or profits analysis is to project but-for earnings[10] and compare the projection to actual earnings or profits received after the date of the incident, creating a difference that is assumed to be lost earnings or profits resulting from the defendant's conduct. In commercial cases dealing with lost profits, the next step in the analysis is to estimate variable costs related to the presumed lost gross revenues and assume that those costs are saved. By subtracting the variable costs saved from the presumed lost gross revenues, the analyst derives the estimate of lost profits. In both personal and business cases, depending on the timing of the losses, the analyst may add interest to past losses (or not, depending on the law of the jurisdiction), and most likely will discount any future lost profits estimate to present value.

Every step of a lost earnings or profits calculation is an assumption. Since the earnings or profits that are estimated to be lost did not occur, no component of their calculation is a fact. The primary foundational assumption of all lost earnings and profits analyses is the financial projection referred to as the "but-for" projection, the assumption that a certain level of personal income or business activity would have happened, *but for* the conduct of the defendant. The second foundational assumption is that the actual post-incident level of earnings or trend of business activity is lower than it otherwise should have been because of the wrongful conduct of the defendant. This assumption is really one of causation, rather than damages, but it often falls within the province of the damages expert because of the financial and business aspects of the issue. In personal injury cases, this step is not so problematic because the plaintiff has usually suffered a marked decline in income for reasons that are fairly obvious, but not always. In business damages cases, the lost profits analysis continues to apply other assumptions relating to variable costs, the time period of the loss and discount rate analysis, but these assumptions are not as easy to criticize or difficult to support as the two foundational assumptions. The aggregation of all of the assumptions of a lost profits analysis will result in an expert opinion that must be both economically sound and legally permissible.

A lost earnings or profits analysis can conform to the legal principle of reasonable certainty, even though it is an aggregation of assumptions. In order to do so, however, the analysis of lost earnings or profits should follow a method of inquiry that is based on gathering observable and empirical data that supports a principle of reasoning to arrive at a logical conclusion. The loss analysis must be more than speculation, conjecture and unsupported conclusions or it will not be sustained as expert opinion evidence.

Date of Analysis. Damages are always calculated at a point in time, usually the date of trial. Consequently, they can be thought of as "past" damages and "future" damages. Generally, past damages are somewhat more certain because of the benefit of hindsight; future damage calculations are less certain because they are imbedded with more assumptions and projections about future activity.

---

10. In business damages cases, the analyst often projects but-for gross revenues as the foundational assumption for the lost profits calculation, but it is equally reliable to base a lost profits analysis on a projection of some other measure of but-for activity. Other examples of appropriate measures include profits, units of production, geographic area of penetration, number of transactions, or some other logical measure of business activity. Regardless of the benchmark of activity that is projected, the analyst is faced with the same issues regarding the reliability and reasonable certainty of the projection.

There are complicated financial issues relating to both the use of hindsight, interest calculations on past losses, and interest rates to be used in discounting future losses to present value. Some of these complexities will be addressed in Chapters 11 and 12.

Conclusion

A damages analysis that results in expert opinion testimony must fall within the legal standard of both proximate cause and reasonable certainty to be admitted into evidence. Achieving reasonable certainty, or failing to, can apply to every part of the analysis. The foundational assumptions—the but-for projection and the fact causation assumption of the plaintiff's actual business or personal activity—are critical to the entire analysis and if either of them is found to be unsupported or speculative, the entire analysis will likely fail. Other financial assumptions, particularly in business cases—variable costs, time periods and discount rate—are significant to the overall lost profits conclusion, but somewhat less controversial than the foundational assumptions.

It seems that courts look at the entire loss analysis without always distinguishing the relative importance of different assumptions within it, and the overall analysis can succeed or fail because of the strength or weakness of any one of its components. Consequently, it behooves the financial analyst who is proffering the economic loss analysis to be thorough in his or her research and support for each of the assumptions contained within it. When opposing an economic loss analysis that is believed to be inadequate, the lawyer or financial analyst should question the underlying logic of the projections and causation, and investigate the research and analysis that is being offered in support of the conclusion.

Chapter 11

Personal Economic Losses

Introduction

Personal economic losses derive from tort law, a body of law that addresses civil wrongs that do not arise from contractual obligations. Personal economic losses suffered by individuals are the direct or indirect consequence of a defendant's unlawful conduct. A plaintiff's direct losses can take many forms, including property damage, medical expenses and increased costs of living. Indirect losses, called consequential damages, include lost personal earnings, loss of earnings capacity, lost employment benefits, loss of retirement income, life care expenses, lost household services and other costs or expenses that indirectly result from the injuries that the plaintiff suffered in the incident in question. The focus of this chapter is personal loss of earnings and loss of earnings capacity, as opposed to property damage or other costs that may comprise a plaintiff's damages. This chapter's sections will take the reader through the steps of examining, analyzing and calculating a personal loss of earnings and loss of earnings capacity.

Personal economic losses generally arise from personal injury claims, wrongful death claims or wrongful termination claims. The successful prosecution of these tort claims results in a finding of liability against the defendant and damages to the plaintiff. Assuming liability is found to exist, the plaintiff must offer evidence of the damages that have been suffered (or will be suffered) to obtain a financial recovery from the defendant. Evidence of damages is offered through the expert testimony of a forensic accountant, economist or similarly qualified professional.

Different Types of Losses

A damages calculation seeks to restore the plaintiff to the financial position he would have been in, absent the injury. There are many possible components of damages that a plaintiff may suffer as a result of a defendant's wrongful conduct, but this chapter ultimately focuses on an individual's lost earnings[1] and lost earnings capacity,[2] including employment benefits and loss of household services. These elements of a plaintiff's damages are frequently the largest components of damages and they often include the most complicated and sophisticated assumptions and calculations. Other components of damages, such as property damage or future medical expenses, may require some accounting or economic analysis, but they are often dependent on input from non-financial experts. Other than identifying their existence, they will not be discussed in depth in this chapter, but it is always important to consider the injured plaintiff's total situation and contemplate all of the components of his loss.

---

1. The terms "lost earnings" and "loss of earnings" are used interchangeably. Sometimes, either term is referred to as "lost income" or "loss of income" because the terms "earnings" and "income" are also used interchangeably.
2. The term "loss of earnings capacity" is used interchangeably with "lost earnings capacity."

The following is a list of possible damages that an individual may suffer in a personal economic loss. Keep in mind that all of these components of damages could exist in both the past and in the future, and the date of the damages analysis has significant financial ramifications. The date of the damages analysis, often called the date of valuation, is discussed subsequently in the chapter.

1. **Lost earnings/Lost earnings capacity.** This component of damages is a significant focus of subsequent discussion in this chapter and includes all hourly or salaried earnings, bonuses, earnings from self-employment or earnings from an independent contractor relationship.

2. **Loss of employment benefits.** This component of damages is closely related to a plaintiff's lost earnings from employment and can be a significant component of the loss. Examples of employment benefits are medical benefits, employer 401(k) contributions and employee stock purchase plans. Frequently, the amount of a person's lost benefits is calculated as a percentage of earnings and added to lost earnings for loss calculations.

3. **Lost retirement income.** Lost retirement income often follows the loss of an individual's job and can also be a substantial component of the individual's economic loss. Depending on the details of the retirement plan involved, the retirement loss is sometimes quantified as a percentage of earnings and added to the plaintiff's lost earnings for calculation purposes. In other instances, lost retirement benefits have to be calculated separately from lost earnings.

4. **Vocational retraining costs.** The costs to retrain an injured person would be a component of damages. The amount of these costs is typically determined by a qualified vocational rehabilitation expert, although the economic quantification (inflationary increases and present value analysis) is usually performed by the damages analyst.

5. **Loss of household services.** Lost household services are the economic value of the services that an injured plaintiff can no longer perform as a result of his injury. In concept, they are akin to lost earnings and earnings capacity, but they are not based on employment. Rather, they are based on the value of the types of services that an individual performs for himself and his family.

6. **Medical expenses.** All jurisdictions allow the plaintiff to recover the reasonable value of past medical expenses as well as the present value of expected future medical expenses that are or will be incurred as a result of the defendant's wrongful conduct. The primary limitations on the recovery of medical expenses are that they be medically necessary and quantified at a standard of "reasonable value." The damages analyst should understand that there may be an argument between parties about the extent of necessity of the claimed medical expenses; the forensic accountant should only be involved in the quantification of the damages, not the medical necessity of care.

7. **Life care expenses.** These are the costs (past or future) of providing necessary care to an injured person, beyond actual medical expenses. The category of life care costs is often quite broad, extending to items like medication, medical supplies, wheelchairs and other items of medically related equipment, required nursing or LVN care, residential facility costs, conservator costs and more, depending on the severity of the plaintiff's injuries. As the name indicates, these are the costs that the plaintiff will need in order to be maintained and cared for in a post-injury condition. Obviously, a severely injured plaintiff may have life care costs in the millions of dollars.

8. **Special transportation needs.** The cost of a specialized vehicle or other specialized transportation would be a component of an injured individual's damages. If this component of damages spans a significant future period of time, the damages analyst may perform research regarding inflationary adjustments and present value calculations for these costs. Often, these costs are included as part of the life care expenses.

9. **Specialized housing requirements.** If an individual's residence has to be remodeled in order to accommodate them in an injured condition, that cost would also be a component of damages. It is also often included as part of the life care expenses.

10. **Value of care provided by others.** Oftentimes when a plaintiff is injured, a spouse or other family member will provide services similar to that of an attendant while they are recovering. These types of services can include help with cooking, cleaning, bathing and dressing the plaintiff and providing transportation. Similar to the calculation for a loss of household services, the loss is based on the value of the types of services provided.

11. **Property damage.** Property damage is not normally considered to be a direct damage to the *person* of the plaintiff, but it can certainly be a component of the total economic loss suffered by the plaintiff in a case involving other personal economic losses. Examples include vehicle damage, damage to real property and damages to other personal property. Generally, the measure of damages to property is the loss or diminution in fair market value of the property, or the cost to repair the property, whichever is less.

12. **Other costs and expenses.** The list of other possible costs or expenses that constitute possible losses to a plaintiff is only limited by the legal requirement that the loss be proximately caused by the defendant's conduct. It is not feasible to list every possible type of damage that a plaintiff could suffer.

The above items represent the majority of the types of a person's personal economic loss. Each case is dependent on its own facts and circumstances to determine the possible components of damages that a particular plaintiff may have suffered. The damages analyst should be expansive in contemplating all of the possible types of a plaintiff's loss. The only limitations, which must be carefully considered, are the causal connection between the defendant's wrongful conduct and plaintiff's damages and the reasonableness of the quantification of the components of damage.

Other Important Issues in Personal Economic Loss Calculations

In addition to the types of losses noted above, personal economic losses often include calculations of the following offsetting amounts.

1. **Mitigating[3] earnings (Duty to Mitigate).** Under the law, a plaintiff who has suffered damages has a duty to mitigate his losses and the concept of mitigation is germane to the calculation of damages. The duty to mitigate requires the plaintiff to make reasonable attempts to minimize the loss that has been caused by the defendant. Although the plaintiff may not be in a position to earn as much as he could have in his pre-injury condition, he must make reasonable efforts to continue in the workforce or return to the workforce in a capacity that is commensurate with his post-injury situation. As a practical matter, the duty to mitigate means that the plaintiff cannot sit back and force the defendant to replace his pre-injury earnings capacity; the plaintiff must minimize his losses. Offset earnings can be based on the *actual earnings* of the plaintiff post-injury (if he has returned to work) or on the *opinions of the appropriate mitigating earnings* offered by a vocational rehabilitation specialist as to when the plaintiff will be able to return to work and what earnings he would likely be able to receive.

2. **Mitigating (offset) employment benefits.** All employment benefits that a plaintiff receives as part of his employment subsequent to the incident at question should be included as an offset to the loss of employment benefits. When the plaintiff has not yet returned to work, the vocational rehabilitation expert will often opine as to what benefits a plaintiff will most likely receive when he does return to work. A reasonable estimate of the value of these benefits should be included as an offset to the plaintiff's lost earnings and benefits.

3. **Personal consumption.** In a wrongful death matter, the decedent's personal consumption expenses are the expenses that the decedent would have spent on himself had he lived. A reasonable estimate of personal consumption must be subtracted from the loss of earnings calculation, following the theory that the survivors are not entitled to recover lost earnings that would have been consumed by the decedent and unavailable to the survivors.

Lost Earnings/Lost Earnings Capacity Analysis

A lost earnings analysis is a financial analysis of the plaintiff's former and changed earnings situation that results in the conclusion that the past or future earnings of the plaintiff are less than they would have been, but for the wrongful conduct of the defendant. The analysis is usually dependent on the facts of the plaintiff's historical earnings situation as well as assumptions about the plaintiff's projected earnings after the date of injury. The lost earnings conclusion is ultimately the difference that

---

3. Mitigating earnings are also referred to as "offset" earnings because they are used to offset the plaintiff's total loss of earnings capacity amount.

results from a comparison of what the plaintiff was expected to earn absent the wrongful conduct of the defendant compared to the plaintiff's actual and/or current expected earnings, given the injury sustained in the incident. The strength of the lost earnings analysis and conclusion is dependent on the facts on which it is based and the reasonableness of the assumptions that are embedded in the analysis.

Lost earnings are consequential damages as opposed to direct damages. Consequential damages arise *as a consequence* of the defendant's wrongful conduct, not directly from it. In other words, when a defendant's conduct injures a plaintiff, the defendant doesn't *directly* take the plaintiff's earnings away from him, but the defendant causes some physical or emotional injury which results in the plaintiff's reduced ability to earn income.

Lost Earnings and Lost Earnings Capacity Distinguished

There is a subtle distinction between a lost earnings analysis and a lost earnings capacity analysis, although the underlying issues and the actual calculations are virtually identical. To be precise, a lost earnings analysis is a calculation of the specific earnings that a person has lost as a result of the defendant's wrongful conduct. For example, if a plaintiff had been employed prior to the incident earning $1,000 per week and the plaintiff could no longer work as a result of the incident caused by the defendant, the plaintiff begins to lose $1,000 per week. That amount is a *loss of earnings* to the plaintiff. In contrast, a *loss of earnings capacity* is the economic loss suffered by an individual when that individual loses the ability or capacity to earn some amount of money, usually an amount different from what he was actually earning at the time of the incident in question. For example, assume our plaintiff earning $1,000 per week was injured but he expected to receive a raise to $1,100 a week the day after he was injured. It would be logical to calculate his loss based on $1,100 a week, resulting in a *loss of earnings capacity* to him. In a true lost earnings analysis, the actual earnings are lost; a lost earnings capacity analysis is a loss of the plaintiff's ability to earn an amount different from what he was actually earning at the date of the incident.

There are two reasons why, in most cases, any calculation of a plaintiff's *lost earnings* is really a *lost earnings capacity* analysis. First, the defendant never takes the plaintiff's earnings directly; he only injures the plaintiff's capacity to obtain earnings.[4] Second, in virtually every lost earnings calculation, after a short period of time, the estimate of a but-for earnings amount is changed from the plaintiff's actual historical earnings to some amount that includes growth or other changes. Consequently, what is being estimated in the calculation is an assumed earnings amount, not the actual earnings that the plaintiff was earning prior to the injury. Therefore, almost every analysis is technically a *lost earnings capacity* analysis, not a *lost earnings analysis*, although many forensic accountants and economists use the terms interchangeably. Following this discussion, the remainder of the chapter will discuss only lost earnings capacity, recognizing the subtle distinction discussed in the previous paragraphs.

---

4.   It is difficult to contemplate a situation where the plaintiff's actual earnings are taken directly from him, unless somebody runs him over and steals his paycheck while he is riding his bike to the bank.

A plaintiff's lost earnings capacity conclusion is frequently the largest component of damages (unless the plaintiff has an extensive amount of future life care expenses) and it often includes the most complicated and sophisticated assumptions and calculations. In its simplest form, a lost earnings capacity calculation projects what the plaintiff would have earned, "but-for" the incident, and compares that projection to what the plaintiff has earned and/or is likely to earn in his after-injury condition.

Conceptual Framework of a Lost Earnings Capacity ("LOE") Analysis

An LOE analysis is a blending of underlying facts, reasonable assumptions, financial theory and legal theory. The facts and assumptions of a particular case are woven through a logical financial and legal rationale in order to derive a conclusion. The proper combination of these four components[5] will yield a supportable lost earnings capacity analysis, one that will be defensible in a court of law.

Facts are historical or present truths. In order to connect facts to any conceptual theory (either legal or financial), it is necessary to use assumptions. Assumptions are suppositions, or the supposing of a hypothetical fact to be true. Assumptions are necessary to perform a lost earnings capacity analysis because everything that is presumed to occur after the date of the incident in question is an assumption. Recognizing that assumptions are required in the analysis, it is critically important that the assumptions used by the damages analyst are reasonable in light of the historical facts of the case and a realistic expectation of what would have happened to the plaintiff in the "but-for" world. As a general proposition, in any economic loss analysis, the more uncertain the data supporting an assumption, the more conservative the assumption should be.

The following step-by-step process constitutes a conceptual framework for legal/financial analysis that helps to compress the vagaries of a complex factual situation into a practical financial analysis. It is helpful to analyze every damages calculation by these four steps.

1. **Facts**—Consider the known facts relating to a particular step in the analysis. In the context of financial analysis, facts are known financial occurrences. Examples of facts are a plaintiff's wages, the number of hours per week he worked, the types of benefits he received and the date of the incident.

2. **Assumptions**—Develop reasonable assumptions to fill in gaps or weaknesses in the facts and to connect the facts to the applicable financial and legal theories. For example, if the plaintiff's historical wage has fluctuated and there is no clear trend, consider using some reasonable average of historical earnings as the assumption for the plaintiff's earnings base in the analysis.

---

5.   Facts, assumptions, financial rationale and legal rationale.

3. **Rationale**—Be certain there is sound logic in interpreting the facts, adopting reasonable assumptions, and that there is a reasonable connection between the facts, assumptions and conclusions that are being reached; and

4. **Conclusion**—Relying on historical facts, reasonable assumptions and sound rationale, draw a conclusion that is supportable and defensible in the face of the arguments against it.

The application of this framework to every part of a personal economic loss analysis is very effective, but it quickly shows that there is no absolute way to perform these types of analyses. Personal economic loss analyses are not "black and white." It is impossible to provide a formula to the analyst that will work in all situations. Even though there are general financial models that can be applied, the unique circumstances of each case will require the analyst to apply a flexible framework of analysis that will lead to the best conclusion. The forensic expert must understand that there will always be an argument that his analysis is not supportable.[6] The goal of an "affirmative" calculation should be to make the analysis as supportable as is reasonably practical.

Financial experts (and all experts, for that matter) should understand the difference between an "affirmative" and a "negative" argument. A good forensic accounting analysis is an affirmative argument—it is a positive assertion that a particular financial conclusion (typically an amount of money) is the correct answer, or the most reasonable answer, to a question. "The business is worth $500,000" or "Ms. Smith's loss of earnings is $1,200,000." The analysis should be supported by facts, reasonable assumptions and sound logic and arrive at a reasonable conclusion. The affirmative argument, or position, must be carefully calculated, considering both the strengths and weaknesses of the underlying facts and assumptions, with the goal of reaching a reasonable conclusion.

A negative argument does not contain any positive assertions, but instead is a criticism leveled at an affirmative assertion or opinion. It suggests a number of complaints regarding the affirmative assertion or opinion. Some negative arguments are meritorious, but it should be understood that it is always easier to argue negatively than to argue affirmatively. Negative arguments can be leveled at almost any part of the forensic economic analysis: the facts, the assumptions, the causal connection between the defendant's conduct and the damages, or the conclusions of the analysis. Examples of negative arguments are: "The facts that were relied on are wrong"; "There is an error in the calculation"; "The data is insufficient on which to base the conclusion reached"; and "The investigation did not eliminate all possible reasons that could have caused the problem." A good forensic analysis will anticipate the negative arguments that will be suggested later and try to affirmatively defend against them in the main analysis. There is no question that this suggestion is easier said than done.

---

6. Keep in mind that one tactic of an opposing lawyer is to argue that the economic analysis is not *perfect* and therefore it should be rejected. Perfection is not a reasonable standard to achieve, so it should not be the goal of the financial analyst.

Graphic Presentation of a Lost Earnings Capacity Analysis

It is helpful to visualize a lost earnings capacity analysis. The following graph shows the relationship of the components of the loss analysis to one another and the time period of the overall analysis. The shaded area shows the actual amount of the lost earnings capacity analysis, but the future portion of the loss will be discounted to present value in the final calculation.

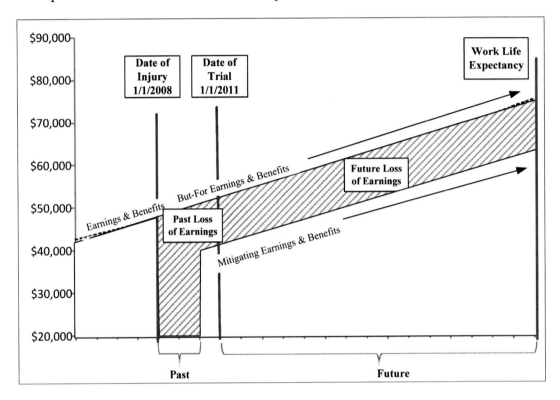

Sample Problem for Chapter 11

Example

The techniques discussed in further detail throughout the remainder of the chapter will be illustrated by the example of Johnny Jones v. ABC Company. Mr. Jones was involved in a car accident with a truck from ABC Company on January 1, 2008. At the time of the incident, he had been a carpenter with DEF Carpentry Company, Inc. for 10 years. Due to the injuries he sustained in the incident, he was unable to return to work as a carpenter. On January 1, 2010, he was able to return to work as an office clerk, earning less money than he had earned while he was employed as a carpenter. In addition, he is unable to perform several of the household services he had performed prior to the incident, and he will require future medical care costs for his injuries.

You were designated as Mr. Jones's economic expert by the law firm of Smith & Smith on July 1, 2009. The trial in the matter is scheduled to begin on January 1, 2011. You decide to use January 1, 2011 as the date of valuation, and past losses will occur from the date of the incident (January 1, 2008) through December 31, 2010. Future losses will begin on January 1, 2011.

Calculating a Plaintiff's Lost Earnings Capacity

Given the types of damages and offsets involved in a personal economic loss calculation as well as the underlying conceptual framework, the decisions necessary and calculations involved in performing a lost earnings capacity analysis can now be discussed.

Important Dates: There are three significant dates that affect a lost earnings capacity analysis:

1. **Date of Incident** ("DOI"; sometimes referred to as date of injury or date of accident, "DOA")—The date of the incident that is the subject of the litigation. The DOI can be the date of the accident giving rise to the plaintiff's personal injury, the decedent's death or the termination of employment of the plaintiff. In most cases, the DOI is a specific date, but occasionally the defendant's alleged wrongful conduct can occur over a period of time, as in the case of some types of employment discrimination or alleged improper long-term conduct of the defendant. In all situations, however, the financial analysis must begin at a specific date so, if the alleged wrongful conduct extends over a period of time, the logical starting point of the financial analysis is the point at which the conduct specifically affects the earnings of the plaintiff. In an employment termination case, this could be the date when the plaintiff finally leaves his employment, is demoted, does not get an expected promotion, or similar event.

2. **Date of Valuation** ("DOV")—The "as of" date at which the financial analysis is performed. In most cases, the DOV is intended to be current, "as of" the date of trial. The date of valuation is very significant because it divides the financial analysis into a past loss component and a future loss component, both of which have significant legal and financial ramifications. Some financial analysts use the actual date that the financial analysis is performed as the DOV while others will push a little bit into the future to estimate the actual trial date for the analysis so the DOV will actually be the date of the trial of the matter. If the analysis is done on an actual date that is earlier than the date of trial (sometimes at the date of the expert deposition), the analysis will often be updated to the date of trial so that the final DOV of the analysis will be as near to the actual date of trial as possible.

3. **End Date of the Analysis**—All financial analyses have an ending date which is, of course, significant. Depending on the facts of the particular situation, the end date can vary significantly from a brief period of loss to the entire remaining life expectancy of the plaintiff. There may be a factual reason to have a relatively short period of loss to the plaintiff, such as a new employment situation that completely mitigates any loss that the plaintiff has suffered, or a complete recovery from injury and return to employment. Many loss of earnings capacity analyses continue to the end of the plaintiff's work life expectancy, and that time period can be many years in the future. Other types of personal economic losses continue to the plaintiff's life expectancy, such as life care needs or the calculation of the loss of household services.

Choosing a Date of Valuation: Past and Future Losses. An economic damages analysis is performed as of a certain date, typically a date near the date of trial. This date is referred to as the date of valuation. Some types of losses may be specific to a point in time and not have any continuing component to them. Property damage, for instance, usually occurs at a point in time and the estimate of the resulting damage is as of a particular date, typically in the past, prior to the date of valuation. Other types of personal economic losses may be ongoing, such as lost earnings capacity, loss of employment benefits or specialized transportation costs, for example. These types of losses will therefore be divided into a past component and a future component. As this chapter proceeds, plaintiff's losses will often be referred to in two different time periods: the plaintiff's *past* lost earnings capacity and the plaintiff's *future* lost earnings capacity.[7]

The division of a loss into past and future components has significant financial ramifications, as well as legal ramifications. First of all, it is easier to contemplate losses that have occurred in the past than losses that will occur in the future. From the current vantage point, the date of valuation, it is easier to look backward to analyze historical losses because many of the factors that merit consideration have already occurred. For example, the plaintiff's health condition has probably become permanent and stationary, external circumstances surrounding his former employment are more defined (the industry is healthy or suffering; the company is doing well or poorly, etc.), and the benefit of hindsight enables the financial analyst to remove some uncertainty from the analysis.[8] In contrast, projected future losses after the date of valuation are entirely dependent on assumptions about economic factors that haven't happened as of the date of valuation, so those loss calculations are always subject to stronger criticism.

From a financial perspective, there is a significant difference between a past loss and a future loss. Financially, an amount of money calculated in the past as owed or owing deserves to have interest added to it to be brought forward to the present date. There can be disagreements about the correct interest rate to assign or whether a simple or compound convention should be applied, but there is no disagreement about the concept of applying interest to a past loss (assuming the amount is owed), at least from a financial perspective.

However, from the perspective of a legal argument, the issue is not so clear. In the law, the application of interest to a past loss, a loss before trial, is called "prejudgment" interest, and it is important to know that not all jurisdictions allow prejudgment interest. In some jurisdictions, awarding prejudgment interest is within the province of the judge, in some others, the jury; and the percentage amount may vary as well. The area of prejudgment interest is an area in which financial analysis is clear, but the law is vague on its acceptance of sound financial theory.

In fairness to the vagaries of the law's position on prejudgment interest, it should be noted that many times the amount of the past loss is in controversy, and that is one of the reasons that many

---

7. All references to a future loss implicitly assume that the future loss is discounted to present value. The details of present value calculations are discussed later in this chapter.
8. There is always an issue about the propriety of considering "after the fact" information in damages analyses. There is no clear answer to the question, but be mindful of it.

jurisdictions are undecided on a strict rule to impose prejudgment interest on an amount found to be owed. It is easy for a financial analyst to state that "interest should be awarded on any amount of past loss from the date of the loss until the present," but when there is uncertainty about both the amount of the loss and the liability of the defendant, the vagueness of the law is more understandable. This is an example of the imperfection of the intersection of finance and the law, and the answers to these complex questions are simply not black and white.

Regarding future loss calculations, basic financial principles would require any calculation of future losses to be discounted to present value. In the law, most jurisdictions properly allow (and some require) calculations of future losses to be discounted to present value. The nuances of discounting future loss calculations are discussed later in the chapter. For now, one must only be aware that losses are frequently divided into "past" and "future" and that basic financial principles of compound interest and present value should be applied. However, as discussed in the discounting portion of this chapter, these immutable financial principles are not always followed in the law, or followed correctly, and the rule of the particular jurisdiction must be carefully noted.

Specific Components of Personal Loss of Earnings Capacity. There are five specific components of a loss of earnings capacity calculation. Each component is incorporated into both the but-for earnings projection and the offset (mitigating) earnings calculation. They are:

1. *Earnings Base*—The foundational assumption of the plaintiff's representative earnings as of the date of the incident. The earnings base should include consideration of the plaintiff's historical salary or hourly wages, bonuses, and any other additional monies that the plaintiff had earned prior to the date of the incident. The earnings base assumption should be designed to reasonably estimate the plaintiff's earning capacity as of the date of the incident, as supported by relevant historical facts and conditions existing at the time of the plaintiff's injury. Later in the analysis when the analyst is estimating mitigating earnings, many of the same underlying factual considerations must be made to properly estimate the amount of mitigating earnings.

2. *Benefits*—This is the monetary value of any and all benefits (such as medical, dental and vision benefits, employer contributions to a 401(k), defined benefit pension plans, employee stock purchase plans, stock options, car allowances, etc.) that a plaintiff would have received had he remained employed but-for the incident. The benefits component also applies to mitigation.

3. *Growth Rate*—The growth rate for the plaintiff's earnings and benefits is estimated by considering the historical growth rate of the plaintiff's earnings, the industry in which the plaintiff is employed, macroeconomic factors relating to wage growth and the conditions at the time of the incident. Generally, the consideration of growth rate must be applied to both past and future lost earnings and benefits, although there might be different conclusions drawn for different time periods.

4. *Time Period*—The amount of time in the past period is typically from the date of the incident up to the date of valuation. The lost earnings capacity calculation must end at some specific date, and the assumption of the future date may be based on the plaintiff's work life expectancy, life expectancy, or some other supportable date in the future. Perhaps the plaintiff had a predetermined retirement date established, or there may be some other factor that drives the conclusion of the end date of the calculation.

5. *Discount Rate*—Future loss estimates must be discounted to present value. The present value is the amount of principal that, when invested at the interest (discount) rate, will yield the plaintiff the future earnings and benefits lost, for the projected time period of the anticipated loss.

Steps of a Lost Earnings Capacity Analysis. The steps of a lost earnings capacity analysis, which require significant further explanation, are as follows:

1. *But-for earnings projection.* Project but-for earnings from the date of injury to the present, and into the future. The but-for earnings projection must include the following components:

   a. an *earnings base* assumption that is supported by the underlying facts;

   b. consideration of the plaintiff's *benefits*, supported by the facts of the case;

   c. consideration of a post date-of-injury *growth rate* in the earnings and benefits, supported by the facts and circumstances; and

   d. a reasonable *time period* for the projection, supported by the facts and circumstances.

2. *Offset earnings analysis.* Identify the actual earnings and/or mitigating earnings from the date of injury to the present, and into the future.

   a. analyze the plaintiff's actual earnings after the date of injury and consider those earnings as an offset;

   b. consider any vocational rehabilitation opinion or relevant opinions of potential post-injury earning capacity; and

   c. recognize that mitigating earnings have the same components that the but-for earnings projection has.

3. *Lost Earnings Capacity.* By comparing the projection of but-for earnings (step #1) with the post date-of-injury offset earnings (step #2), the resulting difference is the presumed loss of earnings to the plaintiff.

4. *Discounting future losses.* To the extent that any of the assumed lost earnings capacity is projected into the future, it must be discounted to present value.

The But-For Projection—Earnings Base. The but-for earnings projection is the foundation of the personal economic loss analysis. By definition, the but-for earnings projection is the projection of *what the plaintiff's earnings would have been, but for the event* that is the subject of the litigation. The reasonableness of this projection dictates the reasonableness of the entire lost earnings capacity analysis and will be the focal point of challenge by the other side of the litigation. If the but-for projection is not credible and supportable, the credibility of the entire personal economic loss calculation can be undermined, and the opposition could argue that the rest of the analysis lacks the same credibility. Therefore, the but-for earnings projection must be based on historical facts and reasonable assumptions that connect those facts to the current and future projections. The assumptions used become defensible and supportable when they are based on facts which are closely connected to the issues being analyzed.

Facts and assumptions related to the earnings base. To analyze the plaintiff's pre-incident situation, first evaluate the foundational facts that existed at the time of the incident. Those foundational facts include the plaintiff's actual historical earnings, job description, earnings trends, any past gaps in earnings, past promotions, tenure of employment and industry trends. The financial analyst should obtain all relevant information regarding the plaintiff's employment as of the date of the incident.

The but-for earnings projection begins with an earnings base that should be closely connected to the historical facts of the plaintiff's situation. The earnings base may be the actual earnings at the time of the injury, an average of historical earnings, a weighted average of historical earnings or some amount that is selected in light of other facts and circumstances. For example, if the injured plaintiff was expected to receive a promotion or a raise at the approximate time of the incident, this greater amount, if supportable, could be used to determine the earnings base. Or, in some instances, the facts may support a conclusion that the plaintiff's historical earnings are not reasonably indicative of the earnings base that should be used in the but-for earnings calculation. An example would be if the plaintiff was about to complete graduate school and his historical earnings were for part-time employment in which he was underemployed while attending school. In this situation, it would not be logical to use the plaintiff's historical earnings as a basis for the but-for earnings projection; a more supportable assumption would probably be a reasonable estimate of his earnings with a graduate degree.

To estimate a reasonable earnings base for the but-for earnings projection, the financial analyst must also consider any unusual aspects of the plaintiff's historical earnings. For example, do historical earnings include overtime hours that are not expected to continue in the future? Are historical earnings overstated or understated by some business trend, such as a boom or a bust, in the particular industry in which the plaintiff was employed? In the past, was the plaintiff entitled to certain monies (such as an annual bonus plan) as part of his annual earnings base that are not anticipated to be continued in the future? Do the plaintiff's historical earnings include periods of unemployment, and, if so, are they explainable? If the earnings gaps can be reasonably explained and are not expected to occur in the future, an assumption that "fills the gaps" can be used to minimize the importance of those time periods. However, if the gaps cannot be logically explained, they should not be ignored in the historical analysis and should be considered in the but-for earnings estimate. If a plaintiff earned $20.00 per hour in the construction industry, but only worked part-time, it is not reasonable to assume that he would have been able to earn $20.00 per hour full-time. The financial analyst must make reasonable assumptions to adjust for any such unusual aspects of a plaintiff's historical earnings.

Rationale related to the earnings base. Rationale is the process of logic that is applied to the facts and assumptions to evaluate them and relate them to a supportable conclusion regarding the issue at hand. After analyzing all aspects of a plaintiff's historical earnings, the financial analyst must apply his or her own rationale to the underlying facts in order to determine a reasonable earnings base. In a straightforward case, the plaintiff may be a federal employee (such as a postal worker) or a member of the military. In these situations, the plaintiff's historical earnings are consistent, uninterrupted and well published. As a result, the but-for earnings estimate is quite predictable. Conversely, a plaintiff may have been an hourly employee in a volatile industry with a sporadic employment history or be self-employed with his own small business and a volatile earnings history. In these types of situations, a defensible conclusion regarding the plaintiff's but-for earnings is much more difficult and the conclusions reached are typically weaker than those for a predictably-employed plaintiff.

Conclusion related to the earnings base. There is no formulaic litmus test that can be applied to every factual situation to tell the financial analyst exactly how to do the analysis. The financial expert is always seeking a degree of predictability that is higher than speculation but, by definition, less than certainty. (Remember, all but-for earnings analyses are assumptions; they are not facts.) The strength of the final conclusion regarding a plaintiff's personal loss of earnings is dependent on the level of certainty and predictability of the underlying facts. The more certain and predictable the situation is, the more defensible the conclusion. The conclusions reached in an economic loss calculation are only as certain as the underlying facts and reasonableness of the assumptions used to reach the conclusion. It is generally advisable to be conservative in light of all historical facts in order to add an additional layer of assurance that the conclusions reached are defensible and can withstand the other side's attacks. In the gray area of damages and litigation, one side will always suggest that the analysis is too speculative while the other side will suggest that it is reasonably certain.

Returning to the chapter's example, Table 1 summarizes the historical earnings analysis of Johnny Jones and a conclusion of the earnings base to use in his but-for earnings projection.

The plaintiff's past but-for earnings projection is normally made on an annual (or monthly) basis. The same assumptions and rationale that were used to determine the past but-for earnings loss amounts should be carried forward into the future period, unless there is some reason to abandon the past but-for earnings assumption. The future but-for earnings projections should continue until the plaintiff's work life expectancy or other assumed end date for the projection. The estimate of work life expectancy is discussed later in the chapter.

Table 1
Johnny Jones v. ABC Company
But-For Earnings Analysis

Facts:

Mr. Jones was employed as a carpenter with DEF Company at the date of the incident, January 1, 2008. He had been employed with the same company for the previous 10 years. A history of his carpenter hourly earnings and hours worked is detailed below.

Year	Hourly Rate	Hours Worked	W-2 Earnings
1998	$15.00	2,000	$30,000
1999	$15.50	2,080	$32,240
2000	$16.05	1,950	$31,298
2001	$16.40	2,000	$32,800
2002	$16.90	2,100	$35,490
2003	$17.40	2,150	$37,410
2004	$17.75	1,900	$33,725
2005	$18.00	2,080	$37,440
2006	$18.65	2,200	$41,030
2007	$18.90	2,080	$39,312

Average Annual Hours Worked   2,054

Assumptions:

1) Assume Mr. Jones would continue to work the same amount of average hours as he had in the previous 10 years. Use 2,050 hours per year for the but-for projection.

Conclusion:

Therefore, conclude that Mr. Jones's but-for earnings base at the date of the incident is:

$18.90   X   2,050   = $38,745

The But-For Projection—Benefits. Employee benefits are the non-cash components of a plaintiff's compensation. A plaintiff who has lost his ability to earn or suffers a diminished earnings capacity has frequently lost the benefits associated with that employment. Therefore, they are clearly a component of a plaintiff's economic loss. In order to analyze and project lost employee benefits, it is first necessary to determine what employee benefits the plaintiff received and then to obtain historical information regarding those benefits. It is usually advisable to analyze the earnings and benefits loss together and then make the but-for earnings projection inclusive of employee benefits. In evaluating the value of a plaintiff's lost benefits, the financial analyst should only include those benefits that the employee received which had a direct economic value to him. Those benefits would typically include:

1. **FICA**—Both the employer and the employee contribute to the FICA tax (Federal Insurance Contributions Act). It is a payroll tax imposed by the federal government to fund Social Security and Medicare. Employers contribute 6.2% of an employee's wages (up to a maximum of $106,800 in annual earnings in 2010). FICA payments are indirectly tied to the amount of Social Security benefits an employee will receive in the future. Most financial analysts include the employer's share of FICA as a component of economic benefit to the employee as part of the LOE analysis.

2. **Health Benefits**—These are the health coverage benefits that an employee receives from an employer. Typically, an employer pays for part, if not all, of the cost to provide the employee with health care benefits. In some instances, an employer will continue to pay for these benefits after an employee has retired and this should be included in the lost benefits amount. The portion of employer-paid health benefits that have been lost should be included as part of the plaintiff's lost benefits.

3. **Dental Benefits**—Like health benefits, an employer can contribute to the cost of providing an employee with dental care benefits.

4. **Vision Benefits**—Similar to health and dental benefits, an employer can contribute to the cost of providing vision benefits to its employees.

5. **Retirement Benefits**—The two most common types of retirement benefits provided by employers are employer contributions to a 401(k) plan or a defined benefit pension plan. The employer's 401(k) contributions can match a certain percent of an employee's contributions or can be some profit sharing amount given to employees each year. When a company offers a defined benefit pension plan, it typically contributes a certain amount into the plan each year and then the employee receives a pre-determined monthly retirement amount for the remainder of his or her life expectancy once the employee retires.

6. **Employee Stock Purchase Plan**—Some employers offer their employees the ability to purchase company stock at a discount. This discounted amount is a benefit to the employee.

7. **Stock Options**—In addition to receiving salaries and bonuses, some employees are granted stock options by their employers. The value of these option grants are a benefit to the employee.

In addition, employees often receive some benefits which are not considered to be an additional, direct economic benefit of employment. Examples of these non-additional benefits would typically include:

1. **Vacation/Holiday/Sick Time**—Often, an employer will include a quantified value for vacation/holiday/sick time in an employee's benefit statement. However, it is not a distinct component of value, but rather, it is effectively a part of the employee's annual compensation.

2. **Other Benefits**—In the but-for situation, it is assumed that an employee would continue to be able to work and would not benefit from any type of benefit that he would receive were he unable to work. Therefore, any employer contributions to these types of benefits would not be considered a direct benefit to the employee. He would only benefit from them if he was unable to work and our assumption is that would not have occurred. These types of benefits, which are not included in the benefits loss are:

    a. Short-Term Disability;

    b. Sickness Insurance;

    c. Accident Insurance;

    d. Long-Term Disability;

    e. Wage Continuation;

    f. Worker's Compensation;

    g. Unemployment Insurance.

There are a number of different methods that can be used to estimate the value of a plaintiff's lost employment benefits. One method is to convert the value of the plaintiff's benefits into a percentage of total annual earnings and then use that percent to estimate the value of future benefits lost. Another method would be to assign specific values to the various types of benefits and add those amounts to the total lost compensation in order to determine a plaintiff's but-for earnings loss.

For example, regarding the employer's contribution to FICA on behalf of an employee, this is typically estimated at 6.2% of the employee's annual wages up to the maximum wage base that is established by the federal government ($106,800 in 2009 and 2010). This benefit is calculated through the end of the plaintiff's work life and is used to estimate the value of the Social Security payments that a plaintiff will then receive once eligible. It is important to note that if the plaintiff involved is close to Social Security retirement age, it can be argued that any additional FICA contributions made by the employer will not have a significant effect on any Social Security benefit received, and therefore, should not be included as an additional economic benefit. It is left to the financial analyst to determine if and when a FICA benefit should be included for the plaintiff. (See Table 2.)

One of the largest components of employee benefits received by a plaintiff can be health, dental and vision benefits. In order to estimate the value of these benefits, the financial analyst must first analyze what information is available with regard to the benefits. The information available will then determine the methodology adopted to assign a value to these benefits. If the financial analyst knows how much the employer was paying each month for the employee's medical coverage, that dollar amount can be used to estimate the value of the benefits. If the plaintiff received a COBRA letter (if he had to leave his employment) and the letter indicates the amount the employee would have had to pay in order to continue the health insurance coverage, that amount can be used to estimate the value of the health insurance provided (less the employee's portion of health insurance he was paying while still employed). An additional valuation method would be to analyze the cost of a similar health coverage plan if the employee were to purchase one in the open market and use its cost. Also, if the cost of the plan or a replacement plan is unavailable, the financial analyst can use various published tables to determine the value of the health benefits as a percent of total compensation. An example of such tables would be the "Employer Costs for Employee Compensation" as published by the Bureau of Labor Statistics. It is left to the discretion of the financial analyst to determine the most reasonable method to value the health benefits lost by the plaintiff. (See Table 2.)

Table 2
Johnny Jones v. ABC Company
But-For Benefits Analysis

Facts:

(1) In our example, Mr. Jones receives medical benefits from his employer, but he does not have any detailed financial information on the value of the health benefits he received from DEF Company.

(2) Mr. Jones contributes 10% of his annual earnings to his employer's 401(K) plan.
DEF Company matches Mr. Jones' contribution as follows:

	Employee	Employer
First 2% - 100 % match of employee contributions	2.00%	2.00%
Next 4% - 50% match of employee contributions	4.00%	2.00%
Next 4% - 25% match of employee contributions	4.00%	1.00%
	10.00%	5.00%

(3) DEF Company pays FICA on behalf of Mr. Jones.

Assumptions:

(1) To estimate the value of Jones's medical benefits, using information from the US Department of Labor is reasonable. The average Employer Cost per hour for Health Insurance as a % of wage is 11.40%.
(2) The employer's cost of matching 401(K) plan is reasonable evidence of the value of that benefit.
(3) The employer's cost of FICA is 6.2% of Jones's hourly wage.

Conclusions:

The value of Jones's benefits is estimated to be (as a % of wage):

Medical	11.40%
Retirement contribution	5.00%
Employer's share of FICA	6.20%
Employee Benefits	22.60%

An additional typical component of employer benefits is retirement benefits received by an employee, whether it be in the form of an employer 401(k) contribution or a defined benefit pension plan. Employer contributions to an employee 401(k) plan are most commonly in the form of an employer match to employee contributions or some amount of profit sharing received annually. The financial analyst must examine the details of the specific plan in order to determine the value of the benefit lost.

If, instead, DEF Company offered a defined benefit pension plan which would pay a set monthly amount to Mr. Jones from the date of his retirement through his remaining life expectancy, the financial analyst would need to analyze the particular details of that pension plan in order to separately calculate the present value of the pension amounts to be received in the future. Such plans are not typically calculated as a percent of a plaintiff's total annual earnings.

Additionally, plaintiffs may have received other types of benefits from their employers including but not limited to participation in employee stock purchase plans, grants of stock options and car allowances. In each particular instance, the forensic accountant must analyze the details of the particular benefit and determine how best to value the loss of that benefit to the plaintiff in the future. These types of benefits are then typically expressed as a percentage of the plaintiff's annual compensation.

As a result of the but-for benefits conclusion of Table 2, a benefits amount of 22.60% of compensation will be used in the loss analysis (see table 4).

The But-For Projection—Growth Rate. Most but-for earnings projections logically include some type of consideration for potential growth in earnings and benefits, either inflationary or productivity related, or both. This growth rate must be considered a component of the plaintiff's economic loss and is a hypothetical element of the earnings projection which extends beyond the date of the incident. The objective of a growth rate is to impute some reasonable assumption of growth into the but-for earnings projection because, had the incident not occurred, it is logical to assume the plaintiff's earnings and benefits would have grown at some rate.

A future growth rate is not an economic fact and, therefore, must be estimated. A financial analyst should consider the following data and information when attempting to assign a reasonable growth rate to a plaintiff's future earnings and benefits.

1. The plaintiff's job description and the industry in which he is employed;

2. The plaintiff's historical earnings increases, particularly the amounts and timing of such increases;

3. The historical employment cost indices for the industry in which the plaintiff was employed;

4. The historical employment cost indices for all workers;

5. The historical rates of inflation for the economy and the industry in which the plaintiff worked;

6. Current inflation projections for the economy and the industry in which the plaintiff was employed;

7. A schedule of the plaintiff's promotions;

8. A schedule of the plaintiff's anticipated promotions, if any; and

9. Information on similarly situated co-workers of the plaintiff in the post-incident period of time (if available).

It is important to note that none of the aforementioned measures of a historical or projected growth rate is absolute. Depending on the facts and circumstances of each individual case, one indicator might prove to be more probative than another. The financial analyst must be careful to consider all of the relevant data in order to estimate a reasonable growth rate to assign to the but-for earnings and benefits projection and must be aware that within the framework of each individual case, there can be a number of reasonable methods to project growth which may be both supportable and defensible.

Table 3 presents an analysis of the historical facts relating to Mr. Jones's wage growth and a conclusion of a reasonable growth rate to use for the lost earnings capacity analysis.

As a result of the analysis in Table 3, a growth rate of 2.60% will be factored into the but-for earnings and benefits analysis in Table 4. In the Jones analysis, a constant growth rate of 2.60% is applied to both earnings and benefits. Note that there may be factual reasons to use a growth rate that is not constant or reasons to use a different growth rate for benefits versus compensation.

The But-For Projection—Time Period. All personal economic loss calculations are prepared for a defined period of time. The loss typically begins at the date of the incident and continues to some finite point in time in the future. As previously discussed with regard to determining a date of valuation, all economic loss calculations are made as of a point in time. This point in time is called the date of valuation and is often determined by the date of trial. The plaintiff's loss that occurred from the date of incident to the date of valuation is defined as the past loss. If a plaintiff's losses are expected to continue beyond the date of valuation, an additional component of the personal economic loss will be a future loss calculation. Most personal economic loss calculations consist of both a past and a future loss calculation. It is at the discretion of the forensic accountant to determine the length of time of the plaintiff's future economic loss calculation.

In some circumstances, the plaintiff's earnings capacity may be impaired for a defined period of time and then return to normal, thus ending the loss of earnings calculation. As an example, consider the lost earnings and benefits of an office worker who suffers a broken leg due to the

---

Table 3
Johnny Jones v. ABC Company
But-For Growth Rate Analysis

Facts:

Mr. Jones was employed as a carpenter with DEF Company at the date of the incident, January 1, 2008. He had been employed with the same company for the previous 10 years. A history of his carpenter earnings and annual increases is detailed below.

Year	Hourly Rate	Increase	Percent Increase
1998	$15.00		
1999	$15.50	$0.50	3.33%
2000	$16.05	$0.55	3.55%
2001	$16.40	$0.35	2.18%
2002	$16.90	$0.50	3.05%
2003	$17.40	$0.50	2.96%
2004	$17.75	$0.35	2.01%
2005	$18.00	$0.25	1.41%
2006	$18.65	$0.65	3.61%
2007	$18.90	$0.25	1.34%

Average Annual Wage Increase (as a percent)		2.60%
Average CPI Growth Over the 1998-2007 Period		2.71%
Average Industry Growth Over the 1998-2007 Period	3.02% -	3.38%

Assumptions:

1) Assume Mr. Jones would have continued to receive an annual increase each January 1st and that this amount would be equal to his past annual increases, 2.60%.

Conclusions:

Therefore, the annual growth rate applied to Mr. Jones' past and future but-for earnings and benefits is: 2.60%

---

negligence of the defendant. Assume the plaintiff is unable to work for six weeks. After that period of time, the plaintiff returns to work with no additional losses. With respect to lost earnings and benefits, the plaintiff has lost six weeks of earnings and any benefits he did not receive during that time period. In many cases, however, the expected amount of time of a plaintiff's lost earnings is not so clear.

In considering a time period for a plaintiff's lost earnings capacity, the financial analyst must also consider mitigating earnings, discussed later in the chapter. In brief, a plaintiff's mitigating earnings capacity may end the economic loss calculation at some time in the future based on the conclusion that the plaintiff's mitigating earnings will converge with the but-for earnings projection amounts. At that time, the plaintiff is said to be "fully mitigated."

Assuming there is no stated reason to end the plaintiff's but-for earnings projection sooner (i.e., a specific date on which the plaintiff's expected loss of earnings will terminate), the plaintiff's work life expectancy is the most logical date on which to end a but-for earnings projection. A

---

plaintiff's work life expectancy is the number of years he is expected to work through the end of his life expectancy. After that number of years has passed, the plaintiff's projected but-for earnings and benefits would have ceased.

There are a number of methods by which to estimate a plaintiff's work life expectancy, and the forensic economic community has done significant research on the issue. Some of the approaches involve sophisticated actuarial analysis, and others incorporate multiple probabilities of living, actual employment, and participation in the workforce. For purposes of this introductory analysis, we will use the most basic work life expectancy tables published by the U.S. government Bureau of Labor Statistics. (I have not duplicated these tables here, but assume that Mr. Jones' statistical work life expectancy is to December 31, 2025.) Table 4 presents Mr. Jones' but-for earnings and benefits projected to his work life expectancy date.

The But-For Projection—Discount Rate. First, as a general rule, past amounts of lost earnings are not usually brought forward with interest to the date of valuation. Although from a financial perspective past damages should be compounded, courts seem to be reluctant to allow prejudgment interest on the past losses in personal economic loss calculations.

The concept of discounting future amounts of money to present value is well understood in finance, and it was discussed in Chapter 8. Discounting is generally accepted for future loss estimates. The present value of future sums of money is the present principal amount that, when invested at the interest rate used in the discounting analysis, will yield the future sums at the future times of the projection. The process of discounting future projected losses to present value is intended to provide the plaintiff a present sum to replace his or her future income.

Although the basic concept of discounting future amounts to present value is universal, there are many slight variations in techniques of discounting that can be applied. It is fair to say that there is no absolute "right or wrong" way to apply discounting methodology; it is only important that future estimated losses be discounted to present value.

In the example in this chapter, the discounting of the future but-for earnings projection and, later, the mitigation projection is done based on the assumption that Zero Coupon U.S. Treasury bonds that mature into each year of the future projection is an appropriate discount rate to apply to the future amounts. For simplicity, we will also assume that each year's future amount "hits" on the last day of the year. (This is a simpler assumption than I would use in the real world, but it enables the reader to replicate the Excel spreadsheet calculations on the Texas Instruments calculator.)

So, in Table 5, we can see the effect of discounting the but-for future earnings projection to present value. The present value ($769,076) is significantly less than the absolute sum of the future value amounts.

In the real world, it is important for the analyst to comprehend and consider more sophisticated approaches to discounting future sums to present value. For instance, it is too simplistic to assume

Table 4
Johnny Jones v. ABC Company
But-For Earnings and Benefits Analysis

Mr. Jones' total earnings and benefits base as of 12/31/2007 are:

Annual Earnings	6.20% FICA	11.40% Health	5.00% 401(K)	Total
$38,745	$2,402	$4,417	$1,937	$47,501

Assume Mr. Jones would continue to receive annual raises each January 1st. Use an annual growth rate of 2.60% to calculate future earnings and benefits. Assume a work life expectancy of 15 years from the date of valuation.

Growth Rate 2.60%

From	To	# of Years	Annual Earnings	[3] 22.60% Benefits	Total Annual Earnings
Past					
01/01/08	12/31/08	1.00	$39,752 [1]	$8,984	$48,736 [2]
01/01/09	12/31/09	1.00	$40,786	$9,218	$50,004
01/01/10	12/31/10	1.00	$41,846	$9,457	$51,303
		3.00	Total Past But-For Earnings		$150,043
Future					
01/01/11	12/31/11	1.00	$42,934	$9,703	$52,637
01/01/12	12/31/12	1.00	$44,050	$9,955	$54,005
01/01/13	12/31/13	1.00	$45,195	$10,214	$55,409
01/01/14	12/31/14	1.00	$46,370	$10,480	$56,850
01/01/15	12/31/15	1.00	$47,576	$10,752	$58,328
01/01/16	12/31/16	1.00	$48,813	$11,032	$59,845
01/01/17	12/31/17	1.00	$50,082	$11,319	$61,401
01/01/18	12/31/18	1.00	$51,384	$11,613	$62,997
01/01/19	12/31/19	1.00	$52,720	$11,915	$64,635
01/01/20	12/31/20	1.00	$54,091	$12,225	$66,316
01/01/21	12/31/21	1.00	$55,497	$12,542	$68,039
01/01/22	12/31/22	1.00	$56,940	$12,868	$69,808
01/01/23	12/31/23	1.00	$58,420	$13,203	$71,623
01/01/24	12/31/24	1.00	$59,939	$13,546	$73,485
01/01/25	12/31/25	1.00	$61,497	$13,898	$75,395
		15.00			
			Total Future But-For Earnings		$950,773
			Total Past and Future But-For Earnings		$1,100,816

[1] $38,745 X 1.026 = $39,752
[2] $47,501 X 1.026 = $48,736
[3] 6.20% FICA + 11.40% Health Benefits + 5.0% 401(K) =   22.60%

that a plaintiff's earnings would all be paid on the last day of a future year, even though the easiest financial calculation to apply to a plaintiff's loss would be an annual ordinary annuity. To make the calculation more closely approximate reality, perhaps a monthly payment assumption would be more reasonable. However, regarding a growth rate to assign to future lost wages, it would not seem logical to assign a monthly growth rate to a person's wages because that isn't the way that wage earners' compensation increases. In order to logically analyze the underlying facts through a financial model, the analyst cannot be constrained by a simple annuity calculation; he must craft a model that truly analyzes the facts of the particular plaintiff's situation but is not so financially complicated that it defies practical explanation. So, consider Table 5 as a simple approach, and then we will look at a more sophisticated alternative.

Based on the facts and assumptions of the damages calculation, the past loss of earnings and benefits for Mr. Jones as a result of the incident on January 1, 2008 is $150,043. Using an end-of-year salary and benefits payment assumption in the calculation, the present value of the future loss of earnings and benefits as a carpenter to Mr. Jones is $769,076. The sum of the past and future but-for earnings loss amounts represents Mr. Jones' total loss, $919,119, before consideration of possible offsetting amounts due to mitigation.

For a more involved discussion of discount rates that are used in personal economic loss analysis, see the Appendix at the end of this chapter. The Appendix presents alternative approaches to discounting that are often used in these types of analyses.

Mitigating Earnings

Mitigating earnings are the plaintiff's earnings in alternative employment, either actual or anticipated. As previously discussed, a plaintiff has a duty to mitigate his loss of earnings claim by making a reasonable attempt to minimize the losses sustained as a result of the defendant's conduct. The amounts that the plaintiff has actually earned post-injury as well as any projected mitigating earnings are used to offset the projected but-for earnings and benefits of the plaintiff. Typically, a plaintiff has been unable to return to work since the incident or has only been able to return in some lesser capacity. However, there are instances, as well, where a plaintiff might be unable to work for a period of time but is then able to return to work earning the same amount or more than his earnings prior to the incident. In these cases, the loss of earnings and benefits ceases when the plaintiff returns to work.

The financial model for mitigating earnings is similar, if not identical, to the model for a loss of earnings capacity analysis. It consists of an earnings base (now the mitigating earnings amount), a benefits amount, a growth rate, a time period and a discount rate (for future mitigating earnings). Frequently, the only difference between the two financial models is a lower amount of assumed earnings and benefits for the mitigating earnings, with the other components (growth rate, time period and discount rate) often being the same. (There can be factual situations where these other factors differ from the but-for earnings model, for instance, if the plaintiff's mitigating earning

Table 5
Johnny Jones v. ABC Company
But-For Earnings and Benefits
Present Value Analysis

Calculations:

Past:

		Growth Rate: 2.60%		[2] 22.60%	Total		Period
From	To	# of Years	Annual Earnings	Benefits	Annual Earnings		Loss
01/01/08	12/31/08	1.00	$39,752 [1]	$8,984	$48,736		48,736
01/01/09	12/31/09	1.00	$40,786	$9,218	$50,004		50,004
01/01/10	12/31/10	1.00	$41,846	$9,457	$51,303		51,303
		3.00			Total Past Loss		$150,043

Future:

		Growth Rate 2.60%		[2] 22.60%	Total		
From	To	# of Years	Annual Earnings	Benefits	Annual Earnings	Discount Rate	Present Value
01/01/11	12/31/11	1.00	$42,934	$9,703	$52,637	0.12%	$ 52,579
01/01/12	12/31/12	1.00	$44,050	$9,955	$54,005	0.30%	53,686
01/01/13	12/31/13	1.00	$45,195	$10,214	$55,409	0.55%	54,506
01/01/14	12/31/14	1.00	$46,370	$10,480	$56,850	0.87%	54,911
01/01/15	12/31/15	1.00	$47,576	$10,752	$58,328	1.23%	54,869
01/01/16	12/31/16	1.00	$48,813	$11,032	$59,845	1.60%	54,411
01/01/17	12/31/17	1.00	$50,082	$11,319	$61,401	1.95%	53,658
01/01/18	12/31/18	1.00	$51,384	$11,613	$62,997	2.20%	52,930
01/01/19	12/31/19	1.00	$52,720	$11,915	$64,635	2.57%	51,462
01/01/20	12/31/20	1.00	$54,091	$12,225	$66,316	2.81%	50,287
01/01/21	12/31/21	1.00	$55,497	$12,542	$68,039	2.97%	49,335
01/01/22	12/31/22	1.00	$56,940	$12,868	$69,808	3.12%	48,314
01/01/23	12/31/23	1.00	$58,420	$13,203	$71,623	3.29%	47,020
01/01/24	12/31/24	1.00	$59,939	$13,546	$73,485	3.37%	46,200
01/01/25	12/31/25	1.00	$61,497	$13,898	$75,395	3.52%	44,905
		15.00			$950,773		

Total present value of future loss	$769,076
Total Past Loss and Present Value of Future Loss	$919,119

[1] $38,745 X 1.026 = $39,752
[2] 6.20% FICA + 11.40% Health Benefits + 5.0% 401(K) =   22.60%

capacity has a lesser growth rate or the plaintiff has a shortened work life expectancy.) Since the financial model for mitigating earnings is usually similar to the loss of earnings capacity model, it can usually be directly incorporated as a subtraction to the lost earnings capacity analysis.

If the plaintiff has returned to work since the incident and prior to the date of trial, the financial analyst can look at the past history of actual mitigating earnings as a possible estimate of future mitigating earnings. However, there may be reasons to not use these earnings in future periods. Some examples where these earnings should not be used is if a plaintiff has not yet achieved an earnings "hardening" or the plaintiff may be underemployed or not otherwise working to his full earnings capacity. Sometimes, the appropriate assumption for the plaintiff's mitigating earnings capacity is the subject of expert testimony of a qualified consultant in the vocational rehabilitation field. When this testimony is provided to the financial analyst, the opinions of these qualified experts should be relied upon in order to calculate any future mitigating earnings the plaintiff will have.

The vocational rehabilitation expert will perform an assessment of the plaintiff and his current abilities and determine which occupations best suit his current limitations. He then also performs job market research in order to determine a reasonable amount of earnings for these types of professions and reasonable benefits he will receive, if any. In addition, the vocational rehabilitation specialist's report might include costs for vocational rehabilitation training that the plaintiff will require in order to become employed in his new profession and any possible reductions in work life expectancy due to his new limitations.

In our example, as shown in Table 6, Mr. Jones will now be able to earn total earning and benefits of \$22,090 + \$338,896 = \$360,986 through the remainder of his work life expectancy. This amount must be subtracted from his total but-for earnings and benefits amount to arrive at a net loss of earnings and benefits to Mr. Jones as a result of the incident. Mr. Jones's total loss of earning and benefits for the past and future period is \$919,119 - \$360,986 = \$558,133. By looking at Table 9 and focusing only on earnings, benefits, and mitigating earnings, you can easily replicate these amounts.

Alternatively, since the time periods, growth rates and discount rates for both the but-for earnings and benefits loss (and mitigating earnings and benefits offset) are the same, one could calculate the difference between the but-for earnings loss amount and the mitigating earnings amount for each time period and then discount that net amount to present value. That would result in the same total net loss of earnings and benefits of \$558,133. When different time periods, growth rates and discount rates are used, the but-for earnings and benefits loss and mitigating earnings and benefits offset must be calculated separately and then the difference is the resulting total economic loss to the plaintiff.

Loss of Household Services

In addition to any loss of income that results from a defendant's actions, a plaintiff might also experience a loss of household services. Household services are services that the plaintiff can no longer perform around the home (such as cooking, cleaning and gardening) that he or she had performed prior to the incident. The economic loss to the plaintiff is the value of these services that he or she once performed.

Table 6
Johnny Jones v. ABC Company
Mitigating Earnings Analysis

Facts:

Mr. Jones returned to work as an office clerk on 1/1/2010, earning $10.00 per hour and working 40 hours per week. He expects a raise to $10.50 an hour on 1/1/2011. He receives a FICA benefit only. He has been assessed by a vocational rehabilitation specialist who has determined that these current earnings are a proper representation of Mr. Jones' current earnings capacity. It is assumed earnings will grow by 2.60% per year and that the earnings and benefits should be discounted to present value using the Zero Coupon Bond rate.

Calculations:

Growth Rate 2.60%

Past: From	To	# of Years	Annual Earnings	6.20% Benefits	Total Annual Earnings	Period Loss
01/01/08	12/31/08	1.00	$0	$0	$0	0
01/01/09	12/31/09	1.00	$0	$0	$0	0
01/01/10	12/31/10	1.00	$20,800 [1]	$1,290	$22,090	$22,090
		3.00		Total Past Mitigating Earnings		$22,090

Future:

Growth Rate 2.60%

From	To	# of Years	Annual Earnings	6.20% Benefits	Total Annual Earnings	Present Value Factor	Present Value
01/01/11	12/31/11	1.00	$21,840 [2]	$1,354	$23,194	0.12%	23,168
01/01/12	12/31/12	1.00	$22,408	$1,389	$23,797	0.30%	23,657
01/01/13	12/31/13	1.00	$22,991	$1,425	$24,416	0.55%	24,018
01/01/14	12/31/14	1.00	$23,589	$1,463	$25,052	0.87%	24,198
01/01/15	12/31/15	1.00	$24,202	$1,501	$25,703	1.23%	24,179
01/01/16	12/31/16	1.00	$24,831	$1,540	$26,371	1.60%	23,977
01/01/17	12/31/17	1.00	$25,477	$1,580	$27,057	1.95%	23,645
01/01/18	12/31/18	1.00	$26,139	$1,621	$27,760	2.20%	23,324
01/01/19	12/31/19	1.00	$26,819	$1,663	$28,482	2.57%	22,677
01/01/20	12/31/20	1.00	$27,516	$1,706	$29,222	2.81%	22,159
01/01/21	12/31/21	1.00	$28,231	$1,750	$29,981	2.97%	21,739
01/01/22	12/31/22	1.00	$28,965	$1,796	$30,761	3.12%	21,290
01/01/23	12/31/23	1.00	$29,718	$1,843	$31,561	3.29%	20,720
01/01/24	12/31/24	1.00	$30,491	$1,890	$32,381	3.37%	20,358
01/01/25	12/31/25	1.00	$31,284	$1,940	$33,224	3.52%	19,788
		15.00			$418,962		

Total Present Value of Future Mitigating Earnings $338,896

Total Past and Present Value of Future Mitigating Earnings $360,986

[1] $10.00 X 2,080 = $20,800
[2] $10.50 X 2,080 = $21,840

The financial analyst can rely on either a self-reported loss of household services hours provided by the plaintiff or on a statistical report which details the average amount of household services hours performed by both males and females in various size households and of various ages. There is no one correct method for determining the total annual loss of household services hours, and, similar to the loss of earnings capacity calculation, it is left to the discretion of the financial expert to analyze the data available, make reasonable assumptions and determine a logical conclusion.

Once a reasonable hourly rate is established for the types of household services that the plaintiff can no longer perform, the present value calculation is similar to that of the but-for earnings loss and the mitigating earnings. A reasonable growth rate and discount rate are determined and then applied to the annual loss of household services amount in order to determine the present value of the total loss of household services of the plaintiff. The loss of household services is typically calculated to the end of the plaintiff's life expectancy.

Although the current example does not include some of the subtleties that may exist in an actual case, the financial analyst should consider the probability that the plaintiff would not likely have performed the same level of household services in the late stages of his life expectancy that he would have performed in earlier years. Also, the notion that the complexion of household services might change because of external factors (retirement, emancipation of minors in the household, etc.) could also be considered in the analysis. Table 7 presents a calculation of lost past and future household services.

Medical, Life Care and Other Expenses

As previously discussed, a plaintiff's possible damages can include past and future medical care costs, life care expenses, special transportation needs and specialized housing requirements. These types of costs (their description, cost, frequency, and duration) are typically quantified by an expert such as a life care planner or other medical professional. It is then the task of the financial analyst to determine the proper growth rates for these particular items as well a proper discount rate in order to calculate the present value of these types of costs. Table 8 shows a calculation of lost past and future medical expenses.

Conclusion of Example

Table 9 summarizes the damages calculations for Mr. Jones's loss of earnings and benefits, mitigation, lost household services and lost medical expenses.

Table 7
Johnny Jones v. ABC Company
Loss of Household Services Analysis

Facts:

Prior to the incident, Mr. Jones reported he performed 10 hours per week of household services, including cooking, cleaning, laundry and car maintenance. He now can only perform 5 hours per week as a result of his injuries. The value of these services has been determined to be $11.00 per hour in 2008. An annual growth rate of 2.5% is applied to this hourly rate and the amounts are discounted to present value using a Zero Coupon Bond rate for a U.S. Government bond maturing into the year of the projection.

Calculations:

Growth Rate   2.50%

Past:

From	To	# of Years	Hourly Rate	250 [1] Annual Hours		Period Loss
01/01/08	12/31/08	1.00	$11.00	$2,750		$2,750
01/01/09	12/31/09	1.00	$11.28 [2]	$2,820		$2,820
01/01/10	12/31/10	1.00	$11.56	$2,890		$2,890
		3.00	Total Past loss of Household Services			$8,460

Future:

Growth Rate   2.50%

From	To	# of Years	Hourly Rate	250 [1] Annual Hours	Present Value Factor	Present Value
01/01/11	12/31/11	1.00	$11.85	$2,963	0.12%	$2,960
01/01/12	12/31/12	1.00	$12.15	$3,038	0.30%	$3,020
01/01/13	12/31/13	1.00	$12.45	$3,113	0.55%	$3,062
01/01/14	12/31/14	1.00	$12.76	$3,190	0.87%	$3,081
01/01/15	12/31/15	1.00	$13.08	$3,270	1.23%	$3,076
01/01/16	12/31/16	1.00	$13.41	$3,353	1.60%	$3,049
01/01/17	12/31/17	1.00	$13.75	$3,438	1.95%	$3,004
01/01/18	12/31/18	1.00	$14.09	$3,523	2.20%	$2,960
01/01/19	12/31/19	1.00	$14.44	$3,610	2.57%	$2,874
01/01/20	12/31/20	1.00	$14.80	$3,700	2.81%	$2,806
01/01/21	12/31/21	1.00	$15.17	$3,793	2.97%	$2,750
01/01/22	12/31/22	1.00	$15.55	$3,888	3.12%	$2,691
01/01/23	12/31/23	1.00	$15.94	$3,985	3.29%	$2,616
01/01/24	12/31/24	1.00	$16.34	$4,085	3.37%	$2,568
01/01/25	12/31/25	1.00	$16.75	$4,188	3.52%	$2,494
01/01/26	12/31/26	1.00	$17.17	$4,293	3.52%	$2,468
01/01/27	12/31/27	1.00	$17.60	$4,400	3.61%	$2,410
01/01/28	12/31/28	1.00	$18.04	$4,510	3.69%	$2,351
01/01/29	12/31/29	1.00	$18.49	$4,623	3.81%	$2,274
01/01/30	12/31/30	1.00	$18.95	$4,738	3.80%	$2,247
01/01/31	12/31/31	1.00	$19.42	$4,855	3.91%	$2,172
01/01/32	12/31/32	1.00	$19.91	$4,978	3.94%	$2,127
01/01/33	12/31/33	1.00	$20.41	$5,103	3.98%	$2,082
01/01/34	12/31/34	1.00	$20.92	$5,230	4.01%	$2,036
01/01/35	12/31/35	1.00	$21.44	$5,360	4.05%	$1,986
		25.00				

Total present value of future lost household services $65,165

Total past and present value of future lost household services $73,625

[1] Annual household services hours calculated as 5 hours/week X 50 weeks per year =   250
[2] The 2008 estimated hourly rate is increased by 2.5% to account for estimated inflationary growth
    in the hourly amount.

Table 8
Johnny Jones v. ABC Company
Past and Future Medical Expenses

Facts:

Dr. White has opined that Mr. Jones has required and will require pain medications for the remainder of his life expectancy at a cost of $150 per month. An annual growth rate of 3.0% is applied to these costs and the amounts are discounted to present value using a Zero Coupon Bond for a U.S. Government bond maturing into the year of the projection. For simplicity, assume that the required payment is at 12/31 of each year.

Calculations:

Growth Rate   3.00%

Past:

From	To	# of Years	Monthly Cost	Annual Cost	Period Loss
01/01/08	12/31/08	1.00	$150	$1,800	$1,800
01/01/09	12/31/09	1.00	$155	$1,854	$1,854
01/01/10	12/31/10	1.00	$159	$1,910	$1,910
		3.00		Total Past Medical expenses	$5,564

Future:

Growth Rate   3.00%

From	To	# of Years	Monthly Cost	Annual Cost	Present Value Factor	Present Value
01/01/11	12/31/11	1.00	$164	$1,967	0.12%	$1,965
01/01/12	12/31/12	1.00	$169	$2,026	0.30%	2,014
01/01/13	12/31/13	1.00	$174	$2,087	0.55%	2,053
01/01/14	12/31/14	1.00	$179	$2,149	0.87%	2,076
01/01/15	12/31/15	1.00	$184	$2,214	1.23%	2,083
01/01/16	12/31/16	1.00	$190	$2,280	1.60%	2,073
01/01/17	12/31/17	1.00	$196	$2,349	1.95%	2,053
01/01/18	12/31/18	1.00	$202	$2,419	2.20%	2,032
01/01/19	12/31/19	1.00	$208	$2,492	2.57%	1,984
01/01/20	12/31/20	1.00	$214	$2,566	2.81%	1,946
01/01/21	12/31/21	1.00	$220	$2,643	2.97%	1,916
01/01/22	12/31/22	1.00	$227	$2,723	3.12%	1,885
01/01/23	12/31/23	1.00	$234	$2,804	3.29%	1,841
01/01/24	12/31/24	1.00	$241	$2,889	3.37%	1,816
01/01/25	12/31/25	1.00	$248	$2,975	3.52%	1,772
01/01/26	12/31/26	1.00	$255	$3,064	3.52%	1,761
01/01/27	12/31/27	1.00	$263	$3,156	3.61%	1,729
01/01/28	12/31/28	1.00	$271	$3,251	3.69%	1,695
01/01/29	12/31/29	1.00	$279	$3,349	3.81%	1,647
01/01/30	12/31/30	1.00	$287	$3,449	3.80%	1,636
01/01/31	12/31/31	1.00	$296	$3,552	3.91%	1,589
01/01/32	12/31/32	1.00	$305	$3,659	3.94%	1,563
01/01/33	12/31/33	1.00	$314	$3,769	3.98%	1,538
01/01/34	12/31/34	1.00	$323	$3,882	4.01%	1,511
01/01/35	12/31/35	1.00	$333	$3,998	4.05%	1,482
		25.00				
				Present Value of Future Medical Expenses		$45,660
				Total Past and Present Value of Future Medical Expenses		$51,224

Table 9
Johnny Jones v. ABC Company
Economic Loss Conclusions

Past Losses:

Loss of earnings and benefits	$ 150,043
Less: Offset earnings	(22,090)
Lost Household Services	8,460
Medical expenses	5,564
Total Past Losses	141,977

Future Losses (at present value):

Loss of earnings and benefits	769,076
Less: Mitigating earnings	(338,896)
Lost Household Services	65,165
Medical Expenses	45,660
Present Value of Future losses	541,005
Total Economic Losses	$ 682,982

Personal Consumption

In a wrongful death matter, personal consumption is the amount of expenses that the decedent would have consumed if he had lived. A reasonable estimate of the amount of the decedent's personal consumption must be subtracted from the loss of earnings or loss of household services calculation. Personal consumption expense is an amount that would not have been available to the decedent's survivors had the decedent lived, and it should not be included as part of the economic damages to the survivors. Similar to household services, the details of a decedent's estimated annual expenditures can be provided by the surviving members of the family, or, as is more typical in wrongful death cases, personal consumption may be estimated based on household expenditure tables provided by the U.S. government.

If a family can provide the details of their annual expenditures, the financial analyst can categorize the various types of expenses to determine those expenses which would have been greater had the decedent lived compared to those which would not have experienced a change. For example, if a husband, wife and their two children were living in a home that they had purchased at the time of the husband's death, the monthly mortgage amount they are expected to pay would not decrease as a result of the husband's death. However, their monthly food expenditures would decrease as they are now only purchasing food for three individuals compared to four before the decedent's death. Additionally, some types of expenditures may have both a fixed component that would not change with the death of one of the family members and a variable component which would decrease as a result. For example, if the family had only one car, the amount of the car payment would not decrease due to the death, but the monthly amount spent on gasoline might as there is now one less adult who would be using the automobile for personal errands.

If the survivors do not provide a detailed record of household expenditures prior to the decedent's death, then the financial analyst can use expenditure tables in order to determine a reasonable amount of annual consumption to be subtracted from the but-for earnings loss calculation. The Bureau of Labor Statistics provides tables of household expenditures by various socioeconomic and other categories. Most often, household expenditures are determined by the level of household income. The total expenditures are expressed as a percent of total household income for each individual living in the household. When one member the household is deceased, this percent is then applied to the total household earnings to determine his level of personal consumption.

Similar to the mitigating earnings offset, the financial analyst will determine the time period, growth rate and discount rate for the consumption calculation in order to bring the amounts back to present value dollars. The present value calculation would be the same as in the previous examples.

Conclusion

Personal economic losses are those losses an individual suffers as a result of actions of a defendant in a litigation matter, typically a personal injury, wrongful termination or wrongful death matter. There is no "right way" to perform an economic analysis or any particular step in an analysis. Since fact patterns can vary so substantially between cases, it is virtually impossible to set forth a mechanical formula or an absolute rule for determining the value of any particular component of a person's economic loss. The challenge of a good forensic economic analysis is to understand the economic consequences of a particular act or event, and consider and evaluate the possible approaches to determine its economic consequences. In the final analysis, the strength of the conclusion of damages depends on the quality of the financial analysis and its relation to the underlying facts of the case.

Discount Rate Calculations

The discount rate is the interest rate that is used to reduce a future value estimate of any monetary amount to present value. There are many ways to estimate the appropriate discount rate to apply to different types of future monies, and these are discussed in Chapter 12. Here, we will limit our discussion to some of the mechanics of properly applying a discount rate to a personal economic loss. This discussion will ignore the methods of estimating a *correct* discount rate and will focus on the *mechanics of applying* the discount rate to future losses.[9]

Discount rate theory. In personal economic loss calculations, courts have generally followed the theory that a plaintiff should be provided a sum of money that can be invested at a risk-free rate to compensate for the lost earnings suffered. As a matter of concept, the analyst must realize that this legal policy doesn't really conform to strict principles of finance. In reality, a person's lifetime earnings are not a risk-free investment–they contain an element of risk (unemployment, injury, death) and to be perfectly comparable, the discounting of a projected lifetime earnings stream should consider an equivalent risk factor in the discount rate, causing it to be higher than risk-free. But courts aren't constrained to follow perfect financial principles, and it is understandable that the policy of the law would favor an injured plaintiff and place him in a lower risk position after the injury than he was in before the injury for purposes of calculating his economic loss.[10] Consequently, the usual approach for discounting future personal economic losses is to use some proxy for a risk-free rate.

Selecting a "proper" discount rate. Given the conceptual mandate that a risk-free interest rate is the appropriate rate to use, there are many reasonable approaches to applying the concept. In finance, the benchmark for "risk-free" has historically been securities backed by the full faith and confidence in the United States government. To apply this benchmark to a person's projected lifetime earnings, analysts use different measures of U.S. Treasury rates in their analyses. There is no absolute right or wrong way to make the calculation.

To some extent, the selection of a discount rate is a process of determining the best conceptual approach to the particular facts of the problem at hand, where it is understood that there is no perfect answer. Assuming that the analyst is going to use some measure of a U.S. government security as a proxy for the risk-free rate, here are some questions to consider:

---

9. Remember that personal economic losses are generally discounted at a risk-free rate. So, financial analysts can slightly disagree about the correct proxy for the rate, but the concept of using a risk-free rate is not usually in dispute. Consequently, this discount rate discussion doesn't focus on the amount of the discount rate, only on the mechanics of applying the rate. The "mechanics" will include a discussion about annual discounting, monthly discounting, a mid-year convention and the use of the net discount rate methodology.

10. This is a perfect example of the occasional, logical incongruity of legal principles and financial principles.

---

1. Which of the following three choices[11] for the time period of the interest rate should be chosen?

   a. A rate that is in effect at the time of the calculation?

   b. A rate that is derived from some historical average of risk-free interest rates?

   c. A rate intended to reasonably estimate what interest rates will be during the period of the projection?

2. Should more than one rate be used for the projection on the theory that the projection discounts future amounts over different time periods to present value?

3. Should some average of present (or past) interest rates be used to apply one discount rate to the future projection?

4. Should an average of interest rates from some blend of risk-free securities be used that enables you consider different characteristics of the proxy securities?

5. Should the "net discount rate" convention be used in the personal economic loss situation (discussed subsequently)?

There is no perfectly correct answer to these subtle discount rate issues. The financial analyst must consider the rationale that supports each approach and decide which one best conforms to the facts of the particular situation. In making a decision about the best approach to use, three other considerations should be made. First, the reality of making financial calculations in a litigation context is that the calculations must be explained to a trier of fact. If the analysis becomes so complex that it cannot be easily explained, there is a risk that the analysis will fail. Simplicity is not a rationale to do something wrong, but it is a reason to opt for an alternative that contains fewer complexities. A second consideration that affects the analyst's choice of discount rate rationale (and every judgment in an economic analysis, for that matter) is the reality that the opposing side of the litigation will be arguing against the analyst, regardless of the conceptual purity of the analysis. Consequently, the choice of discount rate rationale should be made with a view toward defending the choice against a somewhat confusing argument against the choice. Finally, in a litigation context, a financial expert is exposed to cross-examination on the issue of consistency of the present analysis as compared to other analyses that have been performed in the past. It is often difficult to explain subtle differences in methodology that a financial analyst might legitimately choose to use in different cases, so the backdrop of consistency is worthy of consideration. Similar to the concept of simplicity, consistency is not a reason to do something wrong, but the analyst must be mindful that he or she could be challenged with the allegation

---

11. As you consider these questions, think through the reasoning—always imperfect—that would support your choice of any one of these approaches to determining a discount rate.

---

that any inconsistency between present and former analyses is indicative of bias. These are some of the complicated considerations that a financial analyst must contemplate while determining the methodology for each project.

The mechanics of using different discounting conventions. The components of a present value discounting calculation are a future value amount, a time period and a discount rate. The time period can be divided into any fraction of the total time to the future date, but the logical fractions are years, portions of years, months or days. The time period selected for the present value calculation—the "N"—will be the compounding period that will be used in the calculation. Recall from Chapter 8 the significance of different compounding periods in the calculation of future values and be aware that present value calculations are also affected by differing compounding calculations.[12]

There is no absolutely correct answer to the proper compounding period to use to calculate the present value of a future sum in a personal economic loss analysis. The analyst may choose to match the time periods of the present value calculation to the timing of the anticipated losses. For instance, if a wage earner's compensation is lost, it might make sense to treat the future losses as monthly losses rather than annualizing the person's income and assuming that the entire loss for the annual period would have occurred on the last (or first, or middle) day of the year. Alternatively, if the future loss is a cost of surgery that is anticipated to occur five years from today, it might be logical to treat that future loss as a one-time loss that can be discounted on an annual basis.

The relationship of discount rates and growth rates.[13] There is a relationship between the interest rate that is used to discount a future sum to the present value and the amount of growth that is embedded in estimating the future sum. Recall from Chapter 8 that the interest rate, conceptually, has three components: the real rate of interest, the inflation rate, and a risk premium to compensate for the risk inherent in the income stream (or future sum). Let's ignore the risk premium for this discussion (or assume that it is zero), and focus only on the real rate of interest plus the inflation rate. If we assume that the item being projected has some growth expectation (inflation) embedded in it, and the discount rate that is used to bring it to present value has some inflation component in it, then the inflation component is duplicative since it is included in both parts of the financial equation.

The relationship is most easily explained with an example. Assume that Paul Plaintiff is required to have an expensive surgery at some time in the future to repair an injury caused by Danny Defendant. There is credible expert testimony that the surgery presently costs $20,000 and the

---

12. Calculate, for example, the present value of a 20-year stream of annual payments of $60,000 per year, assumed to occur on the last day of each year and discounted at 5% annual interest (answer: PV = $747,732.62). Now, make the payments $5,000 per month instead and calculate the present value (Answer: PV = $757,626.53).

13. "Growth" can be more or less than inflation, but inflation is certainly part of growth. For this discussion, assume that the growth in the sum being projected into the future equals the inflation rate of the item.

medical inflation rate is presently 2.6%.[14] Assume that the present risk-free interest rate is 5%. Finally, assume that Paul's doctor testifies that he will need the surgery in two years. What are Paul's damages related to the medical expenses? Or, how much does Paul have to be awarded today to exactly compensate him for his anticipated surgery?

First, based on the present testimony and the expected inflation rate, the cost of the surgery in two years is expected to be $21,053.52. ($20,000 increased by 2.6% for each of the next two years.) So, there is a future value sum ($21,053.52) that must be discounted to the present value at some discount rate, assumed to be 5% in this illustration. The present value of $21,053.52 at a discount rate of 5%, two years into the future, is $19,096.16. (Check the calculation on your BA – 35 calculator.) Those are the financial facts, and the basis for the next part of the discussion.

Net Discount Rate Method ("NDR").

A net discount rate is a discounting convention by which the growth in the future value amount being discounted is included within the discount rate, as opposed to being calculated in the future amount. The NDR approach enables the analyst to apply a "net" discount factor to a present sum without having to first compound the amount forward to future value. Net discounting can be used to determine the present value of any future amount, but it is most helpful when it is applied to a list of present amounts that have many different future maturities, like medical expenses or a life care plan.

There is a simplified application of the net discount method that is frequently used in calculations; that is the method that will be explained here, even though it is not precisely financially correct.[15] Here is the simplified formula for determining the net discount rate (accepting the interest and growth rates as given):

Nominal interest rate	5.0%
Less: growth rate	(2.6%)
Equals: Net discount rate	2.4%

Let's apply the net discount method to Paul Plaintiff's medical facts above. If we take today's cost of Paul's anticipated surgery, $20,000, assume that it is two years delayed, and discount the present $20,000 at a net discount rate of 2.4% for two years, the calculated PV is $19,073.49. The "net" effect of using the net discount rate method is to implicitly apply the 2.6% growth rate to the present amount (today's cost of Paul's surgery) for the period of the projection (two years), and to discount the future amount to present value at the nominal interest rate (5.0%). (Note that the

---

14. In 2011, the medical inflation rate is really higher than 2.6%, but this amount is being used to simplify the example.

15. The precise financial formula for a net discount rate calculation is $[(1 + r) / (1 + g) – 1]$ where r = the discount rate and g = growth rate. Applied to the facts here, the calculation is $(1.05 / 1.026) – 1 = 2.339\%$. This precise calculation is slightly different from the approximate calculation of 2.4%, but the effect of the difference in most calculations is immaterial. As a practical matter, the net discount rate can be approximately calculated as the discount rate minus the growth rate.

NDR calculation is a few dollars different from the amount of the precise calculation of the present value in a preceding paragraph of $19,096.16. This is not a rounding error; it is an example of the magnitude of the "error" of using a simplified NDR calculation in lieu of the exact calculation.)

In order to be able to use the NDR methodology, both the growth rate and the discount rate must be constant. You can't apply the NDR method to a situation where the expected growth will be 1.5% next year, then 2.2% the following year, and so forth. Even if the analyst doesn't ultimately use the NDR methodology in final calculations, applying the simplified NDR method can be very helpful to ascertain a preliminary conclusion. Consider the following example:

Assume a 30-year-old plaintiff who was earning $35,000 per year suffered a total and permanent loss of earnings. A very informal, preliminary calculation of the loss of earnings could be made with NDR methodology, given some very broad assumptions. Assume the following: the plaintiff's benefits were equal to an additional 20% of salary (therefore, total compensation = 1.2 X $35,000, or $42,000); the plaintiff would have worked to age 65, or another 30 years. Next, assume a long-term inflation rate (growth in earnings rate) of 2.2% (equal to present long-term inflation projections) and finally, assume a reasonable risk-free interest rate of 4.5% (equal to long-term U.S. government bonds. The facts and calculation would be:

PMT = $42,000
N = 35
I/Y = 2.3% (4.5% – 2.2%)
PV = $1,002,187

Obviously, the NDR methodology can be used for a single sum projected into the future, or a stream of cash flows (an "annuity," like a person's lost earnings).

Typically, the net discount rate is estimated as the average difference between the nominal interest rate and the nominal rate of wage growth over some reasonable period of time. The NDR method allows both the growth rate and the discount rate to be broadly or nonspecifically estimated and combined into a single net rate.

Some states have adopted the "total offset" method for discounting future amounts to present value. The implicit assumption of the total offset method is that the growth rate for the present amount is the same as the discount rate for the future value of the amount. The total offset method is a conclusion of a net discount rate of zero percent, and a zero NDR is appropriate when the appropriate growth rate for the amount happens to be the same as the current market discount rate.

Conclusion of discounting conventions. There is no right or wrong convention for discounting future losses to present value. The convention of NDR is no better or worse than the specific growing and discounting of a future projected amount; it is just a different way of estimating the components of discounting. Practicing lawyers must be familiar with the concepts of present value and discounting and it is extremely helpful to be able to make these calculations on behalf of clients.

Chapter 12

Commercial Damages

Introduction

Commercial damages are losses suffered by a plaintiff business enterprise as a result of a defendant's wrongful conduct, usually either the breach of a contract or the commission of a tort. In general, assuming that the liability of the defendant is established, the harmed business enterprise is entitled to be placed in the same financial condition that it would have been in, absent the conduct of the defendant. This theoretical premise is easy to understand, but the application of the concept can be very complicated.

This chapter will provide a general overview of all commercial damages, but it ultimately focuses on two areas: damages from breach of contract and lost business profits. A business can suffer other types of damages, such as property damage or increased costs, but the most complicated calculations generally relate to measuring the lost profits of a business resulting from a defendant's breach of contract or commission of a tort. Lost profits calculations involve the analysis of historical financial activity, financial projections, an understanding of fixed and variable costs and sophisticated concepts of discounting future projections to present value. We will address all of these issues in this chapter.

As in all areas of damages calculations, the financial analyst and the lawyer must be aware of the relevant laws in the jurisdiction so the opinion of lost profits conforms to the cases and statutes that control the particular situation. Sometimes, unfortunately, the law of the jurisdiction is vague and ambiguous regarding the particular factual situation, and the financial analyst must work closely with the legal team to determine the proper approach to apply.

Also, recall that damages are a financial compensation remedy; they aren't the only remedy available to a harmed plaintiff. The plaintiff may be entitled to specific performance of a contract, rescission of a contract or declaratory relief by the court (the court ordering someone to do something). This chapter focuses on damages.

Damages from Breach of Contract

A contract is a legally enforceable promise. In the law, there are a number of elements to a contract: offer, acceptance, mutuality, capacity, consideration and performance. A legal discussion of contract law is beyond the scope of this text; all damages analyses assume that the contract under consideration was breached. Ignoring the remedies of rescission, restitution and specific performance, if damages are claimed, the question for the financial analyst is the amount of damages that result from the breach.

As discussed generally in Chapter 10, there are two alternative theories of contract damages: the out of pocket rule and the benefit of the bargain rule. The particular theory that applies to the present case is a matter of law in the jurisdiction of the litigation and should be discussed with legal counsel. Under either theory, the plaintiff may be entitled to lost profits.

Out-of-Pocket Rule. Under this theory, the plaintiff will receive as damages the amount that he is "out of pocket." The first measure of this damage is the amount that the plaintiff paid under the contract. Depending on the circumstances, the plaintiff might also claim related out of pocket costs, such as site preparation (for the delivery of a machine, for example) or possibly lost profits that were foreseeable to the parties to the contract. The focus of this theory of contract damages is what the plaintiff lost, not what he would have gained if the contract had been performed.

Benefit-of-the-Bargain Rule. Under the benefit of the bargain rule, the non-breaching party is entitled to everything that he would have received, including profits, if the breach had not occurred. The focus under this theory is the benefit that the plaintiff was entitled to under the contract. If, for example, the performance of the contract would have garnered an economic benefit to the plaintiff, the plaintiff is entitled to that benefit as damages.

Cover. "Cover" is the same as mitigation and must be considered in contract damages. The harmed party can't just sit there and claim damages against the breaching party while he does nothing to minimize the harm that he claims was caused by the breach.

Commercial Damages from Torts

A tort is a civil wrong, other than a breach of contract, that results in injury to a person or property for which relief may be obtained in the form of damages or injunction. Intentional torts are intentional acts that are reasonably foreseeable to cause harm to another. Negligence is a tort stemming from the breach of a duty that is imposed on individuals to act in a manner that does not cause harm to others. Economic torts are largely the creation of statutes over the last hundred years, and they have been created to protect people and businesses from harm to commercial enterprise. Examples of economic torts are interference with contractual relations, fraudulent misrepresentation, unfair competition, interference with prospective economic advantage, unfair business practices, infringement of intellectual property rights, and others.

Commercial damages awards fall into three categories: 1) those that intend to make the plaintiff whole (compensatory); 2) those that intend to prohibit the defendant from benefiting from his wrongful conduct (restitution); and 3) those that intend to punish the defendant (punitive). The first category includes the plaintiff's property damage, increased costs, and any lost profits resulting from the defendant's wrongful act. The second category includes the concept of disgorgement of the defendant's profits from the wrongful conduct, a damages remedy that may be allowed in situations where the law considers the defendant's conduct to rise to a higher level of wrongfulness, even if the plaintiff hasn't suffered any lost profits. Examples of situations in which disgorgement would be allowed include theft of trade secrets, trademark infringement or patent infringement. In these types of cases, it is possible that the defendant has profited from its conduct even though the plaintiff hasn't lost any profit and the remedy of disgorgement will allow the plaintiff to recover the defendant's wrongfully obtained profits. For example, perhaps the plaintiff operated a relatively new business that was not yet profitable, but had developed a very good technology or product, and the technology was wrongfully infringed on by a profitable defendant. It is important to note, however, that a plaintiff may not recover both its own lost profits and disgorgement of the defendant's profits; the plaintiff must elect its remedies so there is no double recovery.

The final category of damages is punitive damages, those intended to punish the defendant for egregious or outrageous conduct. Because punitive damages are not economically based, they are not directly within the province of financial expert testimony. Forensic accountants are involved in one aspect of punitive damages, however, and that aspect is analyzing and testifying about the net worth and/or income of the defendant. Because punitive damages are intended to punish a defendant, the defendant's net worth and income is a relevant fact for the jury to consider. A punitive damage award of $100,000 may be a huge punishment against a 25-year-old employed person, but it probably wouldn't get the attention of Microsoft or Citibank.

Commercial damages can involve the loss of, or damage to, property; increased costs or expenses to maintain a pre-injury condition or prevent additional damage; additional expenses incurred to correct a harm caused by the defendant; or the loss of profits caused by the defendant's wrongful conduct. The focus of the remainder of Chapter 12 is lost business profits.

Lost Profits as Damages

Lost net profits. Ultimately, the economic loss suffered by a business is defined as a loss of net profits, not a loss of gross revenue or other decline in business activity. The loss of a gross sale is not necessarily an economic loss to a business, unless the business earned some profit on the sale. Lost profits damages are usually defined as lost net profits; all costs must be deducted.[1] For breach of contract, this means the contract price less cost of performance. For lost profits generally, this means the lost gross revenue minus all "expenses saved." Recovery of lost gross revenues or lost gross profits is only correct when gross revenues or gross profits are the same as net profits.

Theoretical basis of lost profits as damages. The objective of a competent lost profits analysis is to place the plaintiff in the same financial position that it would have been in if the defendant had not breached a contract or interfered with the plaintiff.[2] Lost profits are the difference between what

---

1.   Dunn, Robert L., *Recovery of Damages for Lost Profits, 6th Ed.* (Westport, CT: Lawpress Corporation, 2005), p. 469.
2.   Brinig, B.P., "Achieving Reasonable Certainty In Quantifying Lost Profits Damages," *Dunn on Damages: The Economic Damages Report for Litigators and Experts,* Spring 2011, page 7.

the plaintiff's profits would have been "but for"[3] the wrongful act of the defendant and the actual profits experienced by the plaintiff after the wrongful conduct. The algorithm for estimating lost profits is quite simple, but its application is complicated. Although there can be variations depending on specific facts and circumstances of each case, the typical approach to a lost profits analysis is to project but-for gross revenues[4] and compare the projection to actual revenues earned after the date of the incident, creating a difference that is assumed to be lost gross revenues resulting from the defendant's conduct. The next step in the analysis is to estimate the costs that would relate to the presumed lost gross revenues because it is assumed that those costs would be saved. These costs are usually measured by determining the business's variable costs.[5] By subtracting the variable costs saved from the presumed lost gross revenues, the analyst derives the estimate of lost profits. Depending on the timing of the losses, the analyst may add interest to past losses (or not, depending on the law of the jurisdiction), and most likely will discount any future lost profits estimate to present value.

Steps of the lost profits analysis. The previous paragraph summarized the following steps that are generally undertaken in a lost profits analysis:

1. Project *but-for* revenues[6] since the date of the incident to the present, and on into the future.

2. Identify *actual* revenues that have occurred since the date of the incident and project actual revenues into the future.

3. Calculate the *difference* between #1 and #2, representing gross revenues lost from the incident in question.

4. Analyze the *variable costs* that are saved as a result of the gross revenues that are lost, and *subtract the costs saved* from the lost revenues.

5. *Calculate lost net profits*, both past and future.

6. For past lost profits, *consider adding pre-judgment interest* to the calculation.

7. *Discount future lost profits to present value* at an appropriate discount rate.

---

3. The phrase, "but-for" or "but-for world," is often used in damages terminology to describe the hypothetical condition that is projected to have happened after the wrongful conduct, assuming the wrongful conduct had not occurred. By definition, the "but-for world" is a hypothetical situation that is projected, based on reasonable assumptions and in light of all the facts and circumstances. The strength of the damages calculation depends on the reasonableness of the but-for projection, and the projection should be grounded in historical fact and reasonable assumptions.

4. The analyst often projects but-for gross revenues as the foundational assumption for the lost profits calculation, but it is equally reliable to base a lost profits analysis on a projection of some other measure of but-for activity. Other examples of appropriate measures include profits, units of production, geographic area of penetration, number of transactions, or some other logical measure of business activity. Regardless of the benchmark of activity that is projected, the analyst is faced with the same issues regarding the reliability and reasonable certainty of the projection.

5. Variable costs are costs that tend to vary directly with the level of production, within a relevant range. In relation to damages, they are discussed later in the chapter.

6. Or other relevant measure of business activity.

Every step of a lost profits calculation is an assumption. Since the profits that are estimated to be lost did not occur, no part of the calculation of them is a fact. The primary foundational assumption of all lost profits analyses is the financial projection referred to as the "but-for" projection, the assumption that a certain level of business activity would have happened, *but for* the conduct of the defendant. The second foundational assumption is that the actual post-incident level or trend of business activity is lower than it otherwise should have been because of the wrongful conduct of the defendant. This second assumption is really one of causation rather than damages, but it often falls within the province of the damages expert because of the financial and business aspects of the issue. Following the first two foundational assumptions, the lost profits analysis continues to apply other assumptions relating to variable costs, the time period of the loss and discount rate analysis. All of these steps are discussed subsequently in this chapter. The aggregation of all of the assumptions of a lost profits analysis will result in an expert opinion that must be both economically sound and legally permissible.

Three conceptual areas of lost profits. Lost profits damages claims fall, generally, into three conceptual areas: those in which a business suffers reduced income but continues to exist; those in which a business ceases or terminates some or all of its operations; or those in which a business never commenced operations. Each of these areas presents some unique financial (and legal) issues.

Reduced income cases (lost profits). In a reduced income case, the business usually suffers a loss for a specific period of time, but it is expected to return to "normal" at some point. The length of the loss period can vary depending on the underlying cause of action and upon the underlying facts of the case.[7] In a breach of contract action, the loss period will generally be projected over the remaining term of the contract.[8] In the case of tort actions, the loss period is usually from the date of the wrongful act until the date operations return "to normal." The plaintiff is entitled to recover earnings lost as a result of the defendant's actions for that period of time "proximately" related to those actions.[9] Recall, however, that the plaintiff has a duty to mitigate its losses and that duty requires that steps be taken to minimize the ongoing losses; the plaintiff cannot sit back and unfairly profit from the defendant's wrongdoing after reasonable steps would have ended the losses. The following graph depicts a reduced income situation:

---

7.   AICPA Practice Aid 06-4, *Calculating Lost Profits* (2006: New York, NY), p. 23. This publication contains an excellent discussion of the entire subject of lost profits and is recommended to all practitioners.

8.   *Id.*

9.   Brinig, B.P., et al., *PPC's Guide to Litigation Support Services*, 10th Ed. (July 2005).

Reduced Income

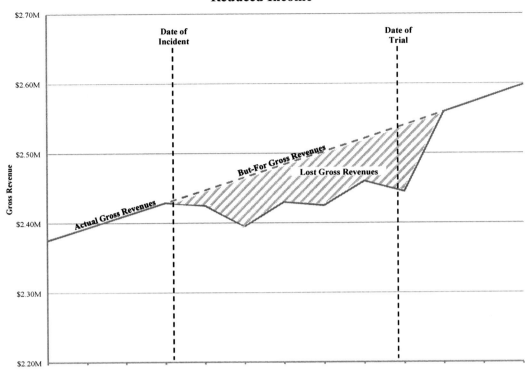

Destruction of business. In these cases, the issues of lost business profits or loss in value of the business, or both, is presented. Obviously, if the business is completely destroyed, all the future profits of the business into perpetuity are lost. But complete destruction of the business raises complicated questions. First, during the demise of the business, additional costs may have been incurred to attempt to save it. Those additional or increased costs are a proper component of the plaintiff's damages and can add to the lost profits. Many financial analysts ask the question: can the plaintiff's losses from lost profits be greater than the value of the business? Although the question remains open, it seems that the majority of practitioners believe that the value of the business is the upper limit on the plaintiff's lost profits, excluding damages for extra costs that were incurred while trying to save the business. Also note, however, that the timing of the loss calculations (ex-post or ex-ante, discussed subsequently) can affect the total amount of the lost profits. The graph on the adjacent page shows the total loss of anticipated revenues from the destruction of a business.

New business venture. From a financial perspective, there is no reason why a new business venture that is stopped by the wrongful conduct of a defendant should not be able to recover its lost profits. Most recent cases reject the once generally accepted rule that lost profits damages for a new business are not recoverable. The development of the law has been to find damages for lost profits of an unestablished business recoverable when they can be adequately proved with reasonable certainty.[10] The great difficulty in analyzing new business ventures, however, is for the damages analyst to find a reasonable basis to project "but-for" revenues and profitability.

---

10. Dunn, *op. cit.*, p. 378.

Destruction of Business

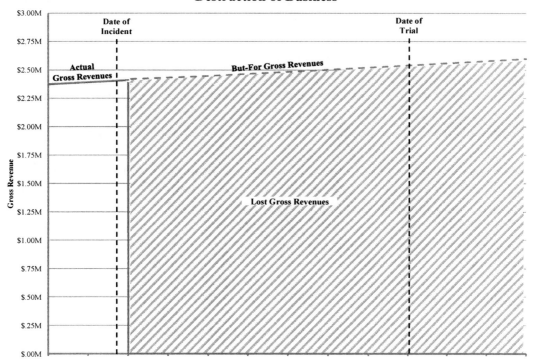

Calculating Lost Profits Damages

1. Project but-for revenues since the date of the incident to the present, and on into the future.

"Methods" of projecting but-for revenues. Most practitioners approach a lost profits analysis from the perspective of first identifying lost revenue by projecting but-for revenues and comparing the projection to actual revenues after the incident. A calculation of lost profits invariably requires certain assumptions about the level of profitability that would have been attained, but for the happening of some tort or breach of contract. Some authors have referred to three bases for making but-for projections as *methods* of calculating lost profits,[11] but intellectual scrutiny indicates that only one of the three is actually a method of estimating; the other two are really only characterizations of assumptions. The following paragraphs discuss the yardstick approach, the before-and-after approach and the sales projections approach.

The yardstick approach. This technique is a method of estimation and it requires the analyst (a) to identify some comparable, independent financial statistic related to the plaintiff's activity to

---

11. Pratt, Riley and Schweihs, *Valuing Small Businesses & Professional Practices*, 3rd Ed. (New York, NY: McGraw-Hill, 1998), p 830. See also Weil, Wagner and Frank, Eds., *Litigation Services Handbook, The Role of the Accountant as Expert*, 2nd Ed. (New York, NY: John Wiley & Sons, Inc.) p 30-32.

be projected, and (b) to plot the but-for performance of the plaintiff's activity based on the post-incident performance of the benchmark activity. When properly applied, the yardstick approach can be a scientific method that supports the validity of a but-for projection and convincingly removes the projection from the realm of speculation. The difficulty with the method lies in identifying substantially similar financial statistics or industry benchmarks to compare to the plaintiff's business activity. A second complication is that the approach may require adjustments to the statistics or industry data to make them more comparable to the subject. The very necessity of making adjustments raises questions about the comparability of the benchmark data.

The yardstick method is best suited when an independent financial benchmark can be found that can be statistically correlated to the plaintiff's historical activity. When a benchmark statistic exists that provides adequate data and it can be closely correlated to the plaintiff's activity, the yardstick method is the most valid and reliable method for estimating but-for activity. In some cases, a regression analysis can be used to establish the level of correlation existing between the yardstick data and the historical data of the subject company. Conceptually, a regression analysis is a time-series method which measures the extent to which one set of data depends upon, or is influenced by, another. If a close historical correlation is shown between some yardstick and the plaintiff's activity, it is very logical to use the continuation of the yardstick measure to plot the hypothetical performance of the plaintiff.

An example of a situation in which a yardstick method could be applied would be one where there was a comparable, but unaffected, division or branch of the plaintiff that could be shown to have the same characteristics as the affected branch, except for the alleged unlawful conduct of the defendant. Another example would be a situation where there was valid secondary data on the sales of a particular product in a relevant market, assuming it could further be shown that the plaintiff would have participated in those sales on some type of pro-rata basis. Immediately, though, one can begin to think of reasons for distinctions between the market data and the plaintiff's presumed sales.

The application of the yardstick method is impractical in the majority of damages cases because of the uniqueness of most plaintiffs' situations as well as the unavailability of adequate data to use as a benchmark. Where could one find competent secondary data to use to compare to the sales of a highly specialized machine tool company in Atlanta, Georgia? Or assume, for example, that there are five ethnic restaurants in the ethnic part of a city and that they each control approximately 20% of the market. The landlord of Restaurant A breaches the lease and forces Restaurant A out of business. It is unlikely that there is a study of sales of the particular type of ethnic food in the particular city that can be used as a yardstick measure of Restaurant A's lost sales. Further, it is unlikely that the other restaurants will disclose their financial information, although it could be suggested that this information would be an excellent "yardstick" to use as a measure of the plaintiff's lost sales. These examples of the yardstick method's limitations demonstrate why the use of the yardstick method is fairly limited.

Before-and-after method. Under this "method," the but-for activity of the plaintiff is projected based on some historical results, assuming the defendant's conduct had not occurred. The before-and-after approach is not really a methodology; it is merely a characterization of the assumption that is being made. It is a statement that says: "I think that X projection would have occurred, but for the unlawful conduct of the defendant." The approach is best suited to a business situation in which there is no practical application of a yardstick method available and one that has an established pattern of activity or track record. The supportable application of the approach depends on the financial analyst's ability to establish and support a proven historical track record of the plaintiff so that the pre-incident period can serve as a benchmark for the but-for projection. The rationale for relying on the pre-incident activity as the basis for the but-for activity must be articulated and proven. Obviously, a showing of the similarity of factors that affect the projected activity from before the incident to the post-incident period is helpful, if not essential, to validate the use of the before-and-after approach. The very use of the approach assumes, of course, that the plaintiff's operations before and after the complained-of event were comparable.

A typical application of the before-and-after approach is the showing of an historical trend of gross revenues, identification of the act of the defendant that is alleged to have altered the trend, and the claim that the trend would have continued but for the defendant's act. There must be reasonable factual support for the but-for projection. To support the analysis, the financial analyst will conduct studies of the numerous factors that could affect the projected activity with a before-and-after quantification of relevant factors, if possible. For example, the analyst may seek a quantification of the economic conditions in the immediate area that affect the business, a quantification of traffic counts or customer counts in the before-and-after condition, and information on the relevant industry and its recent growth or decline. If the results show that none of the factors has materially changed or negatively affected the activity that is being projected, the but-for projection may be free from contamination. Obviously, the more thorough and complete the study of other possible factors is, the more reasonably certain the basis of the but-for projection is.

Sales projections (but-for) method. Under this approach, some activity of the plaintiff, usually revenue, is projected during the post-incident period, based on the assumption that the projection would have occurred but for the alleged effects of the defendant's actions. The sales projections approach is not really a methodology; like the before-and-after approach, it is a characterization of the assumption that is being made. The attempted use of this "method" requires the creation of some type of forecast of business activity during the post-incident period based on certain "but-for" assumptions and the application of the method implicitly assumes that the only material reason that the plaintiff's performance is below the projection is the conduct of the defendant. The existing descriptions of the sales projections method in the literature do not appear to truly distinguish it from the before-and-after method.

Summary of methods. There are many observable, measurable factors that can be studied to assist the financial analyst in arriving at a reasonable but-for projection. The financial history of the enterprise as it relates to the matter in question should be thoroughly analyzed. The historical profitability of the business should be studied and compared to the profitability after the incident. The trends in revenues related to the issue in question should be scheduled out and compared to the post-incident activity. The analyst should contemplate and consider the myriad factors that could have affected the business post incident and consider their effect on the but-for projection.

Working closely with representatives of management, the analyst should identify relevant business factors that existed at the time of the incident and during the presumed damage period, and undertake to investigate whether the factors can be studied and quantified to inform the but-for projection. Frequently, industry data can be obtained from trade associations or other sources that will show trends in product demand, industry sales or other relevant macroeconomic data. Sometimes the information is directly helpful, but even if it is not directly relevant, this type of data provides general background information that is worthy of consideration in the analysis.

Regardless of the approach used to estimate the but-for projection, the financial analyst should carefully consider the logical basis for assuming the reasonableness of the projection. The but-for projection should take into account the existence of factors other than the defendant's conduct that could influence the projection (i.e., seasonality, business cycles, competitive forces, general economic conditions, industry conditions, etc.). In determining the magnitude of but-for projections, the analyst must also account for the managerial and financial ability of the plaintiff to achieve the projections (i.e., production capacity, capital structure, human resources, management capabilities, etc.). And finally, the but-for projection should be tested for overall reasonableness in relation to the plaintiff's historical operating activity and in light of all the facts and circumstances surrounding the damages issue. Because the but-for projection is the foundational assumption of the entire lost profits analysis, it will be closely scrutinized for reasonableness by the court. A thoughtful, objective analysis by the financial analyst can help assure that the projection will be found to be reasonably based, with the analyst's ability to defend it being paramount.

At the end of this first step of the lost profits analysis, the analyst should have a reasonable projection of but-for lost revenues (or other measure of business activity) from the date of the incident to the present, and on into the future, if applicable.

2. Identify actual revenues that have occurred since the date of the incident, and project actual revenues into the future.

The actual operating results during the past damage period are identified and related to the same time periods (weeks, month, years) that the but-for projection is made. If the harm is anticipated to continue into the future, it will be necessary to project actual revenues into the future because the reduced activity is not yet known, but can only be projected.

3. Calculate the difference between #1 and #2, representing gross revenues lost from the incident in question.

The actual and projected results are subtracted from the but-for projections during the past and future damage period. This calculation yields a "difference" in financial activity expected and financial activity achieved. The result of this calculation will yield the assumed lost gross revenues (or other activity) and form the basis for the damages calculation.

4. Analyze the variable costs that are saved as a result of the gross revenues that are lost, and subtract the costs saved from the lost revenues.

If the differential measure is gross revenues, those revenues should be reduced by expenses "saved" because the revenues were not achieved. All direct and/or variable costs relating to the lost gross revenues should be subtracted to compute net profits lost. Absent unusual circumstances, these costs are *saved* or *avoided*. Estimating costs is essential to any lost profits analysis.

The plaintiff's historical financial data (including cost data) is usually the basis upon which to estimate the "but for" incremental costs. An analysis of variable expenses, semi-variable expenses and fixed expenses will be undertaken. The costs that should be deducted from presumed lost revenues in order to calculate lost profits are generally referred to as avoided costs. Avoided costs are those costs that would have been incurred in connection with the generation of the lost revenues but were not incurred.[12] Simply stated, because certain revenues are assumed to be lost, it is only logical to assume that the plaintiff will not experience the related costs; those costs must be deducted from lost gross revenue to determine lost net profits.

"Plaintiffs occasionally argue that proof of expenses is a matter of mitigation of damages and that the burden of coming forward with the evidence of expenses is on defendant. This is wrong. Evidence of net profits is part of the plaintiff's case. It is the plaintiff's burden to prove all elements of expense and deduct them."[13]

In this type of analysis, it is important to differentiate fixed expenses and variable expenses. Fixed expenses are those expenses that do not vary with the level of gross revenues (within a relevant range of production). Rent expense, insurance expense and administrative salaries are examples of fixed expenses. These types of expenses remain, even if some of the company's revenue is lost. Variable expenses are those that vary with the level of revenues. Food costs in a restaurant, direct labor in a factory, water expense in a Laundromat, etc. are examples of variable expenses. If a business doesn't make a particular sale, the expenses related to that sale are not incurred. So if Joe's Mower Shop doesn't sell a lawn mower for $500, Joe "saves" the cost of the mower ($300) and the sales commission to the salesman ($50). Regardless of whether he made the sale, his rent expense, insurance expense and utilities expense would have been the same. If Joe had sold the mower, his net profit from that sale would have been $150, and that is what he lost if he wasn't able to make the sale.

In addition to fixed expenses and variable expenses, there is a category of expenses called semi-variable[14] expenses that are part fixed and part variable. For example, telephone charges may have a fixed monthly component plus a variable component relating to long distance or high volume use. To properly treat semi-variable expenses in a damages analysis, only the variable component would be subtracted from the presumed lost gross revenue.

---

12. AICPA Practice Aid 06-4, *op. cit.*, p. 29
13. Dunn, *op. cit.*, p.479.
14. Sometimes semi-variable expenses are called semi-fixed expenses. There is no difference.

Finally, there is a category of expenses called overhead. Overhead is a broad category of expenses that may include both variable and fixed expenses. Overhead expenses are generally not directly traceable to the finished goods (or services) that are produced. In sophisticated cost accounting systems, overhead expenses are allocated to finished goods through some overhead allocation system. It is a complicated factual question whether overhead expenses are "saved" when gross revenues are lost, but, technically, the variable component of overhead, if it can be determined, should be subtracted from lost gross revenue because the variable component is saved. According to Dunn:

> The weight of authority, however, holds that fixed overhead expenses need not be deducted from gross income to arrive at the net lost profits properly recoverable. Most cases that have considered the argument that fixed overhead must be allocated and deducted have rejected it.[15]

And again from Dunn:

> A number of cases hold that an allocation of fixed overhead must be deducted. They do not, however, state any rationale for the conclusion beyond the assertion that overhead is a cost of doing business.[16]

Generally, tax benefits are not to be considered in computing lost profits damages. Damages analyses are usually calculated before income tax considerations because the damage award will be taxable, the same way that the profits would have been taxable had they been earned. Depreciation expense should probably not be deducted from lost gross revenues to derive lost net profits, although some cases have held to the contrary (see Dunn).

The result of the costs saved analysis (usually referred to as variable cost analysis) is a conclusion that some of the lost gross revenue is offset by the related costs that have been saved because the plaintiff did not obtain the revenue. These saved costs will be subtracted from the lost gross revenue to arrive at estimated lost net profits (both in the past and projected into the future).

5. Calculate lost net profits, both past and future.

The result of reducing the presumed lost revenues by the costs saved is a conclusion of lost net profits, both in the past and on into the future.

6. For past lost profits, consider adding pre-judgment interest to the calculation.

Most jurisdictions are reluctant to allow interest on past lost profits because their calculation was uncertain, but almost all jurisdictions require future estimates of losses to be discounted to present value.

---

15. Dunn, *op. cit.*, 483.
16. Dunn, *op. cit.*, 494.

7. Discount future lost profits to present value at an appropriate discount rate.

Future lost profits should be discounted at an appropriate rate because the purpose of the award of damages is to provide a fund that, with principal and interest, will yield plaintiff an amount equivalent to its loss. Discounting is a significant part of damages analysis, and it is discussed separately in the next section of the chapter.

Discounting Future Lost Profits

There is no disagreement that expected future economic losses must be discounted to the present to avoid over-compensating a plaintiff for the harm that some wrongful act will inflict in the future.[17] Financially, discounting is necessary for two reasons:

1. Time value of money: a dollar today is more valuable than a dollar in the future because today's dollar can be invested at an interest rate that earns more than a dollar a year from now. Damage awards should account for this fact.

2. Risk associated with cash flows: future cash flows are uncertain. Investments with lower risk are preferred to projects with higher risk. Damage awards should account for the risk in achieving expected future profits.

Although the concept of discounting future economic losses is not controversial, experts frequently disagree about the theoretical and practical issues of incorporating the concept of risk in measures of economic damages and business valuation. The challenge to the damages analyst is to determine an appropriate discount rate that takes into account both the time value of money and a component which recognizes the risk of achieving the profit expectation. This second component is frequently referred to as the "risk premium."

Many approaches are recognized to empirically determine the appropriate discount rate for a stream of anticipated future business income. The approaches include the Cost of Equity, the Cost of Debt, and the Weighted Average Cost of Capital.[18]

a. Cost of Equity. A company's cost of equity is typically calculated using either a "build-up" approach or the Capital Asset Pricing Model.

b. Cost of Debt. Some practitioners have used a variation of the subject company's borrowing rate as the basis for determining an appropriate discount rate to apply to projected lost profits.[19]

---

17. Brinig, B.P., and Kinrich, J.H., "Discount Rate, Risk and Economic Damages: Practical Considerations," *Business Valuation Update*, Vol. 15, No. 9, September 2009.
18. AICPA practice Aid 06-04, *op cit.*, p. 26.
19. *Id* at 28.

---

c. Cost of Capital. The Weighted Average Cost of Capital (WACC) is the cost of incremental capital to a firm considering its blended cost of debt, equity and other capital.

Importantly, all the methods of determining an "appropriate" discount rate incorporate a significant amount of judgment by the analyst or appraiser. Consequently, it must be concluded that the proper discount rate is, among other steps of *objective* financial analysis, a matter of subjective judgment.

In layman's terms, the question is: What is the appropriate level of risk that should be embedded in the expectation of the continuity of the business income flow that is being projected to be lost in the present analysis? Is it the marketplace discount rate for this type of income flow? In other words, if this lost profit projection is from a business with a publicly traded price/earnings ratio of 10X, isn't the marketplace saying that it "values" the risk of the continuity of income from this business at a 10% discount rate? (Exclude growth from the discussion for simplicity.) Is the risk of the current loss projection the same risk (or higher or lower) as the overall risk for the income flow from this business?

Proffered theories of discount rate rationale. Following are some proffered theories of discount rate rationale that may or may not be appropriate in certain circumstances (and not necessarily agreed to by the author of this text):

1. *Market value discount rate.* The correct rate for discounting anticipated profits is the discount rate for the business as a whole (market value discount rate). Theoretically, this is a detached assessment of the risk of the continuity of anticipated profits.

2. *Investment value discount rate.* Since the income flow is owned by the present, existing business, the appropriate discount rate to assign to the anticipated income flow is the subjective risk of that income flow to its owner (investment value[20]). The investment value discount rate would usually be lower than the market value discount rate, resulting in a higher present investment value than present market value. Theoretically, a plaintiff would not be over-compensated in this type of analysis because the plaintiff already owns the present value of the anticipated profits, given the plaintiff's subjective risk of receiving those profits.

   a. A question presented in this type of analysis is how much negative risk premium should be assigned to the owner of the business. In other words, how much "less risky" is the income flow because it is "owned" by someone who is intimately familiar with the operations of the business, the competition and the industry.

---

20. *The Dictionary of Real Estate Appraisal*, 3rd Ed. (Chicago, IL: Appraisal Institute, 1993) defines investment value as value to a particular investor based on individual investment requirements, as distinguished from the concept of market value, which is impersonal and detached.

3. *Risk-free discount rate.* The correct discount rate for determining the present value of anticipated lost profits is a risk-free rate. This proposition is based on the assumption that the expected future profits are determined as a fact by the trier of fact, thereby reducing them to a virtual certainty. Consequently, those "certain" profits should be reduced to present value using a risk-free discount rate.

   a. The question presented from using this approach is the problem of awarding the plaintiff a dollar amount of damages that is greater than what was lost. If the plaintiff's business was a 20% risk business (marketplace discount rate), and the income flow was $100,000 per year, the total value of the business was $500,000. If the plaintiff's loss of $100,000 per year is discounted at a risk free rate, say 5%, then the calculated "present value of plaintiff's loss" is $2,000,000. Can this make sense?

4. If the loss in profits is measured by a particular increased expense, it can be suggested that the increased expense (cost, or implicit loss of profits) should be discounted at a risk-free rate because this "loss of profit" is a virtual certainty. Arguably, there is a different risk of this "certain" increased expense as opposed to the risk of anticipated future profits.

5. The marginal profits that are assumed to be lost in the present dispute are higher risk than the normal, anticipated profits of the business. Therefore, a higher discount rate should be used for those lost profits, resulting in a lower present value. An example of this situation would be lost anticipated profits when those profits strain the existing capacity of the business, or stem from some new and unproven technology of the business, or some other factor that causes them to be more speculative than the ongoing profit from regular operations. Or, it could simply be said that the marginal or incremental profits of the business (those assumed to be lost in the present dispute) are always riskier than the overall anticipated profits of the business.

6. The marginal profits that are assumed to be lost in the present dispute are lower risk than the normal, anticipated profits of the business. Therefore, a lower discount rate should be used for those lost profits, resulting in a higher present value. An example of this situation would be lost anticipated profits from an identifiable segment of the business that is considered lower risk than the "average" operations or profitability of the business as a whole.

The AICPA Business Damages Study. In the fall of 2002, The American Institute of Certified Public Accountants conducted a Business Damages Survey[21] that found a wide diversity in practices and approaches in many of the technical aspects of business damages calculations. The survey results indicate practitioners may need a better understanding in the area of the appropriate discount rate to determine the present value of future lost profits and its relationship to the income stream. Of 398 practitioners surveyed, when asked what discount rate they used to determine the present value of future lost profits in which the company is not totally destroyed, 27% said they

---

21. *Diversity in Calculating Business Damages*, American Institute of Certified Public Accountants, www.cpa2biz.com, June 2003.

used a risk-adjusted rate based on the riskiness of the forecast; 21% used a safe rate of return; 16% used the company's weighted average cost of capital; 12% used the rate of return of a similar business; and the remainder answered some other rate. When asked about the discount rate typically used when the business is totally destroyed, 22% used a risk-adjusted rate based on the riskiness of the forecast; 29% used the rate of return of a similar business; 17% used a safe rate of return; 13% used the company's weighted average cost of capital; and the remainder used some other rate.

Summary. If the risk of the future profits is measured by the subjective risk to the present owner (investment value), the present value of future profits can be greater than fair market value of the business. If the risk of the future profits is measured by the hypothetical objective risk of those profits in the marketplace (to hypothetical investors), the present value of profits will equal fair market value. If the projected future profits are discounted at a rate that is lower than the discount rate for the business, then the present value of the profits will be greater than the fair market value of the business. There are other theories of rationale for discount rates for lost profits. Proper discounting will always depend on the facts and circumstances of each case and a careful financial analysis of the risk of the anticipated (or lost) profits.

Another Issue: Date of Valuation

The Issue. The date from which lost profits are calculated can have a significant effect on both the amount of the lost profits determined and the facts that can be considered in the damages analysis. The choices are:

1. Date of Trial ("ex-post" method)

2. Date of Incident ("ex-ante" method)

Date of Trial ("ex-post" method). Under this method, the damages analyst stands at the date of trial with *full knowledge of all facts that have occurred since the date of the incident* and calculates both past and future losses. Using methodology discussed in the previous sections of this chapter, the analyst estimates the plaintiff's past lost profits from the date of the incident to the present time. *Using all factual information available as of the date of trial,* the analyst projects and estimates future lost profits to the end of the presumed damaged period and discounts those future losses to the present.

Because the ex-post method relies on information available after the date of the incident, it effectively removes any financial risk from the calculation of past lost profits. The method simply "sums up" years of presumed past lost profits without consideration of discounting those profits to the date of the incident. For determining the present value of future profits under the ex-post method, the damages analyst can use information that was not available at the date of the incident. It does appear that most analysts perform a lost profits analysis as of the date of trial dividing the lost profits into past losses and the present value of the future losses. Under this methodology, various calculations of interest can be offered, as follows:

1. Interest on past losses can be ignored.

2. Interest on past losses can be calculated at a simple or compound interest rate.

3. Past losses can be brought to the present, without interest, but with some inflation factor applied to the past losses to bring them to the present.

4. Future losses are discounted to present value at an assumed appropriate discount rate.

Date of Incident ("ex-ante" method). The ex-ante methodology assumes that all lost profits are future profits and must be discounted back to the date of the breach or commission of the tort. There is no "past" component to losses and the damages analyst relies only on information that was known or knowable as of the date of the incident. Once the present value of all future lost profits is determined, the resulting damage award is brought forward to the date of the award by applying pre-judgment interest.[22]

Discussion of Alternatives. The alternative of ex-post or ex-ante is a legal decision that can have a dramatic effect on the calculation of damages. The ex-post method effectively converts relatively risky income projections (from the date of incident to the date of trial) into a certain stream by using the benefit of hindsight. Proponents of this methodology argue that the plaintiff has been deprived of its income flow in the past and it should be replaced with a sum that replaces the lost income stream, regardless of the risk of the stream. The ex-post method generally results in a finding of a higher amount of damages to the plaintiff.

The argument in support of the ex-ante methodology is that, at the time of the incident, the plaintiff had an expectation of earning a future flow income at a particular level of risk. When the plaintiff was injured, that future expectation was damaged, but the remedy for that loss should not give the plaintiff more than the present value of the loss at the date of the incident. By calculating the loss at the date of trial (with a look-back to the date of the incident), the calculation of past loss effectively "makes certain" the historical lost profits suffered by the plaintiff. By removing the element of risk from the past lost profits, the proponents of ex-ante argue, the ex-post method over-compensates the plaintiff. Generally, an ex-ante calculation results in a lower calculation of damages than an ex-post calculation.

Conclusion

The calculation of lost profits is a complex matter that is heavily dependent upon the unique facts of each particular case. In its simplest form, the calculation is simply a projection of the hypothetical profits that would have existed "but for" the defendant's action, minus the actual profits that did exist after the defendant's action. The basis of the calculation is primarily factual. The financial analyst should have a logical, defensible position supporting his or her assumptions regarding

---

22. AICPA Practice Aid 06-4, *op. cit.*, p. 23.

anticipated revenues and all costs associated with those revenues. The discounting of lost profits will always require some subjective judgment on the part of the analyst, but the result of the discounting of lost profits should have a relationship to the current value (either fair market value or investment value) of the plaintiff business entity. If the present value of lost profits is significantly greater than the current value of the business entity (or portion that was damaged), compensation to the plaintiff may be greater than the *value* of what the plaintiff lost.

Chapter 13

Opinion Evidence and Expert Testimony

Introduction

This chapter discusses the subject of presenting finance and accounting information in litigation. It introduces opinion evidence and discusses methods for using financial experts in a litigation setting. The role of the lawyer is distinguished from the role of the expert witness, and the reader is introduced to legal privileges that apply to experts in litigation.

A significant part of the chapter is devoted to using expert witnesses in depositions and trials and cross-examining opposing expert witnesses in these litigation proceedings. Some of the discussion is from the perspective of the lawyer, and some is from the perspective of the expert witness.

Opinion Evidence

As a general rule, witnesses are only permitted to testify about facts that they have observed, and not their opinions or conclusions about the consequences of the facts. Subject to two exceptions, the opinions of witnesses are considered to be irrelevant and therefore not admissible. The attorneys will make arguments about the meaning and significance of the proven facts of the case and ask the jury to make findings of fact and conclusions based on their findings, but witnesses may only testify about the facts. Generally, witnesses may not testify about their beliefs, impressions, opinions or conclusions about the facts.

There are two exceptions to the prohibition of opinion testimony: non-expert opinion testimony about subjects that are matters of common daily experience, and expert evidence. A lay witness will be allowed to give opinions and testify about matters that are within the common experience of people. Examples of admissible areas of non-expert opinions are estimates of speed or distance, the emotional state of a person (upset, agitated, angry), or other everyday estimates (size, weight, etc.). Lay opinion testimony of this sort is allowable where the witness has personal knowledge of the facts, the witness's conclusion conveys a definite conception of the facts, and the conclusion is one that people in general are capable of drawing. This exception is rationalized as a way to get necessary facts to the jury from a witness whose knowledge cannot otherwise be articulated.

Expert opinion testimony is admissible in situations where the testimony will assist the trier of fact in understanding an issue that is beyond the common knowledge of lay persons. Federal Rule of Evidence 702:

> Rule 702: Testimony by Experts. If specialized, technical, or scientific knowledge will aid the trier of fact to better understand the presented evidence or to assist in the

determination of a fact in issue, a witness qualified as an expert may testify to that fact in the form of an opinion. This is applicable if the testimony is based upon a sufficient amount of information or facts, if the testimony is the product of credible and reliable methods and principles, and if the expert witness has diligently applied those methods and principles reliably to the facts presented in the case.

State law generally follows the federal rules although there are numerous subtle differences that should be considered in a particular jurisdiction. In California, testimony of expert witnesses is governed by California Evidence Code §§720-723 and §§801-805. California and federal statutes are generally similar and confer upon the trial judge broad discretion in ruling on the admissibility of expert testimony. California Evidence Code Section 801 states:

> 801. If a witness is testifying as an expert, his testimony in the form of an opinion is limited to such an opinion as is:
>
> (a) Related to a subject that is sufficiently beyond common experience that the opinion of an expert would assist the trier of fact; and
>
> (b) Based on matter (including his special knowledge, skill, experience, training, and education) perceived by or personally known to the witness or made known to him at or before the hearing, whether or not admissible, that is of a type that reasonably may be relied upon by an expert in forming an opinion upon the subject to which his testimony relates, unless an expert is precluded by law from using such matter as a basis for his opinion.

California Evidence Code Section 720 states:

> 720. (a) A person is qualified to testify as an expert if he has special knowledge, skill, experience, training, or education sufficient to qualify him as an expert on the subject to which his testimony relates. Against the objection of a party, such special knowledge, skill, experience, training, or education must be shown before the witness may testify as an expert.
>
> (b) A witness' special knowledge, skill, experience, training, or education may be shown by any otherwise admissible evidence, including his own testimony.

In California courts, Evidence Code §801(a) permits an expert to testify on subjects which are "sufficiently beyond common experience that the opinion of an expert would assist the trier of fact." In federal courts, Federal Rule of Evidence 702 allows expert testimony "if scientific, technical, or other specialized knowledge will assist the trier of fact to understand the evidence or to determine a fact in issue." The U.S Supreme Court's decisions in *Daubert v. Merrell Dow Pharmaceuticals, Inc.* (509 U.S 579 (1993)) and *Kumho Tire Co. v. Carmichael* (526 U.S 137 (1999)) made it clear that the trial judge must act as a gatekeeper to exclude expert testimony that is likely to mislead the trier of fact, and much has been written to guide the courts when scientific evidence is in question.

Expert testimony is not required or appropriate when an issue is within the realm of "common knowledge" of the trier of fact.[1] Most financial testimony (damages, forensic accounting or valuation) involves issues beyond common knowledge of the trier of fact. Accordingly, the testimony of a qualified expert is admissible on these questions.

The Attorney's Role Versus the Expert's Role Generally, and the Financial Expert[2] Specifically

There is an important distinction between the role of the expert and the role of an attorney representing a client in litigation. "When providing litigation services, the [C.P.A.] practitioner is an objective consultant offering opinions about facts that may be in dispute to the trier of fact and is subject to the Statement on Standards for Consulting Services."[3] The attorney's role is to advocate the client's position within the bounds of the ethical practice of law.

Once the financial expert has competently derived a financial or accounting opinion, the financial expert has a duty to present and defend that opinion against positions that are adverse to that opinion. The financial expert, or any expert for that matter, is not an advocate on behalf of the client, but is an advocate for a competently derived financial or accounting opinion. It is generally recognized that the C.P.A.'s obligation is to arrive at an unbiased, objective financial or accounting opinion. The C.P.A.'s conclusion should not be tainted by the desires of the client.

The attorney is ethically bound to strenuously advance the interests of his or her client within the adversarial system. The attorney's focus will emphasize the facts that support the client's position and minimize the importance of the facts that contradict the client's position.

An important distinction must be drawn between "substantive" advocacy and "procedural" advocacy. Substantive advocacy is altering the objectivity of a financial analysis or opinion to advance the interest of a client. An ethical expert witness will not be a party to substantive advocacy. Procedural advocacy is an awareness of the tactics and strategies of litigation. If the technical expert witness is to be effective, he or she must be able to advance the expert opinion successfully within the litigation context. Consequently, it is essential for the expert witness to be aware of the tactics and strategies of litigation.

A complete discussion of the strategies and tactics of the financial expert witness's role in litigation is beyond the scope of this text, but a few paragraphs on the subject are relevant to the lawyer's understanding of the witness's role. An awareness of the witness's responsibilities is helpful to the attorney for both using experts and cross-examining them.

---

1. See *Jorgensen v. Beach 'N Bay Realty, Inc.*, 125 Cal. App. 3d 155. 177 Cal. Rptr. 882 (1981).

2. In this chapter, the financial expert is assumed to be a Certified Public Accountant, but the law does not distinguish between qualified experts based specifically on professional licensing other than to consider a license to be one indicia of sufficient education or experience.

3. *Application of AICPA Professional Standards in the Performance of Litigation Services*, Consulting Services Special Report 93-1, American Institute of Certified Public Accountants, 1993.

Assumptions. In most cases, a financial or accounting analysis will be significantly based on assumptions such as but-for projections, discount rates and other components of damages calculations. By definition, an assumption is the act of conceding or taking for granted; supposing something to be a fact. Certain assumptions are within the realm of the C.P.A.'s knowledge and experience and should be subject to the C.P.A.'s opinion as to their reasonableness. For instance, a typical assumption in the analysis of a business is the assumption that the business will continue to operate as a going concern. Most C.P.A.s would agree that this assumption falls within the purview of the C.P.A.'s experience. Since it is an assumption that is within the purview of the C.P.A.'s professional judgment, the reasonableness of the going concern assumption is within the scope of the opinion of the C.P.A.

Some assumptions are not within the scope of the financial expert's experience, for instance, the viability of a particular scientific technology or the reliability of management's sales penetration projections. Consequently, the financial expert should probably not opine as to the reasonableness of the assumption about technology or marketing, but rather should defer to the opinions of others. Some assumptions fall in the "gray area" of the financial expert's or C.P.A.'s knowledge and experience. For instance, the importance of a particular chief executive officer to the operations of a business and the resulting "key person" discount issues may be an area where the C.P.A. has familiarity in some cases but not in others. Care should be exercised when dealing with these "hybrid" assumptions.

A cross-examining lawyer should inquire about the basis of all assumptions that an opposing expert is using in deriving an expert opinion. The reasonableness of the assumptions is critical to the witness's ability to support the ultimate opinion, so the cross-examining lawyer should be penetrating the basis of the assumptions for weaknesses. Also, if the cross-examining lawyer can push the expert into defending assumptions that are outside of the expert's area of knowledge, this area can be fertile ground for undermining the credibility of the expert's analysis.

Rationale is the process of applying logic to facts and assumptions to derive supportable conclusions. By definition, rationale is the fundamental reason, or rational basis, for something. Stated informally, rationale is the "smell test" of reason as it is applied to facts and assumptions to derive conclusions. The process of applying rationale to facts and assumptions is undertaken many times in a financial or accounting analysis.

If every step of the financial analysis includes good, defensible rationale, the ultimate conclusion should make sense. It is important to ensure that that sound rationale be applied in every "sub-step" of the analytical process. In litigation, the importance of good rationale is heightened because the opposing side is challenging every step of the financial analysis, particularly the rationale of every step.

There are two ways to test rationale, negatively and affirmatively. In litigation, the opposition generally challenges rationale negatively by pointing out what *wasn't* done in support of the analysis. They also ask, "What's wrong with this analysis?" Or, "How could this have been done differently?" Rationale can also be supported affirmatively by the logical process of affirmatively asserting the steps of the analysis. For instance: X conforms to traditional analysis, **AND** X conforms to the way that a presumed buyer and/or seller of the business would look at the issue, **AND** X conforms to the financial expert's experience, **AND** X makes intuitive sense. However, it is important to recognize and accept that rationale is never perfect. There is always some disconnect among the facts, assumptions and conclusions. Competent opposing counsel will always try to stress the imperfections or disconnections in the rationale.

Every conclusion or sub-conclusion in an accounting or financial analysis should be supported by several theories of rationale, if possible. These "layers" of rationale support the conclusion and make it very defensible. For example, to determine the amount of "fair compensation" for the owner/operator of a particular business enterprise, the financial expert would ideally employ as many of the following lines of rationale as possible:

1. Develop an understanding of the background, education and experience of the particular owner/operator along with a detailed description of the current duties, management skills and number of hours worked.

2. Undertake statistical studies of reported compensation of similarly situated officers in similar type businesses.

3. Analyze the compensation of the next level of management in the company and add some reasonable premium to those amounts as an indication of the reasonable value of the subject owner/officer.

4. Obtain data on salaries of chief executive officers in the geographic area in which the company is located.

5. If the company is not 100% owned by the subject owner/operator, seek to obtain some historical evidence of a negotiated salary amount among owners.

6. Obtain the opinion of the owner as to the reasonable value of his or her services.

It is not possible to create a formula for perfect rationale for solving any one issue, but it is important for the financial expert to understand that broad-based rationale results in very defensible conclusions. It is usually very easy for a conclusion to be supplanted if it has only one line of rationale (i.e. one study, one method or one "comparable" sale).

The attorney must educate the substantive expert about the strategies and tactics of litigation, and the differences in their respective roles in the process. Although the expert is not an advocate for the client of the attorney, the competent presentation of opinion evidence requires knowledge of the litigation process, and it is the attorney's job to make sure the retained expert is properly advised.

Legal Privileges Relating to Expert Witnesses

Perhaps the most important point to note about the subject of legal privileges and expert witnesses is that there are none that apply. Once an individual is designated as an expert witness, everything that he or she considered, reviewed, discussed or rejected in arriving at the expert opinion is discoverable by the opposing party to the litigation. Some lawyers and many experts either don't know this fact or forget it, and the results can be devastating to a client's position in a litigated matter. It is critical to realize that anything that is said or transmitted to a designated expert is fully discoverable by the other side of the litigation.

Attorney work product rule. An attorney can hire a consultant to assist him or her in the preparation of a case and the work product and knowledge of the consultant can be privileged under the attorney work product rule. The attorney work product rule is the legal doctrine that provides that materials prepared by an attorney in preparation for litigation are protected from discovery by the opposing side to the litigation. The rule has been extended to agents of the lawyer working at the lawyer's direction, although the privilege is not absolute. Generally, however, a lawyer can retain a consultant to assist in the preparation of a matter, and the work of the consultant is privileged from discovery.

The attorney work product rule has given rise to the term "consulting expert," meaning a consultant who will perform services for the lawyer related to the litigation but will not be designated as an expert witness in the matter. The consultant's work is protected from discovery in the same way that the lawyer's secretary or paralegal's work is protected. In many cases, an attorney will initially hire a technical professional as a consultant to investigate an issue relevant to the litigation. Frequently, the consultant will perform some initial research and/or investigation and report back preliminary findings to the attorney. The attorney may then designate the consultant as an expert witness in the case. If that occurs, there is no privilege shielding the consultant-turned-expert from discovery.

Attorney-client privilege. The attorney-client privilege is the privilege that protects certain communications between a client and his or her attorney and keeps those communications confidential. Although there are minor variations, the elements necessary to establish the privilege are: the asserted holder of the privilege is a client; the person to whom the communication is made is a member of the bar (or subordinate) and is acting as an attorney; and the communication was for the purpose of securing legal advice. There are a number of exceptions to the privilege; most noteworthy relating to expert witnesses is the exception that the communication was made in the presence of individuals who were neither the attorney nor the client. Although some lawyers and experts think that the attorney-client privilege insulates expert witnesses from discovery, that position does not seem to be supportable. The only privilege that has anything to do with the use of experts is the attorney work product rule and it is only applicable if the expert is not designated as an expert witness to testify in the matter.

Using and Opposing Experts in Litigation

Lawyers must effectively use experts to introduce opinion evidence to advance their clients' positions in litigated matters. Conversely, there are techniques that can be used to minimize the effect of an opposing expert's testimony.

Taking Effective Expert Depositions

A deposition upon oral examination is a pretrial discovery procedure used to obtain facts relevant to the litigation. The witness is asked questions under oath by an examining lawyer. The questions and answers are transcribed by a court reporter verbatim. If testimony at trial is different from the deposition testimony, the witness can be impeached with the deposition transcript at trial. Depositions and other discovery procedures are governed by Federal Rules of Civil Procedure 26 to 37. Because of liberal discovery rules, almost any question can be asked during the deposition. The deposition is often considered to be the most important event during the course of business litigation because most cases settle before trial based on the opposing lawyer's evaluation of testimony and the demeanor of witnesses.

The role of experts in depositions. The expert should assist the lawyer for his party in preparing for the deposition of the opponent's expert by providing the lawyer with background information about the education, experience and reputation of the opponent's expert. The expert should advise the lawyer where to probe for weaknesses in the methodology and analysis used by the opponent's expert in reaching his opinion. For example, the opponent's expert may have skipped some steps in his analysis or failed to review financial records which would affect his conclusions. The expert should suggest deposition questions to his party's lawyer and, if possible, attend the deposition of opponent's expert.

The expert must prepare for and give an effective deposition. The expert's analysis should be completed before the scheduled deposition; however, the expert should not prepare a report or reduce his conclusions to writing unless he is asked to do so by his party's lawyer. The expert should insist on a detailed briefing with his party's lawyer before the deposition to discuss his testimony. It is advisable to conduct a rehearsal with mock cross-examination to ferret out potential weaknesses in testimony.

The role of the lawyer in depositions. Depositions are used to find facts, evaluate witnesses, learn the expert's analysis and opinion, evaluate the case for settlement, and for use at trial. Practically, it is important for the lawyer to memorialize the expert's complete analysis so there is no surprise at trial. Strategically, the lawyer should not disclose his or her trial tactics in the process of the expert deposition.

A good deposition gets to the core of the issues that the expert has analyzed by forcing the expert to reduce a complex analysis to basic steps and understandable terms. Good deposing attorneys are not intimidated because they possess a lack of substantive knowledge of the expert's field. The lawyer doesn't need to know as much substance as the expert; he or she only seeks to learn the totality of the expert's opinions and the basis of them.

The lawyer's preparation should include:

1. A discussion with his or her own expert about the nature of the analysis, anticipated opinions of opposing expert, and the reputation of the opposing expert.

2. Inquiry of the lawyer's colleagues about previous opposition or retention of the opposing expert.

3. Performing some research in the substantive area of the expert so that the lawyer has some familiarity before the deposition.

4. Review of other deposition transcripts of the opposing expert.

5. An agreement with opposing counsel to obtain the expert's file prior to the deposition.

6. Consideration of video deposition, a more expensive but very effective tool for obtaining more candid testimony on important issues.

An effective deposition is usually executed pursuant to a plan in which the attorney has formulated objectives for the deposition. The deposition plan should identify the lawyer's purpose of this deposition: Learn opinions? Test opinions? Evaluate strengths? Pin down a particular point? Gauge effectiveness of expert? Discredit expert? Recognize, however, that an argumentative penetration of the witness's weak points serves to educate the witness and prepare him or her for cross-examination at trial.

The notice of deposition should include a subpoena that requires the expert's production of the *entire* file, including all notes, memoranda, billing records, computer discs and research material. It is helpful if the lawyer can obtain the file several days before the deposition.

The Effective Expert Deposition

Sequencing. Carefully planned sequencing of the areas of inquiry is critical for conducting an effective expert deposition. In the deposition of an experienced expert witness, there is a very narrow window of opportunity for the deposing attorney to gain advantage. At the outset of the deposition, the expert should be quickly asked about the assignment and the expert's opinions, leaving less important areas of inquiry for later.

Admonitions. The extent of the use of admonitions in an expert witness deposition requires judgment on the part of the deposing attorney. The attorney may need to make a record about the expert's understanding of the deposition procedure, the force of the oath and the fact that the expert understands the questions that he will answer. In the deposition of an experienced expert witness, however, lengthy admonitions are usually an unnecessary waste of time. If the expert has significant deposition experience, the lawyer should simply establish that fact and that the expert is thoroughly familiar with the deposition procedure. The lawyer can then directly proceed into the substance of the expert's analysis.

Background, Education and Experience. Several considerations are important in this area. If this inquiry is even necessary, it should not be made at the beginning of the deposition. This subject is the expert's most comfortable area and he/she should not be given the opportunity to get comfortable at the beginning of the deposition. If you, the opposing counsel, anticipate that the deposition will be used at trial in lieu of testimony, why should you qualify the opposing expert witness?

Attitude and Demeanor. The deposing attorney may vary his/her attitude and demeanor depending on many different factors. A less experienced witness may be somewhat intimidated by an aggressive approach. A cool, calm and collected approach is probably more effective with an experienced expert witness. The chance is that the "nice guy" will get more information than the obnoxious antagonist.

Administrative. Near the outset of the deposition, the lawyer should cover the following areas:

1. Review the deposition subpoena with the witness and ask the witness to confirm that he/she brought everything that was requested with him to the deposition.

2. Ask the witness to describe everything in the file.

3. Ask the expert what documents were requested for the case. What documents were provided? What requested documents were omitted?

4. Inquire about billing to date. How much time has the expert spent on this case? How much time has been spent by the expert's employees?

Mechanics of Taking the Deposition. Take prepared notes to the deposition which include a broad outline, a checklist and a *few* specific questions in key areas. Don't be obsessive about pre-planned questions or note taking in the deposition; much more is learned by listening intently and going with the flow of the answers.

Substance of Expert's Analysis. The deposing attorney should first identify each step of logic taken by the expert in developing his/her conclusion. Example: "Give me a broad overview of the steps you have taken in your analysis." (Chronologically, in order of importance, or any way the expert will provide the steps.)

Methodical Approach. Once the expert's analysis is reduced to five or six major steps of logic, each step should be examined methodically. With respect to each major step, the following inquiry should be made:

1. Why is this particular step necessary at all?

    a. Could this step have been eliminated?

    b. Has the expert performed this type of analysis in the past without including this step?

2. What was the specific outcome of this particular step?

    a. On what facts is the outcome based?

    b. On what observations is the outcome based?

    c. On what assumptions is the outcome based?

    d. On what judgments is the outcome based?

3. Generally, what other outcomes are possible for this step in an analysis?

    a. What facts would cause a different (lower, higher, stronger, weaker, etc.) outcome at this step of the analysis?

    b. If expert opines to some *inadequacy* about the underlying situation, what in his/her opinion would constitute *adequacy*?

    c. If expert opines to some *failure*, what in his/her opinion would constitute *success*?

4. When inquiring about the expert's opinion about a quantifiable issue, what is the range of reasonable outcomes, if a range can be quantified?

    a. For example, if lost profits are stated to be $50,000, what is the reasonable *range* of lost profits?? $40,000 to $60,000?? Zero to $10,000,000??

Make the Expert Argue with Himself/Herself. With respect to a particular outcome for one of the expert's logical analytic steps, ask what facts of this case support a higher outcome or a lower outcome? A similar outcome? A different outcome? Try to force the expert to argue the strengths and weaknesses of his/her conclusion.

1. Follow through on equivocal answers.

a. Answer: *X* is *generally* true. Question: When would it not be true? Not *generally* true?

b. Answer: True, based on what I know now. Question: What else would you need to know to make it unequivocal?

Communications with Others. It is well known that experts' communications with counsel and others are not privileged.

1. Ask the expert to name every person with whom he or she has communicated in connection with the particular case. The reason for and nature of each of these communications should be explored in the deposition.

2. The expert should be asked about every meeting he has had with his client's attorney. The date, time, place, reason for the meeting and parties in attendance should be inquired about. The lawyer should fully inquire about the purpose of each meeting and the results of that meeting. Also, were any documents or reports given to the lawyer at the meeting?

3. All discussions by opposing counsel with opposing expert witnesses are discoverable. After every break, inquire about the details of any discussions that the expert witness had with his/her client's attorney.

4. Review all notes of meetings that are present in the expert's file. If notes are not included in the file, ask if notes were taken. Were they destroyed/discarded? Does the expert normally attend meetings without taking notes?

Two-way Street. A deposition is a two-way street, requiring the lawyer to disclose his/her questioning strategies to the expert witness. Be sensitive to this fact and try to be discreet about inquiring into areas in which you believe the expert is somewhat weak and you intend to explore more heavily at trial. Don't argue with the witness and don't heavily pursue areas in which you feel the expert is weak. Consider saving your inquiry for trial.

Some Practice Pointers:

1. Treat objections as though they are just a formality of the deposition. After the objection, refocus attention on the witness and seek the answer to the question that was just asked.

2. Try to avoid arguments with opposing counsel. Arguments tend to increase the tension in the room and make an experienced witness less inclined to offer valuable information. A less experienced witness may respond differently, however.

3. As you conclude your inquiry into each substantive area or "step" of the expert's analysis, ask the expert if there is anything about step x "that you haven't told me." An experienced expert will respond, "not that I can presently think of." At this point, the lawyer should

seek a commitment that if the expert does think of anything about step x between now and the signing of the deposition, the expert will write in the fact that he/she has thought of.

4. Inquire if the expert has any other work planned in this matter. Specifically, are there any steps that he/she intends to complete? Has his lawyer asked him *not* to perform any steps?

5. Inquire about the expert's availability for trial on the scheduled trial date.

6. When you are defending the deposition of your client's expert witness and the deposing attorney has brought the opposing expert witness as a consultant, ask that consulting expert witness to preserve a copy of his/her notes for production at the time of that witness's deposition. (They are notes; they were taken in the course of the expert's work; there seems to be no good reason why they should not be preserved and produced.)

Some additional questions the lawyer may wish to consider:

1. Have all your professional opinions or conclusions reached in this case been explored in this deposition?

2. Is there anything you would like to add so as not to be misunderstood?

3. How sure are you about your opinions?

4. If you had an unlimited budget in this case, what additional steps would you perform?

5. Have you been involved in drafting any legislation in your field?

6. How many other cases have you performed for the lawyer who has retained you in this matter?

7. How many other cases have you handled for this lawyer's law firm?

8. Have you socialized with this lawyer?

9. Have you removed anything from your file?

10. Were you asked to remove anything from your file?

11. Have any written materials been destroyed or discarded?

12. Have you retained previous drafts of your analysis?

13. Have you provided any written materials to your client's lawyer that are not photocopied in your file?

14. Do you have a computer disk that has a copy of any documents that are not presently in your file?

15. Have you discussed any weaknesses in your analysis with your client's lawyer?

16. You have made calculations based on the opinions of other experts [retained by your clients] in this matter. Have you made any calculations based on the other side's experts? If not, why not?

Other questions that the expert may answer. (These questions are really irrelevant and should be answered with "I don't know" or "I don't have an opinion," but many experts will answer them.)

1. Are you familiar with the opposing expert?

   a. Is he/she credible?

   b. Tell me about his/her reputation

2. Do you think the opinion of Dr. Expert, another expert on the deponent's same side of the case is reasonable?

   a. Why?

Conclusion of the Effective Expert Deposition. The deposition is often the most important aspect of the litigation process. It is essential that the deposition be used to effectively explore the strengths and weaknesses of the opposing expert's position to avoid surprise at trial. The deposing attorney should thoroughly explore the expert's analysis and conclusions without disclosing the strengths, weaknesses or strategies of his or her case.

Eliciting Opinion Evidence at Trial

The majority of litigated matters settle before trial based on both parties' evaluation of the strengths and weaknesses of their respective positions and consideration of the risks and costs of litigation. In most of those cases, opinion evidence was obtained during discovery in the form of deposition testimony and written reports of expert testimony. In the cases that go to trial, opinion evidence is only effective if it is carefully planned and properly presented at trial. The strength of the financial expert's opinion is ultimately dependent on the thoroughness of the investigation, the soundness of the economic assumptions, an accurate perception of the facts, and a proper application of the facts to economic theory. However, the most competently derived expert opinion will be ineffectual if it is not presented in a way that resonates with the trier of fact.

The lawyer and the expert must effectively prepare and plan the expert testimony that will be offered at trial. During direct examination, the expert witness will testify about: (i) his qualifications as a financial expert; (ii) the scope of the assignment; (iii) the methodology of the financial or accounting analysis; and (iv) the conclusions he or she has reached as a result of the analysis.

Foundational questions and testimony. In California, Evidence Code §720(a) provides that a witness is qualified to testify as an expert "if he has special knowledge, skill, experience, training, or education" on the subject at issue. Federal Rule of Evidence 702 is in substantial accord. The determination as to whether a witness is qualified to testify as an expert is made by the trial judge whose decision is reversible only for an abuse of discretion.[4] The qualifications of a witness to testify as an expert must relate to the subject about which he is asked to express an opinion.[5] A C.P.A. is qualified to testify as an expert witness on a wide range of subjects including the results of an audit and whether financial statements were prepared in accordance with generally accepted accounting principles.

Although the legal purpose of foundational testimony is to qualify the witness as an "expert witness," the practical purpose of the foundational testimony is to establish the expert's credibility and professional expertise. In business litigation, the relative credibility of the expert witnesses may be dispositive of the case. The general subjects of foundational testimony are:

1. Education—general and specialized.

2. Professional credentials.

3. Employment experience, particularly as it relates to the issue being considered.

4. Academic affiliations, particularly teaching of accounting, finance or appraisal.

5. Publications or lectures.

6. Previous qualifications as an expert witness.

The lawyer should not allow the expert's qualifications to be removed from issue by stipulation because such a stipulation will deprive the expert of the opportunity to establish his credibility and strength. The lawyer and the expert should review and prepare the specific foundational questions to assure that the expert's qualifications are presented completely and in an organized fashion. The breadth of the foundational testimony will vary depending upon the type of the case and the circumstances of the trial. The lawyer and expert must be prepared to condense the testimony if they sense that the judge is becoming impatient or the jury is becoming bored. At the

---

4.   See *Naples Restaurant, Inc. v. Coberly Ford Co.*, 259 Cal. App. 2d 881, 66 Cal. Rptr. 835 (1968).
5.   See *Miller v. Los Angeles County Flood Control Dist.*, 8 Cal. 3d 689, 106 Cal. Rptr. 1 (1973); *Reno-West Coast Distribution Co., Inc. v. Mead Corp.*, 613 F.2d 722 (9th Cir. 1979).

end of the foundational testimony, the lawyer should ask the judge for a ruling on the qualification of the witness as an expert. There is a psychological benefit to obtaining a confirmation from the judge that the expert has met the legal requirements to qualify as an expert.

Expert testimony—analysis and opinion. In California, Evidence Code §801(b) provides that an expert witness may base the testimony on matter "perceived by or personally known to the witness or made known to him at or before the hearing . . . that is of a type that reasonably may be relied upon by an expert in forming an opinion upon the subject to which his testimony relates." Federal Rule of Evidence 703 is in substantial accord. Information relied upon by an expert need not necessarily be admissible into evidence. An expert may rely on hearsay or other inadmissible evidence as a basis for his opinion if it is the type of matter upon which an expert may reasonably rely in forming an opinion.[6] The opinion of the financial or accounting expert will commonly be based in part upon inadmissible evidence, including inquiries made with other persons involved in a similar business or trade.

After the expert's qualifications are established, the expert and the attorney should set forth the origination of the expert's involvement in this case. An outline of the testimony should include:

1. Who retained the expert?

2. What investigation or analysis the expert was asked to undertake.

3. When the investigation was commenced and when concluded.

4. The basis of expert's compensation.

5. An assurance that no suggestion was made as to the conclusion the expert should reach.

6. An assurance that the expert has no financial interest in the outcome of the case.

The expert will be asked what he or she did in carrying out the investigation or analysis. The expert's response should provide a detailed discussion of each step of his analysis and investigation. It should show the judge or jury that the expert's procedures covered every facet of the damages or valuation assignment.

When the expert has performed a technical financial or valuation analysis, the testimony should include an economic overview of the available methods for the analysis with a discussion of the strengths and weaknesses of each method and its applicability to the facts of the case. Clear reasoning should be stated for the rejection of methods that were not ultimately used in reaching the expert's conclusions. The general economic support for the method(s) ultimately chosen should be presented at this stage of the testimony.

---

6.   See *Brown v. Colm,* 11 Cal. 3d 639, 114 Cal. Rptr. 128 (1974); *U.S. v. Sims,* 514 F.2d 147 (9th Cir. 1975).

One of the challenges of effective expert testimony is being complete and educational while avoiding a detailed explanation of elaborate economic theories. Generally, these theories cannot be adequately explained in a trial setting and result in confusion. Also, complicated theories are fertile ground for stiff cross-examination.

It is critically important to present the weaknesses of an economic position during direct examination. Every economic position has some weaknesses, and the expert has presumably considered and incorporated them into his opinion. Strategically, it is advisable to disclose the weakness in an "offensive" posture, rather than to "defend" against a challenge during cross-examination. Examples of real weaknesses in an economic analysis are:

1. Inability to investigate important information.

2. Inaccuracy of financial information.

3. Lack of confirming, external data.

4. Choice of one damages or valuation method to the exclusion of others.

5. An error in the expert's calculations.

Regardless of the existence of real weaknesses in the analysis, in virtually every case, the opposition will assert that there are weaknesses in the expert's analysis. Examples of asserted weaknesses are:

1. Imprecision of conclusions.

2. Discounting of comparable data, i.e., "it is not comparable enough."

3. Statistical impurity in any outside study.

4. Other methods of valuation that could have been used.

5. The analysis could have been more thorough.

6. Conclusion could have been different (even if only $1 different).

The expert and the lawyer should carefully plan the technique of direct examination. The options include specific questions with relatively narrow answers or more generalized questions (why's and how's) with narrative answers. If the expert is experienced in litigation, narrative testimony can resemble an economics class. The difficulty here is that the lawyer relinquishes control to some extent. Furthermore, the testimony may be subject to an objection as non-responsive to the question asked. If the testimony is to proceed on the basis of specific questions, the lawyer must be extremely versed in the nuances of the expert's field.

The most important consideration is preparation. The lawyer and the expert must be in agreement about the techniques and strategy to be employed during the trial. In addition, lawyer and expert must be prepared to alter the technique and strategy in response to rulings from the judge. The expert should feel free to volunteer an important point, by way of explanation, during direct examination. A very important aspect of the expert witness function is to take a reasonable amount of control of his aspect of the case, including direct examination. Frequently, a lawyer is hesitant to disclose how little he knows about accounting, finance and economics and is somewhat intimidated by the expert. A competent lawyer will be glad to share control of the case to benefit his client.

The demeanor of the expert witness will have an effect on his testimony. Although the expert's analysis may have incorporated very sophisticated financial techniques, it must be explained in a relatively simple, understandable manner. This must be accomplished without being condescending or patronizing to the judge or jury. No economic position is ironclad. It is important that the expert present his case with recognition of the uncertainty inherent in his analysis. At any stage in the litigation process, the expert should be willing to concede uncontroverted facts and graciously acknowledge minor errors.

Economic testimony should not be presented in an absolute fashion. The expert has simply undertaken a study, made certain assumptions that he considers reasonable, and derived conclusions. Reasonable minds could differ at any point in the analysis.

Cross-Examination

During cross-examination, the opponent's lawyer will attempt to expose and exploit any weakness of the expert's position as it was presented on direct.

Legal rules governing cross-examination. An expert witness may be cross-examined to the same extent as any witness, and, in addition, as to his qualifications, the subject to which his expert testimony relates, the matter upon which his opinion was based, and the reasons for his opinion. See, Cal. Evid. Code §721(a); Fed. R. Evid. 705. An expert witness may not be cross-examined as to the content of any scientific, technical or professional treatises or journals unless the witness referred to or considered such publications in arriving at his opinion, or such publications have been admitted into evidence. See, Cal. Evid. Code §721(b).

Technique of the expert's withstanding cross-examination. The best preparation for cross-examination is a thorough, professional job on the affirmative financial analysis. Nothing is easier than defending a sound economic position. Each assumption in the financial expert's analysis is subject to question on cross-examination. During the development of the damages or valuation process, the expert should have questioned each of his assumptions and weighed alternative positions. The expert should be thoroughly versed in any opposing expert's financial analysis because that analysis will certainly be one of the foundations of the cross-examining lawyer's questions.

Frequently, a series of facts or premises will be compounded into a question (or a series of questions). A simple "yes" or "no" answer will then be asked for. If the question cannot be fairly answered with a "yes" or "no," the expert should not hesitate to state that the question cannot be so simply answered. The response to such a narrow question should be to attempt to shift the burden back to the lawyer to frame a proper question or require that a more general question—permitting fair explanation—be asked.

The expert witness should be mindful of not varying his or her personal style, but should be aware of negative habits that may be distracting from the quality or credibility of the expert testimony. Under the challenge of cross-examination, it is easy to become defensive or argumentative, and this emotional style may reflect negatively on the witness. The witness should endeavor to remain polite. It is generally more effective to answer questions in a pondering or reflective manner, rather than answering them defensively.

Certain facts or arguments will go against any economic position. The expert witness should not hesitate to acknowledge this reality when he or she is challenged with these facts. Also, the competent expert will not hesitate to concede an error, but the expert should not blindly accept the opponent's lawyer's characterization of the facts of the direct testimony. Examples:

1. "So, you just *picked* a number?"

2. "So, your study *isn't accurate* then, is it?"

3. "So, after this *brief, informal interview*, you decided to . . ."

Technique of lawyer's cross-examination of opposing expert. First, recognize that the substantive area of inquiry of cross-examination is in the area of expertise of the witness, and the lawyer does not want to give the expert the opportunity to restate or reinforce his direct testimony. So it is important for the lawyer to control the cross-examination with closed questions that do not give the witness significant opportunity to explain subtle concepts. Rather, the lawyer should be trying to show weaknesses in the expert's analysis by eliciting errors, steps not taken, improper judgments and facts and approaches not considered.

In the planning phase of cross-examination, the lawyer must decide if the opposing expert has made significant errors in the analysis, in which case the lawyer will directly and substantively attack the expert testimony. If the expert has made errors or adopted unsupportable assumptions, the lawyer must decide how to best show these weaknesses through well-structured cross-examination questions. If the expert's analysis is reasonable, the cross-examination should be more indirect, with the goal of "ruffling the edges" of the testimony. The lawyer should consider using the opposing expert to obtain agreement with certain underlying assumptions that favor the lawyer's client's position, rather than just trying to disagree with the substance of the opposing expert's position.

The lawyer's greatest resource in challenging his opponent's economic position is his own expert. The lawyer should obtain his own expert's critique of the opposing expert's opinion. The critique should outline erroneous facts and assumptions contained in the opposing report. It should also include written questions for the cross-examination. Some lawyers want their own expert witness to be present at the counsel table during the cross-examination of the opposing expert. Careful consideration should be given to the problem of the appearance of advocacy on the part of the expert. It would appear that sufficient preparation could eliminate the need to have the expert present at counsel table.

Conclusion

With minor exceptions, most financial testimony is opinion testimony. Expert opinion testimony is admissible in situations where the testimony will assist the trier of fact in understanding an issue that is beyond the common knowledge of lay persons.

There is an important distinction between the role of the expert rendering opinion testimony and the role of an attorney representing a client in litigation. The attorney's role is to advocate the client's position within the bounds of the ethical practice of law. The expert's opinion testimony should be objectively supportable and based on facts learned prior to the hearing and also supported by reasonable assumptions where facts are not available. Substantive advocacy is altering the objectivity of a financial analysis or opinion to advance the interest of a client. An ethical expert witness will not be a party to substantive advocacy. Procedural advocacy is an awareness of the tactics and strategies of litigation. If the technical expert witness is to be effective, he or she must be able to advance the expert opinion successfully within the litigation context.

The attorney work product rule is the legal doctrine that provides that materials prepared by an attorney in preparation for litigation are protected from discovery by the opposing side to the litigation. The attorney-client privilege is the privilege that protects certain communications between a client and his or her attorney and keeps those communications confidential. Once an individual is designated as an expert witness in a litigated matter, the opposing side of the litigation is entitled to discover everything that the expert has learned or relied on in the course of the expert's work. No privileges apply to the expert's work in the matter.

The strength of the financial expert's opinion is ultimately dependent on the thoroughness of the investigation, the soundness of the economic assumptions, an accurate perception of the facts, and a proper application of the facts to economic theory. To be effective, however, expert testimony must be presented at trial in a manner that educates the trier of fact and compels a finding that conforms to the opinion. In order to accomplish this goal, the lawyer and the expert must effectively prepare and plan the expert testimony that will be offered at trial.

Glossary/Index

Accelerated depreciation: methods of depreciation that expense a greater proportion of the cost of a fixed asset in the earlier years of its estimated useful life, and a lesser proportion in the later years. *[82]*

Account: the account is an individual record of increases and decreases in specific assets, liabilities, equity, revenues and expenses; the device used to accumulate increases and decreases in a specific item. *[31]*

Account balance: the difference between the total debits and total credits in the account. *[36]*

Accounting: the system of recording & reporting the financial transactions of an entity culminating in the presentation of financial statements. *[1, 8, 11]*

Accounts payable: a current liability of an entity representing a short-term obligation to trade creditors for the purchase of goods and services, usually in the ordinary course of the entity's operations. *[69]*

Accounts receivable: a current asset that represents the expected receipts from customers created by the sale of goods and services on credit. *[123]*

Accounts receivable turnover ratio: a financial ratio that states the relationship between a company's credit sales and its average accounts receivable balance; the ratio shows the number of times per year, on average, that the entity "turns over" its accounts receivable balance to earn its total credit sales. *[124]*

Accrual: the accumulation of an asset or a liability for which the cash has not yet been received or paid. The accumulation of the asset, accounts receivable, corresponds with the accrual of revenue; the accumulation of the liability, accounts payable, corresponds with the accrual of an expense. *[55, 57]*

Accrual basis revenue: accrual basis revenue is the total of all revenue that is earned during an accounting period, regardless of when the related cash is received. See Realization Principle, page 58. The formula for converting from cash basis revenue to accrual basis revenue is shown on page 68.

Accrual basis accounting: measures the performance and position of a company by recognizing events based on true economic activity regardless of when cash transactions occur; recognizes revenue when it is earned and expenses when they are incurred, regardless of when the related cash is exchanged. *[56]*

Accumulated depreciation: a contra asset account that shows the accumulation of an asset's cost expiration (depreciation expense) up to the date of the balance sheet. *[77]*

Acquisition cost: the overall cost of purchasing an asset; all costs required to place the asset in service to the company. *[79]*

Activity methods of depreciation: the calculation of depreciation expense based on the level of activity or usage of the particular fixed asset. Under these methods, depreciation expense is calculated by estimating the asset's useful life (at the time of acquisition) in terms of the total activity or usage that is anticipated, then the depreciable base is divided by that total activity life, resulting in an amount of depreciation expense per unit of activity. *[85]*

Adjusted book value: a valuation term related to a balance sheet; it is the total of the assets, net of liabilities, with the assets adjusted to their realizable market value; it is a cost approach to valuation of a business. *[162]*

Adjusting journal entries: journal entries made and posted at the end of the accounting period to adjust accounts internally within the business enterprise; used to account for the changes in business resources that occur as a result of internal activity within the business, as opposed to external transactions. *[48]*

Affirmative argument: in relation to expert testimony, a positive assertion that a particular conclusion is the correct or most reasonable answer to a problem. *[219]*

Aging of accounts receivable: the process of listing all of the accounts receivable that exist at a particular date, by customer, outstanding balance amount and date of invoice, then identifying the age of the outstanding balance in categories (usually 30-day increments); each "aged" category of accounts receivable is assigned an estimated uncollectible percentage based on the firm's historical experience; the process is used to estimate the total uncollectible portion of the accounts receivable. *[63]*

Allowance method (for uncollectible accounts receivables and bad debt expense): a method of accounting for uncollectible accounts receivable and bad debt expense that estimates the amount of uncollectible receivables during the accounting period and charges that amount as bad debt expense in the period; the allowance method attempts

to properly match the bad debt expense with the revenue that was recognized by the accrual of the related accounts receivables; applies the Matching Principle. *[64]*

Allowance for doubtful accounts: a contra asset account created to show the estimated uncollectable portion of accounts receivable; estimated uncollectible accounts receivable are usually determined by preparing an aging of the accounts receivable, although there are other bases of making the estimate. *[64]*

Amortization: In accounting, "amortization" is the method of allocating the cost of an intangible asset over its estimated useful life; it is calculated using a straight-line method and the reduction in the asset can be accounted for using a contra asset account, accumulated amortization, or the asset can be directly written down when the period expense is recorded. *[89]* In finance, "amortization" is the term used to describe the systematic reduction of a loan principal balance resulting from a stream of regular repayments of principal and interest. *[144]*

Amortization schedule: In finance, the financial schedule that shows the ongoing loan balance, the amount of the monthly payment, and the portion of the monthly payment that comprises interest and principal reduction. The mortgage (or loan) is said to "amortize" according to the schedule. At any point during the loan's amortization schedule, there is a remaining unpaid principal balance that is owed, which is referred to as the "balloon payment" required to repay the loan completely at that point in time. *[144, 146]*

Annual Depletion Expense: equal to the per-unit depletion expense multiplied by the units during the year. *[88]*

Annuity: a constant stream of equal payments (or receipts); a series of consecutive, equal cash flows occurring for N equal time periods with a fixed interest rate calculated at the end of each cash flow. An annuity with payments at the end of each period is called an ordinary annuity; an annuity with payments at the beginning of each period is called an annuity due. *[149]*

Annuity due: an annuity with payments occurring at the beginning of each time period, similar to rental payments. *[149]*

Appraisal: a professional opinion, usually written, of the market value of real or personal property whose market price is not usually readily determinable. *[155]*

Articulation: the interrelationship between the real/permanent accounts contained in the balance sheet and the temporary accounts contained in the income statement. *[53]*

Assets: the economic resources owned by a business entity; they are a permanent accounts of the balance sheet. *[12]*

Assumption: this is a supposition, or the supposing of a hypothetical fact to be true. *[218, 272]*

Auditing: the examination of a company's accounting records by a Certified Public Accountant to opine whether or not they conform to Generally Accepted Accounting Principles and fairly present the results of operations of the entity. *[7]*

Average Age of Inventory: a financial ratio determined by dividing 365 days by the Inventory Turnover Ratio; the result measures the average age (in days) of the entity's inventory. *[123]*

Average collection period (of accounts receivable): a financial ratio determined by dividing 365 days by the Accounts Receivable Turnover Ratio; the result measures the average collection period (in days) for the entity's accounts receivable. *[124]*

Avoided costs: In lost profits analyses, these are costs that would have been incurred in connection with the generation of the lost revenues but were not incurred; often referred to as "variable costs saved." *[261]*

Balance sheet: the financial statement that presents the financial status (assets, liabilities and equity) of a business at a point in time. *[12]*

Balloon payment: the unpaid principal balance (unamortized balance) of a loan; the amount required to repay the loan at any point in time. *[144, 146]*

Before-and-after method: in commercial damages analyses, a "method" of projecting the but-for activity of a plaintiff based on some historical results, assuming the defendant's conduct had not occurred; it is more of a characterization of an assumption than a true methodology. The approach is best suited to a business situation in which there is no practical application of a yardstick method available and one that has an established pattern of activity or track record. *[258]*

Below the line: a colloquial expression that usually refers to certain business expenses that are considered below the gross profit line of the income statement. *[94]*

Benefit-of-the-bargain-rule: a measure of contract damages in which the non-breaching party is entitled to everything that he would have received, including profits, if the breach had not occurred; the non-breaching party can recover the value of what he was promised in the contract as well as other benefits that were foreseeable at the time of the contract; the focus under this theory is the benefit that the plaintiff was entitled to under the contract. *[252]*

Book value: As it relates to an individual asset, "book value" is the net amount that the asset is presented on the balance sheet, after subtracting any contra asset that relates to the asset, such as accumulated depreciation or allowance for doubtful accounts. As it relates to the entire company, "book value" is the term used to describe the total equity of the firm, as measured by the total of the assets minus the total of the liabilities. *[78]*

But-for projections (revenues, earnings, benefits, growth rate, time period): In damages calculations, a "but-for" projection is the hypothetical condition that is projected to have happened after the wrongful conduct, assuming the wrongful conduct had not occurred. *[224, 225, 254, 257]*

Capital: in financial theory, a measure a measure of the accumulated wealth of an individual or entity that has been created by sacrificing present consumption in favor of investment to generate future returns above investment costs; it is the measure of wealth, not the wealth itself. *[128]*

Capital expenditure: the purchase of an asset that is expected to benefit to company for a period longer than one year; for tax purposes, capital expenditures are costs that cannot be deducted in the year in which they are paid or incurred and must be capitalized, or made into an asset, as opposed to being expensed, or written off during the present accounting period. *[76]*

Capitalization of earnings: an income approach to determining the value of an asset, usually applied to a business. Under this method, the value of the enterprise is estimated by capitalizing the representative earnings base at an appropriate capitalization rate that represents the required rate of return to an investor in consideration of the perceived risk of the expected earnings stream; it is also referred to as a "price/earnings" method and it is a two-factor method to determine the value of the business; in order to apply the method properly, the analyst must add or subtract any "excess" or "deficient" assets to the two-factor conclusion. *[160]*

Capitalization of excess earnings: a method of business valuation that considers the adjusted book value of the assets and liabilities of the business, as well as an estimate of the intangible asset value of the enterprise based on excess earnings generated by the business. *[162]*

Capitalization of gross revenues: an expression of the value of a business in relation to its annual gross revenue. As a business valuation methodology, it has very limited application. *[161]*

Capitalization of other benefit streams: income approaches to valuation that rely on the capitalization of other measures of net economic benefit streams to the enterprise such as Debt-Free Cash Flow, Earnings Before Interest and Taxes (EBIT) or Earnings Before Interest Taxes Depreciation and Amortization (EBITDA). *[161]*

Cash basis accounting: a method of accounting that relies entirely on the receipt or payment of cash as the determinant for the recognition of revenue or expense; not accepted for GAAP purposes, but routinely used by small businesses and individuals for tax reporting purposes; does not properly recognize all the revenue earned in the accounting period and does not properly account for all the expenses of the period. *[61, 66]*

Cash basis revenue: the total of all cash receipts from sales during the accounting period. *[66]* The formula for converting from cash basis revenue to accrual basis revenue is shown on page 68.

Cash flow insolvency: exists when an enterprise cannot pay its debts when they become due, regardless of its overall solvency; also known as income statement insolvency. *[119]*

Chart of accounts: a listing of all of the general ledger accounts that are used for the enterprise. *[33]*

Closing the books: the process of "zeroing out" the temporary accounts (revenue and expense accounts) at the end of the accounting period and making a final adjustment of net income or net loss to equity. *[49]*

Collateral source rule: a rule of evidence that prohibits the defendant from showing that the plaintiff has been compensated for his loss from another source, usually insurance; under the collateral source rule a plaintiff is entitled to recover the full measure of his damages from the defendant, regardless of the fact that the plaintiff may have been compensated for his loss from another source. *[201]*

Commercial damages: damages suffered by a plaintiff business enterprise as a result of a defendant's wrongful conduct. *[251]*

Common size technique: The restatement of the financial statements of a business into

percentages to facilitate comparison (by vertical and horizontal analysis) to other accounts and categories within the financial statement as well as to other companies in the relevant industry; a benefit of this technique is the ability to compare companies of different sizes to one another on a percentage basis, rather than an absolute basis. *[111]*

Common stock: a form of corporate equity ownership, a type of security; it is an equity account. *[52]*

Comparable business sales: a market approach to valuing a business that compares the subject to the sale of "comparable" businesses; some private companies have developed databases that report the details of sales of businesses. The databases contain information about the types of business, location, date of sale, selling price and financial information about the operations of the business prior to its transfer. This information is helpful to assist in understanding how the marketplace views the particular type of business. *[161]*

Comparability: In financial analysis, valuation and damages analysis, the degree to which the subject is comparable to statistics relating to other companies or industries. *[161, 258]*

Comparative analysis: The comparison of significant financial statistics of a business to those of other businesses or composites of relevant industry information. *[110]*

Compensatory damages: an amount paid to compensate the claimant for loss, injury, or harm suffered by another's wrongful conduct; they can be both special (economic) or general (noneconomic) because they compensate the plaintiff for harm suffered, whether or not the harm is economic; also known as "actual damages." *[203]*

Compound interest: the interest rate convention by which the original principal balance is increased by the amount of accumulated interest at the end of each compounding period; then, interest is computed on the new balance as well as the original principal. *[133]*

Compound journal entry: a journal entry that affects more than two accounts. *[44, 50]*

Consequential damages: indirect losses suffered by the plaintiff as a consequence of the defendant's wrongful conduct. *[202, 207, 209]*

Conservatism principle: a fundamental accounting principle that applies to accounting judgments made in uncertain situations; supports the choice of the option least likely to overstate assets and profits. *[25]*

Consistency principle: a fundamental accounting principle that requires that accounting reports be prepared using methods and estimates that are consistent with those of prior periods. *[25]*

Contra asset account: a general ledger account that is presented with the assets of the business that "goes against" the asset that it is attached to, and when considered with its corresponding asset, the contra asset account effectively reduces the net balance of the asset shown on the balance sheet. Contra asset accounts are increased by credits and reduced by debits. *[64, 64]*

Contract: a legally enforceable promise. *[251]*

Copyright: the exclusive legal right to reproduce, publish, sell, or distribute the matter and form of something (as a literary, musical, or artistic work), with a life of 50 to 70 years past the death of its owner. *[89]*

Corporate finance: the science of allocating a company's sources of capital with a view toward optimizing the balance between the cost of the capital and the benefits received from using the capital. *[127]*

Cost: the amount of money or property paid for a good or service. *[21]*

Cost accounting: the process of identifying, recording and analyzing the costs of production and distribution; contains sophisticated methods for allocating different cost components to manufactured goods. *[106]*

Cost approach: In appraisal, a method of determining value based on the summation of all of the costs required to reproduce the property in its present condition. It is most reliable when it is applied to newer properties and it is also used for special use properties. Its application to business appraisal focuses on the balance sheet. *[156]*

Cost principle: a fundamental concept of GAAP; assets are recorded at the amount of cash or cash equivalents paid or the fair value of the consideration given to acquire them at the time of their acquisition; liabilities are recorded at the amount of proceeds received in exchange for the obligation. *[24]*

Cost of goods available for sale: equal to the beginning inventory plus all of the purchases during the year. *[94]*

Cost of goods sold: equal to the cost of goods available for sale (beginning inventory plus purchases) minus the ending inventory; the total of the direct costs of the products that compose a company's sales. *[96]*

Cost of natural resources: determined by the direct cost of the resource plus related costs such as exploration and development costs, as well as consideration of the costs to restore the property to its original condition. *[87]*

Credit: amounts entered on the right-hand side of a T-account. *[35]*

Credit balance: when the credits exceed the debits in the account. *[36]*

Current assets: cash and other assets that are expected to be converted into cash, sold or consumed within one year or the normal operating cycle of the business. *[13]*

Current liabilities: short-term obligations due in less than one year. *[14]*

Current ratio: a financial ratio used to measure liquidity; equal to the current assets divided by the current liabilities; another representation of a firm's working capital, only the metric is stated in a ratio, rather than an absolute number. The current ratio enables comparison of the subject company to industry norms because the status of the firm's liquidity is presented as the ratio of current assets to current liabilities, indicating how many times the current liabilities can be "covered" by the theoretical liquidation of all the current assets. By using a ratio, different sized firms can be compared to one another, and an individual firm can be compared to an industry average. *[120]*

Damages: the financial compensation that is claimed by or awarded to a plaintiff as a result of a defendant's misconduct as compensation for loss or injury; the monetary amount that is intended to "make the plaintiff whole" after suffering the harm caused by the defendant. *[199, 200]*

Damages analysis: a financial analysis that estimates damages. *[213 et seq., 251 et. seq.]*

Date of incident: the date of the incident that is the subject of the litigation; sometimes referred to as date of injury or date of accident. *[221]*

Date of valuation: the "as of" date at which the financial analysis or valuation is performed; it is significant because it divides a damages analysis into a past loss component and a future loss component, both of which have significant legal and financial ramifications. *[page 266]*

Debit: amounts entered on the left-hand side of a T-account. *[35]*

Debit Balance: when the debits exceed the credits in the account. *[36]*

Debt: liabilities to outsiders; capital provided by creditors as opposed to owners. *[14,121]*

Debt ratio: a financial ratio used to measure leverage; measures the percentage of the total assets of the firm that are financed with debt, as opposed to equity; equal to the total liabilities divided by the total assets; indicates to creditors how well protected they are in the event the firm becomes insolvent. A high ratio has a negative influence on a company's ability to obtain additional financing. *[121]*

Debt to equity ratio: a financial leverage ratio used to measure leverage; sets forth the relationship of the company's debt to its equity; equal to the total liabilities divided by the total equity; the most meaningful use of the ratio is in relation to the company's industry. *[121]*

Declining balance method: a method of accelerated depreciation that is calculated at different multiples of the straight-line rate; different percentages are used for different types of assets in the Internal Revenue Code. *[82]*

Deferral: deferral is the accounting mechanism that is used when the related cash transaction occurs before the revenue or expense recognition should occur; deferral results in the creation of an asset or liability. *[57]*

Deferred revenue: the liability account that is created when a customer pays cash in advance of the required services being rendered. Deferred revenue represents the amount of money that is owed back to the customer/client until the services are performed and the related revenue is earned. *[57]*

Deferred tax item: an asset or liability account that results from temporary timing differences between the accounting treatment of tax items and the financial treatment of the tax items. The difference in the tax treatment creates a future detriment or betterment that is recognized as an asset or liability. *[73]*

Deferred tax asset: a present benefit that the company owns that can be used to offset some taxes that it might otherwise owe in the future; used to offset taxes that are owed for income in the future. *[73]*

Deferred tax liability: results from the company's ability to defer or delay the payment of some amount of taxes on its income because of some beneficial tax treatment that it takes advantage of in its tax accounting, but not in its financial statement reporting. *[73]*

Defined benefit pension plan: a pension plan in which the employee's benefit is determined based on a pre-determined formula, regardless of the balance, if any, of the funded amount of the plan. *[228]*

Depletion (expense): the process of allocating the cost of natural resources to expense over the estimated life of the resource; usually calculated by an activity method of depletion, such as units of production measured by individual units of the resources are extracted. *[87]*

Depletable cost: the total cost of the natural resource plus any restoration cost less any salvage value remaining after the resources are extracted; similar to depreciable base. *[87]*

Depreciable base: the acquisition cost of a fixed asset minus its salvage value. *[87]*

Depreciated replacement cost: a valuation term, depreciated replacement cost of an asset is the current cost of a new replacement asset minus an allowance for the percentage of the asset's useful life that has expired. *[165]*

Depreciation: the mechanism for allocating the cost of a fixed asset to the operations of the business over the estimated useful life of the asset; a systematic write off of the cost of the asset against, or matched to, the revenue that the asset is used to produce. *[75, 76]*

Depreciation expense: reflects the current accounting period's expiration of part of the fixed asset (unexpired cost); the consequence of this deduction is to lower the company's net income and, if the company pays taxes, to lower the current taxes that the company will pay. *[77]*

Depreciation schedule: a fixed asset register that records all of the details of the accounting (acquisition date, cost, depreciation method, current period depreciation expense, and the accumulated depreciation) for each fixed asset of an entity. *[81]*

Direct damages: direct losses suffered by the plaintiff as a result of defendant's unlawful conduct. *[202]*

Direct labor: the labor cost that can be directly traced to manufactured goods; a component of cost of goods sold; usually excludes labor costs of supervision or management. *[106]*

Direct write-off method (for uncollectible accounts receivables and bad debt expense): a method of determining bad debt expense under which an uncollectible account receivable is written off (expensed) in the period in which it is determined to be uncollectible, which may be in an accounting period later than the related revenue was recorded. *[64]*

Discounted future benefits stream: A method by which the value of the enterprise is estimated by projecting the anticipated net income, cash flow or other economic benefit into the future, and discounting the projection to present value at an appropriate risk-adjusted rate. *[161]*

Dividend: in a corporation, a payment to shareholders that represents a return of capital or accumulated income. *[18]*

Double declining balance method: an accelerated depreciation method that results in higher depreciation expense in the earlier years of the life of an asset; this method begins by calculating 200% of the straight line rate, applied to the book value of the asset. *[82]*

Double entry accounting system: the method of bookkeeping in which every financial transaction is expressed as a debit to one account and a credit to another account, so that the totals of the debits and credits for every transaction are always equal. *[37]*

Draw: a return of capital to an owner in a proprietorship. *[18]*

Duty to mitigate: As an offset to a plaintiff's damages, the law requires the plaintiff to make reasonable attempts to minimize the loss that has been caused by the defendant. *[216]*

Earnings base: the foundational assumption of the plaintiff's representative earnings as of the date of the incident. It should include consideration of the plaintiff's historical salary or hourly wages, bonuses, and any other additional monies that the plaintiff had earned prior to the date of the incident. *[223]*

Economic torts: largely the creation of statutes over the last hundred years; they have been created to protect people and businesses from harm to commercial enterprise. *[252]*

Employee benefits: a component of a personal economic loss, benefits are the non-cash components of a plaintiff's compensation. *[223]*

Employee stock purchase plan: a benefit offered by employers to their employees in which employees are able to purchase company stock at a discount. *[228]*

End date of analysis: the end date of a damages analysis can vary significantly from a brief period of loss to the entire remaining life expectancy of the plaintiff. *[221]*

Entity concept: a fundamental accounting principle that identifies and separates an organization from its owners or managers; the individual entity stands alone and its financial activity is measured independently. *[24]*

Equity: the owners' residual claim on the assets of the business, after the creditors' claims have been satisfied; equity is also called capital, stockholder's equity or net worth; it is a permanent account of the balance sheet. [14]

Ex-ante calculation of damages: a calculation of damages with the date of valuation being the date of the wrongful conduct. [267]

Excess earnings: the amount of income earned by the business beyond the value of the owner's services and the capital employed in the business; they are attributable to intangible assets in the business and must be present for goodwill to exist. [171]

Expected future deviations in business income: in valuation, anticipated changes from the historical level of revenue sources, access to new markets or changes in labor or other costs; should be considered when determining representative earnings. [167]

Expenses: the costs that expire during the creation of revenue; expense accounts are temporary accounts in the general ledger that are closed at the end of the accounting period. [21]

Ex-post calculation of damages: a calculation of damages at a later date than the day of the wrongful conduct, usually the date of trial. [267]

External transactions: transactions of a business entity that are executed with outsiders. [31]

Facts: historical or present truths; known financial occurrences. [218]

Fair market value: the price at which the property will change hands between a willing seller and a willing buyer, neither party being under compulsion to buy or sell, and both having reasonable knowledge of the relevant facts. [157]

Fair market value, in continued use: the present value of an item of property as part of a larger assemblage of assets; generally considered to be the depreciated replacement cost of the asset, giving consideration to the age and condition of the asset. [158]

Fair value: a standard of value; there are a number of definitions for fair value, depending on the context of its use. See [157].

Fair value of officer services: In valuation, the fair market value of the services provided by the owner are subtracted from revenues to arrive at net income; the amount necessary to replace the services performed by the owner. [171]

Fees earned: revenues earned from the performance of services. [20]

228: Federal Insurance Contributions Act; it is a payroll tax imposed by the federal government to fund Social Security and Medicare. [228]

FIFO: first-in, first-out; an inventory costing assumption used to determine the cost of ending inventory; the first goods purchased are assumed to be the first to be sold. [100]

Finance: the science of funds management; involves the interrelationships of money, interest, time and risk; the study of the allocation of scarce capital resources, measured by money, over time; seeks to weigh the relative cost of taking current action compared to the anticipated future benefit from foregoing the current action, to allow people to choose between the two alternatives. [1, 127]

Financial statement: the end result of the accounting process; the primary mechanism for disclosing an entity's financial performance to management, investors and the public. [11]

Financial statement analysis: the quantitative analysis of financial information of a company with a view toward determining important facts about the firm (i.e. liquidity, solvency, profitability, leverage and certain aspects of management effectiveness); used to determine the financial health and stability of a firm at the present time and it is also often used as the basis for projections of the anticipated performance of the company in the future. *[109]*

Finished goods: a type of manufacturing inventory; the amount of manufactured product on hand that awaits sale to customers. *[107]*

Fixed assets: tangible capital assets that are purchased for long-term use in furtherance of the activities of the business; these are not items that are normally consumed or used up in the regular course of business operations or production; these are not assets that are held as financial investments or assets held for resale to customers. *[13, 13]*

Fixed costs (expenses): costs or expenses of a company that do not vary with the level of sales over a relevant range of production. *[110, 261]*

Full disclosure principle: the accounting principle requires that all facts needed to make the financial statements not misleading be disclosed. *[27]*

Fundamental accounting equation: Assets = Liabilities + Equity; the total of the resources of a business is exactly equal to the total of the claims on the resources of the business. *[15]*

Fundamental analysis: the investment philosophy that is based on the financial strength and profitability of the individual company as opposed to technical analysis, which is based on statistical analysis of stock price trends. *[109]*

Fundamental value: see Intrinsic Value. *[157]*

Future value: the future value of a sum of money is the total future accumulation of principal plus interest on a present sum of money; the amount to which an investment will grow at a point in the future, assuming it earns interest for a period of time. *[131]*

Future value ordinary annuity: the accumulation of principal and interest at the end of the annuity period. *[150]*

General damages: noneconomic damages which compensate the plaintiff for the aspects of the specific harm suffered that are not objectively quantifiable; they are are based on the fact finder's opinion of the amount of money that will financially compensate the plaintiff for some noneconomic harm. *[202]*

General journal: the book of original entry; the accounting record where each transaction of the business is initially recorded in the books of the business; a list of every transaction undertaken by the business, stated in the form of debits and credits. *[42]*

General ledger: the book of final entry; contains all of the individual accounts of the business. *[45]*

Generally Accepted Accounting Principles (GAAP): the conventions, rules, and procedures that define accepted accounting practice at a particular time; includes not only broad guidelines of general application but also detailed practices and procedures that provide a standard by which to measure financial presentations; the "common law" of accounting. *[23]*

Generally Accepted Auditing Standards (GAAS): the body of accounting literature that governs the field of auditing. *[7]*

Going concern assumption: a fundamental accounting assumption that requires that a company is assumed to be in business indefinitely unless there is evidence to the contrary. *[24]*

Goodwill: an intangible asset of a business that can result from the cumulative benefits of reputation, location, long establishment, efficient management, proprietary processes or other intangibles attributes; the value of an entity over and above the value of its tangible assets, net of liabilities. *[155 et seq.]*

Gross profit: the profit that a company earns directly from the sale of its merchandise, before consideration of the expenses of operating the business. *[93]*

Gross profit margin: stating a company's gross profit as a percentage of the company's sales; also known as gross margin; a very important financial statistic that shows the performance of a company with respect to its industry, its pricing and its cost structure; equal to the company's gross profit divided by its sales. *[93, 116]*

Half-year convention: an assumption used to estimate the starting date for the depreciation of a newly-acquired asset; assumes that the asset was purchased exactly in the middle of the accounting period, thereby allowing one-half of one year's depreciation in the first year of service. *[80]*

Hedonic damages: a category of damages that seek to objectively measure the loss of the quality of a person's life as a result of suffering some injury. *[203]*

Historical cost assumption: a fundamental concept of GAAP; assets are recorded at the amount of cash or cash equivalents paid or the fair value of the consideration given to acquire them at the time of their acquisition; liabilities are recorded at the amount of proceeds received in exchange for the obligation. *[24]*

Horizontal analysis: a technique in the analysis of financial statements; after the financial statements are reduced to percentages, each year (or period) is compared to other periods for the purpose of observing trends or anomalies that are worthy of further consideration. *[111]*

Household services (loss of): a component of possible economic loss to a plaintiff in a personal injury or wrongful death case; services that the plaintiff can no longer perform for himself/herself or the family (such as cooking, cleaning, gardening, home maintenance, etc.) that he/she had performed prior to the incident. *[238]*

Income approach: an appraisal approach based on the assumption that the value of a property is the present value of all of its future economic benefits; also referred to as the "capitalization of earnings" method or, in public stock market parlance, the "price/earnings" ratio method. *[156]*

Income statement: the financial statement that summarizes the revenues and expenses of an entity for a period of time. *[19, 48]*

Income statement ratios: financial ratios that are useful for analyzing a company's operating performance, both by itself and relative to its industry. *[112–118]*

Income summary: a nominal account into which all income statement revenue and expense accounts are transferred at the end of the accounting period; the account is only used in the process of closing the books; it is completely closed out at the end of the closing process. *[50]*

Inflation rate: a component of the market rate of interest. *[130]*

Insolvency: the condition in which the firm's liabilities exceed its assets. *[109]*

Installment sale: the sale of property at a gain where at least one payment is to be received in a later tax year; under GAAP, it may be an allowable method of revenue recognition. *[59]*

Intangible assets: identifiable non-physical economic resources that have been acquired or created through time and effort and are identifiable as a separate asset, excluding monetary assets such as stocks, securities, accounts and notes receivable; under GAAP, they are only booked as assets if they are purchased. *[89]*

Intellectual property: a generic term that describes the form of intangible asset that exists because it is legally defined and gives its owner legal rights against infringers. *[89]*

Intentional torts: intentional acts that are reasonably foreseeable to cause harm to another. *[252]*

Interest: the "rental value" of money; interest is measured by a percentage rate on the principal amount in question; it is a measure of the time value of money; equal to the principal multiplied by the interest rate multiplied by the time period. *[128 et seq.]*

Interest income: revenue from interest earned. *[20]*

Internal transactions: accounting transactions within an entity that reapportion costs among different accounts. *[31]*

International Financial Reporting Standards (IFRS): principles-based standards, adopted by the International Accounting Standards Board. *[23]*

Intrinsic value: a standard of value also known as Fundamental Value; it differs from investment value in that it represents an analytical judgment of value based on the perceived characteristics inherent in the investment, not tempered by characteristics peculiar to any one investor, but rather tempered by how these perceived characteristics are interpreted by one analyst versus another. *[157]*

Inventory: stock in trade that is owned by a company and held for resale, or materials held to be used in the manufacture of goods for sale; exists in merchandising and manufacturing companies. *[92]*

Inventory turnover ratio: a financial ratio that measures the number of times a firm's inventory is sold in a year; calculated by dividing the cost of goods sold by the average inventory during the year. *[122]*

Investment value: a standard of value; the specific value of an investment to a particular investor or class of investors based on individual investment requirements; distinguished from market value, which is impersonal and detached. *[157]*

Investment value discount rate: in commercial damages analyses, the discount rate for the business as a whole including an adjustment for the subjective risk of the continuation of the income flow to the particular owner. *[264]*

Journal: an accounting record used to summarize transactions; the General Journal is the book of original entry *[42]*; special journals are used to record repetitive transactions like cash disbursements or cash receipts. *[42–44]*

Journalizing the transaction: the initial recording of a transaction in the accounting records of a business. *[37]*

Journal entry: the expression of a transaction in the form of debits and credits; the initial entry of a transaction in the accounting records. *[37]*

Leverage: a measure of the amount of a firm's capital that is provided by lenders as opposed to the amount that is provided by equity investors, or owners; the use of debt to finance the assets of a company in addition to the use of equity capital; the degree to which a company is leveraged is an element of the firm's financial risk. *[121]*

Liability: debt owed to an outsider; a present obligation of the enterprise arising from past events, the settlement of which is expected to result in an outflow from the enterprise's resources; liability accounts are permanent accounts, presented on the balance sheet. *[14]*

Life care expenses: a component of possible economic loss to a plaintiff in a personal injury case; the costs (past or future) of providing necessary care to an injured person, beyond actual medical expenses; these are the costs that the plaintiff will need in order to be maintained and cared for in a post-injury condition. *[240]*

LIFO: last-in, first-out; an inventory costing assumption used to determine the cost of ending inventory; the most recently purchased goods are assumed to be the first to be sold. *[101]*

Liquidity: the ability of a company to easily convert assets into cash and meet its current debts; a firm's liquidity is a measure of the current status of the firm's cash and its ability to convert other assets into cash in the short term without discount or penalty; three measures of a company's liquidity are: working capital, the current ratio, and the quick ratio. *[110, 119, 121]*

Long-term liabilities: long-term obligations due in more than one year. *[14]*

Lost earnings (analysis): a component of personal economic loss; the terminology is used interchangeably with "loss of earnings"; it is a calculation of the specific earnings that a person has lost as a result of the defendant's wrongful conduct; a financial analysis of the plaintiff's former and changed earnings situation that results in the conclusion that the past or future earnings of the plaintiff are less than they would have been, but for the wrongful conduct of the defendant. *[217]*

Lost earnings capacity: a component of personal economic loss; the terminology is used interchangeably with "loss of earnings capacity"; the economic loss suffered by an individual when that individual loses the ability or capacity to earn some amount of money, usually an amount different from what he was actually earning at the time of the incident in question. *[217]*

Lost household services: see household services. *[238]*

Lost profits (Lost net profits): the economic loss suffered by a business; generally defined as the difference between what the plaintiff's profits would have been "but for" the wrongful act of the defendant and the actual profits experienced by the plaintiff after the wrongful conduct. *[253 et seq.]*

Management effectiveness: through financial statement analysis one can see the effectiveness management, including the effectiveness of the company's credit management (collection of accounts receivable) or the utilization of the amount of the company's inventory. *[110]*

Management ratios: financial ratios that are used as a tool to evaluate management's performance in some areas of business operations; usually derived from both the balance sheet and the income statement; used to evaluate how effectively certain assets are converted into cash, to provide information on how efficiently the enterprise uses its assets, and to assist in evaluating how well the company has operated during the year. *[122]*

Manufacturing: the process of producing finished goods from raw materials by fabricating or assembling the materials, adding labor and performing the activity in an organized process. *[105]*

Market approach: see Sales Comparison Approach. *[156]*

Market approaches to value: In business valuation, market approaches valuation are a usually a variation of income approaches, but they rely on some market data for the determination of the capitalization rate, or multiple, to apply to the net income flow of the business to determine value. *[161]*

Market rate of interest: referred to as the nominal interest rate; contains three components: the real rate of interest; an estimate of the anticipated inflation rate; and, for loans that have any risk above risk-free, an additional component for risk, called a risk premium; determined by the marketplace, as a function of supply and demand. *[129]*

Market value discount rate: in commercial damages analyses, the discount rate for the business as a whole; this is a detached assessment of the risk of the continuity of anticipated profits. *[264]*

Matching principle: a fundamental accounting principle that requires the matching of revenues and expenses; the principle states that when specific revenues are recognized in a period, the expenses incurred to generate those revenues should also be assigned to that period. *[27]*

Materiality principle: a fundamental accounting principle that addresses the relative importance or significance of specific financial information; if the amount in question or the characterization of the transaction is considered significant, then it should be specifically reported as part of the accounting process and in the preparation of financial statements. *[25]*

Mitigating earnings: earnings used to offset the plaintiff's total loss of earnings capacity amount; can be based on the actual earnings of the plaintiff post-injury (if he has returned to work) or on the opinions of the appropriate mitigating earnings capacity offered by a vocational rehabilitation specialist as to when the plaintiff will be able to return to work and what earnings he would likely be able to receive; also referred to as "offset" earnings. *[216, 236]*

Mitigating employment benefits: all employment benefits that a plaintiff receives as part of his employment subsequent to the incident; if plaintiff has not yet returned to work, these benefits can be estimated by a vocational rehabilitation expert. *[216, 236]*

Mitigation of damages: the policy of the law that requires the aggrieved party to make efforts to minimize his damages; the plaintiff cannot passively sit back and allow damages to accumulate without undertaking some responsibility to lessen them. *[201, 216, 236]*

Monetary damages: financial compensation claimed by or paid to the plaintiff to attempt to make him whole, after the wrong committed by the defendant or to return him to the status quo ante, the way he was before the wrong occurred. *[199]*

Monetary finance: addresses the time value of money, a concept that underlies all economic transactions; the study of money and the relationship between its current purchasing power and its ability to earn interest. *[127]*

Monetary wealth: anything that can be bought and sold, and for which there is a market, and therefore a price. *[128]*

Money: a medium of exchange, a unit of account, a measure of value and a standard of deferred payment; a means of facilitating commercial transactions and allocating wealth; it has no inherent value; it is merely a means of measuring capital (human, natural, industrial). *[128]*

Money measurement concept: a fundamental accounting concept that recognizes that accounting data only records transactions that are capable of being expressed in monetary terms. *[26]*

Monthly convention: an assumption used to estimate the starting date for the depreciation of a newly-acquired asset; breaks the year into months and assumes that the asset is placed in service on the first day of the month if it is placed in service during the first half of the month, or if it is purchased in the second half of the month it assumes that the asset is placed in service on the first of the next month. *[81]*

Mortgage (loan): a loan secured by real property through the use of a mortgage note; in common usage, the term "mortgage" usually refers to the loan; the typical mortgage loan contains a fixed number of equal payments and a constant interest rate, although there are many variations on the terms of mortgage loans. *[140]*

Natural resources: long-term capital assets that can be owned by a business and used up, or depleted, during the course of the operations of the business; they are wasting assets, physically extracted from the earth through business operations and they are only replaceable through natural processes. *[87]*

NAICS: the North American Industry Classification System; it is the standard used by Federal statistical agencies in classifying business establishments for the purpose of collecting, analyzing, and publishing statistical data related to the U.S. business economy; includes definitions for each industry, background information, tables showing changes between years, and a comprehensive index. *[115]*

Negative argument: in relation to expert testimony, a criticism leveled at an affirmative assertion or opinion; it suggests a number of complaints regarding the affirmative assertion or opinion. *[219]*

Negligence: a tort stemming from the breach of a duty that is imposed on individuals to act in a manner that does not cause harm to others. *[252]*

Net book value: see "Book value." *[78]*

Net income: the income statement result during an accounting period if the entity's revenues exceed its expenses; revenues minus expenses; shows the net positive change in the equity of the business during the accounting period as the result of business operations. *[19]*

Net loss: the result of expenses exceeding revenues in the accounting period; see net income. *[19]*

Net profit margin: a financial ratio that states an entity's net profit (net income) as a percentage of its revenue; this ratio enables the analyst to compare a company's return on sales with a performance of other companies in the industry. *[117]*

Net tangible asset value (NTAV): total adjusted tangible assets less liabilities; also referred to as net book value. *[171]*

Net worth: the total assets minus the total liabilities stated at a particular year in time; also referred to as book value. *[14]*

Nominal accounts: these accounts are T-accounts that are only used at the very end of the accounting period, in the mechanical process of closing the books. *[50]*

Nominal damages: a category of damages that represents a token amount awarded to a plaintiff to recognize that the loss or harm suffered was technical rather than actual, in some cases to show that some right of the plaintiff was violated by the defendant, but the actual damage was slight. *[10, 203]*

Non-operating items: income and expenses which are not essential to the normal operations of the business or professional practice; in business valuation, non-operating items are added back to the income statement to determine income for valuation purposes. *[166]*

Non-recurring items: revenues or expenses which are either the result of unique events or outside of their normal expected ranges; in business valuation, non-recurring items are usually adjusted to the income statement to determine income for valuation purposes. *[166]*

Objectivity principle: a fundamental accounting principle requiring that accounting data be unbiased and based on the most objectively verifiable information available. *[26]*

Operating profit margin: a financial ratio that states an entity's operating profit as a percentage of its revenue; operating profit is profit from continued operations before interest and taxes; it is an important measure of management's ability to control operating costs and raise productivity; it is often a better measure of management skill than a company's net profit margin because net income is influenced by income taxes, which are not always within the control of management; also known as net income from operations, operating income, or earnings before interest and taxes (EBIT); this ratio enables the analyst to compare a company's return on sales with a performance of other companies in the industry. *[117]*

Ordinary annuity: a constant stream of equal payments (or receipts); a series of consecutive, equal cash flows occurring for N equal time periods with a fixed interest rate calculated at the end of each cash flow. An annuity with payments at the end of each period is called an ordinary annuity; an annuity with payments at the beginning of each period is called an annuity due. *[149]*

Out-of-pocket rule: a measure of contract damages in which the non-breaching party is entitled to receive as damages everything that he is "out of pocket" pursuant to trying to perform the contract; the focus of this theory of contract damages is what the plaintiff lost, not what he would have gained if the contract had been performed. *[252]*

Overhead: a grouping of expenses that are indirectly related to the manufacturing process; these are generally not directly traceable to the finished goods (or services) that are produced; overhead includes factory supervision expenses, factory utilities, factory rent and other expenses of operating the manufacturing process that cannot be directly tied to the products that are manufactured. *[106]*

Patent: the exclusive right for the manufacture, use and sale of a particular product, granted in the United States for a period of 20 years. *[89]*

Payment: the amount of a regular cash flow (usually monthly) that includes interest and principal; a component of an annuity calculation or a mortgage loan amortization schedule. *[131]*

Percentage of completion method: a method of revenue recognition under the Realization Principle by which a portion of the total revenue of a long-term contract is recognized in an accounting period; the percentage of the contract that has been completed to date is measured (usually based on the percentage of the total costs that have been incurred to date), then that percentage is used to recognize a portion of the total revenue of the project in the current accounting period; used for companies engaged in long-term contracting projects. *[58]*

Periodic method of inventory accounting: a method of accounting for physical inventory by which the amount of inventory on hand is determined by a physical count at the end of the accounting period; the physical inventory

is then "costed" by applying different inventory costing assumptions (LIFO, FIFO, average cost) resulting in an estimate of the cost of the ending inventory. *[97]*

Periods per year (Payments per year) (P/Y): the number of compounding periods per year; as a component of an interest or annuity calculation, the number of compounding periods per year is an important component of any interest calculation; compounding periods are usually daily, monthly, quarterly, semi-annually or annually. *[131]*

Permanent accounts: these accounts are maintained for the assets, liabilities and equities of a business; contain balances that change over time based on the activity posted to them, but remain open after the books of the business have been closed at the end of the accounting period. *[33]*

Perpetual method of inventory accounting: a method of accounting for physical inventory by which the amount of inventory on hand is constantly monitored; every item of inventory is specifically identified in the inventory accounting records, its cost is recorded, and it is specifically accounted for during the time that it is held by the business. When an item is sold, the exact cost of the specific item is removed from the asset account (inventory) and the expiration of that cost is recorded in the income statement as a cost of goods sold. *[96]*

Personal consumption: a factor of economic loss in wrongful death cases; an estimate of the expenses that the decedent would have spend on himself had he lived; personal consumption is subtracted from lost earnings because the decedent's personal expenses would not have been available to the survivors. *[243]*

Personal economic losses: losses suffered by individuals that result directly from or as an indirect consequence of a defendant's unlawful conduct. *[213]*

Personal finance: an individual's personal financial planning. *[127]*

Per-unit depletion: a calculation within natural resource accounting, per-unit depletion is equal to the depletable cost divided by the units of resource. *[87]*

Point of sale recognition: under the Realization principle, revenue is recognized at the time of sale. *[58]*

Posting: the process of transferring the debits and credits from the journals to the proper general ledger account. *[45]*

Prejudgment interest: the application of interest to a past loss, a loss calculated before the date of trial. *[222,267]*

Premise of value: an assumption about the likely set of transactional circumstances that apply to the valuation process. *[158]*

Prepaid asset (or "item"): a purchased economic resource that will be used up in the near term future operations of the business; an unexpired cost that will soon be expensed/expired in the operations of the business. *[70]*

Present Value: a present sum of money; the "principal" amount in a financial calculation. *[131, 138]*

Present value ordinary annuity: an annuity in which the payments are discounted to a present value; the present value of N payments occurring at the end of each payment period

discounted back to the beginning of the first payment period. *[149, 152]*

Principal: a present sum of money; in financial calculations, this amount is called "Present Value." *[131, 138]*

Principle of Anticipation: The appraisal principle that bases the value of property on the expectation of benefits to be derived in the future. *[155]*

Principle of Contribution: The appraisal principle that requires an appraiser to measure the value of any improvement to a property by the amount it contributes to the market value of the property, not by the cost of the improvement. *[155]*

Principle of Substitution: The appraisal principle that states that a buyer of property will pay no more for the property than the amount for which a property of like utility may be purchased; that a property's value tends to be limited by the cost of acquiring an equally desirable substitute. *[155]*

Profitability: A firm's ability to earn income and, as a result, sustain growth in both the short- and long-term; a company's degree of profitability is usually based on the income statement, but analysis of the firm's financial statements will show that the amount of assets and equity are relevant to understanding the company's profitability. *[109, 116]*

Proprietor's Equity: in proprietorships, the equity account that shows the owner's residual claim on the assets of the entity; at the end of the accounting process (closing the books), net income or net loss is assed to (subtracted from) Proprietor's Equity. *[14, 49]*

Proximate cause: a legal principle which governs the recovery of all compensatory damages, whether the underlying claim is based on contract, tort or on both; requires that the harm suffered, for which damages compensate, be logically connected—and relatively closely connected—to the defendant's act; there is no absolute definition of proximate cause that will dictate a hard and fast rule to define the connection between the damages and the wrongful conduct. *[200]*

Public Company Accounting and Oversight Board (PCAOB): oversees and investigates the audits and auditors of public companies; created by the Sarbanes-Oxley Act of 2002. *[6]*

Public finance: deals with taxation, government spending and government financing issues. *[127]*

Publicly traded comparables: a consideration in both the market approach and income approach to valuing a business; here the analyst seeks price information about publicly traded stocks in the same or similar industries and draws comparisons about the publicly traded price in relation to earnings per share. This information is used to assist in "pricing" the stock of the subject company. *[161]*

Punitive damages: a type of general damages that are charged against a defendant to punish the defendant for egregious, intentional or reckless conduct; also known as "exemplary damages." *[203]*

Purchases: an expense account in which all of a company's purchases are accumulated; a temporary account that gets closed out at the end of the period with the other revenue and expense accounts. *[94]*

P/Y: see "Periods per year." *[131]*

Quick ratio: a financial ratio used to measure liquidity; equal to the current assets minus inventory, divided by current liabilities; measures a company's liquidity without considering its inventory (which is the least liquid of a company's current assets). It is a measure of highly liquid assets that are mostly composed of cash, short term securities and accounts receivable. It measures the firm's ability to meet its current obligations even if none of its inventory can be sold. It is also known as the "acid test" ratio. *[120]*

Ratio analysis: the comparison of different accounts, categories or elements of a firm's financial statements to one another to derive meaningful information about the financial health of the organization; the most common form of financial analysis; provides relative measures of the firm's financial condition and performance. *[110]*

Rationale: the process of logic that is applied to the facts and assumptions to evaluate them and relate them to a supportable conclusion regarding the issue at hand. *[219, 226]*

Raw materials: a type of inventory in a manufacturing concern; a company purchases raw materials inventory to hold until it is needed for the production process. *[105]*

Realization principle: a fundamental accounting principle that addresses the proper timing of the recognition of revenue; it states that items of revenue should be recognized when the entity has completed or virtually completed the exchange and it can reasonably estimate the probability of payment. *[26, 58]*

Real rate of interest: equal to the market rate of interest minus the current inflation rate; the base rate for the rental of money without consideration of inflation; reflects the real cost of funds and, in a world in which there was no inflation, the real rate of interest would equal the nominal, or market, rate of interest. *[129]*

Reasonable certainty: a legal principle governing the calculation of damages that requires that damages be proven with reasonable certainty; however, most courts have recognized that the rule applies only to the fact of damages, not to the amount of damages. *[201]*

Regression analysis: a time-series method which measures the extent to which one set of data depends upon, or is influenced by, another. *[258]*

Relevant information: information is relevant to the extent that it can potentially alter a decision. *[23]*

Reliable information: reliable information is verifiable, representationally faithful, and neutral. *[23]*

Replacement value: the amount necessary to replace an asset (at its current level of utility) at current market prices. *[158]*

Reproduction value: the amount necessary to reproduce an exact replica of the asset. *[158]*

Rescission: an equitable contract remedy that places both parties back in the same situation that they were in before the alleged breach. *[199, 208]*

Restitution: an equitable contract remedy that requires a defendant to restore all of his ill-gotten gains to the plaintiff. *[199, 208]*

Retained Earnings: an account in the equity section of a corporation's balance sheet; retained earnings represent the residual equity claim of the stockholders on the assets of a corporation arising from the accumulated, retained net income of the corporation. Retained earnings are increased by net income, and reduced by net losses and/or dividends paid to stockholders. *[52]*

Return on equity: a financial ratio that shows the percentage return on the owners' net equity investment in the business; calculated by dividing the current year's net income by the average total equity. *[118]*

Return on total assets: a financial ratio that measures how efficiently profits are being generated from the business' assets; calculated by dividing the current year's net income by the average of the total assets from the beginning of the year and the end of the year; it is best to compare this ratio with the ratios of companies in similar businesses or industry, a ratio that is low compared to the industry average indicates that business assets are being used inefficiently. *[118]*

Revenue: the gross increase in assets that flows into an entity as a result of business operations; the measure of the business' sales of goods and services to its customers; also referred to as "sales," "fees earned" or "interest income"; it is one of the temporary accounts of the income statement. *[20]*

Revenue expenditure: distinguished from a capital expenditure; revenue expenditures are outlays that benefit the business currently, and are therefore treated as an expense to be matched against revenue in the current accounting period, as opposed to the acquisition of capital assets. *[76]*

Revenue Ruling 59-60: the Internal Revenue Service's seminal pronouncement on the valuation of closely held corporations; it outlines the approach, methods and factors to be considered in valuing the shares of closely-held corporations for estate and gift tax purposes. *[189]*

Revenue Ruling 68-609: outlines the "formula" approach to be used in determining the fair market value of intangible assets of a business only if there is no better basis available for making the determination. *[197]*

Risk premium: a component of an interest (or discount) rate to compensate the lender or investor for the risk of the investment; it is a component that increases the "price" (or cost, or required rate of return) of the investment (or loan) to account for the possibility of the default of the debtor or failure of the investment to achieve the expected return. *[130, 263]*

Sales: revenues obtained from the sale of goods. *[20]*

Sales comparison approach: a fundamental approach to appraisal; relying on the principle of substitution, the sales comparison approach is a method of estimating the fair market value of a property by comparing it to the sale of similar properties in the marketplace; also known as the "Market Approach." *[156]*

Sales projection method: in commercial damages analyses, a "method" of projecting the but-for activity of a plaintiff based on the assumption that the projection would have occurred, but-for the alleged effects of the defendant's actions; it is more of a characterization of an assumption than a true methodology. *[259]*

Sales to working capital ratio: a financial ratio that measures the efficiency with which an entity's working capital is employed; calculated by dividing the total current sales by the average working capital balance. A low ratio may indicate inefficient use while a high ratio may signify over trading–a vulnerable position for creditors. 124]

Salvage value: the estimated value that a fixed asset will have at the end of its useful life; also called residual value or scrap value. *[79]*

Sarbanes-Oxley Act of 2002: set new or enhanced standards for all U.S. public company boards, management and public accounting firms; applies in general to publicly held companies and their audit firms. *[6]*

Semifixed and semivariable costs (expenses): costs or expenses that are partially fixed and partially variable; the terms are used interchangeably. *[110]*

Simple interest: a simplified convention for calculating interest on a principal amount; equal to the principal multiplied by the interest rate multiplied by the time period; the interest rate is applied to the original principal balance (only), at the agreed-on rate and for the time period of the loan. There is never an adjustment to the principal balance for the accumulation of unpaid or accrued interest. *[132]*

Solvency: a firm's ability to pay its obligation to creditors and other third parties in the short term; the condition of a firm's assets exceeding its liabilities. *[109, 119]*

Special damages: specifically identifiable economic losses that a plaintiff claims or has suffered as a proximate result of the defendant's conduct; they are intended to compensate the plaintiff for the quantifiable losses suffered. *[202]*

Special journals: subsets of the general journal used to enter repetitive journal entries; examples of special journals are the cash disbursements journal and sales journal. *[44]*

Specific performance: an equitable contract remedy that requires each party to do what was required under the contract; a contract remedy which requires that the defendant do exactly what was promised in the contract, for instance, transferring the title to a promised parcel of land, rather than just paying money (damages) for the breach of the contract. *[199, 208]*

Standard of value: a definition of the type of value (i.e. fair market value) being sought in an appraisal; usually reflects an assumption as to who will be the buyer and who will be the seller in the hypothetical or actual transaction regarding the subject property of the appraisal; it can be legally mandated, either by statute or contract. *[156]*

Stockholders' Equity: in corporation accounting, the equity section of the balance sheet is called Stockholders' Equity; the total of Stockholders' Equity represents the stockholders' residual claim on the assets of the entity. *[52]*

Straight-line depreciation: a method of allocating the cost of a fixed asset evenly over the estimated useful life of the asset; under this method, the same amount of depreciation expense is taken each year; calculated as the cost of the asset minus the estimated salvage value, divided by the estimated useful life. *[79]*

Subrogation: related to insurance, a contract provision that provides that the insurance carrier has the right to recover the amount of the paid claim from the plaintiff if the plaintiff prevails against the defendant. *[202]*

Sum of the years' digits method: an accelerated method of depreciation that results in a more accelerate write-off than straight-line depreciation, but less than the double declining balance method; the annual depreciation expense under this method is calculated by multiplying the depreciable base by a schedule of fractions that are determined by the sum of the total years of the asset's useful life, the numerator of the fraction is the number of years left to be depreciated and the denominator is the sum of the total years of the useful life. *[85]*

Tangible assets: assets that have a physical substance and can be touched; examples include cash, inventory, buildings, vehicles, and equipment. *[12]*

Temporary accounts: these accounts record revenue and expense activity for a period of time, and then they are closed at the end of the accounting period, meaning they are adjusted to zero. *[33, 49]*

Time period: the length of time for which an interest calculation will be made; in financial calculations, it is the number of compounding periods ("N") in the calculation. *[131]*

Time value of money: money has the ability to earn interest, the economic measure of its time value; the concept of the time value of money is economically the same to both the lender and the borrower; to the lender, the time value of money is a benefit; to the borrower, it is a cost. *[128–131]*

Tort: a civil wrong, other than a breach of contract that results in injury to a person or property for which relief may be obtained in the form of damages or injunction. *[252]*

Total cost of inventory: a component of a company's cost of goods sold; the original cost of the inventory plus all the costs to get it in place to sell; does not include the carrying cost of holding the inventory for sale nor the other ongoing expenses of the business. *[94]*

Transaction: an event or condition recorded in the books of account; an event that effects a change in the assets, liabilities, or capital of a business; transactions can be internal or external. *[30]*

Trend Analysis: analyzing portions of historical financial statements of a firm to determine relevant historical trends of activity, such as growth (or decline) in revenues, costs and expenses, and net income. *[110]*

Trial balance: a listing of all of the account balances of the business in columnar form, listed in the order in which they appear in the general ledger. *[46]*

Units of production method: the most common activity method of depreciation; to calculate depreciation under this method, first determine the depreciation per unit by taking the cost minus the salvage value divided by the useful life of the asset, then determine depreciation for the period by multiplying the depreciation per unit by the number of units used in the accounting period. *[85]*

Useful life: the period of time that it will be economically feasible to use the fixed asset. *[79]*

Value as a forced liquidation: a premise of value; value in exchange, on a piecemeal basis (not part of a mass assemblage of assets), as part of a forced liquidation; this premise contemplates that the assets of the business enterprise

will be sold individually and that they will experience less than normal exposure to their appropriate secondary market. *[158]*

Value as a going concern: a premise of value; value in continued use, as a mass assemblage of income-producing assets, and as a going-concern business enterprise. *[158]*

Value as an assemblage of assets: a premise of value; value in place, as part of a mass assemblage of assets, but not in current use in the production of income, and not as a going-concern business enterprise. *[158]*

Value as an orderly liquidation: a premise of value; value in exchange, on a piecemeal basis (not part of a mass assemblage of assets), as part of an orderly disposition; this premise contemplates that all of the assets of the business enterprise will be sold individually, and that they will enjoy a normal exposure of their appropriate secondary market. *[158]*

Variable costs (expenses): costs or expenses of a company that vary with the level of revenues over a relevant range of production. *[110, 261]*

Variable rate loan: a loan that has a varying interest rate; a series a series of fixed rate loans. *[147]*

Vertical analysis: a technique in the analysis of financial statements; after the financial statements are reduced to percentages, each account is compared vertically to view the percentages of the accounts to one another (i.e. assessing the amount of cost of goods sold as a percentage of gross revenue) to observe the reasonableness of the relative amounts; it is most informative when it is done on a comparative basis by relating the company to some external benchmark, usually some industry financial data. *[111]*

Vocational retraining costs: the costs to retrain an injured person; a possible component of damages in a personal economic loss calculation. *[214]*

Wealth: the totality of valuable resources or possessions under the ownership or control of a person or an entity; in business, it is the total of all assets (net of liabilities) of an economic unit that can be used in the further production of income. *[128]*

Weighted average cost: an inventory costing assumption used to determine the cost of ending inventory; based on the weighted average of all the goods that comprise the cost of goods available for sale (the beginning inventory and the purchases for the entire year); calculated by dividing the total cost of the beginning inventory plus the cost of all the purchases by the sum of the total number of units purchased plus the units in beginning inventory. *[101]*

Working captial: a financial calculation used to measure liquidity; the amount by which a firm's current assets exceed its current liabilities, indicating the amount of liquidity available to satisfy maturing short-term debts and fund continued short-term operations. *[119]*

Work in process: a type of manufacturing inventory; accounting for work in process involves determining the proper cost of beginning inventory, the costing of the factors that are added to the production process (i.e. raw materials, direct labor, and overhead), and the transfer of work in process to finished goods. *[106]*

Work life expectancy: the number of years the plaintiff is expected to work through the end of his life expectancy. *[234]*

Yardstick approach: in commercial damages analyses, a method of projecting the but-for activity of a plaintiff by comparing the pre-incident activity to an independent variable, correlating the relationship, and then projecting the post-incident activity based on the independent variable. The method is best suited when an independent financial benchmark can be found that can be statistically correlated to the plaintiff's historical activity. It should be noted that the application of the yardstick method is impractical in the majority of situations. *[257]*

CPSIA information can be obtained at www.ICGtesting.com
Printed in the USA
LVOW130117170911

246674LV00003B/2/P